SAVE
58% OFF
THE COVER PRICE!
IT'S LIKE GETTING
ISSUES FREE!

TH
IS
M
M
JA
PREVIEWS, COVERAGE OF ART, MUSIC, JAPANESE CULTURE, STYLE, & MORE!

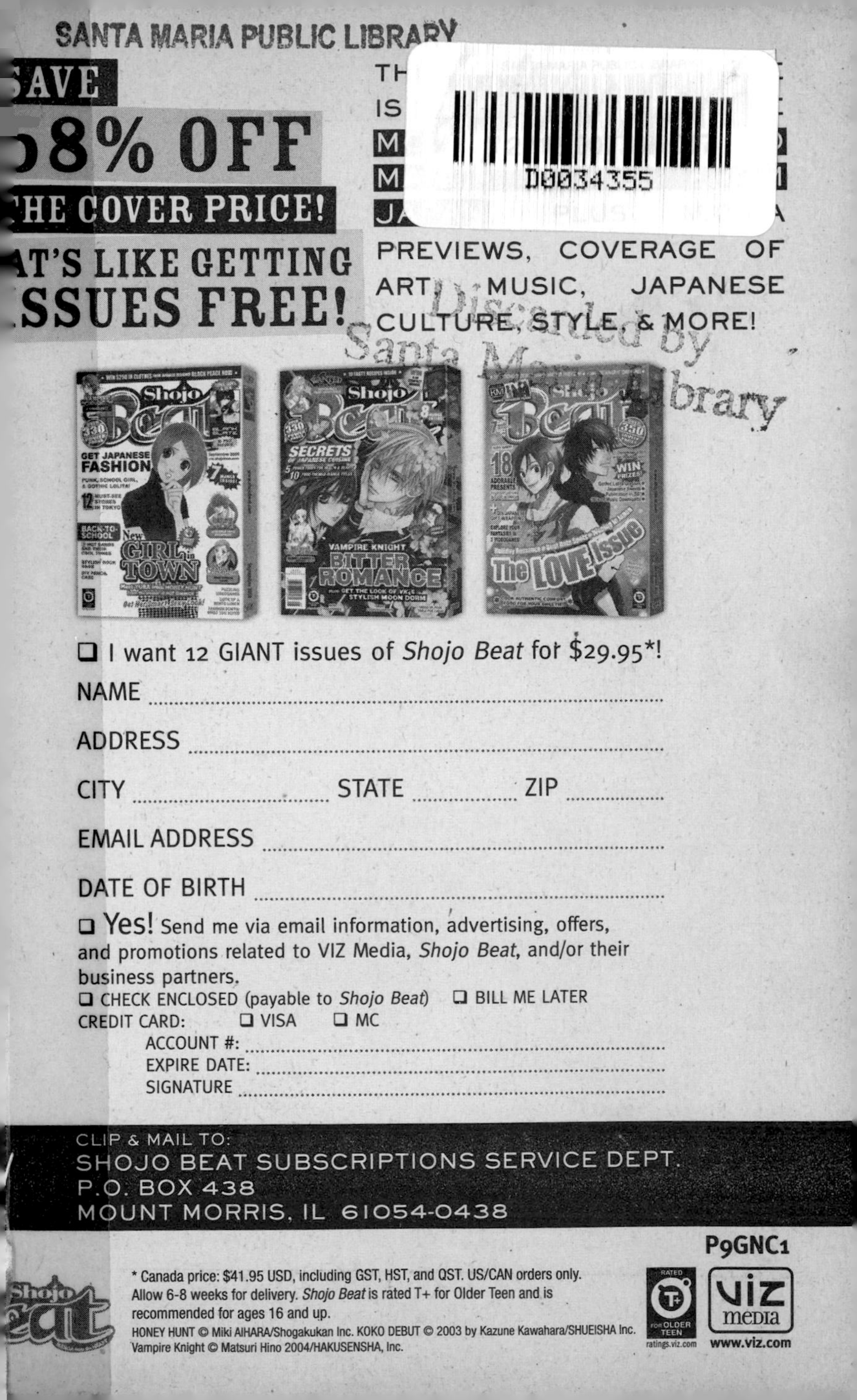
Shojo Beat
GET JAPANESE FASHION
New GIRL in TOWN
Shojo Beat
SECRETS OF JAPANESE CUISINE
VAMPIRE KNIGHT BITTER ROMANCE
Shojo Beat
The LOVE Issue

❑ I want 12 GIANT issues of *Shojo Beat* for $29.95*!

NAME ....

ADDRESS ....

CITY .... STATE .... ZIP ....

EMAIL ADDRESS ....

DATE OF BIRTH ....

❑ Yes! Send me via email information, advertising, offers, and promotions related to VIZ Media, *Shojo Beat*, and/or their business partners.

❑ CHECK ENCLOSED (payable to *Shojo Beat*) ❑ BILL ME LATER

CREDIT CARD: ❑ VISA ❑ MC

ACCOUNT #: ....

EXPIRE DATE: ....

SIGNATURE ....

CLIP & MAIL TO:
SHOJO BEAT SUBSCRIPTIONS SERVICE DEPT.
P.O. BOX 438
MOUNT MORRIS, IL 61054-0438

P9GNC1

* Canada price: $41.95 USD, including GST, HST, and QST. US/CAN orders only. Allow 6-8 weeks for delivery. *Shojo Beat* is rated T+ for Older Teen and is recommended for ages 16 and up.

RATED T+ FOR OLDER TEEN ratings.viz.com

VIZ media www.viz.com

Wild Ones

アラクレ

Vol. 7

Story & Art by
Kiyo Fujiwara

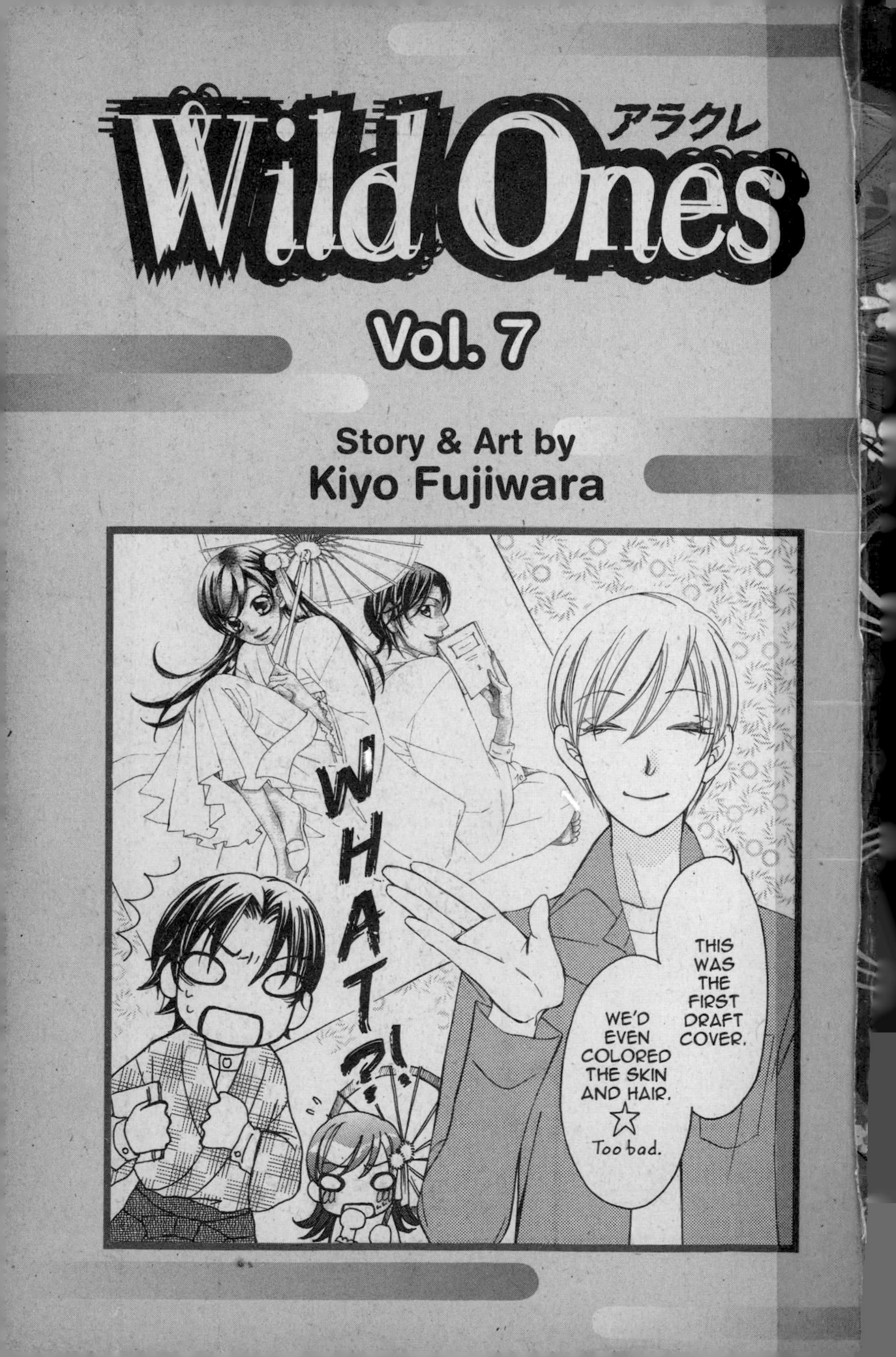
THIS WAS THE FIRST DRAFT COVER.
WE'D EVEN COLORED THE SKIN AND HAIR. ☆ Too bad.
WHAT?!

Wild Ones アラクレ

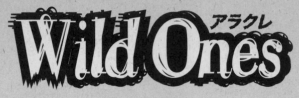

Volume 7

CONTENTS

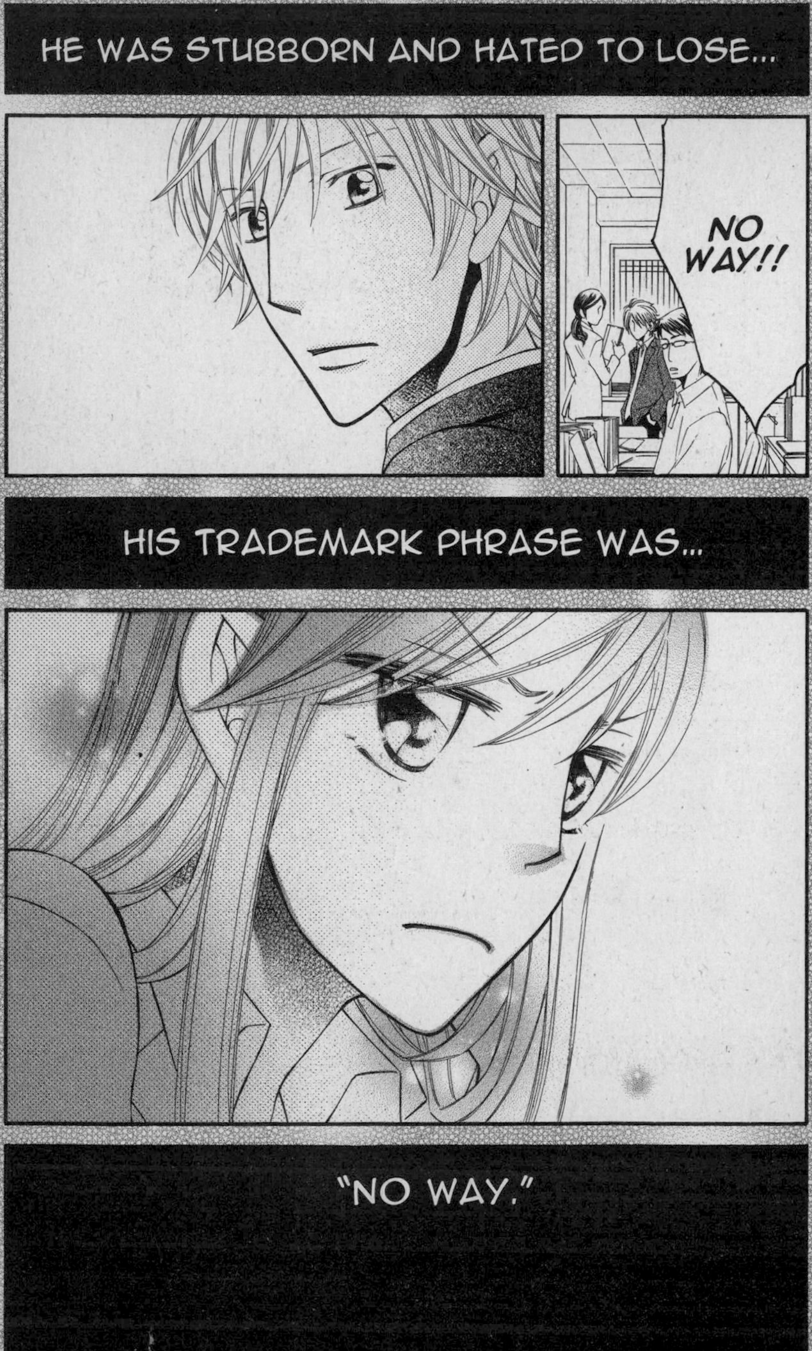
HE WAS STUBBORN AND HATED TO LOSE...
NO WAY!!
HIS TRADEMARK PHRASE WAS...
"NO WAY."

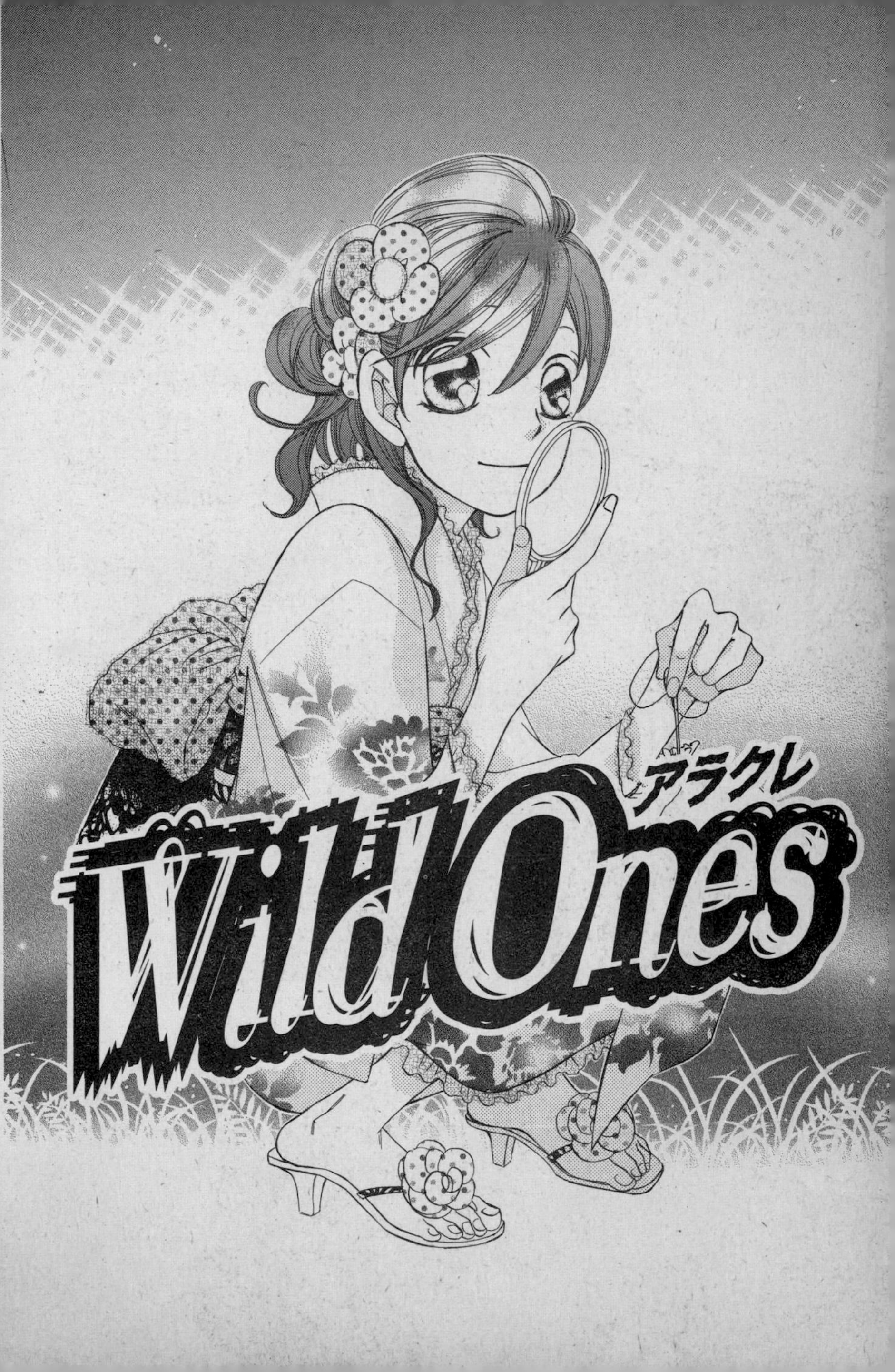
アラクレ
Wild Ones

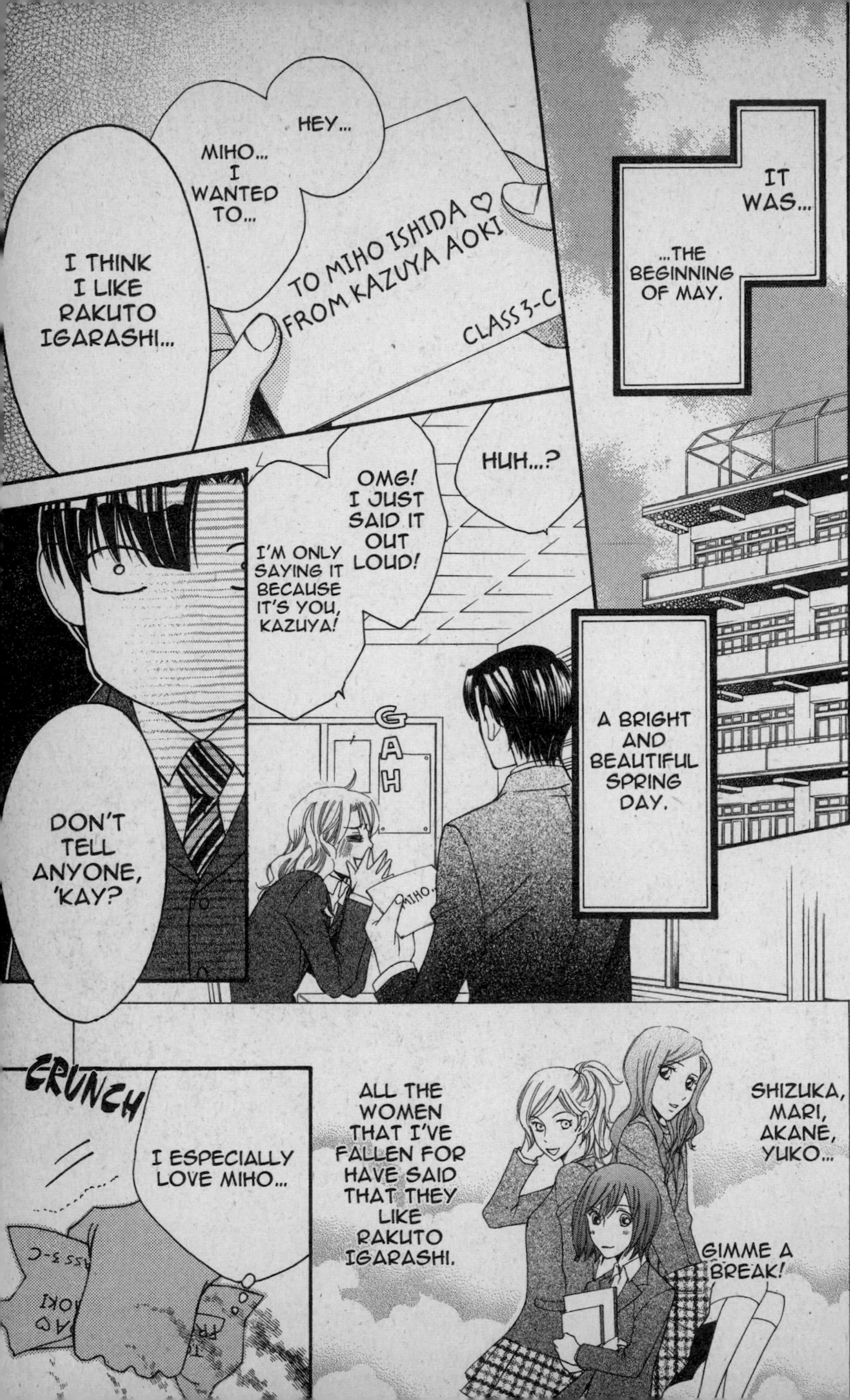
IT WAS...
...THE BEGINNING OF MAY.
A BRIGHT AND BEAUTIFUL SPRING DAY.
HEY...
MIHO... I WANTED TO...
TO MIHO ISHIDA ♡ FROM KAZUYA AOKI
CLASS 3-C
I THINK I LIKE RAKUTO IGARASHI...
HUH...?
OMG! I JUST SAID IT OUT LOUD!
I'M ONLY SAYING IT BECAUSE IT'S YOU, KAZUYA!
GAH
MIHO...
DON'T TELL ANYONE, 'KAY?
SHIZUKA, MARI, AKANE, YUKO...
GIMME A BREAK!
ALL THE WOMEN THAT I'VE FALLEN FOR HAVE SAID THAT THEY LIKE RAKUTO IGARASHI.
CRUNCH
I ESPECIALLY LOVE MIHO...

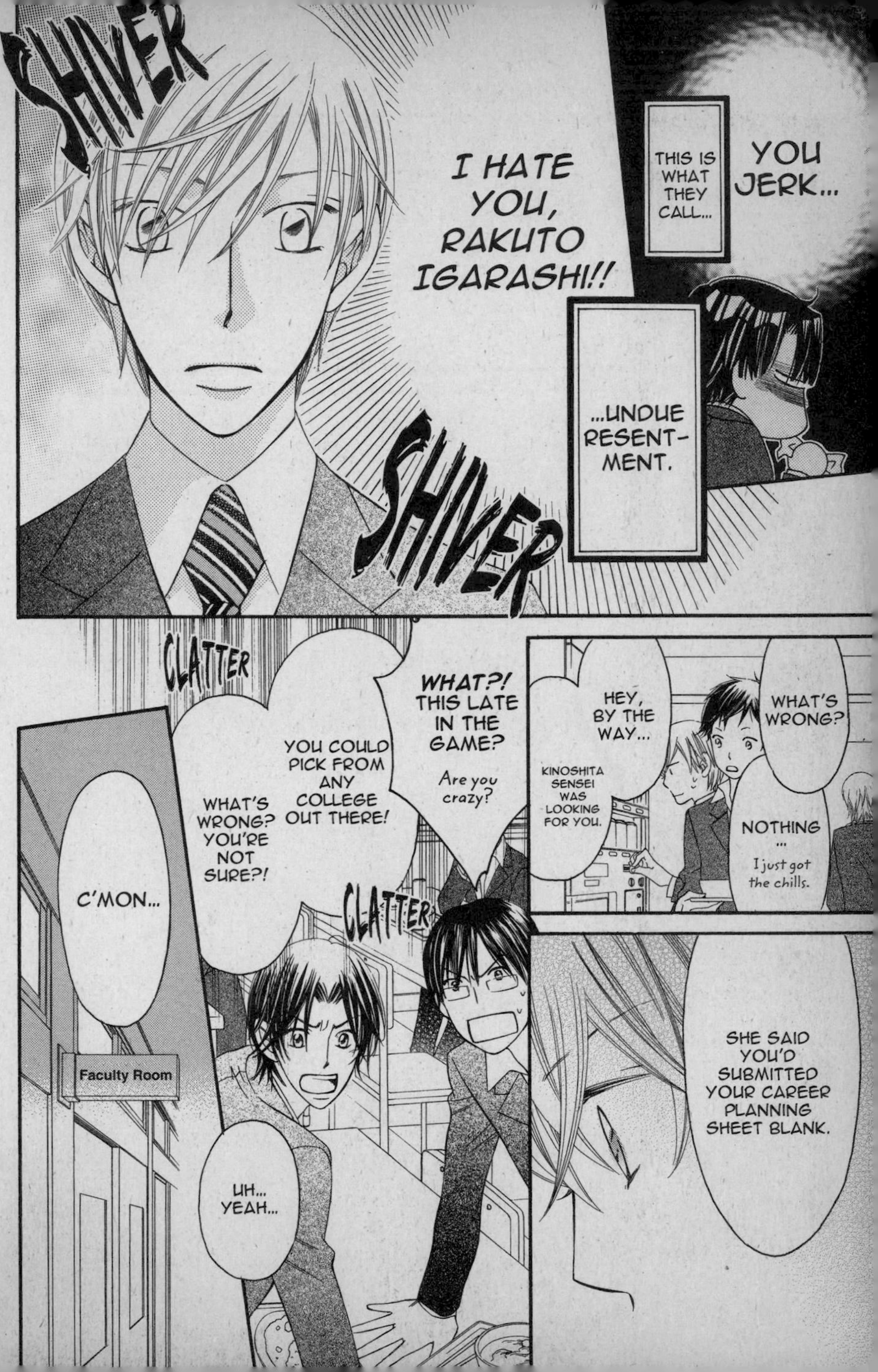

YOU JERK...
THIS IS WHAT THEY CALL...
...UNDUE RESENTMENT.
SHIVER
I HATE YOU, RAKUTO IGARASHI!!
SHIVER
WHAT'S WRONG?
NOTHING... I just got the chills.
HEY, BY THE WAY...
KINOSHITA SENSEI WAS LOOKING FOR YOU.
SHE SAID YOU'D SUBMITTED YOUR CAREER PLANNING SHEET BLANK.
WHAT?! THIS LATE IN THE GAME?
Are you crazy?
CLATTER
YOU COULD PICK FROM ANY COLLEGE OUT THERE!
WHAT'S WRONG? YOU'RE NOT SURE?!
C'MON...
CLATTER
UH... YEAH...
Faculty Room

IT'S VOLUME 7!!

THANK YOU SO MUCH. THANK YOU SO MUCH.

I REALLY REALIZE HOW GREAT THIS IS... VOLUME 7...

BUT JEEZ... I REALLY HAVE TERRIBLE HANDWRITING. AND THIS ISN'T EVEN THAT BAD. I TRY HARD TO MAKE IT LEGIBLE... BUT YOU SHOULD SEE MY LAYOUTS AND ROUGH DRAFTS... IT'S PRETTY BAD.

I THOUGHT SO AS I WENT OVER TO FIX MY WORK. THE LETTERERS TAKE THE DIALOG FROM THE ROUGH DRAFT, BUT BECAUSE MY HANDWRITING IS SO BAD, THEY OFTEN MISTAKE "..." FOR "!" HOW PATHETIC!

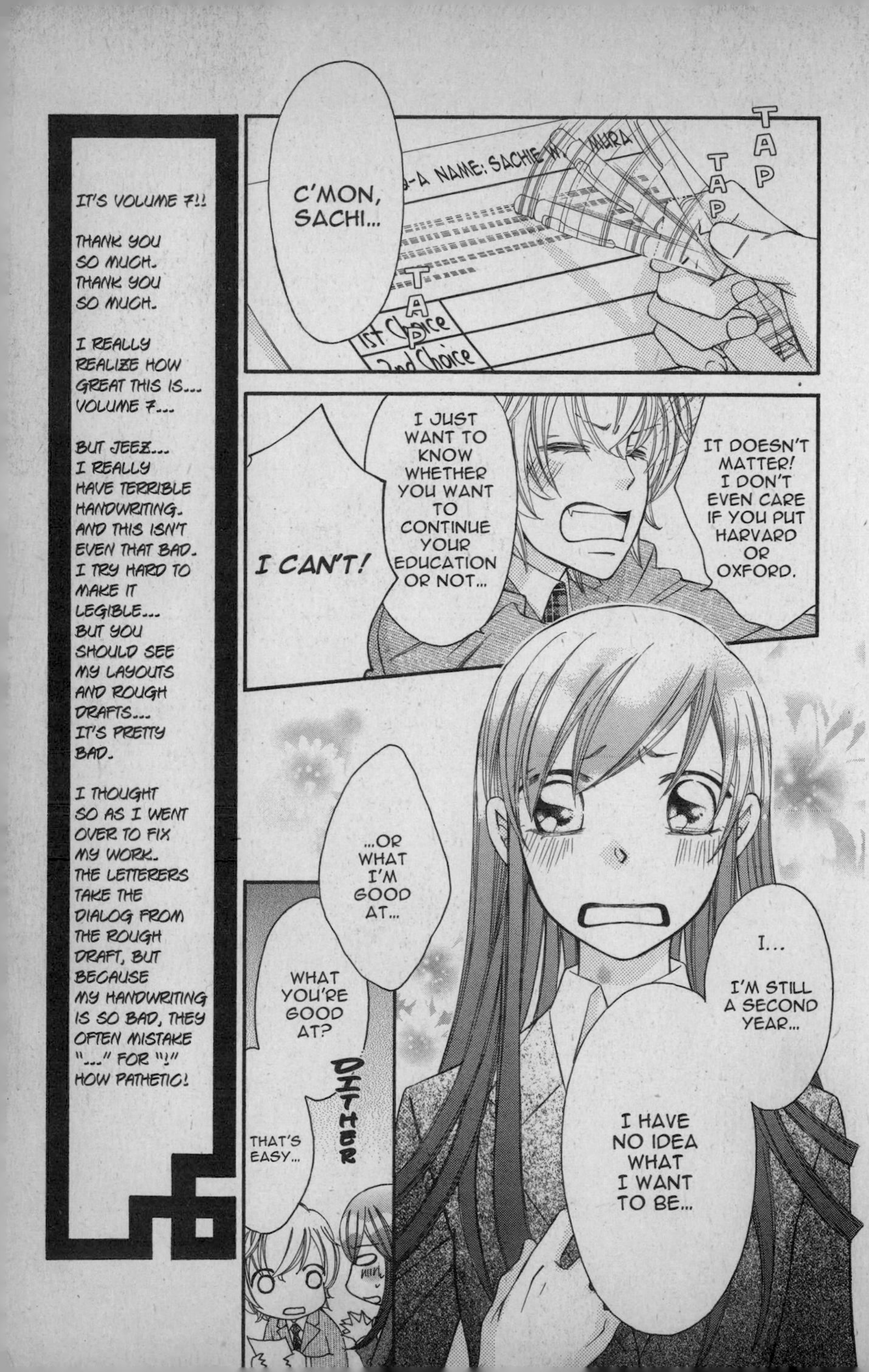
TAP
TAP
TAP
NAME: SACHIE M... MURA
1st Choice
2nd Choice
C'MON, SACHI...
IT DOESN'T MATTER! I DON'T EVEN CARE IF YOU PUT HARVARD OR OXFORD.
I JUST WANT TO KNOW WHETHER YOU WANT TO CONTINUE YOUR EDUCATION OR NOT...
I CAN'T!
I...
I'M STILL A SECOND YEAR...
I HAVE NO IDEA WHAT I WANT TO BE...
...OR WHAT I'M GOOD AT...
WHAT YOU'RE GOOD AT?
DITHER
THAT'S EASY...

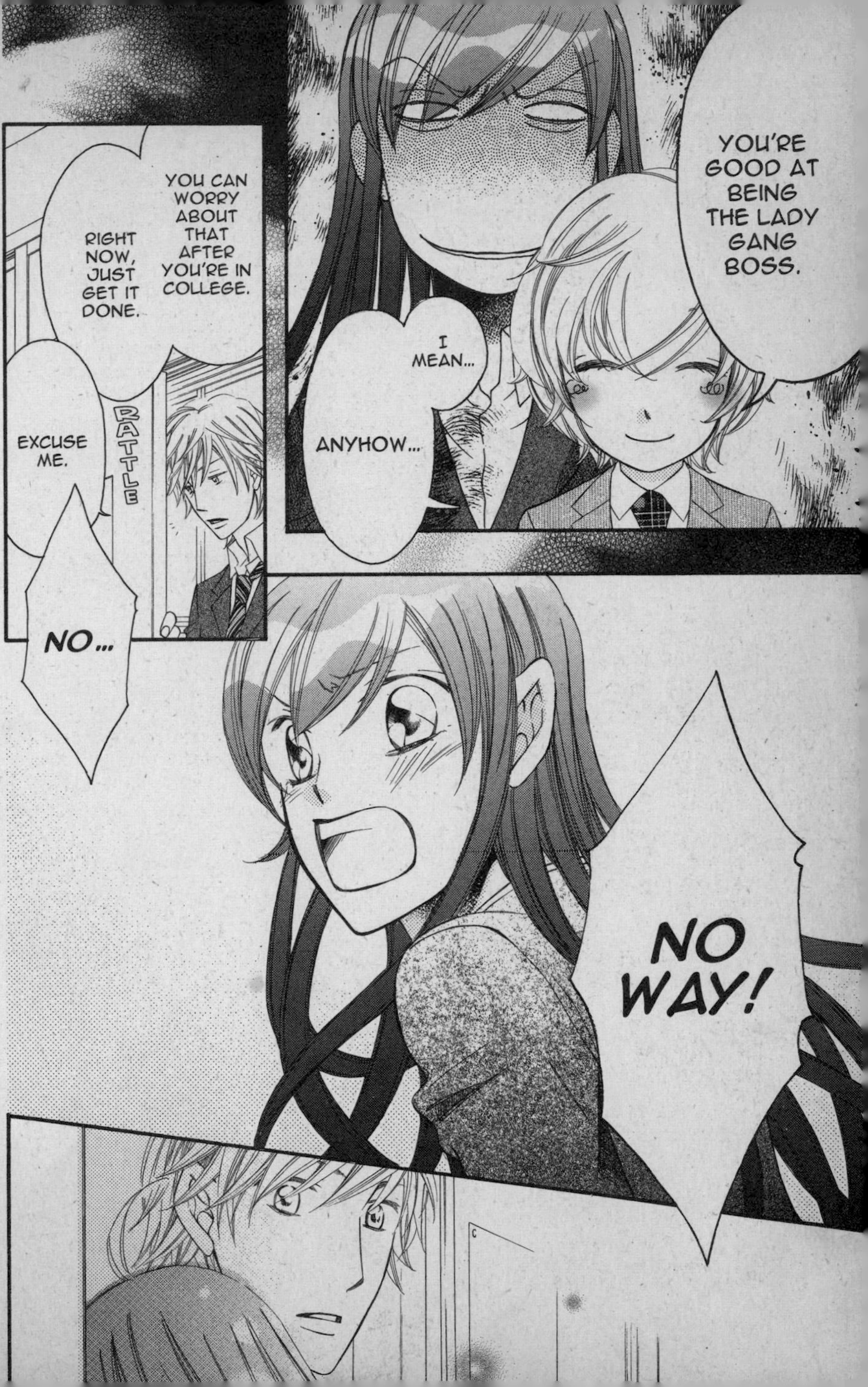

YOU'RE GOOD AT BEING THE LADY GANG BOSS.
I MEAN...
ANYHOW...
RIGHT NOW, JUST GET IT DONE.
YOU CAN WORRY ABOUT THAT AFTER YOU'RE IN COLLEGE.
RATTLE
EXCUSE ME.
NO...
NO WAY!

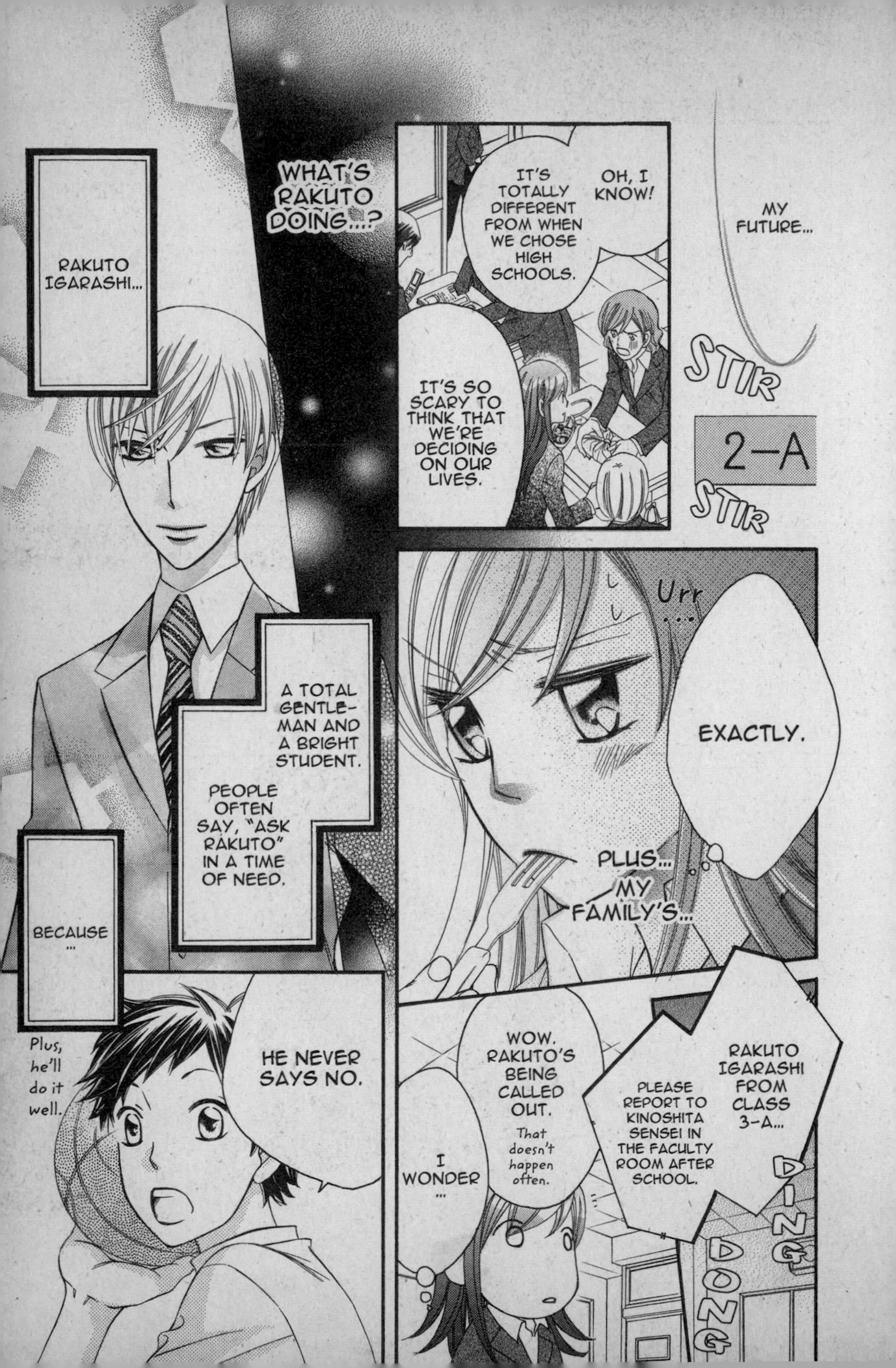
MY FUTURE...
STIR
2-A
STIR
OH, I KNOW!
IT'S TOTALLY DIFFERENT FROM WHEN WE CHOSE HIGH SCHOOLS.
IT'S SO SCARY TO THINK THAT WE'RE DECIDING ON OUR LIVES.
Urr...
EXACTLY.
PLUS... MY FAMILY'S...
DING DONG
RAKUTO IGARASHI FROM CLASS 3-A...
PLEASE REPORT TO KINOSHITA SENSEI IN THE FACULTY ROOM AFTER SCHOOL.
WOW. RAKUTO'S BEING CALLED OUT.
That doesn't happen often.
I WONDER...
WHAT'S RAKUTO DOING...?
RAKUTO IGARASHI...
A TOTAL GENTLEMAN AND A BRIGHT STUDENT.
PEOPLE OFTEN SAY, "ASK RAKUTO" IN A TIME OF NEED.
BECAUSE...
HE NEVER SAYS NO.
Plus, he'll do it well.

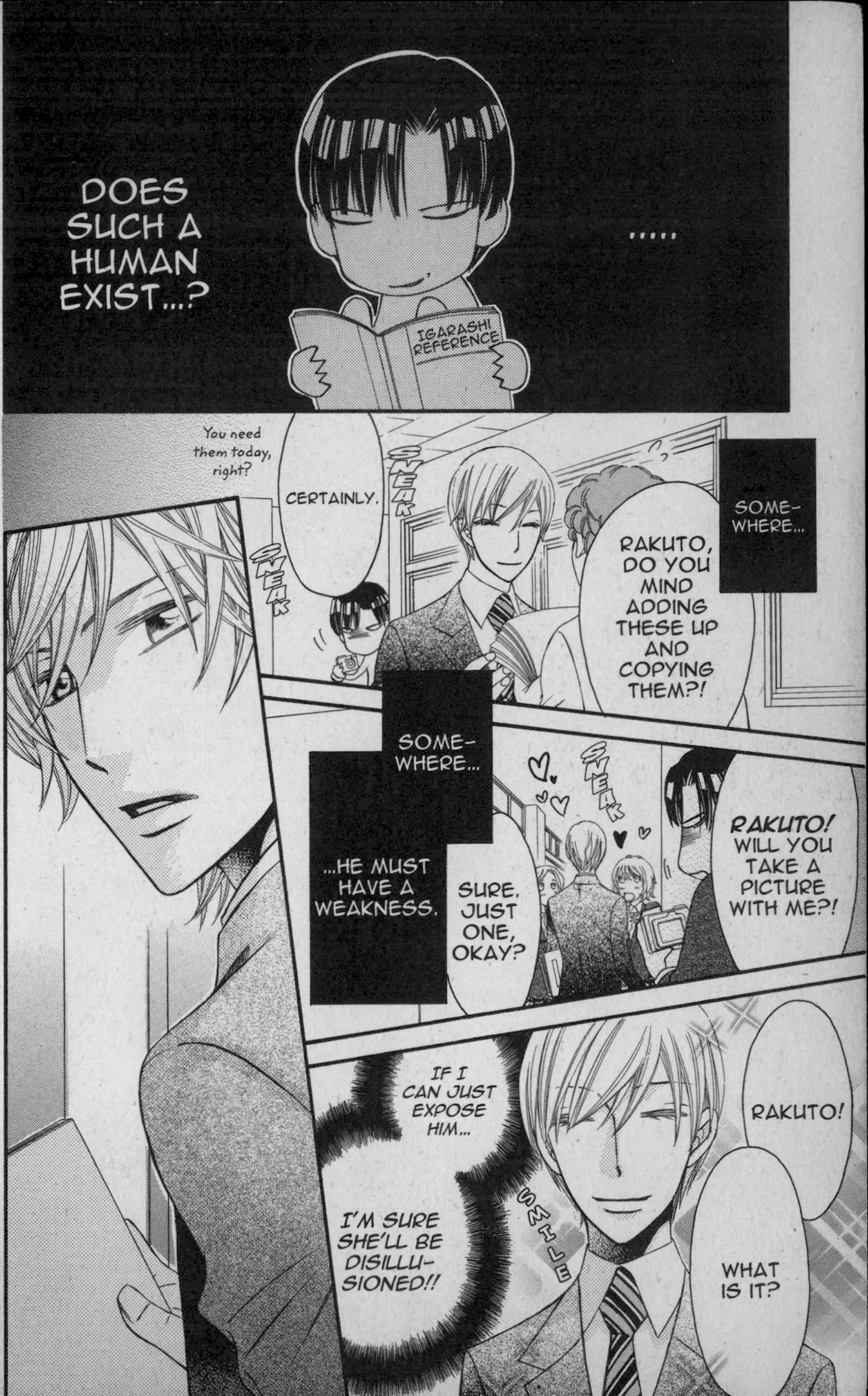
.....
DOES SUCH A HUMAN EXIST...?
IGARASHI REFERENCE
SOME-WHERE...
RAKUTO, DO YOU MIND ADDING THESE UP AND COPYING THEM?!
SNEAK
CERTAINLY.
SNEAK
You need them today, right?
RAKUTO! WILL YOU TAKE A PICTURE WITH ME?!
SNEAK
SURE. JUST ONE, OKAY?
SOME-WHERE...
...HE MUST HAVE A WEAKNESS.
RAKUTO!
WHAT IS IT?
SMILE
IF I CAN JUST EXPOSE HIM...
I'M SURE SHE'LL BE DISILLU-SIONED!!

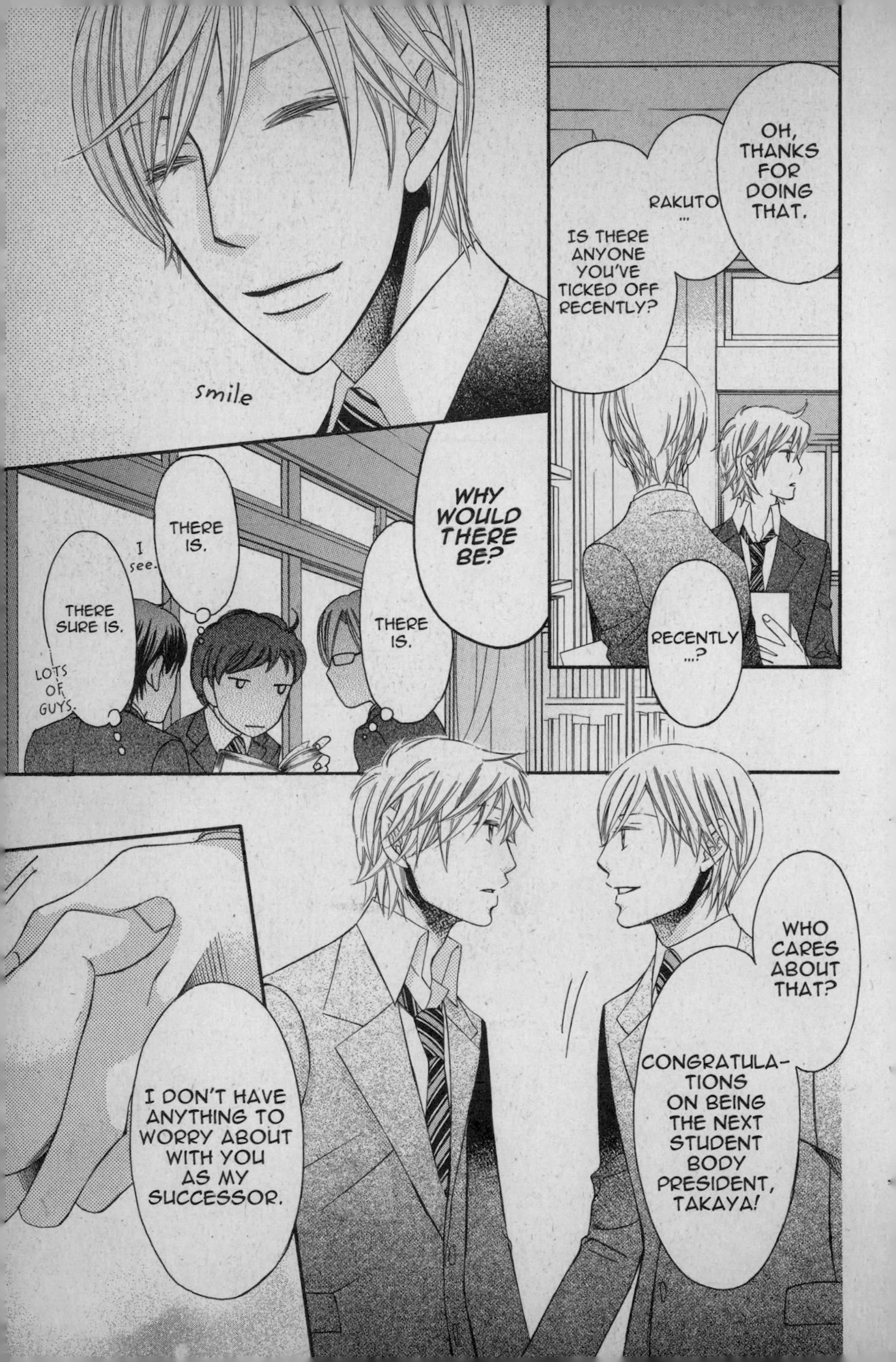
OH, THANKS FOR DOING THAT.
RAKUTO...
IS THERE ANYONE YOU'VE TICKED OFF RECENTLY?
RECENTLY...?
smile
WHY WOULD THERE BE?
THERE IS.
THERE IS.
I see.
THERE SURE IS.
LOTS OF GUYS.
WHO CARES ABOUT THAT?
CONGRATULA-TIONS ON BEING THE NEXT STUDENT BODY PRESIDENT, TAKAYA!
I DON'T HAVE ANYTHING TO WORRY ABOUT WITH YOU AS MY SUCCESSOR.

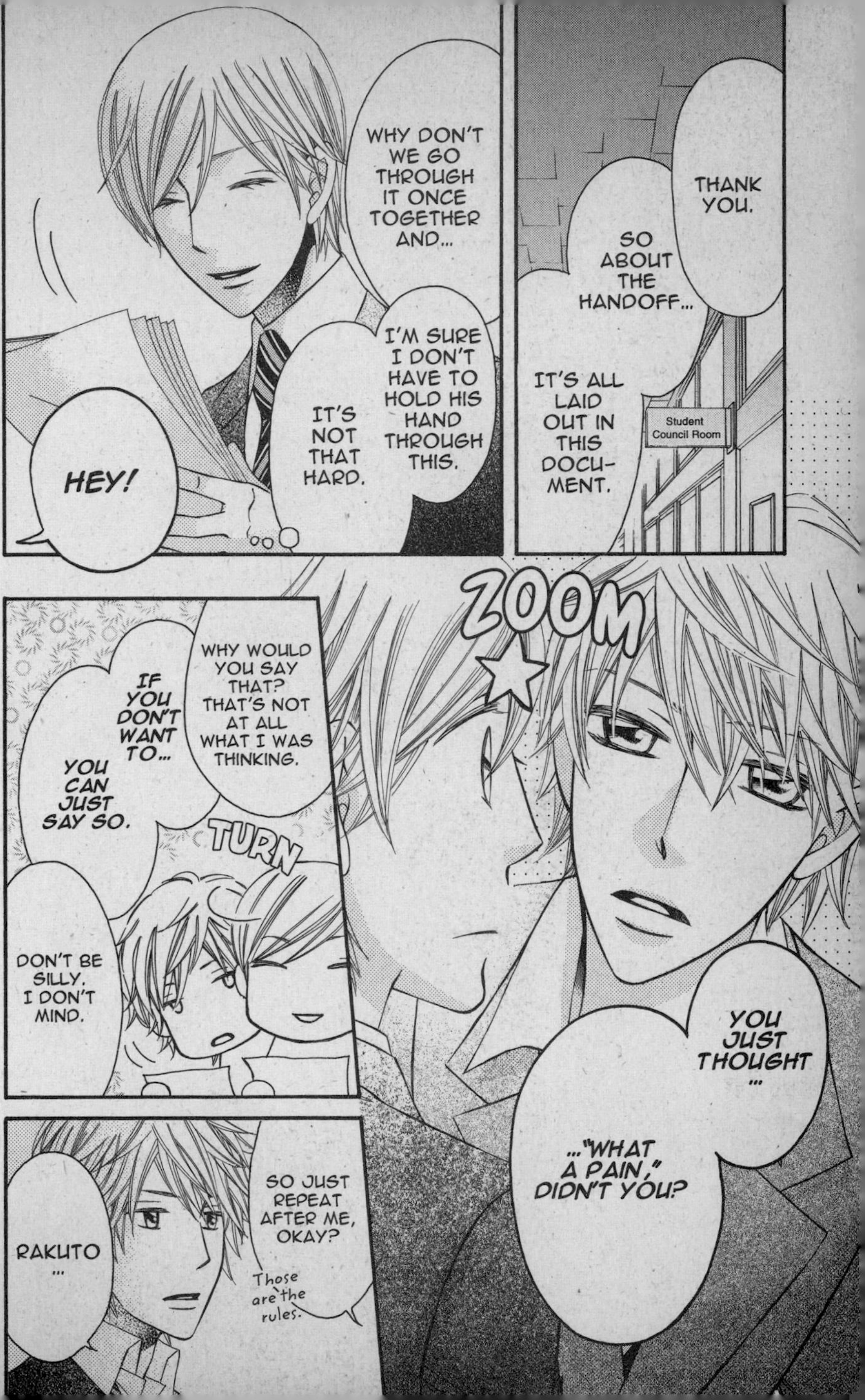

THANK YOU.
SO ABOUT THE HANDOFF...
IT'S ALL LAID OUT IN THIS DOCUMENT.
Student Council Room
WHY DON'T WE GO THROUGH IT ONCE TOGETHER AND...
I'M SURE I DON'T HAVE TO HOLD HIS HAND THROUGH THIS.
IT'S NOT THAT HARD.
HEY!
ZOOM
YOU JUST THOUGHT ...
..."WHAT A PAIN," DIDN'T YOU?
WHY WOULD YOU SAY THAT? THAT'S NOT AT ALL WHAT I WAS THINKING.
IF YOU DON'T WANT TO...
YOU CAN JUST SAY SO.
TURN
DON'T BE SILLY. I DON'T MIND.
SO JUST REPEAT AFTER ME, OKAY?
Those are the rules.
RAKUTO ...

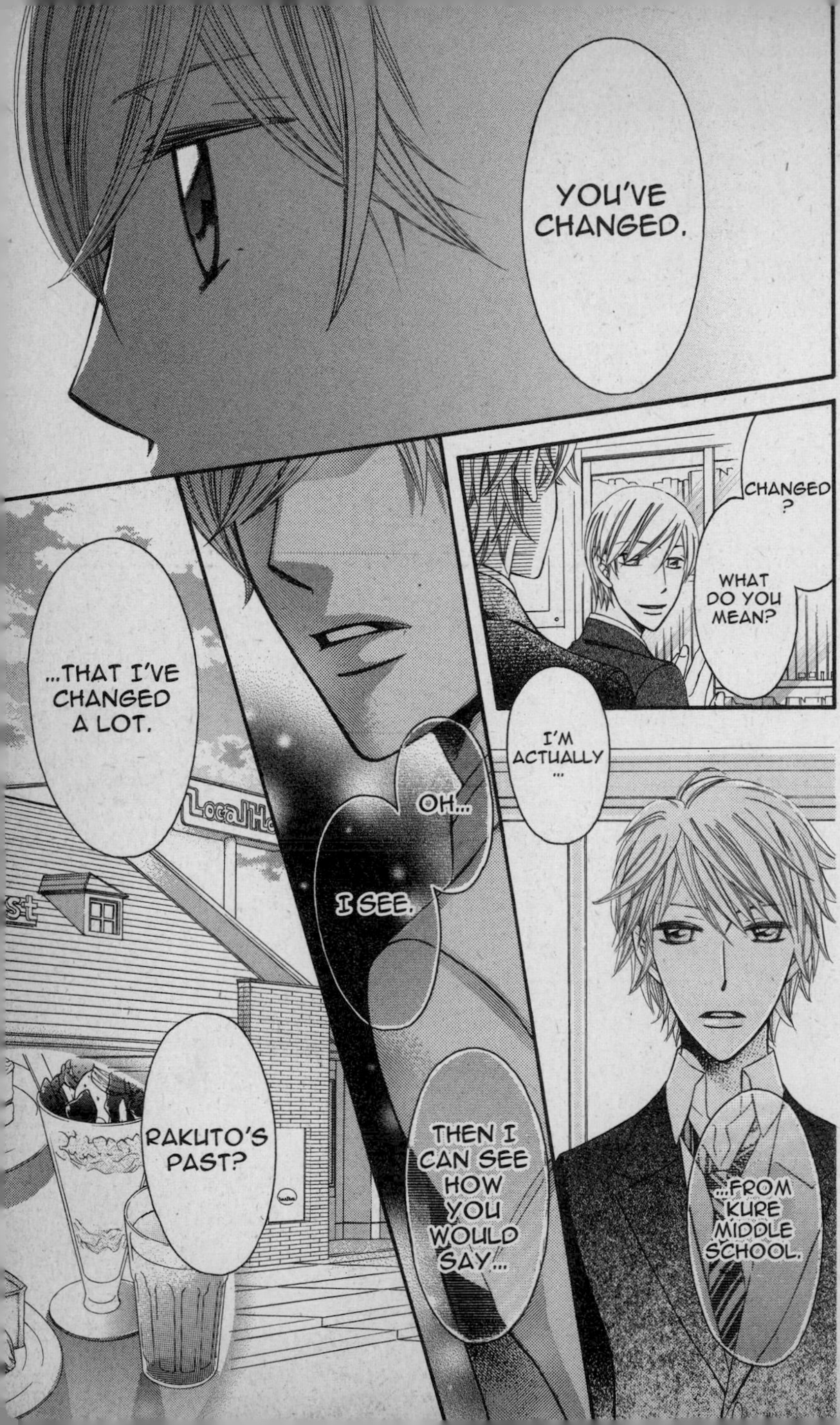
YOU'VE CHANGED.
CHANGED?
WHAT DO YOU MEAN?
I'M ACTUALLY...
...FROM KURE MIDDLE SCHOOL.
OH...
I SEE.
THEN I CAN SEE HOW YOU WOULD SAY...
...THAT I'VE CHANGED A LOT.
RAKUTO'S PAST?

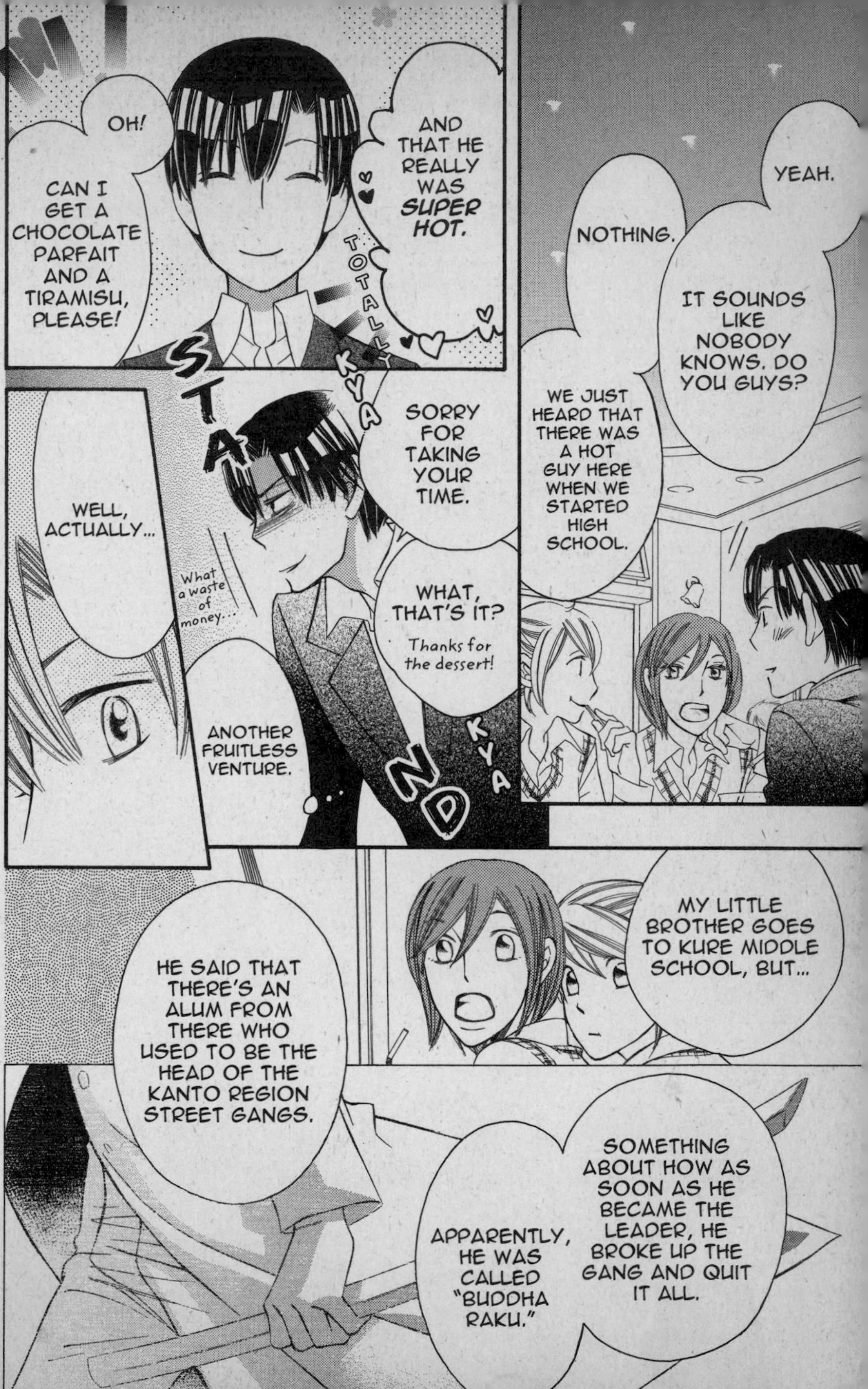
YEAH.
IT SOUNDS LIKE NOBODY KNOWS. DO YOU GUYS?
NOTHING.
WE JUST HEARD THAT THERE WAS A HOT GUY HERE WHEN WE STARTED HIGH SCHOOL.
AND THAT HE REALLY WAS SUPER HOT.
TOTALLY
OH!
CAN I GET A CHOCOLATE PARFAIT AND A TIRAMISU, PLEASE!
KYA
SORRY FOR TAKING YOUR TIME.
STAND
WHAT, THAT'S IT?
Thanks for the dessert!
KYA
WELL, ACTUALLY...
What a waste of money...
ANOTHER FRUITLESS VENTURE.
MY LITTLE BROTHER GOES TO KURE MIDDLE SCHOOL, BUT...
HE SAID THAT THERE'S AN ALUM FROM THERE WHO USED TO BE THE HEAD OF THE KANTO REGION STREET GANGS.
SOMETHING ABOUT HOW AS SOON AS HE BECAME THE LEADER, HE BROKE UP THE GANG AND QUIT IT ALL.
APPARENTLY, HE WAS CALLED "BUDDHA RAKU."

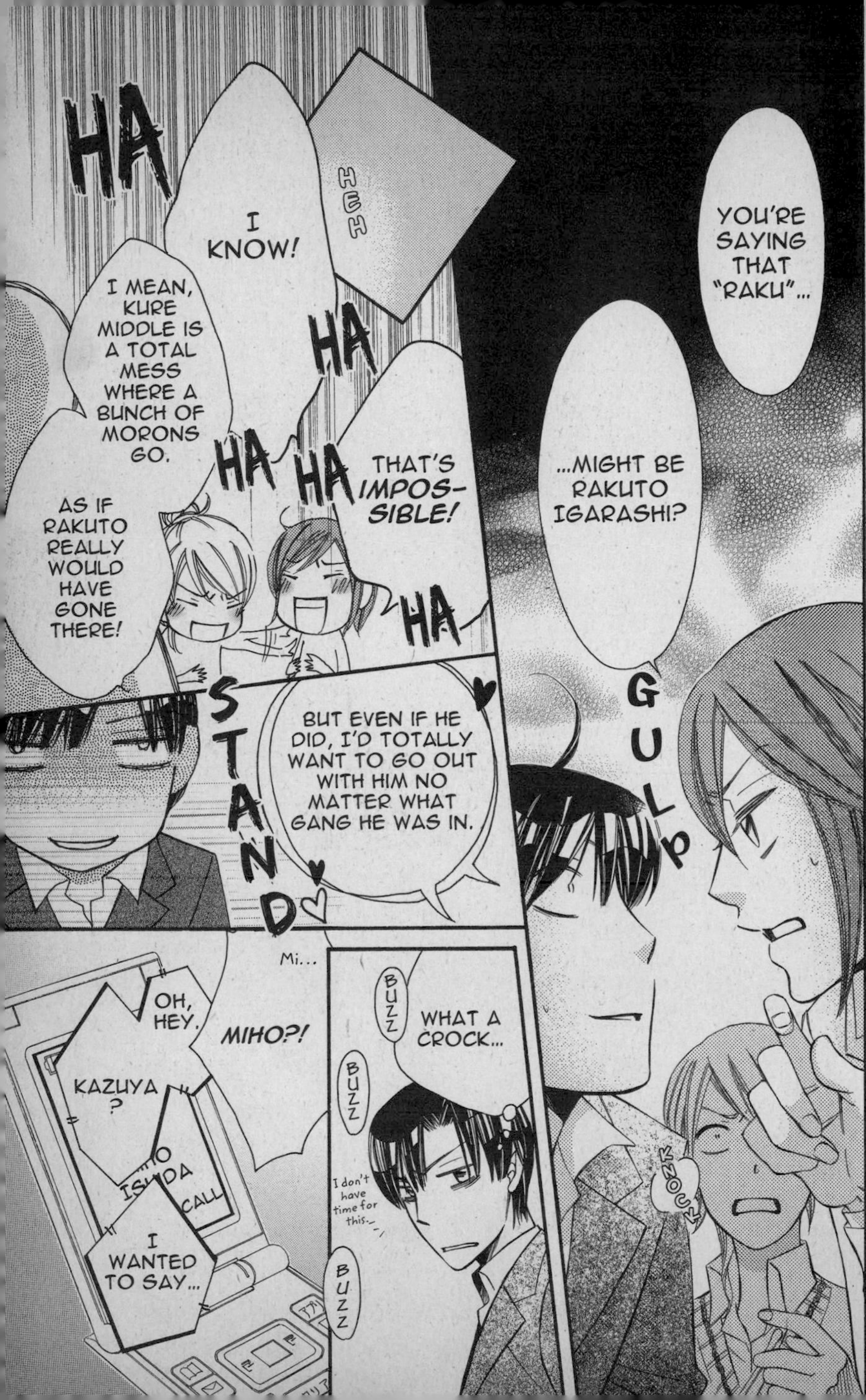
YOU'RE SAYING THAT "RAKU"...
...MIGHT BE RAKUTO IGARASHI?
GULP
KNOCK
HEH
I KNOW!
HA
I MEAN, KURE MIDDLE IS A TOTAL MESS WHERE A BUNCH OF MORONS GO.
HA
THAT'S IMPOSSIBLE!
HA
HA
HA
AS IF RAKUTO REALLY WOULD HAVE GONE THERE!
BUT EVEN IF HE DID, I'D TOTALLY WANT TO GO OUT WITH HIM NO MATTER WHAT GANG HE WAS IN.
STAND
BUZZ
WHAT A CROCK...
BUZZ
I don't have time for this...
BUZZ
Mi...
MIHO?!
OH, HEY.
KAZUYA?
ISHIDA
CALL
I WANTED TO SAY...

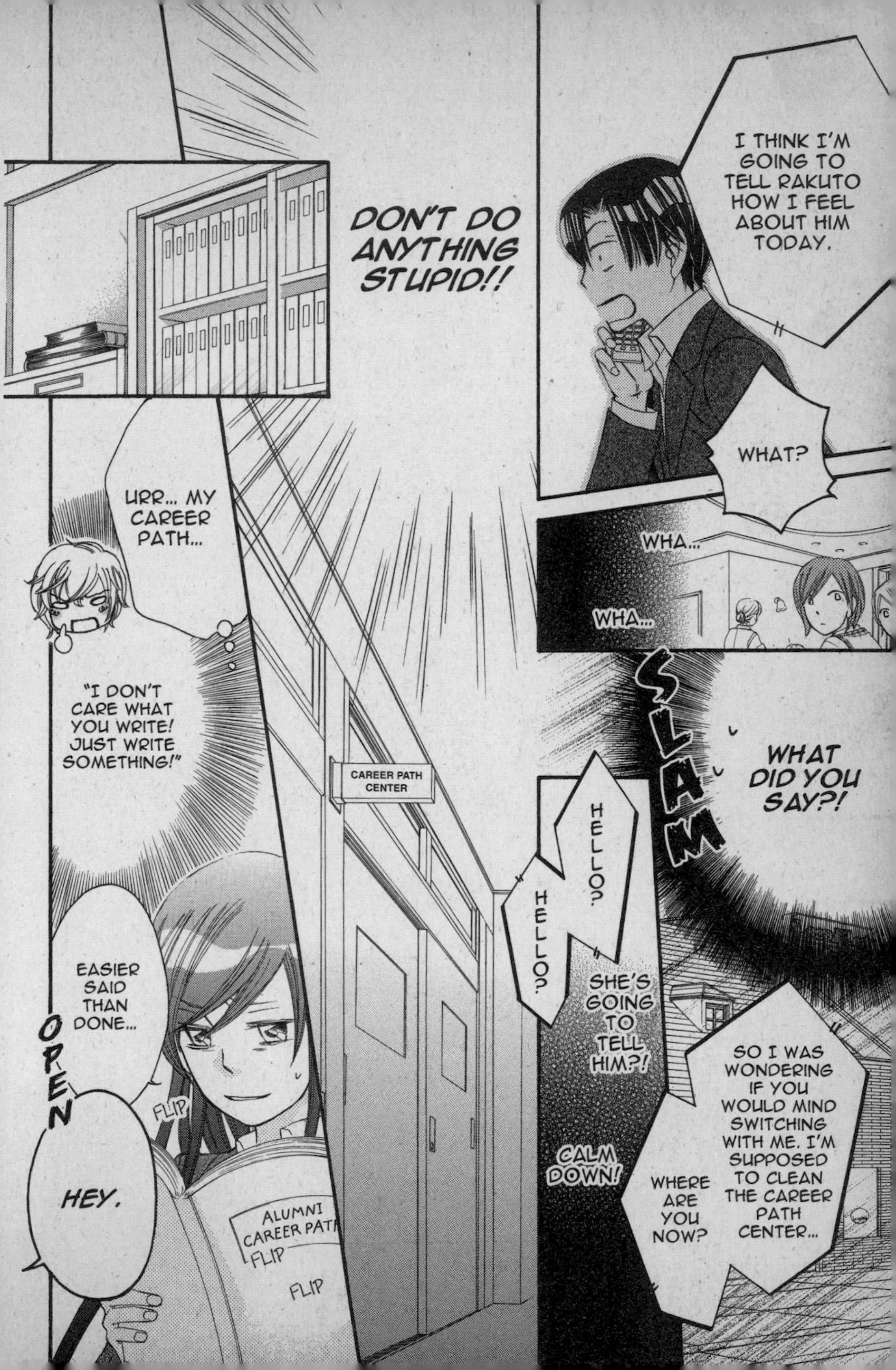
I THINK I'M GOING TO TELL RAKUTO HOW I FEEL ABOUT HIM TODAY.
WHAT?
WHA...
WHA...
SLAM
WHAT DID YOU SAY?!
HELLO?
HELLO?
SHE'S GOING TO TELL HIM?!
CALM DOWN!
SO I WAS WONDERING IF YOU WOULD MIND SWITCHING WITH ME. I'M SUPPOSED TO CLEAN THE CAREER PATH CENTER...
WHERE ARE YOU NOW?
DON'T DO ANYTHING STUPID!!
URR... MY CAREER PATH...
"I DON'T CARE WHAT YOU WRITE! JUST WRITE SOMETHING!"
CAREER PATH CENTER
EASIER SAID THAN DONE...
FLIP
ALUMNI CAREER PATH
FLIP
FLIP
OPEN
HEY.

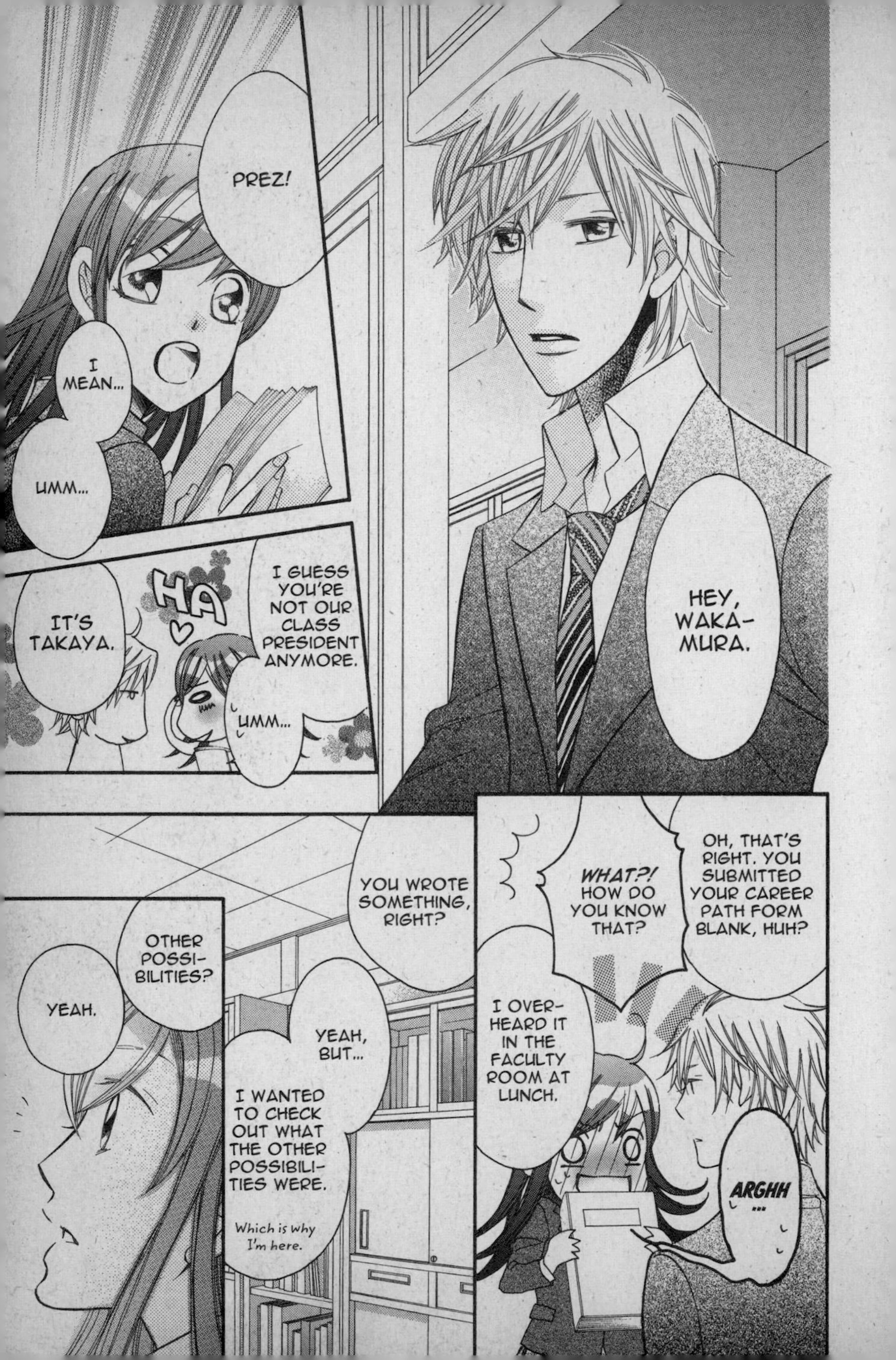
HEY, WAKAMURA.
PREZ!
I MEAN...
UMM...
I GUESS YOU'RE NOT OUR CLASS PRESIDENT ANYMORE.
UMM...
HA
IT'S TAKAYA.
OH, THAT'S RIGHT. YOU SUBMITTED YOUR CAREER PATH FORM BLANK, HUH?
WHAT?! HOW DO YOU KNOW THAT?
I OVERHEARD IT IN THE FACULTY ROOM AT LUNCH.
ARGHH...
YOU WROTE SOMETHING, RIGHT?
YEAH, BUT...
I WANTED TO CHECK OUT WHAT THE OTHER POSSIBILITIES WERE.
Which is why I'm here.
OTHER POSSIBILITIES?
YEAH.

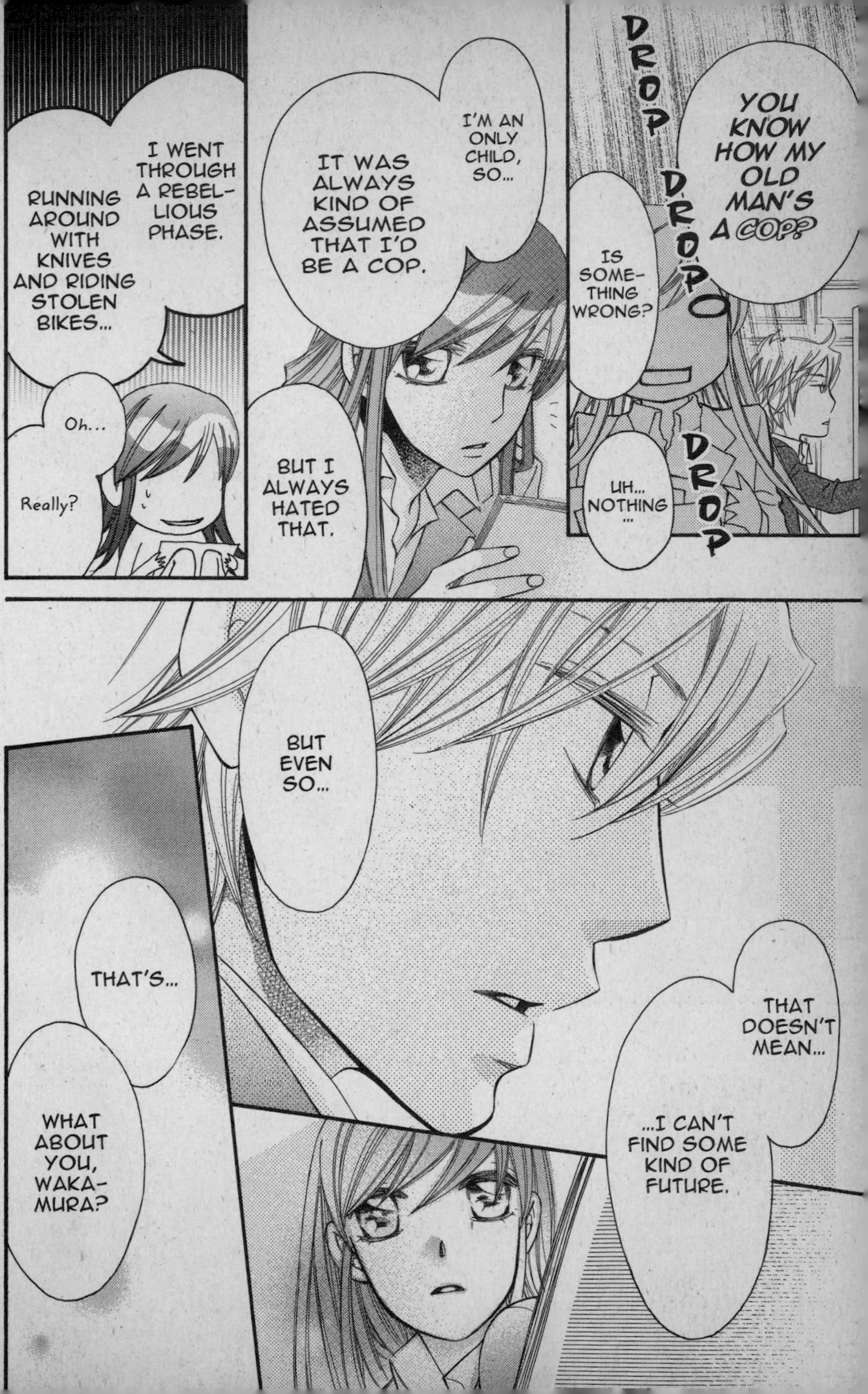
YOU KNOW HOW MY OLD MAN'S A COP?
DROP
DROP
IS SOMETHING WRONG?
UH... NOTHING...
DROP
DROP
I'M AN ONLY CHILD, SO...
IT WAS ALWAYS KIND OF ASSUMED THAT I'D BE A COP.
BUT I ALWAYS HATED THAT.
I WENT THROUGH A REBELLIOUS PHASE.
RUNNING AROUND WITH KNIVES AND RIDING STOLEN BIKES...
Oh...
Really?
BUT EVEN SO...
THAT DOESN'T MEAN...
...I CAN'T FIND SOME KIND OF FUTURE.
THAT'S...
WHAT ABOUT YOU, WAKAMURA?

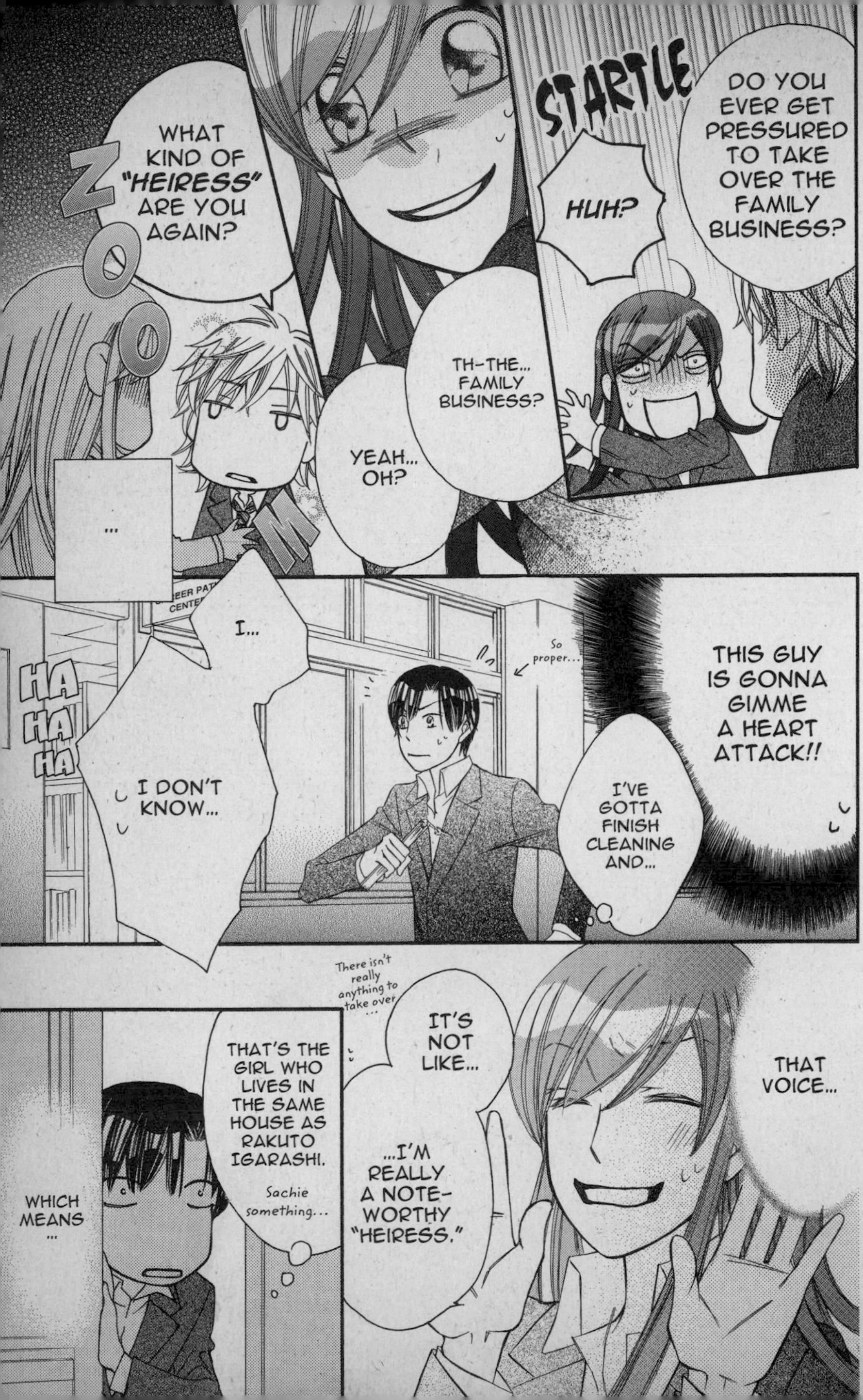
DO YOU EVER GET PRESSURED TO TAKE OVER THE FAMILY BUSINESS?
STARTLE
HUH?
TH-THE... FAMILY BUSINESS?
YEAH... OH?
WHAT KIND OF "HEIRESS" ARE YOU AGAIN?
ZOOM
...
THIS GUY IS GONNA GIMME A HEART ATTACK!!
I'VE GOTTA FINISH CLEANING AND...
So proper...
I...
I DON'T KNOW...
HA HA HA
THAT VOICE...
IT'S NOT LIKE...
...I'M REALLY A NOTE-WORTHY "HEIRESS."
There isn't really anything to take over...
THAT'S THE GIRL WHO LIVES IN THE SAME HOUSE AS RAKUTO IGARASHI.
Sachie something...
WHICH MEANS ...

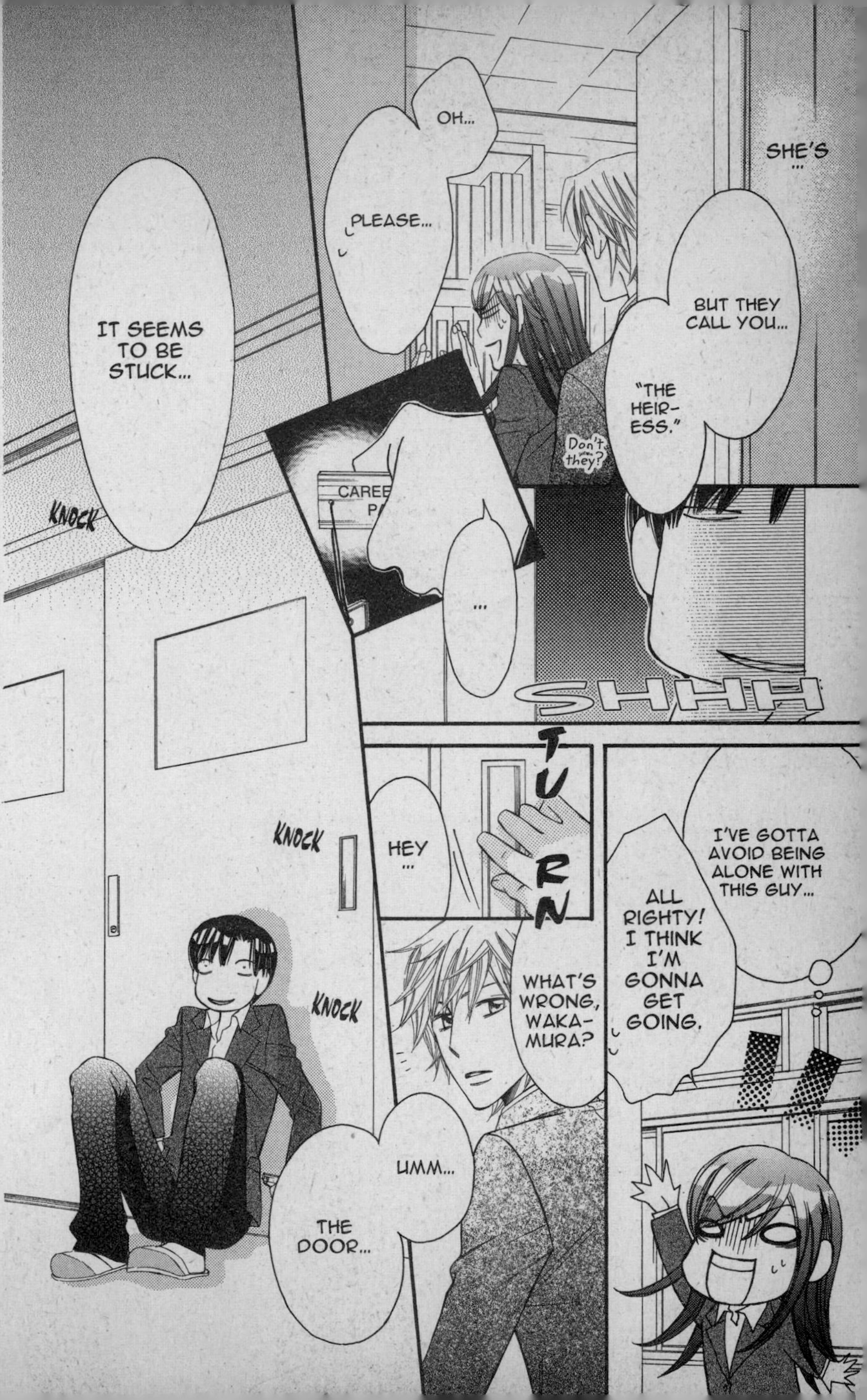
SHE'S ...
BUT THEY CALL YOU...
"THE HEIR-ESS."
Don't they?
OH...
PLEASE...
CAREE
P
...
SHHH
I'VE GOTTA AVOID BEING ALONE WITH THIS GUY...
ALL RIGHTY! I THINK I'M GONNA GET GOING.
TURN
HEY ...
WHAT'S WRONG, WAKA-MURA?
UMM...
THE DOOR...
IT SEEMS TO BE STUCK...
KNOCK
KNOCK
KNOCK

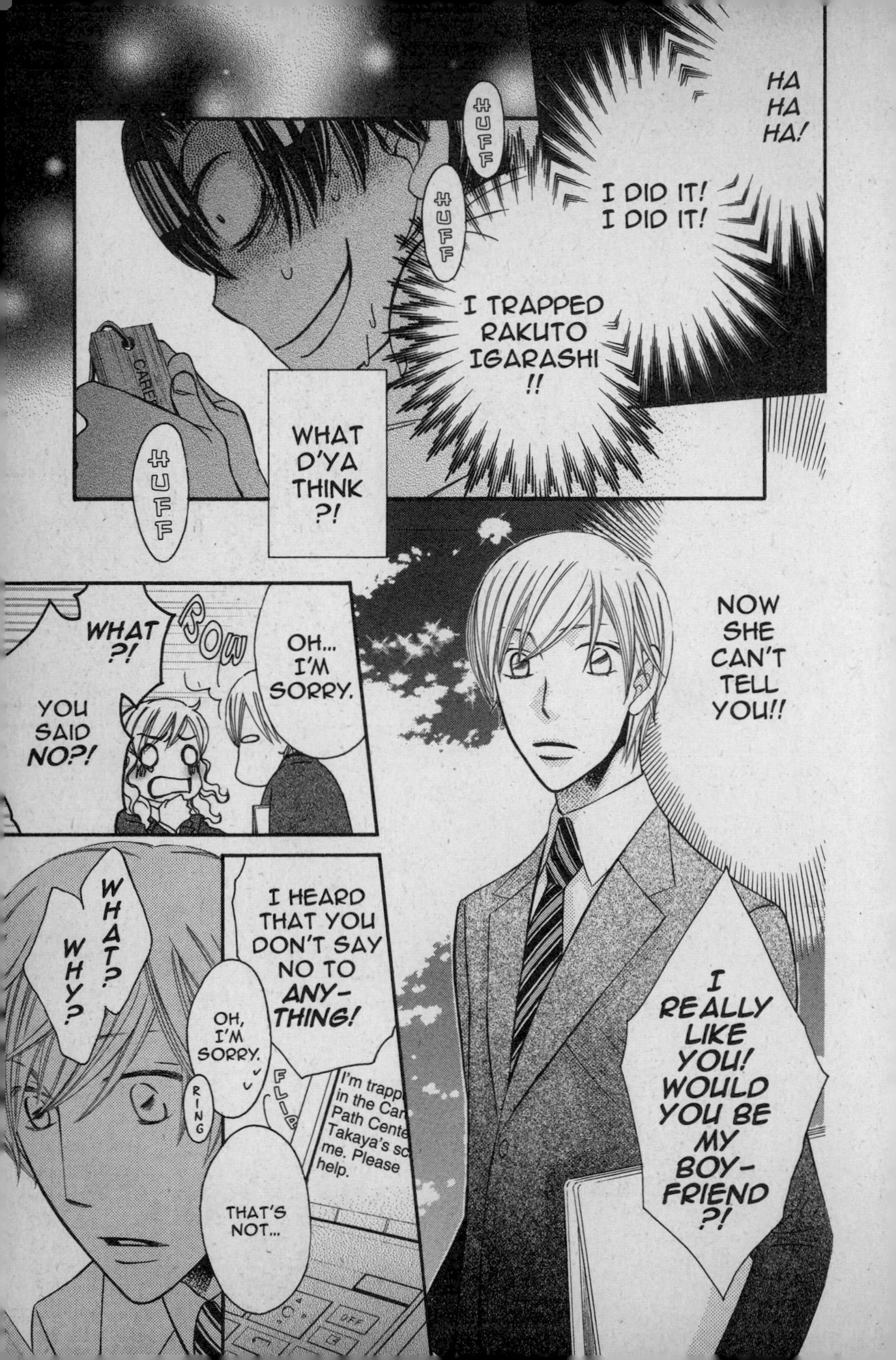
HA HA HA!
I DID IT! I DID IT!
I TRAPPED RAKUTO IGARASHI !!
HUFF HUFF
HUFF HUFF
WHAT D'YA THINK ?!
HUFF HUFF
NOW SHE CAN'T TELL YOU!!
I REALLY LIKE YOU! WOULD YOU BE MY BOY-FRIEND ?!
OH... I'M SORRY.
BOW
WHAT ?!
YOU SAID NO?!
I HEARD THAT YOU DON'T SAY NO TO ANY-THING!
WHAT? WHY?
OH, I'M SORRY.
FLIP
RING
I'm trapp in the Ca Path Cente Takaya's sc me. Please help.
THAT'S NOT...

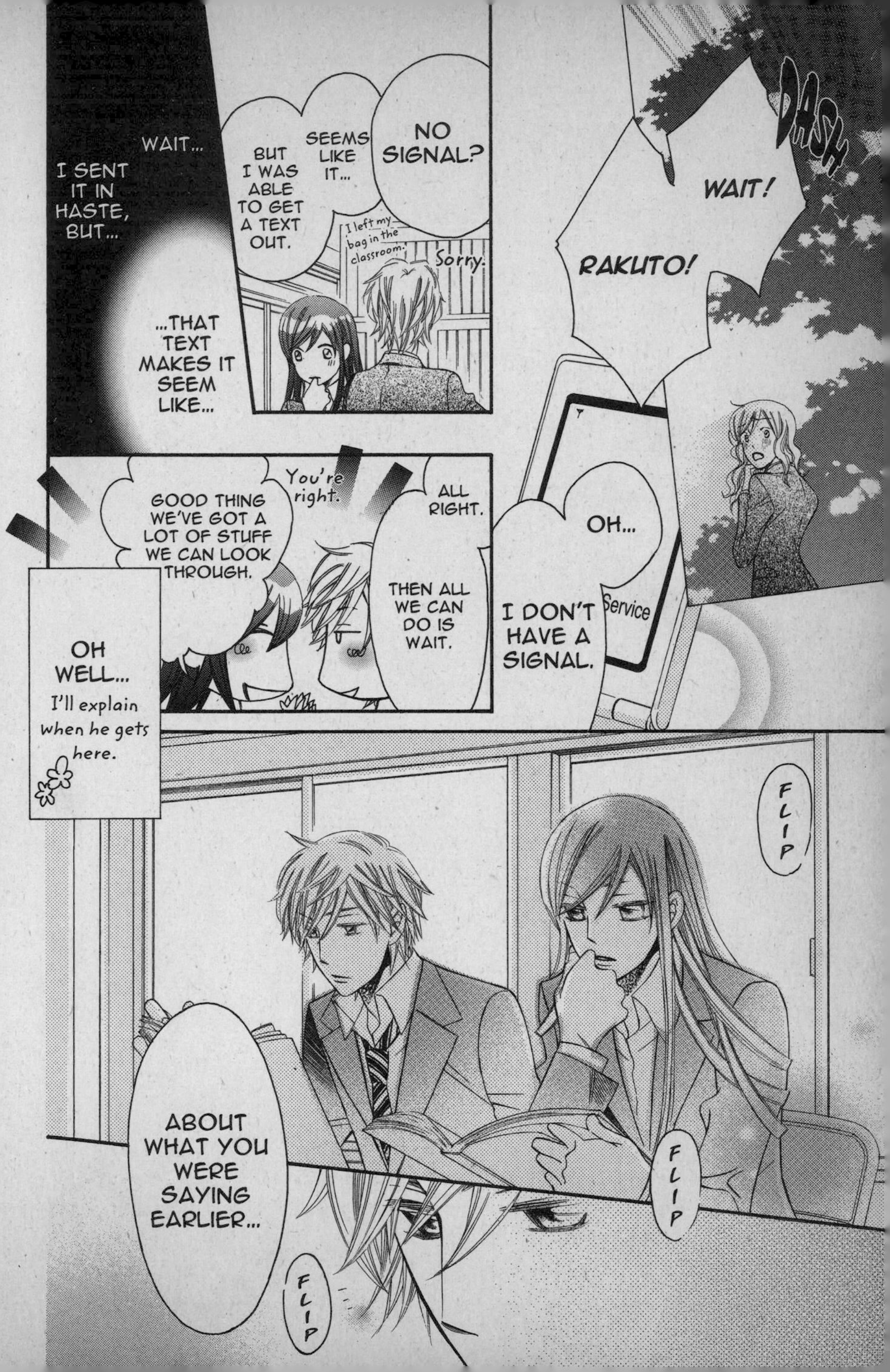
DASH
WAIT!
RAKUTO!
OH...
I DON'T HAVE A SIGNAL.
Service
NO SIGNAL?
SEEMS LIKE IT...
BUT I WAS ABLE TO GET A TEXT OUT.
Sorry.
I left my bag in the classroom.
WAIT...
I SENT IT IN HASTE, BUT...
...THAT TEXT MAKES IT SEEM LIKE...
ALL RIGHT.
THEN ALL WE CAN DO IS WAIT.
You're right.
GOOD THING WE'VE GOT A LOT OF STUFF WE CAN LOOK THROUGH.
OH WELL...
I'll explain when he gets here.
FLIP
FLIP
ABOUT WHAT YOU WERE SAYING EARLIER...
FLIP

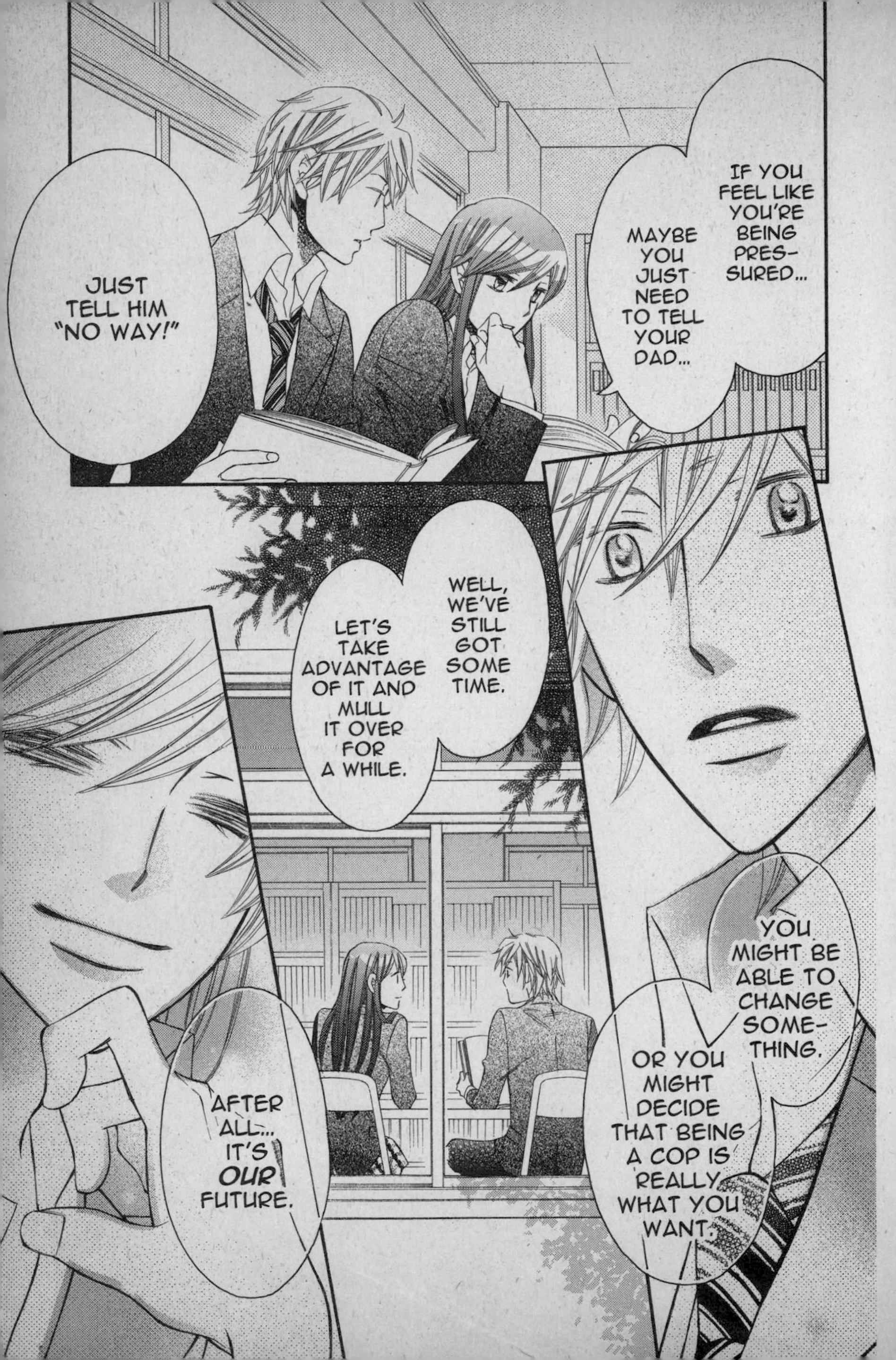
IF YOU FEEL LIKE YOU'RE BEING PRES-SURED...
MAYBE YOU JUST NEED TO TELL YOUR DAD...
JUST TELL HIM "NO WAY!"
YOU MIGHT BE ABLE TO CHANGE SOME-THING.
OR YOU MIGHT DECIDE THAT BEING A COP IS REALLY WHAT YOU WANT.
WELL, WE'VE STILL GOT SOME TIME.
LET'S TAKE ADVANTAGE OF IT AND MULL IT OVER FOR A WHILE.
AFTER ALL... IT'S ***OUR*** FUTURE.

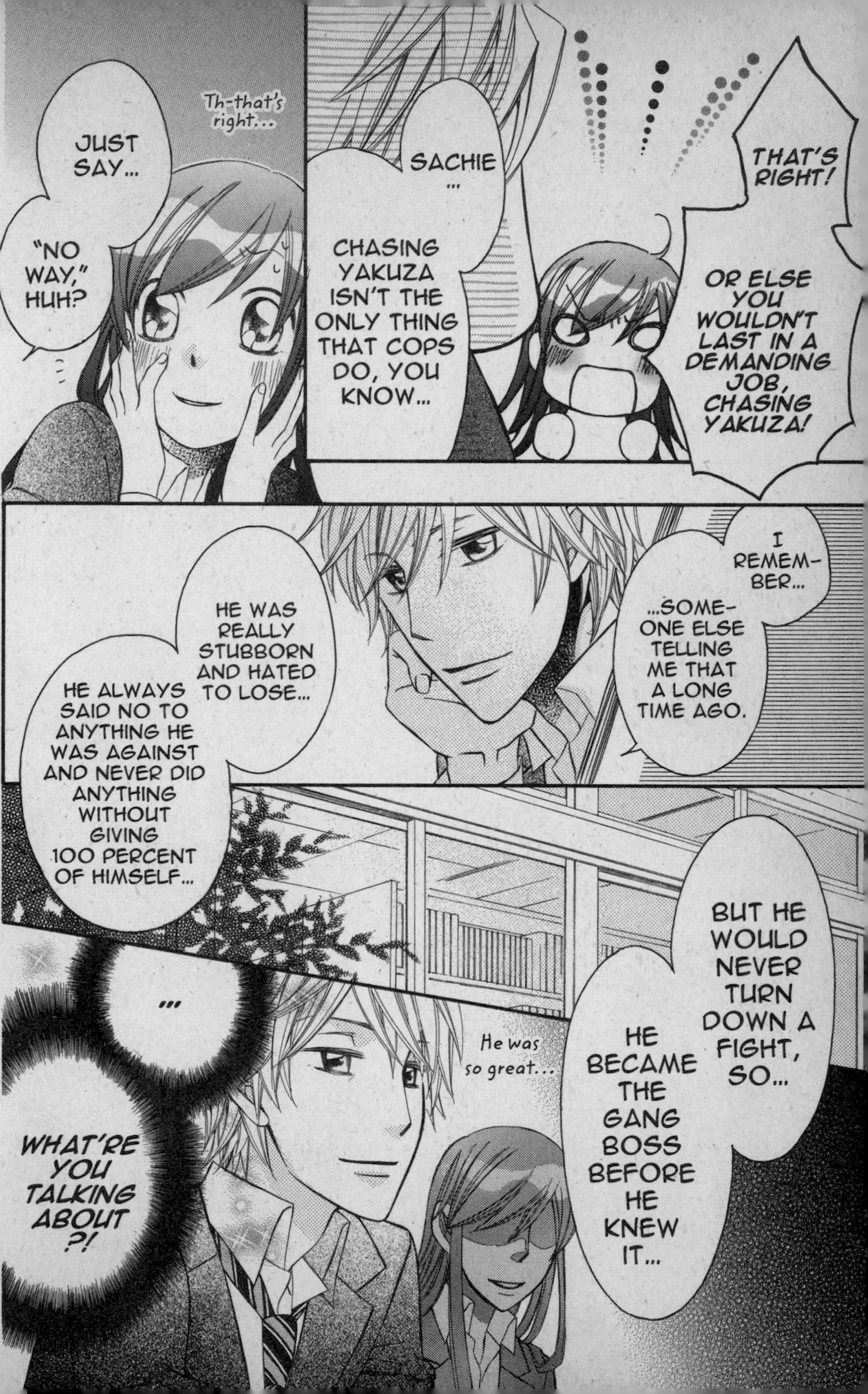
THAT'S RIGHT!
OR ELSE YOU WOULDN'T LAST IN A DEMANDING JOB, CHASING YAKUZA!
SACHIE ...
CHASING YAKUZA ISN'T THE ONLY THING THAT COPS DO, YOU KNOW...
JUST SAY...
"NO WAY," HUH?
Th-that's right...
I REMEMBER...
...SOMEONE ELSE TELLING ME THAT A LONG TIME AGO.
HE WAS REALLY STUBBORN AND HATED TO LOSE...
HE ALWAYS SAID NO TO ANYTHING HE WAS AGAINST AND NEVER DID ANYTHING WITHOUT GIVING 100 PERCENT OF HIMSELF...
BUT HE WOULD NEVER TURN DOWN A FIGHT, SO...
HE BECAME THE GANG BOSS BEFORE HE KNEW IT...
He was so great...
...
WHAT'RE YOU TALKING ABOUT?!

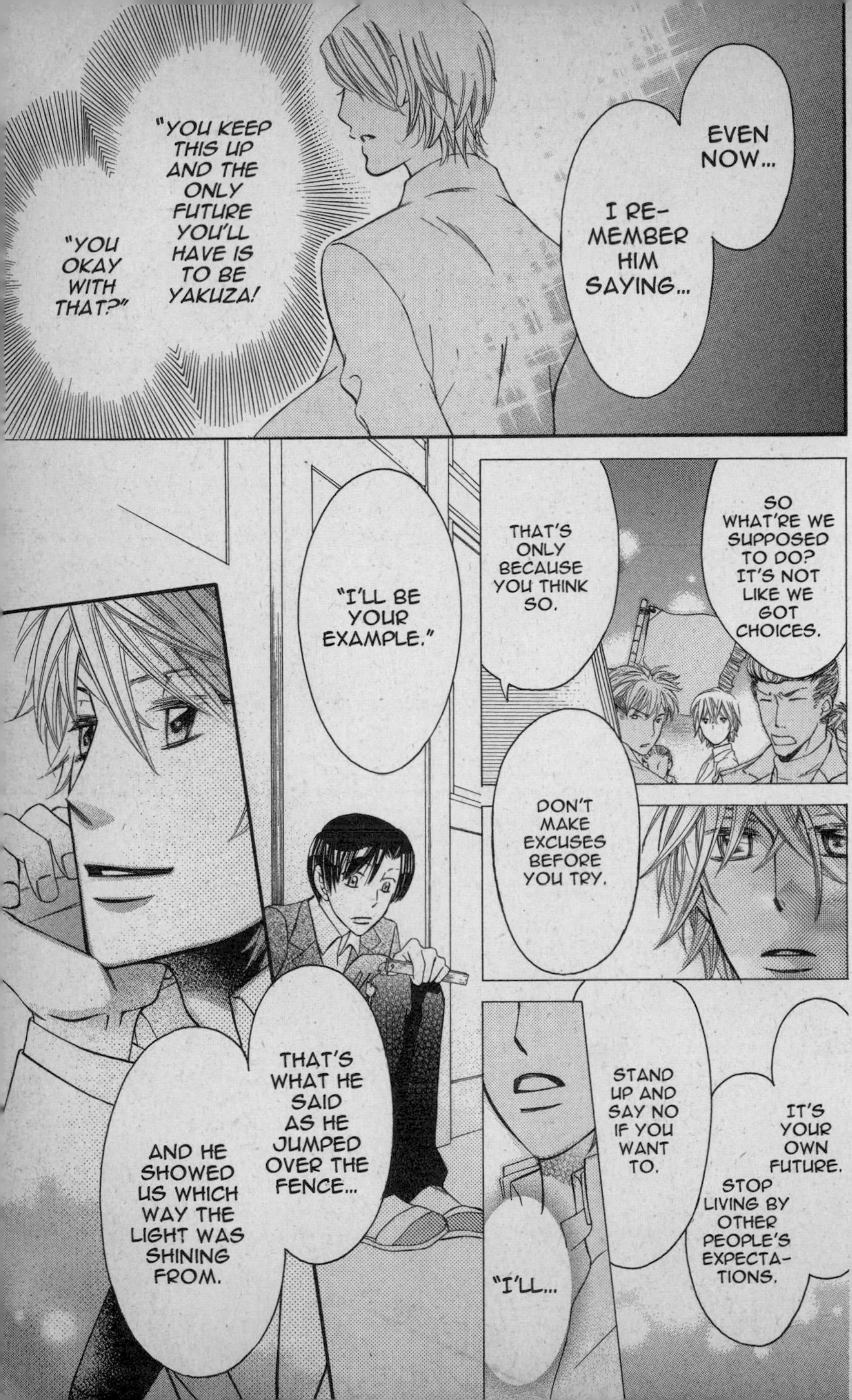
EVEN NOW...
I RE-MEMBER HIM SAYING...
"YOU KEEP THIS UP AND THE ONLY FUTURE YOU'LL HAVE IS TO BE YAKUZA!
"YOU OKAY WITH THAT?"
SO WHAT'RE WE SUPPOSED TO DO? IT'S NOT LIKE WE GOT CHOICES.
THAT'S ONLY BECAUSE YOU THINK SO.
DON'T MAKE EXCUSES BEFORE YOU TRY.
IT'S YOUR OWN FUTURE.
STOP LIVING BY OTHER PEOPLE'S EXPECTA-TIONS.
STAND UP AND SAY NO IF YOU WANT TO.
"I'LL...
"I'LL BE YOUR EXAMPLE."
THAT'S WHAT HE SAID AS HE JUMPED OVER THE FENCE...
AND HE SHOWED US WHICH WAY THE LIGHT WAS SHINING FROM.

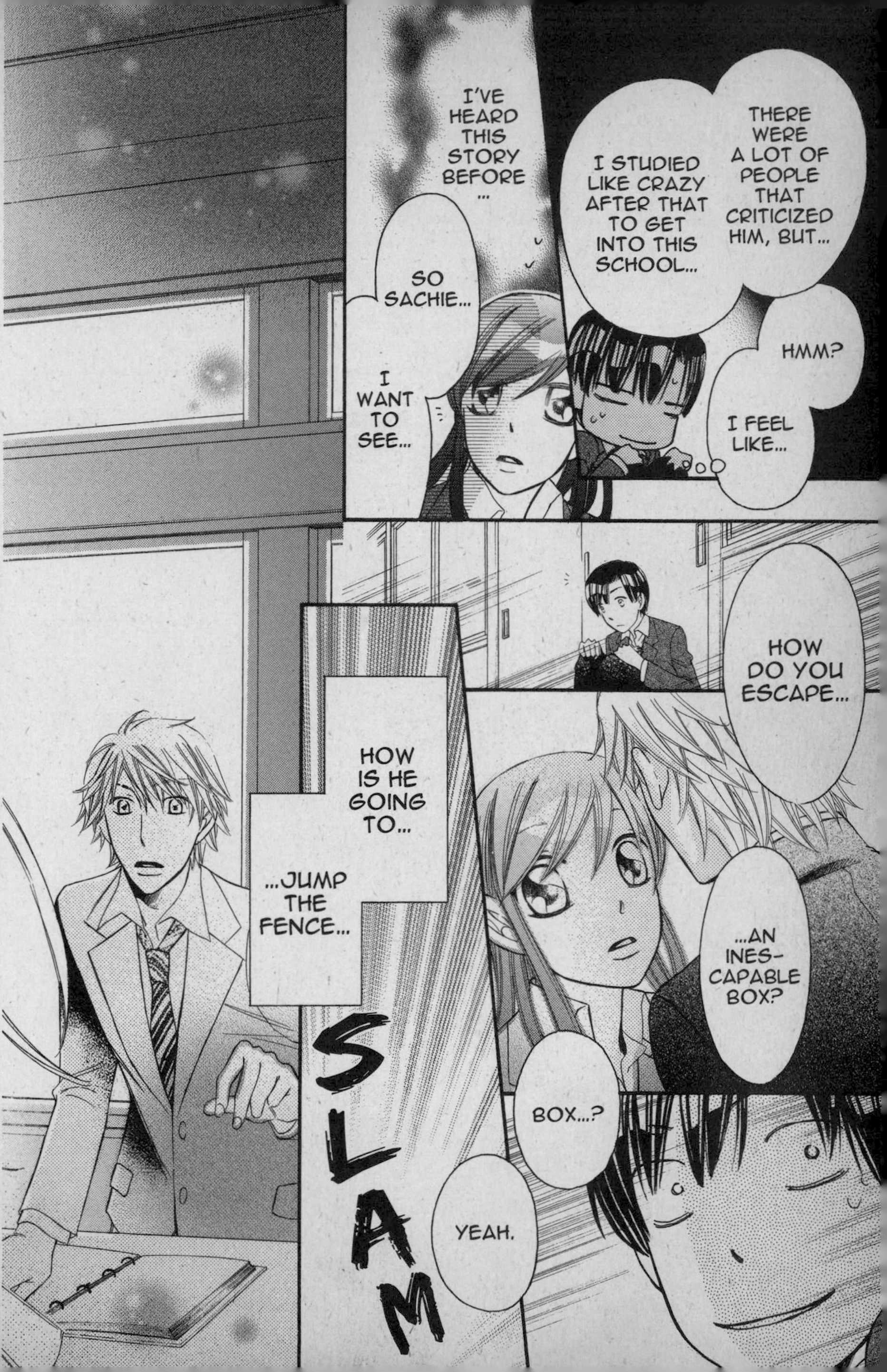
THERE WERE A LOT OF PEOPLE THAT CRITICIZED HIM, BUT...
I STUDIED LIKE CRAZY AFTER THAT TO GET INTO THIS SCHOOL...
HMM?
I FEEL LIKE...
I'VE HEARD THIS STORY BEFORE...
SO SACHIE...
I WANT TO SEE...
HOW DO YOU ESCAPE...
...AN INES-CAPABLE BOX?
HOW IS HE GOING TO...
...JUMP THE FENCE...
BOX...?
YEAH.
SLAM

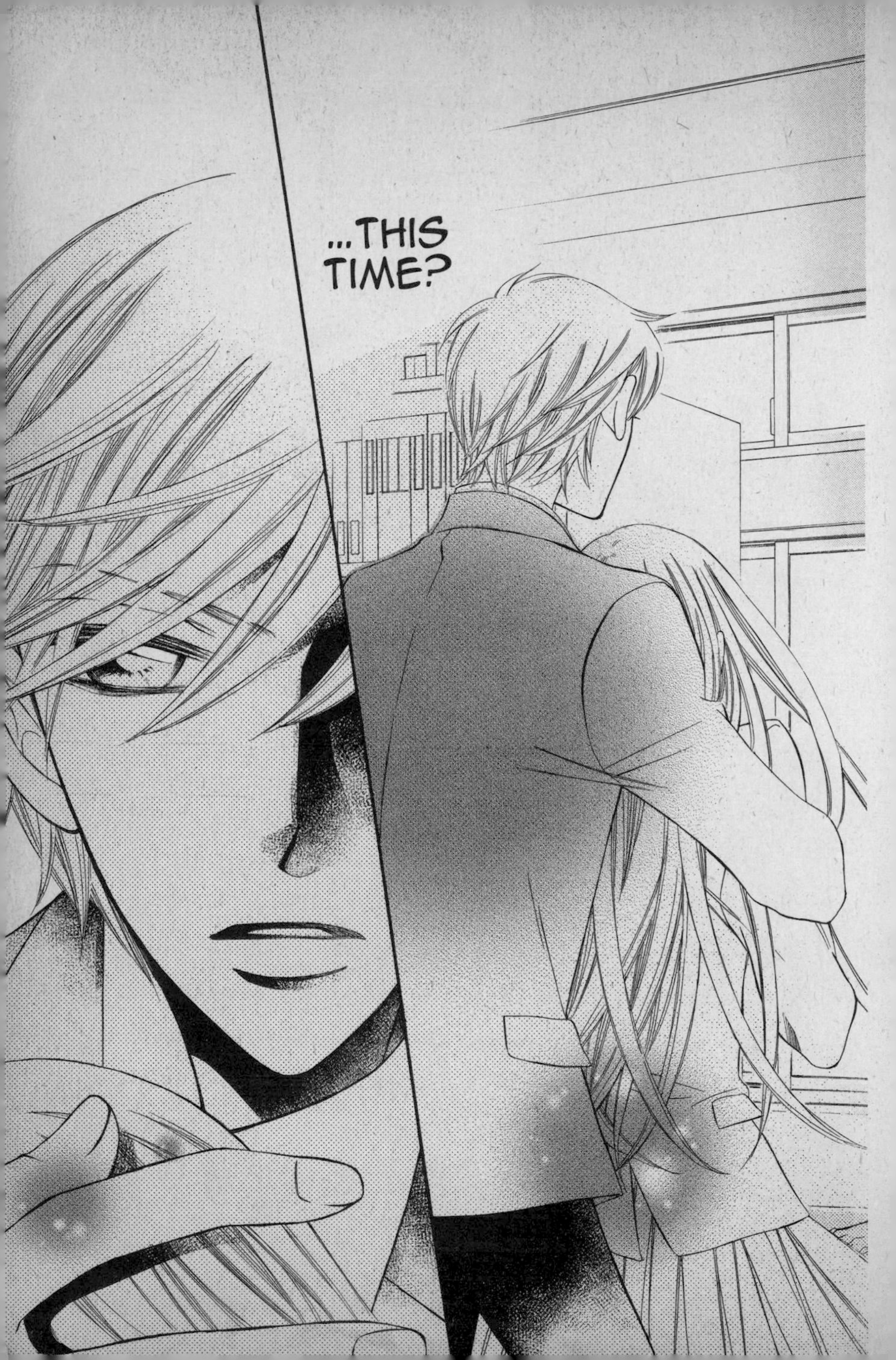
...THIS TIME?

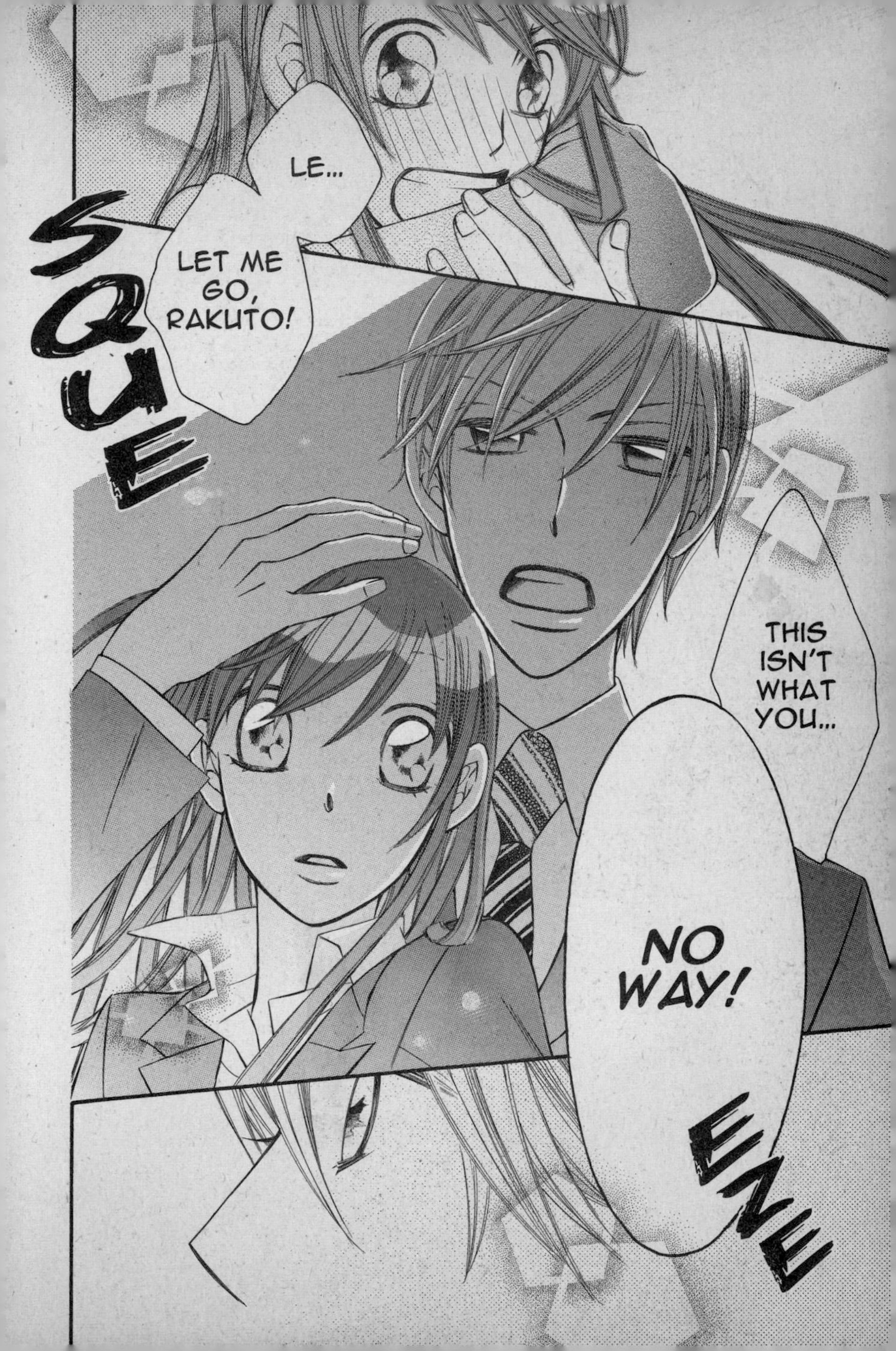
LE...
LET ME GO, RAKUTO!
SQUE
THIS ISN'T WHAT YOU...
NO WAY!
EZE

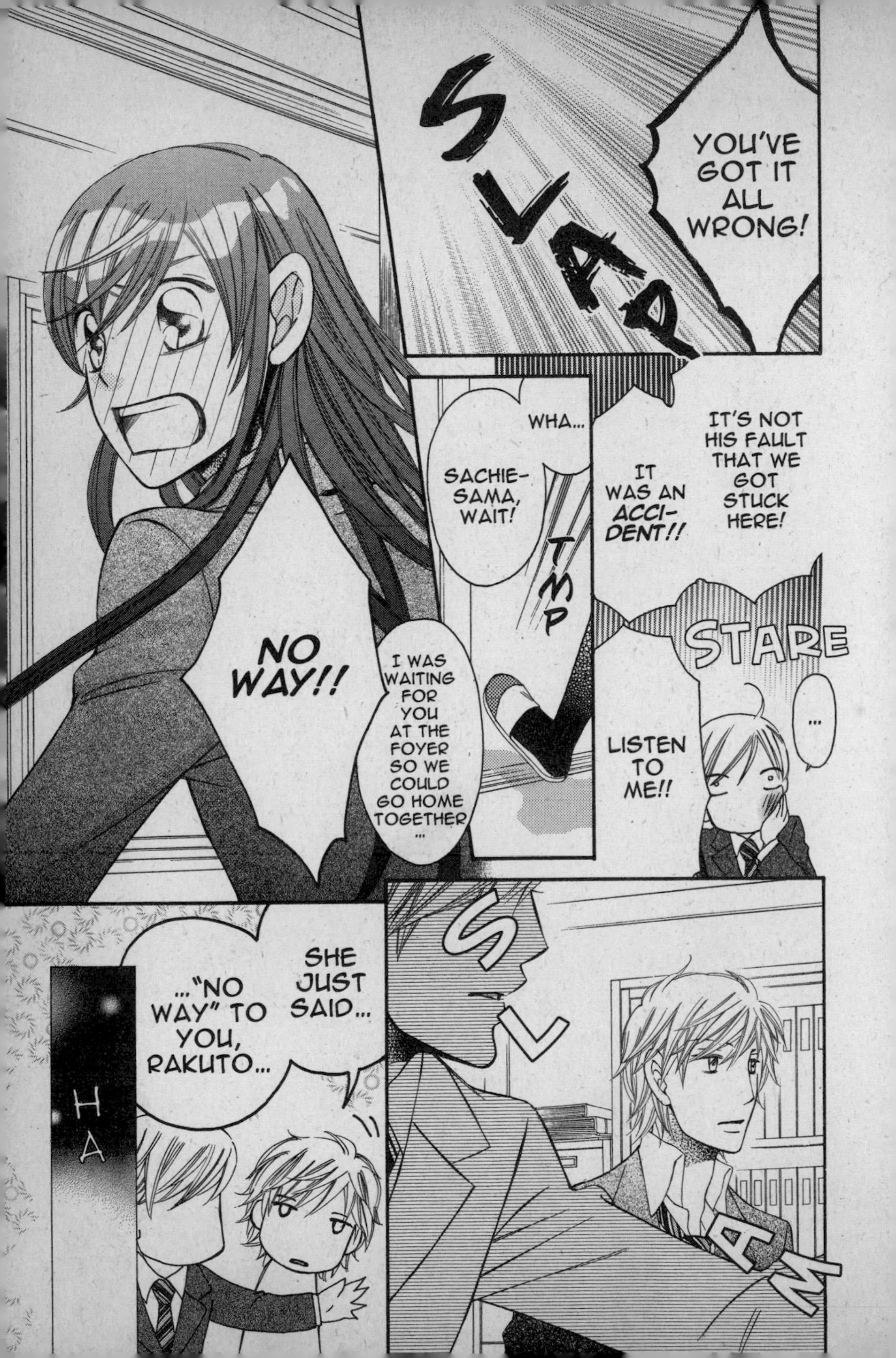
YOU'VE GOT IT ALL WRONG!
SLAP
IT'S NOT HIS FAULT THAT WE GOT STUCK HERE!
IT WAS AN ACCIDENT!!
STARE
...
LISTEN TO ME!!
WHA...
SACHIE-SAMA, WAIT!
TMP
NO WAY!!
I WAS WAITING FOR YOU AT THE FOYER SO WE COULD GO HOME TOGETHER...
SLAM
SHE JUST SAID...
..."NO WAY" TO YOU, RAKUTO...
HA

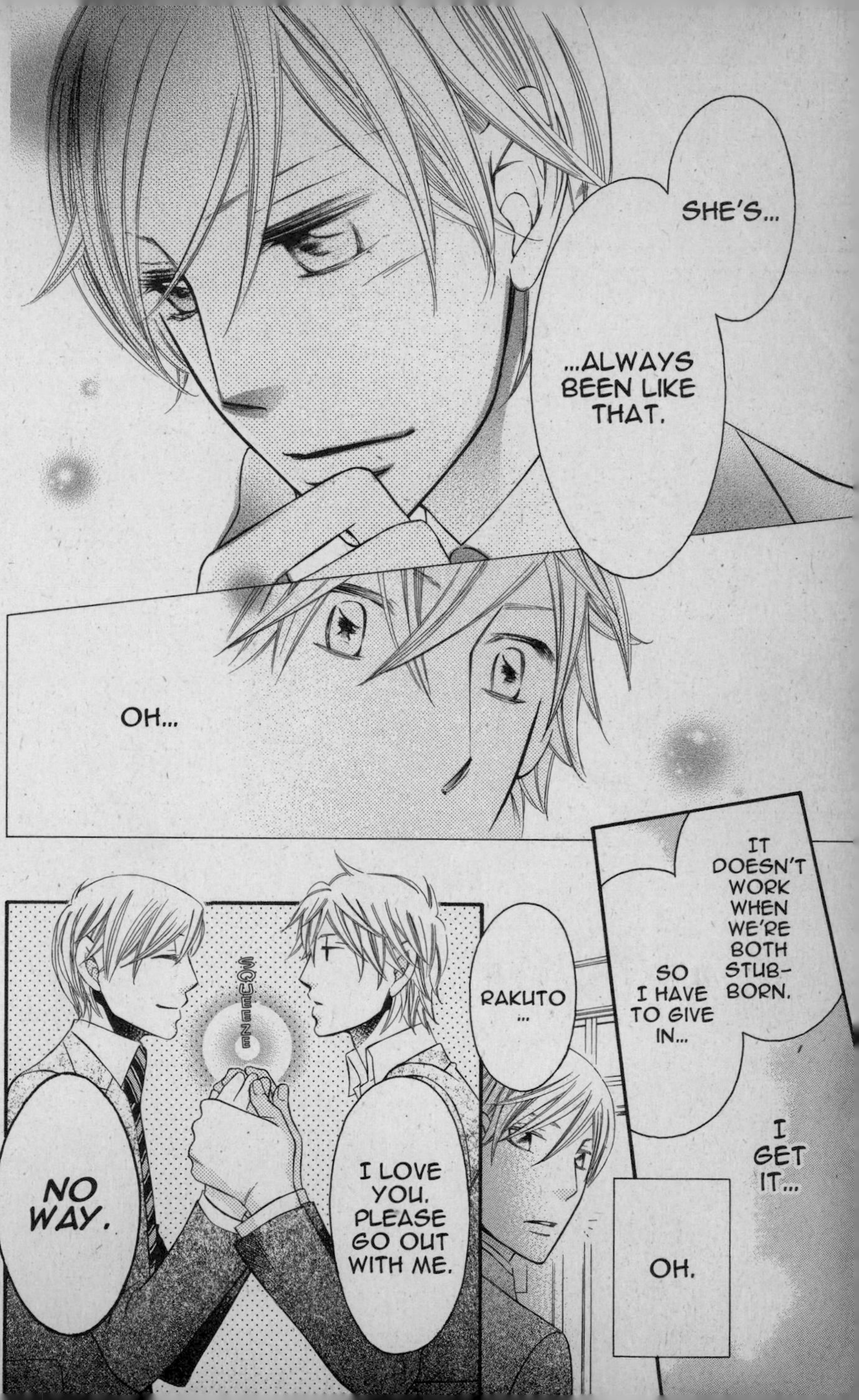
SHE'S...
...ALWAYS BEEN LIKE THAT.
OH...
IT DOESN'T WORK WHEN WE'RE BOTH STUB-BORN.
SO I HAVE TO GIVE IN...
RAKUTO ...
I GET IT...
OH.
SQUEEZE
I LOVE YOU. PLEASE GO OUT WITH ME.
NO WAY.

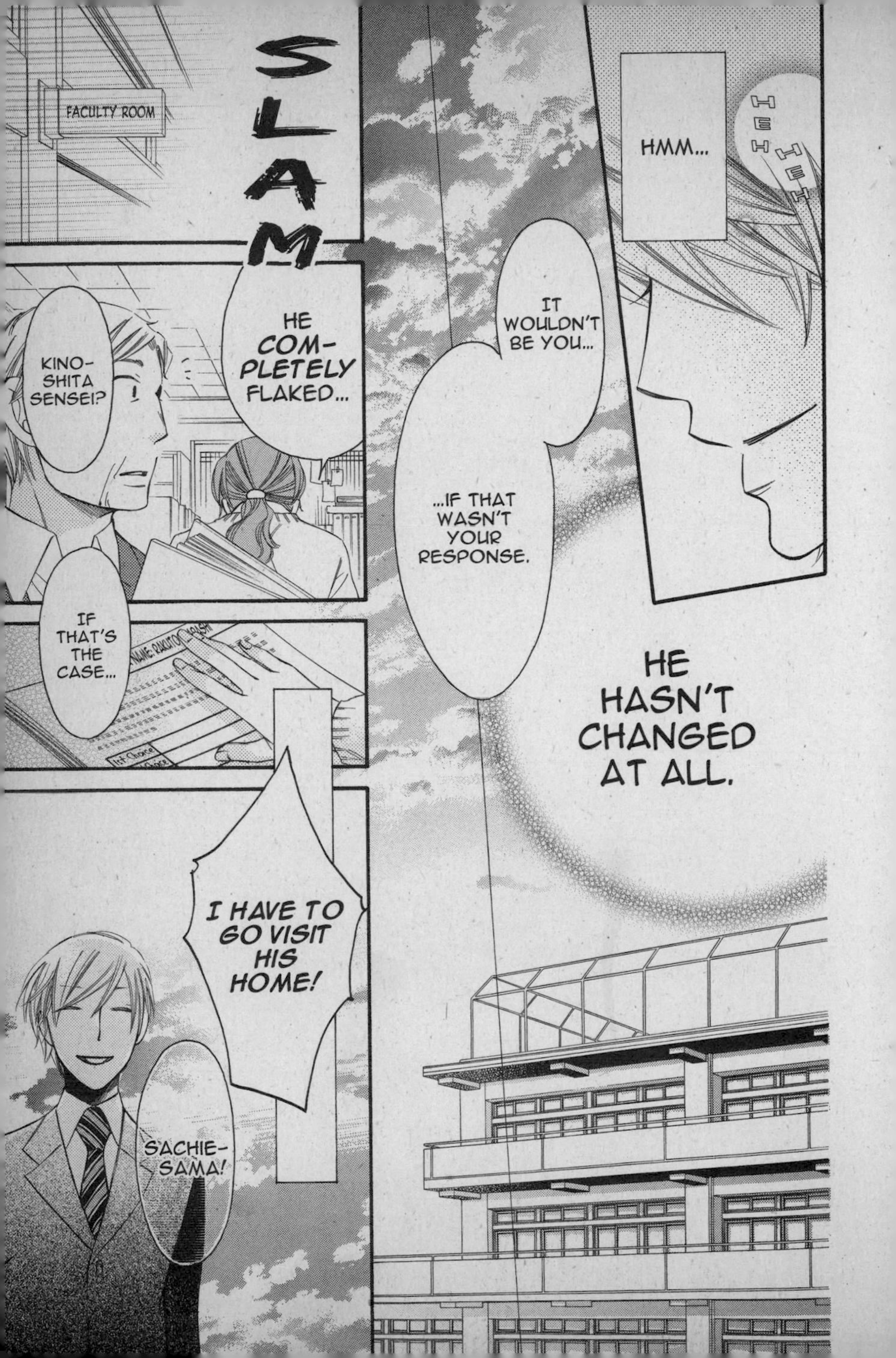
HEH HEH HEH
HMM...
IT WOULDN'T BE YOU...
...IF THAT WASN'T YOUR RESPONSE.
HE HASN'T CHANGED AT ALL.
SLAM
FACULTY ROOM
HE COMPLETELY FLAKED...
KINOSHITA SENSEI?
IF THAT'S THE CASE...
I HAVE TO GO VISIT HIS HOME!
SACHIE-SAMA!

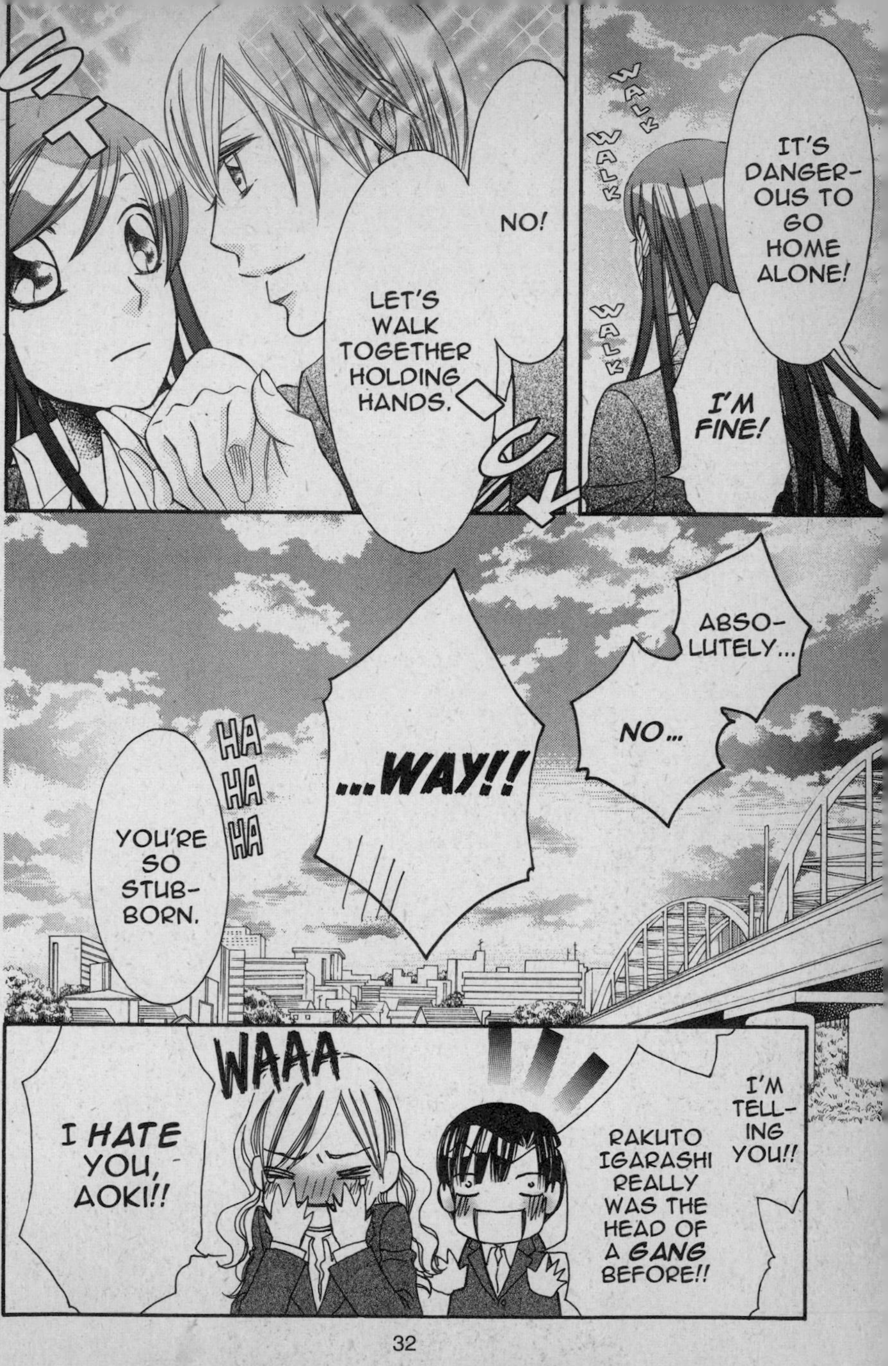
WALK WALK
WALK WALK
IT'S DANGER-OUS TO GO HOME ALONE!
I'M FINE!
STICK
NO!
LET'S WALK TOGETHER HOLDING HANDS.
ABSO-LUTELY...
NO...
...WAY!!
HA HA HA
YOU'RE SO STUB-BORN.
I'M TELL-ING YOU!!
RAKUTO IGARASHI REALLY WAS THE HEAD OF A GANG BEFORE!!
WAAA
I HATE YOU, AOKI!!

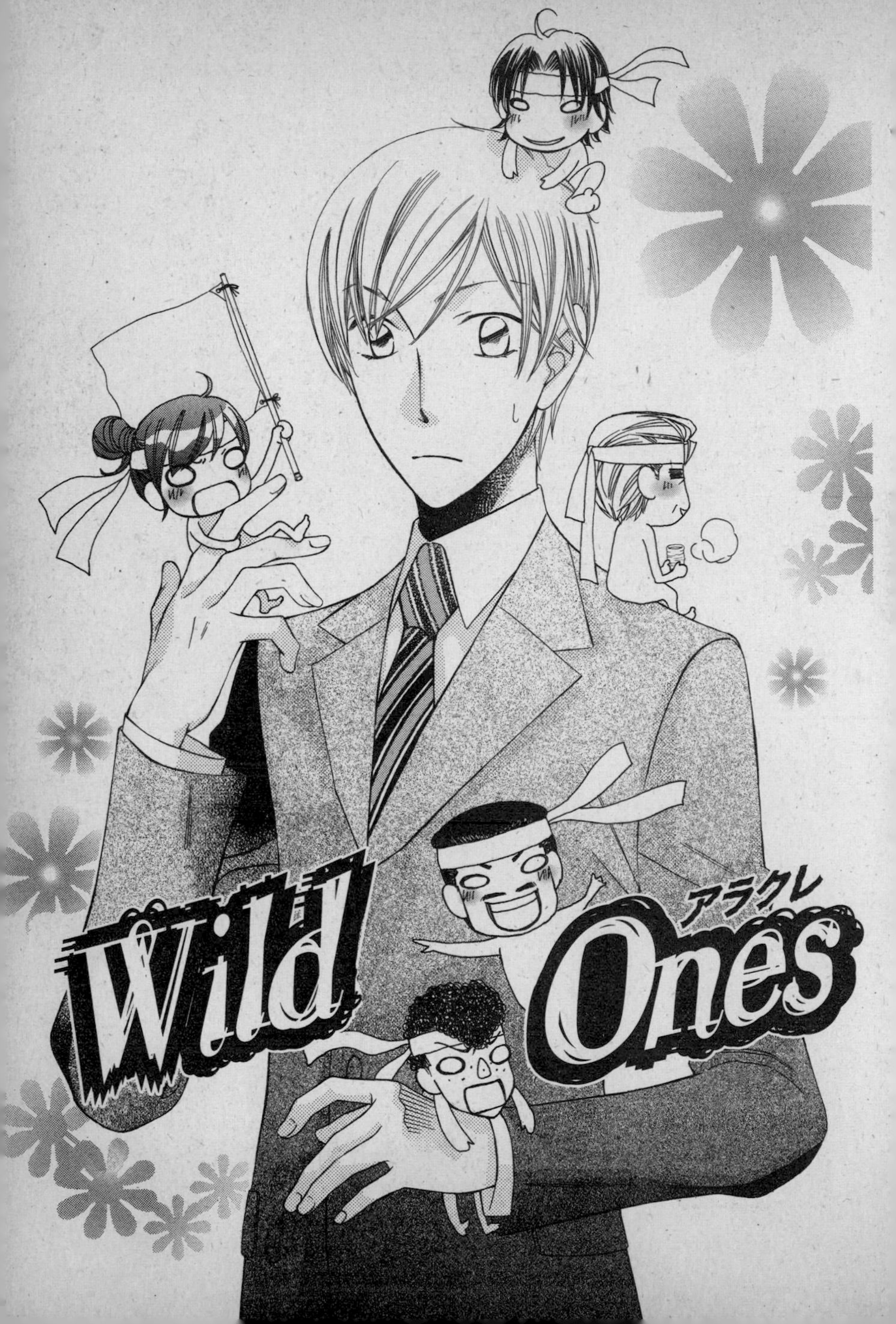
Wild Ones
アラクレ

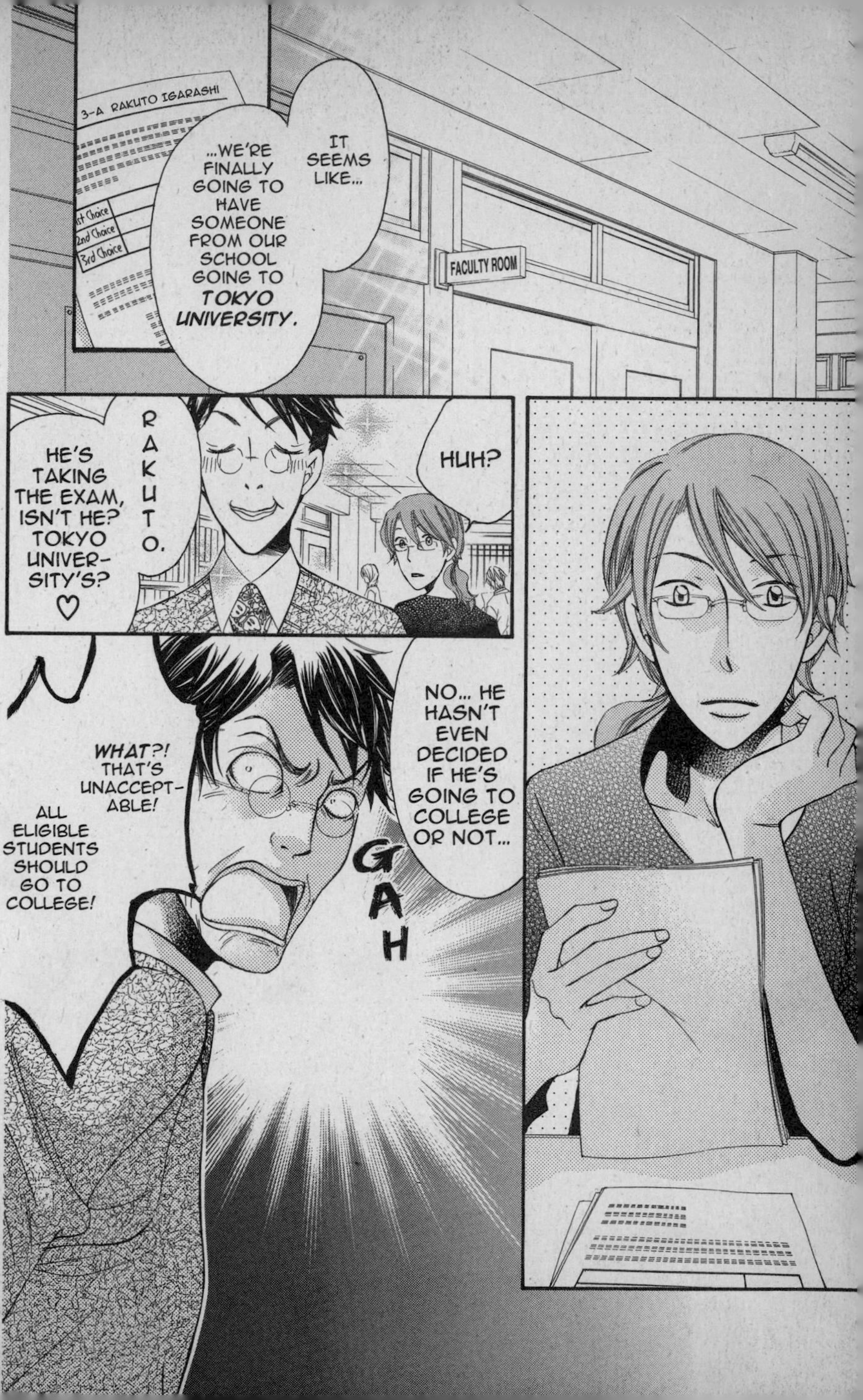
3-A RAKUTO IGARASHI
1st Choice
2nd Choice
3rd Choice
FACULTY ROOM
IT SEEMS LIKE... ...WE'RE FINALLY GOING TO HAVE SOMEONE FROM OUR SCHOOL GOING TO *TOKYO UNIVERSITY*.
HUH?
RAKUTO.
HE'S TAKING THE EXAM, ISN'T HE? TOKYO UNIVERSITY'S? ♡
NO... HE HASN'T EVEN DECIDED IF HE'S GOING TO COLLEGE OR NOT...
GAH
WHAT?! THAT'S UNACCEPTABLE!
ALL ELIGIBLE STUDENTS SHOULD GO TO COLLEGE!

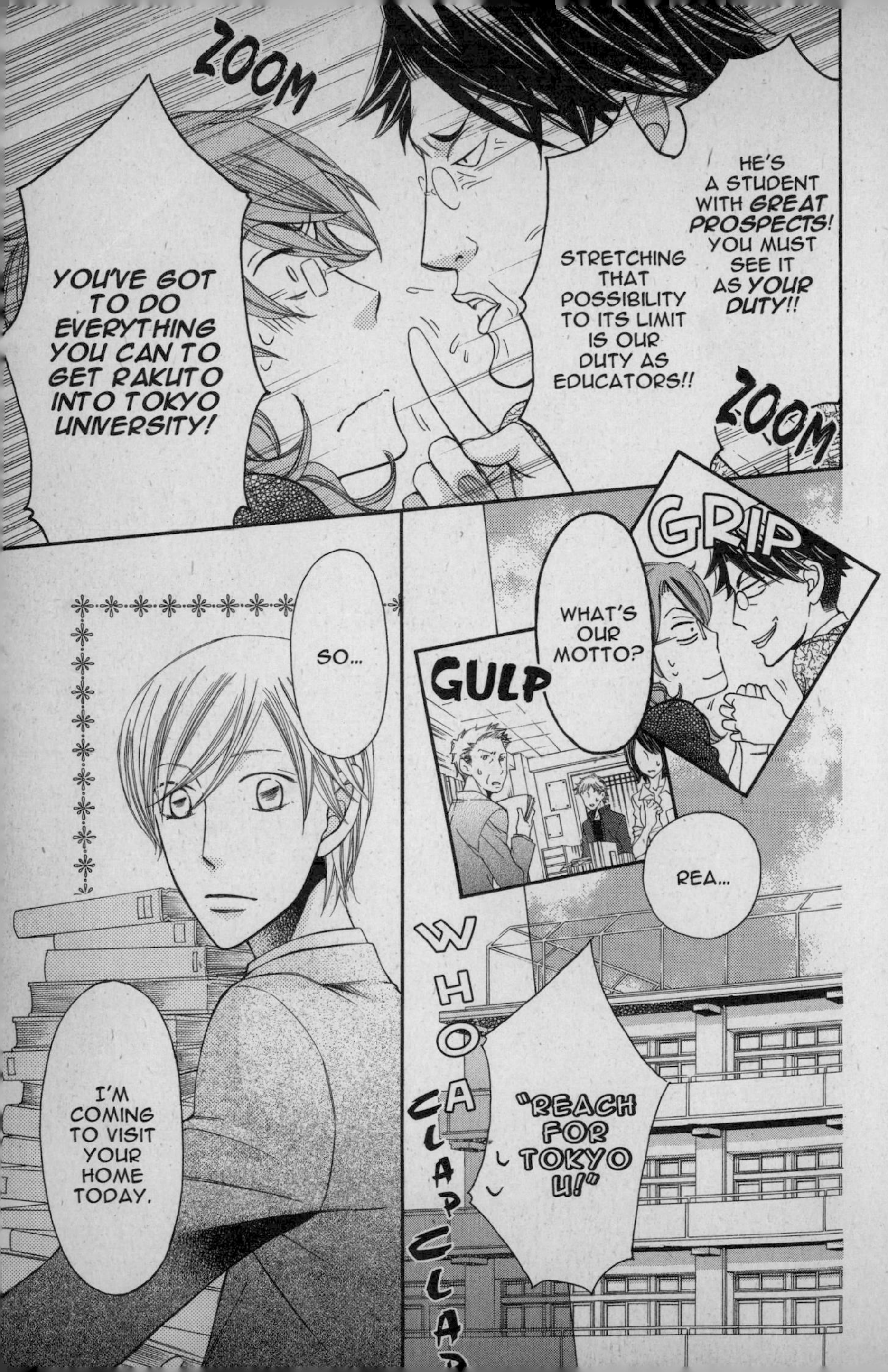
ZOOM
HE'S A STUDENT WITH GREAT PROSPECTS! YOU MUST SEE IT AS YOUR DUTY!!
STRETCHING THAT POSSIBILITY TO ITS LIMIT IS OUR DUTY AS EDUCATORS!!
ZOOM
YOU'VE GOT TO DO EVERYTHING YOU CAN TO GET RAKUTO INTO TOKYO UNIVERSITY!
GRIP
WHAT'S OUR MOTTO?
GULP
REA...
"REACH FOR TOKYO U!"
WHOA
CLAP CLAP
SO...
I'M COMING TO VISIT YOUR HOME TODAY.

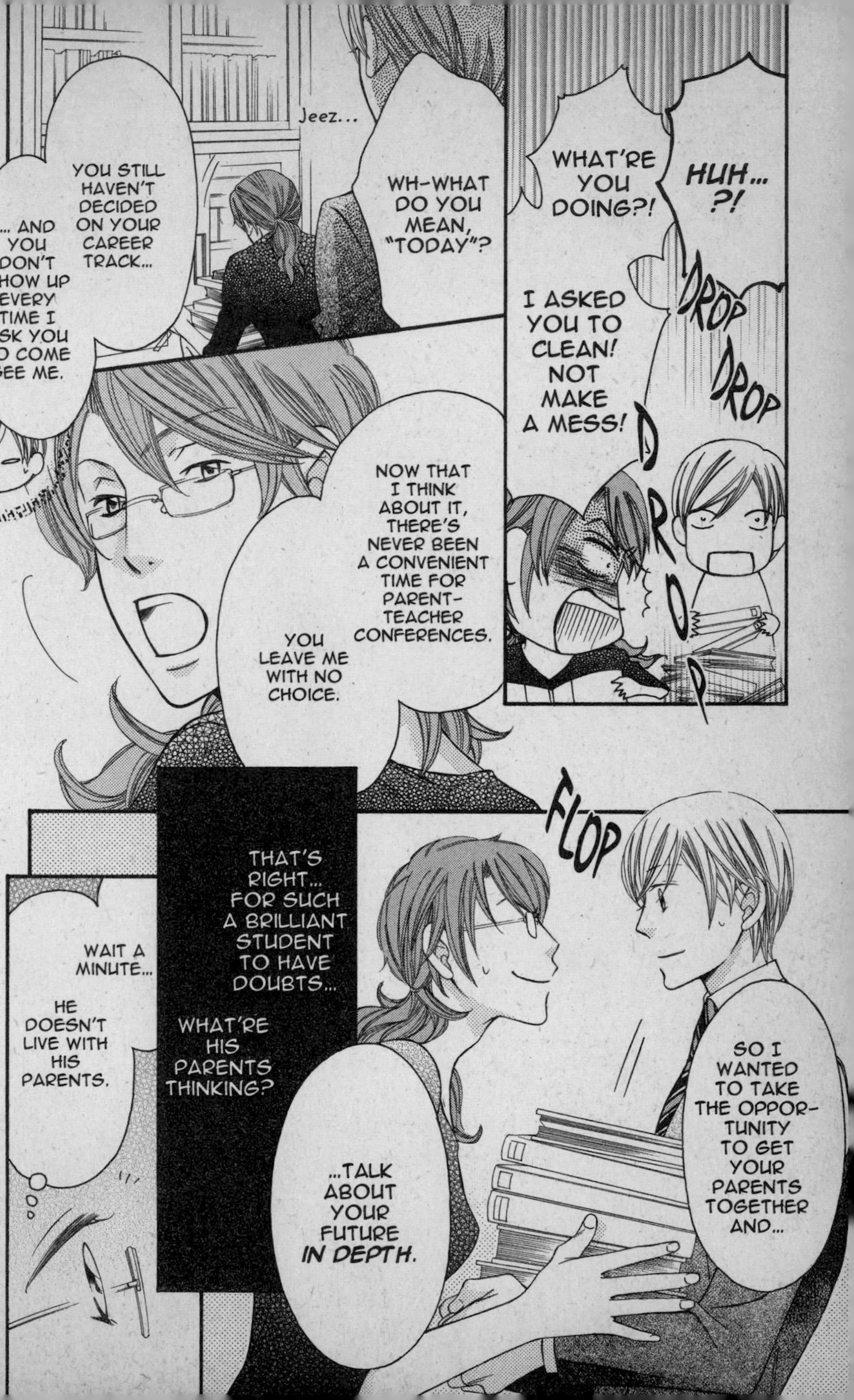
WHAT'RE YOU DOING?!
HUH... ?!
I ASKED YOU TO CLEAN! NOT MAKE A MESS!
DROP DROP
DROP
Jeez...
WH-WHAT DO YOU MEAN, "TODAY"?
YOU STILL HAVEN'T DECIDED ON YOUR CAREER TRACK...
... AND YOU DON'T SHOW UP EVERY TIME I ASK YOU TO COME SEE ME.
NOW THAT I THINK ABOUT IT, THERE'S NEVER BEEN A CONVENIENT TIME FOR PARENT-TEACHER CONFERENCES.
YOU LEAVE ME WITH NO CHOICE.
FLOP
SO I WANTED TO TAKE THE OPPOR-TUNITY TO GET YOUR PARENTS TOGETHER AND...
...TALK ABOUT YOUR FUTURE IN DEPTH.
THAT'S RIGHT... FOR SUCH A BRILLIANT STUDENT TO HAVE DOUBTS...
WHAT'RE HIS PARENTS THINKING?
WAIT A MINUTE...
HE DOESN'T LIVE WITH HIS PARENTS.

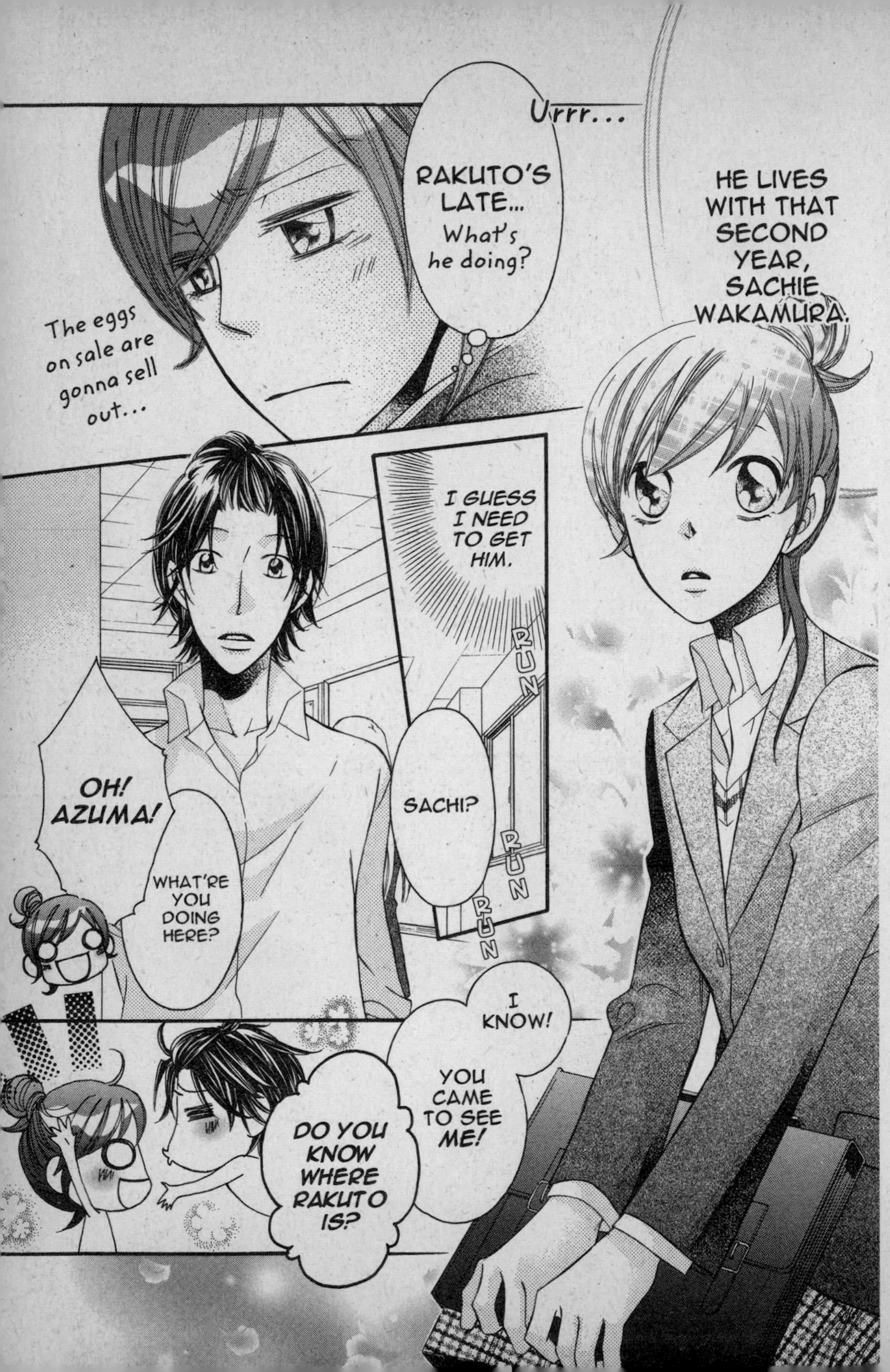
Urrr...
RAKUTO'S LATE... What's he doing?
The eggs on sale are gonna sell out...
HE LIVES WITH THAT SECOND YEAR, SACHIE WAKAMURA.
I GUESS I NEED TO GET HIM.
RUN RUN RUN RUN
SACHI?
OH! AZUMA!
WHAT'RE YOU DOING HERE?
I KNOW! YOU CAME TO SEE ME!
DO YOU KNOW WHERE RAKUTO IS?

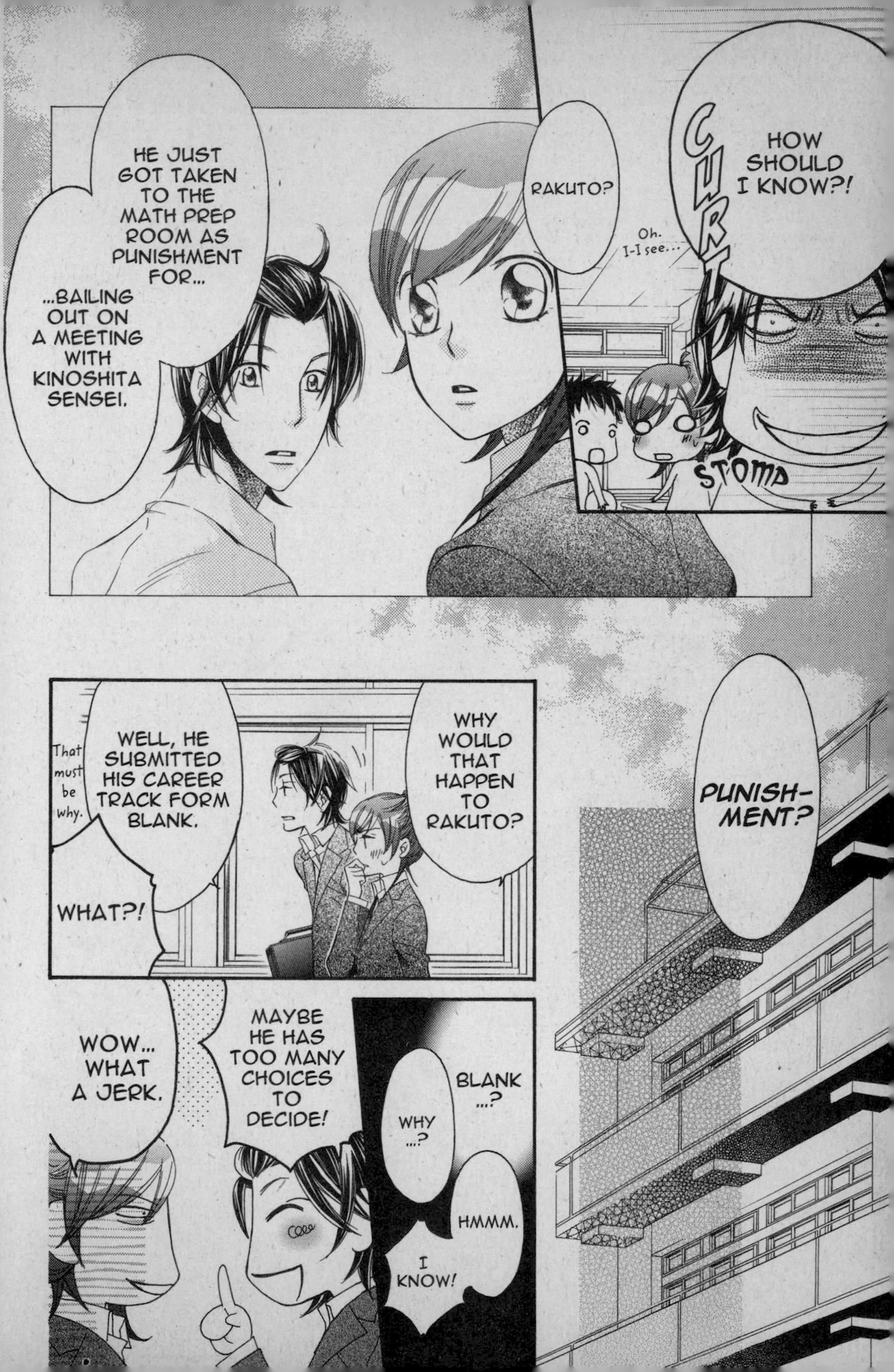
RAKUTO?
HOW SHOULD I KNOW?!
CURT
Oh. I-I see...
STOMP
HE JUST GOT TAKEN TO THE MATH PREP ROOM AS PUNISHMENT FOR...
...BAILING OUT ON A MEETING WITH KINOSHITA SENSEI.
PUNISH-MENT?
WHY WOULD THAT HAPPEN TO RAKUTO?
WELL, HE SUBMITTED HIS CAREER TRACK FORM BLANK.
That must be why.
WHAT?!
BLANK ...?
WHY ...?
HMMM.
I KNOW!
MAYBE HE HAS TOO MANY CHOICES TO DECIDE!
WOW... WHAT A JERK.

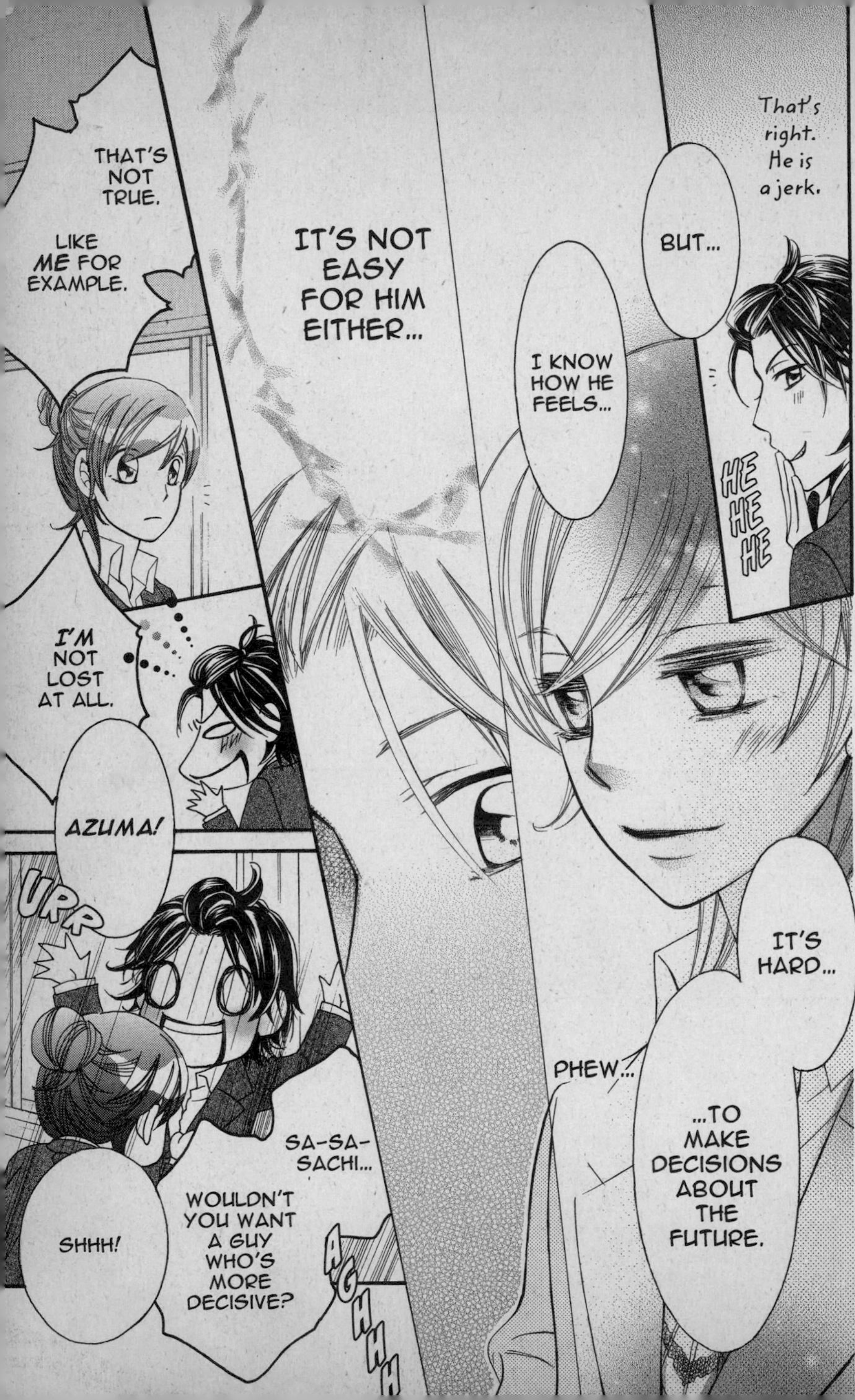
That's right. He is a jerk.
BUT...
HE HE HE
I KNOW HOW HE FEELS...
IT'S HARD...
...TO MAKE DECISIONS ABOUT THE FUTURE.
PHEW...
IT'S NOT EASY FOR HIM EITHER...
THAT'S NOT TRUE.
LIKE *ME* FOR EXAMPLE.
I'M NOT LOST AT ALL.
AZUMA!
URR
WOULDN'T YOU WANT A GUY WHO'S MORE DECISIVE?
SA-SA-SACHI...
SHHH!
AGHHHH

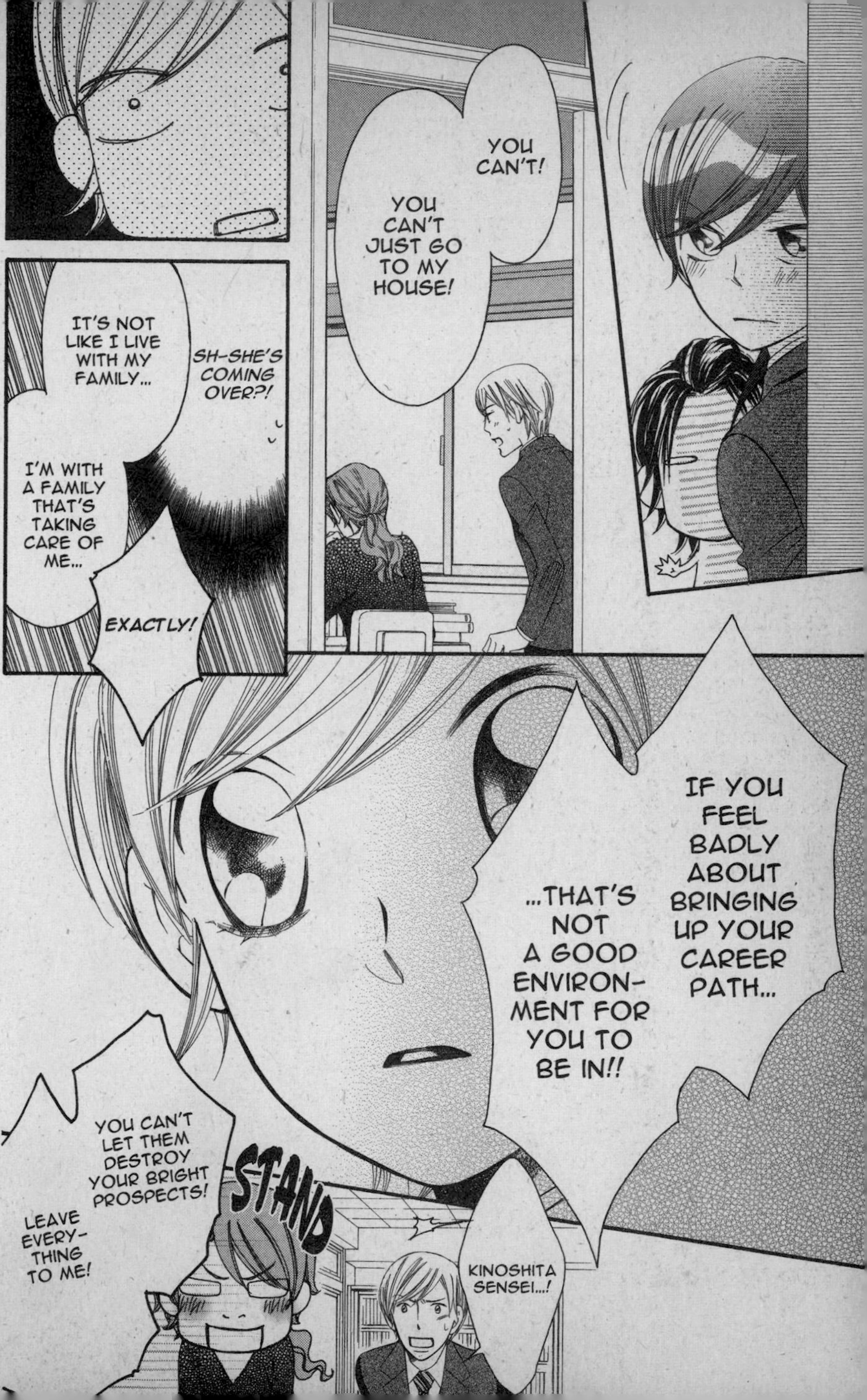
YOU CAN'T!
YOU CAN'T JUST GO TO MY HOUSE!
IT'S NOT LIKE I LIVE WITH MY FAMILY...
SH-SHE'S COMING OVER?!
I'M WITH A FAMILY THAT'S TAKING CARE OF ME...
EXACTLY!
IF YOU FEEL BADLY ABOUT BRINGING UP YOUR CAREER PATH...
...THAT'S NOT A GOOD ENVIRON-MENT FOR YOU TO BE IN!!
YOU CAN'T LET THEM DESTROY YOUR BRIGHT PROSPECTS!
STAND
KINOSHITA SENSEI...!
LEAVE EVERY-THING TO ME!

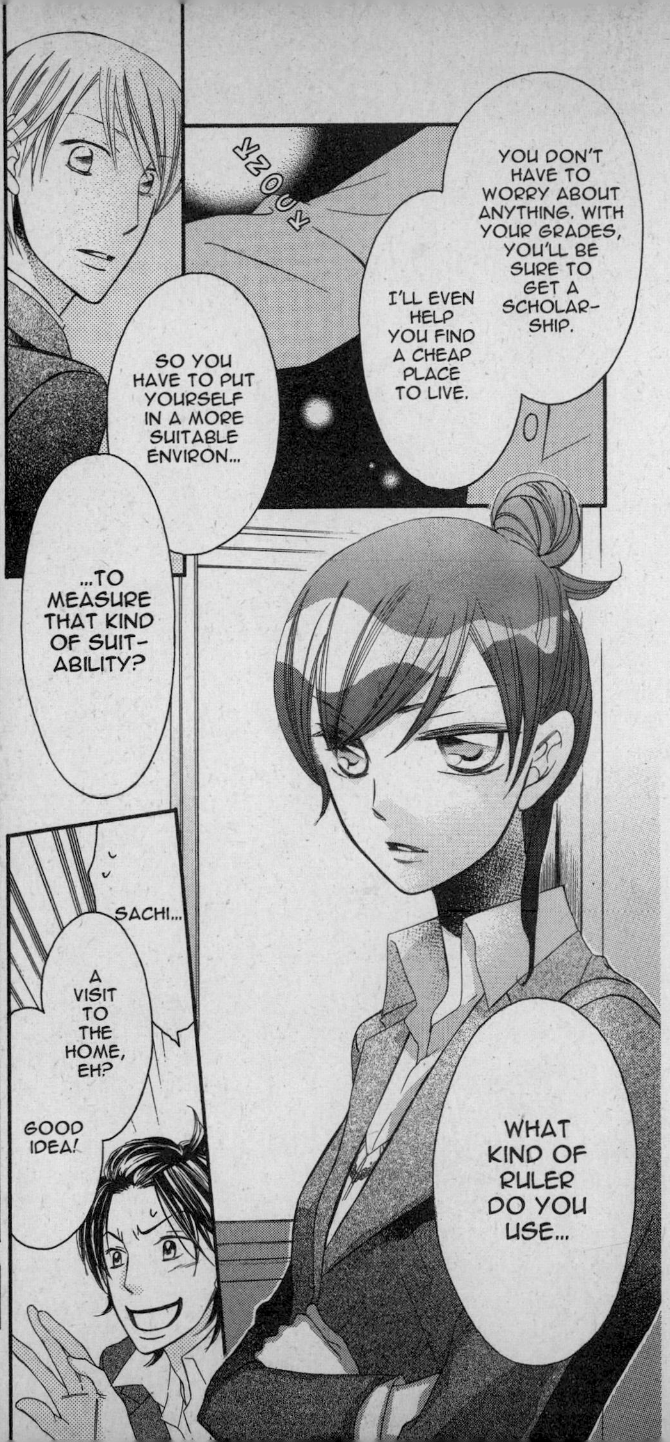
YOU DON'T HAVE TO WORRY ABOUT ANYTHING. WITH YOUR GRADES, YOU'LL BE SURE TO GET A SCHOLAR-SHIP.
I'LL EVEN HELP YOU FIND A CHEAP PLACE TO LIVE.
SO YOU HAVE TO PUT YOURSELF IN A MORE SUITABLE ENVIRON...
...TO MEASURE THAT KIND OF SUIT-ABILITY?
WHAT KIND OF RULER DO YOU USE...
SACHI...
A VISIT TO THE HOME, EH?
GOOD IDEA!

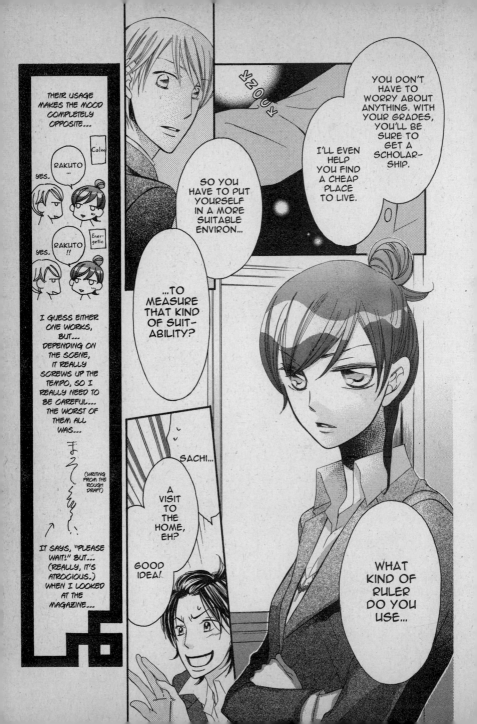

THEIR USAGE MAKES THE MOOD COMPLETELY OPPOSITE...

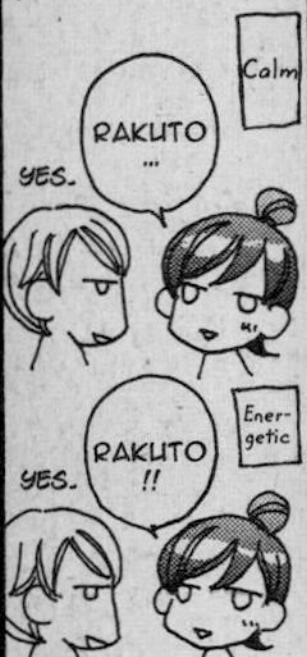
Calm
RAKUTO...
YES.
Ener-getic
RAKUTO!!
YES.

I GUESS EITHER ONE WORKS, BUT... DEPENDING ON THE SCENE, IT REALLY SCREWS UP THE TEMPO, SO I REALLY NEED TO BE CAREFUL... THE WORST OF THEM ALL WAS...

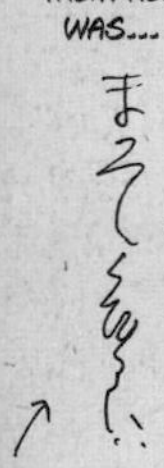

(WRITING FROM THE ROUGH DRAFT)

IT SAYS, "PLEASE WAIT!" BUT... (REALLY, IT'S ATROCIOUS.) WHEN I LOOKED AT THE MAGAZINE...

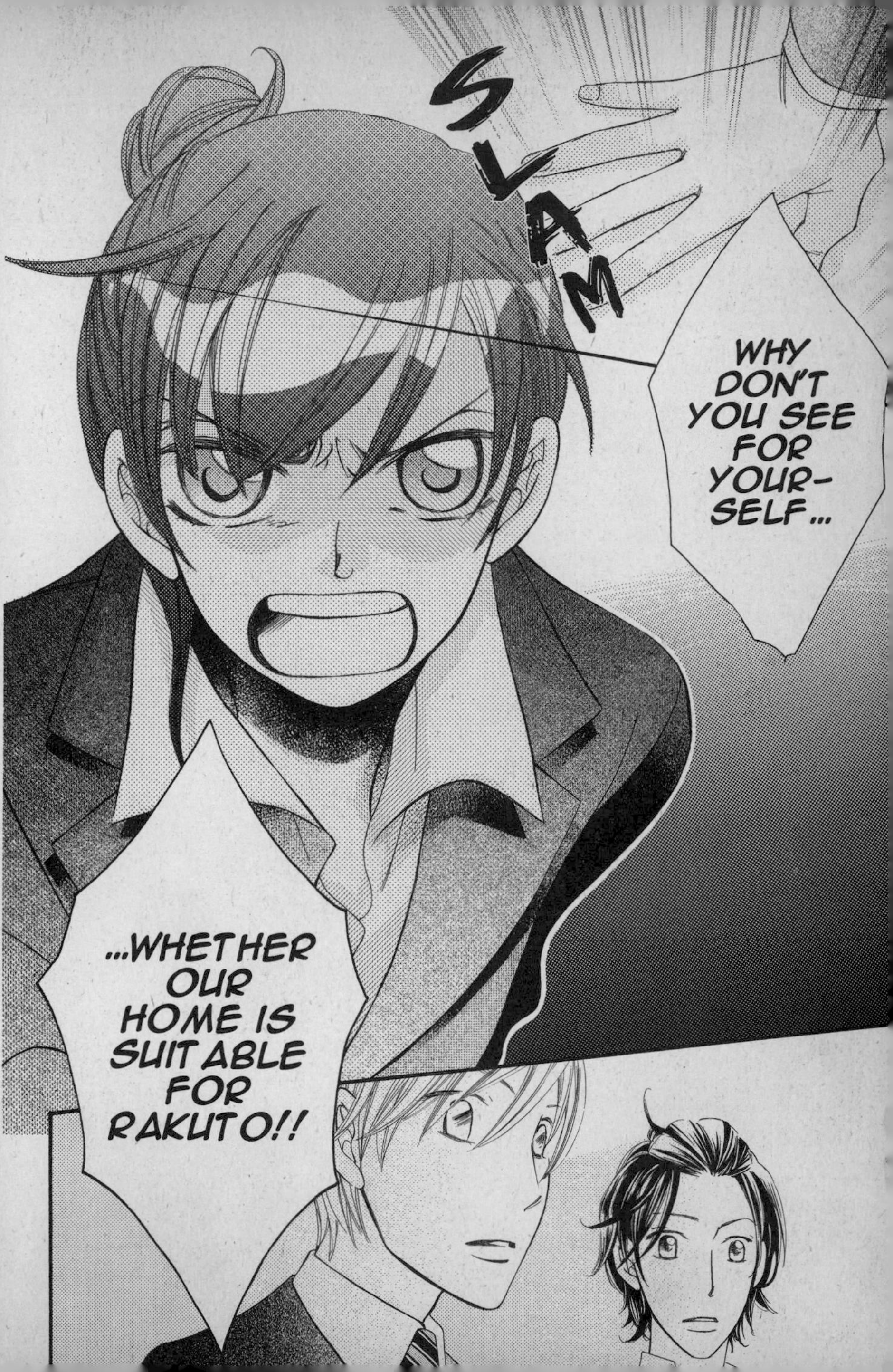
SLAM
WHY DON'T YOU SEE FOR YOURSELF...
...WHETHER OUR HOME IS SUITABLE FOR RAKUTO!!

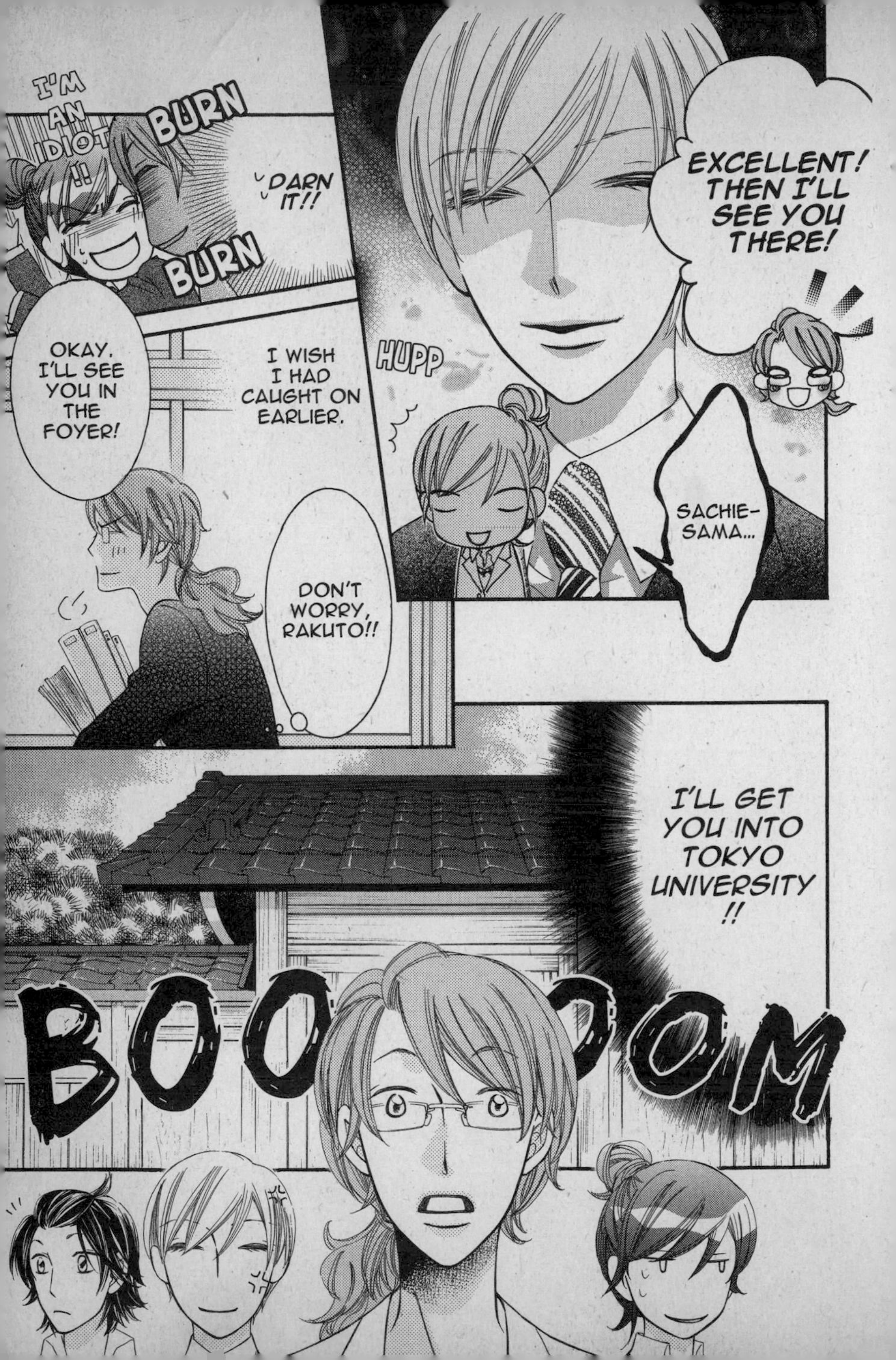
EXCELLENT! THEN I'LL SEE YOU THERE!
HUPP
SACHIE-SAMA...
BURN
DARN IT!!
I'M AN IDIOT!!
BURN
I WISH I HAD CAUGHT ON EARLIER.
OKAY. I'LL SEE YOU IN THE FOYER!
DON'T WORRY, RAKUTO!!
I'LL GET YOU INTO TOKYO UNIVERSITY!!
BOOOOOM

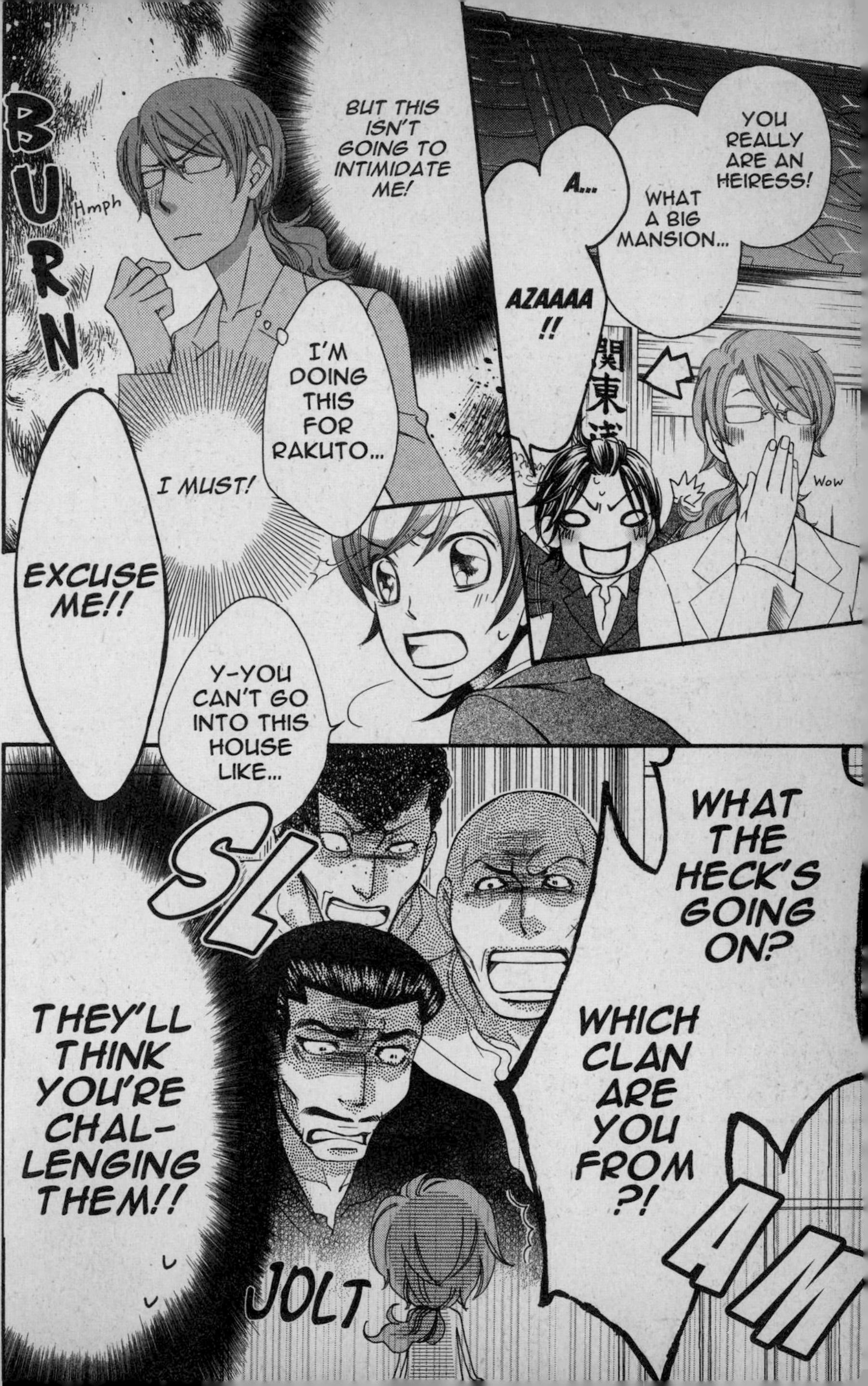
YOU REALLY ARE AN HEIRESS!
WHAT A BIG MANSION...
A...
AZAAAA!!
Wow
BUT THIS ISN'T GOING TO INTIMIDATE ME!
BURN
Hmph
I'M DOING THIS FOR RAKUTO...
I MUST!
EXCUSE ME!!
Y-YOU CAN'T GO INTO THIS HOUSE LIKE...
SLAM
WHAT THE HECK'S GOING ON?
WHICH CLAN ARE YOU FROM?!
THEY'LL THINK YOU'RE CHAL-LENGING THEM!!
JOLT

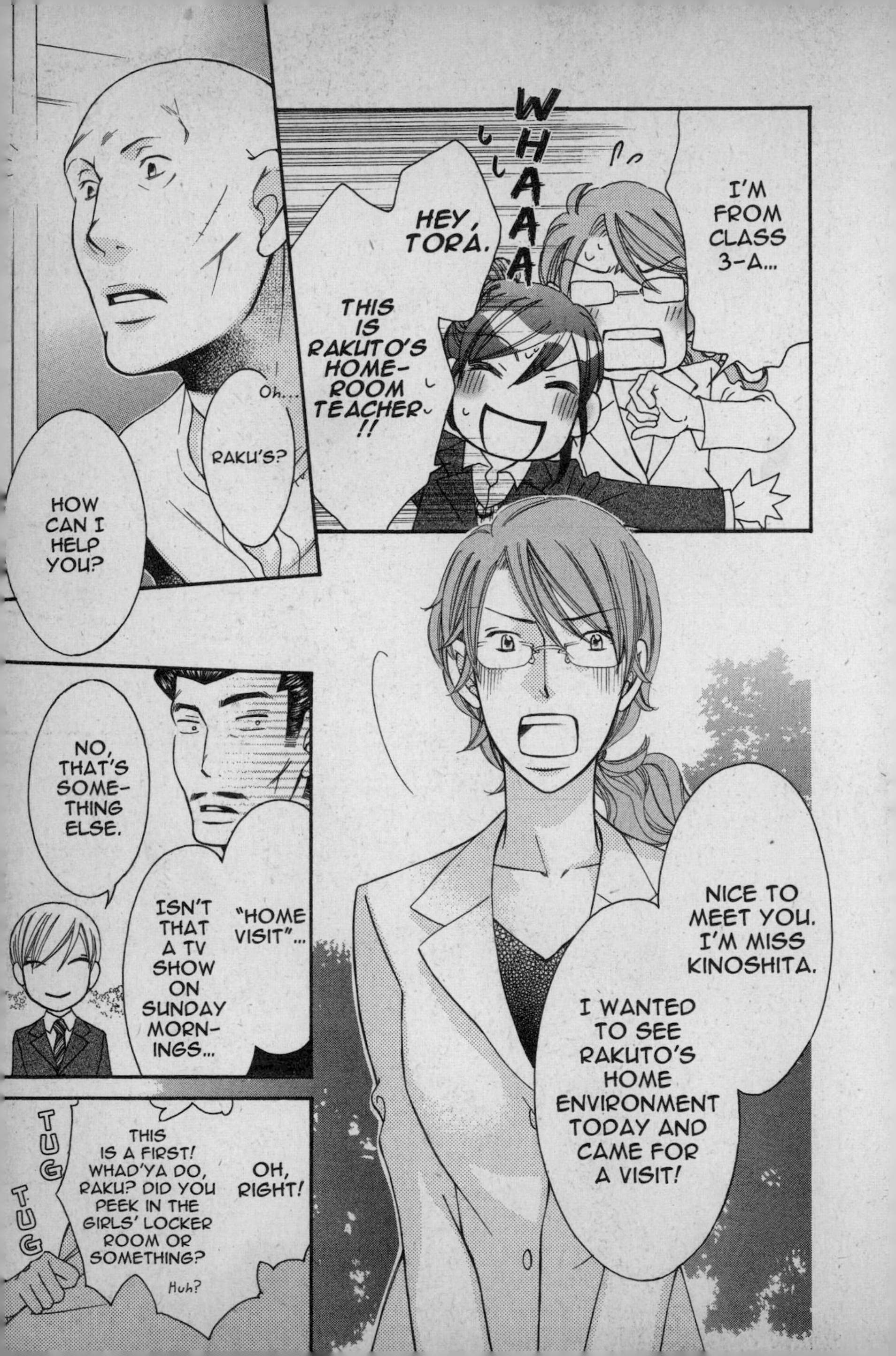
I'M FROM CLASS 3-A...
WHAAAA
HEY, TORA.
THIS IS RAKUTO'S HOME-ROOM TEACHER!!
Oh...
RAKU'S?
HOW CAN I HELP YOU?
NICE TO MEET YOU. I'M MISS KINOSHITA.
I WANTED TO SEE RAKUTO'S HOME ENVIRONMENT TODAY AND CAME FOR A VISIT!
"HOME VISIT"...
ISN'T THAT A TV SHOW ON SUNDAY MORN-INGS...
NO, THAT'S SOME-THING ELSE.
OH, RIGHT!
THIS IS A FIRST! WHAD'YA DO, RAKU? DID YOU PEEK IN THE GIRLS' LOCKER ROOM OR SOMETHING?
Huh?
TUG
TUG

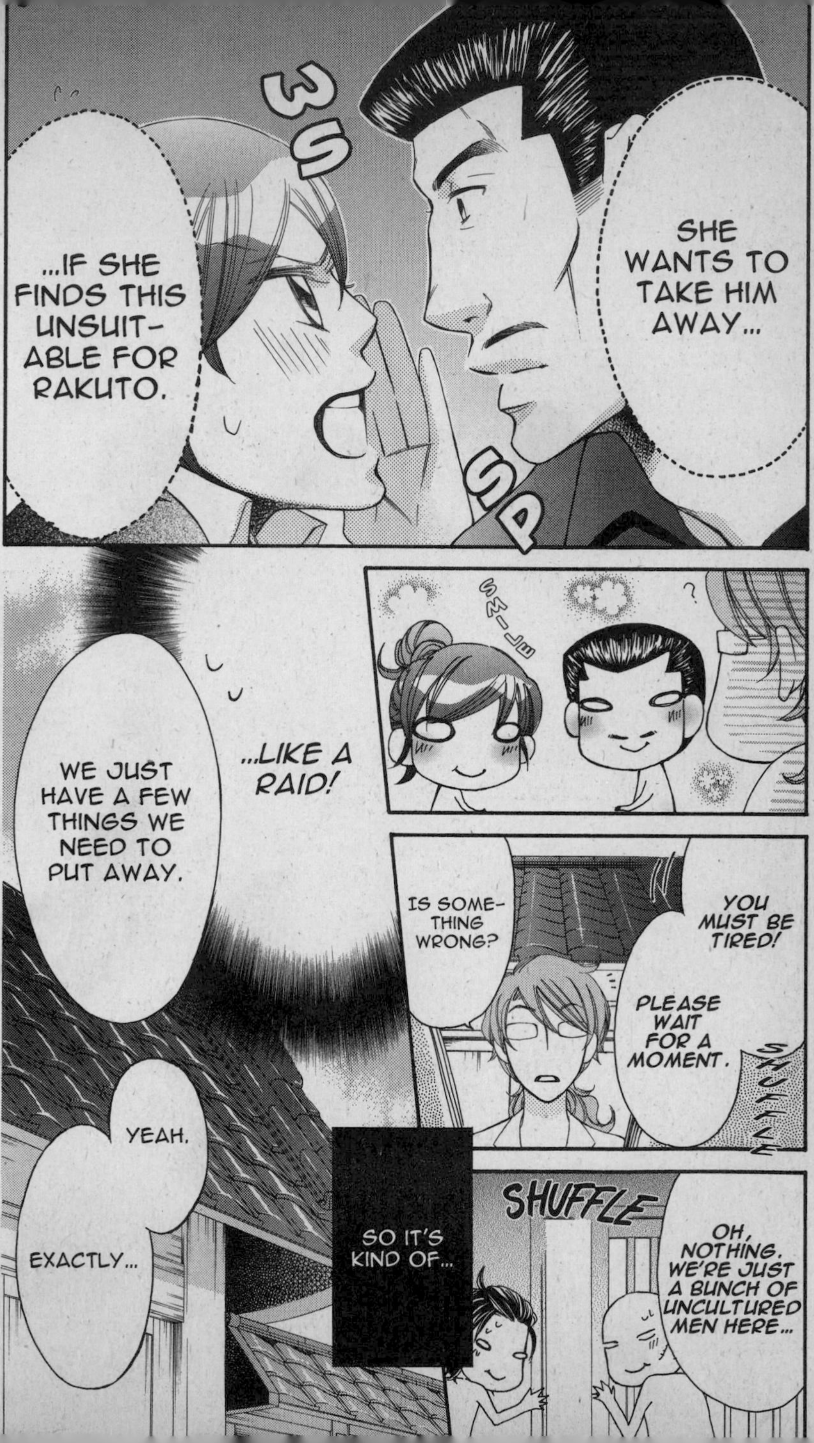
SHE WANTS TO TAKE HIM AWAY...
...IF SHE FINDS THIS UNSUIT-ABLE FOR RAKUTO.
SP
YOU MUST BE TIRED!
PLEASE WAIT FOR A MOMENT.
SHUFFLE
IS SOME-THING WRONG?
SHUFFLE
OH, NOTHING. WE'RE JUST A BUNCH OF UNCULTURED MEN HERE...
SO IT'S KIND OF...
...LIKE A RAID!
WE JUST HAVE A FEW THINGS WE NEED TO PUT AWAY.
YEAH.
EXACTLY...

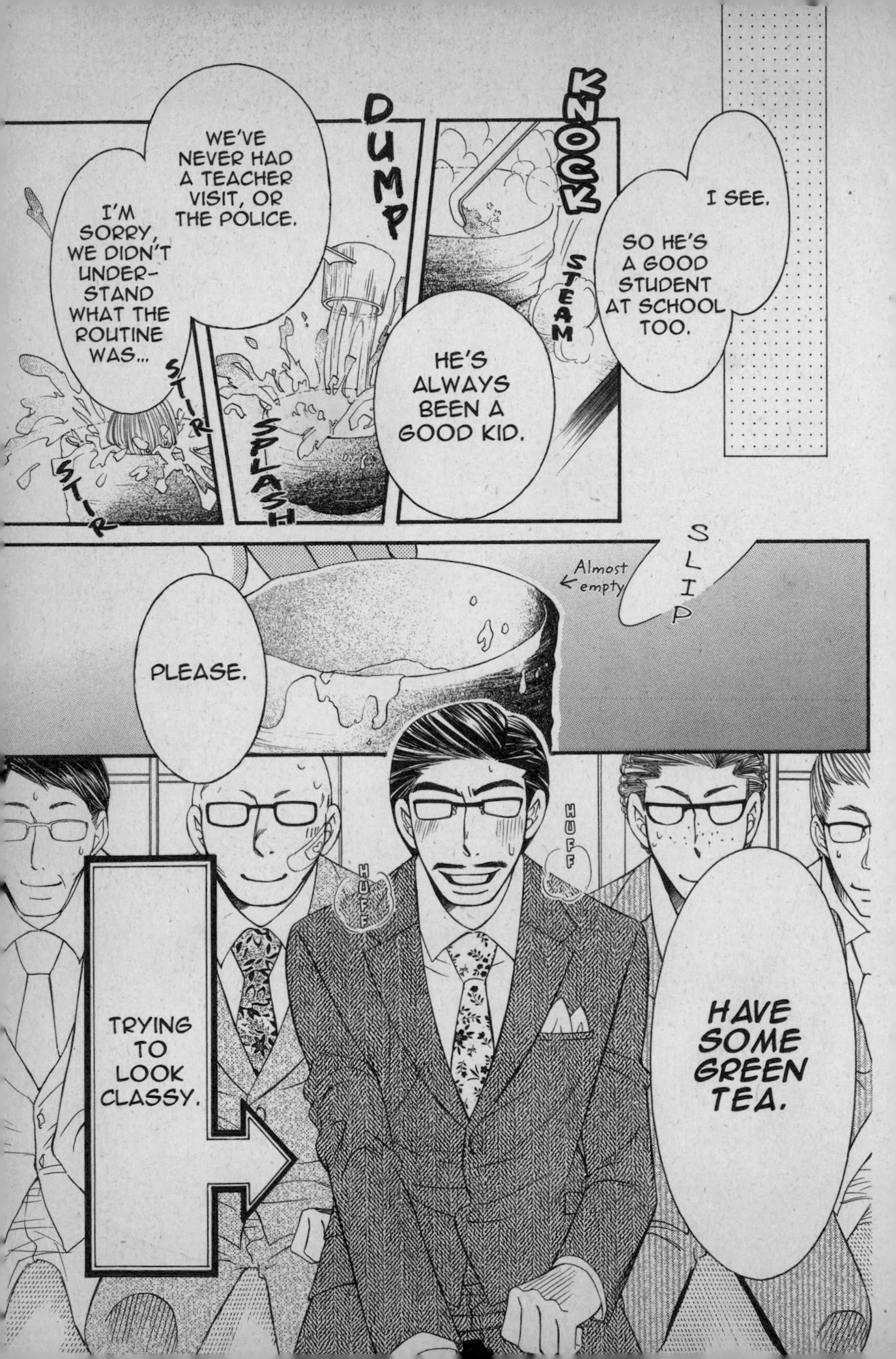
I SEE.
SO HE'S A GOOD STUDENT AT SCHOOL TOO.
KNOCK
STEAM
HE'S ALWAYS BEEN A GOOD KID.
DUMP
SPLASH
WE'VE NEVER HAD A TEACHER VISIT, OR THE POLICE.
I'M SORRY, WE DIDN'T UNDER-STAND WHAT THE ROUTINE WAS...
STIR
STIR
SLIP
Almost empty
PLEASE.
HAVE SOME GREEN TEA.
HUFF
HUFF
TRYING TO LOOK CLASSY.

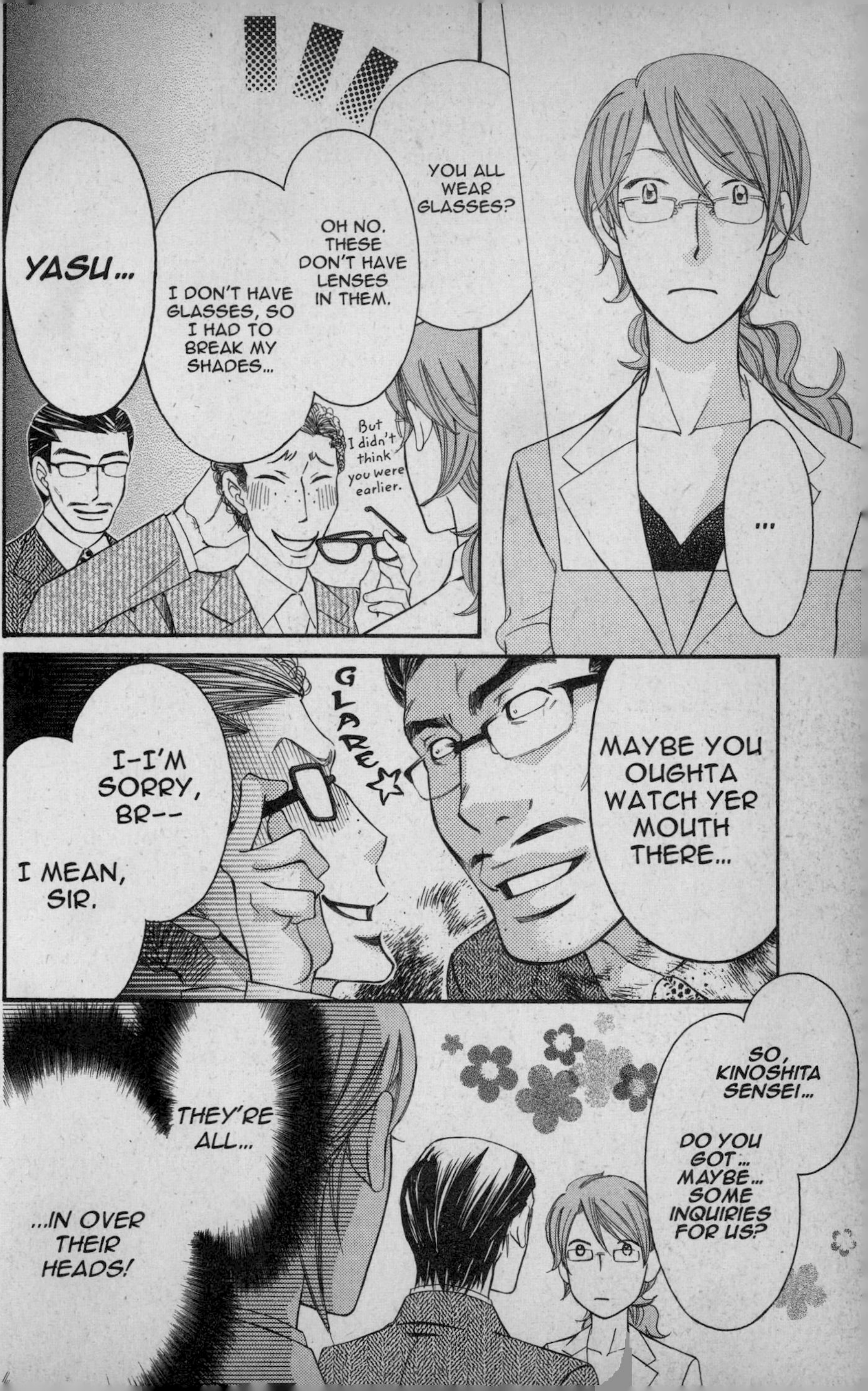
...
YOU ALL WEAR GLASSES?
OH NO. THESE DON'T HAVE LENSES IN THEM.
I DON'T HAVE GLASSES, SO I HAD TO BREAK MY SHADES...
But I didn't think you were earlier.
YASU...
MAYBE YOU OUGHTA WATCH YER MOUTH THERE...
GLARE
I-I'M SORRY, BR--
I MEAN, SIR.
SO, KINOSHITA SENSEI...
DO YOU GOT... MAYBE... SOME INQUIRIES FOR US?
THEY'RE ALL...
...IN OVER THEIR HEADS!

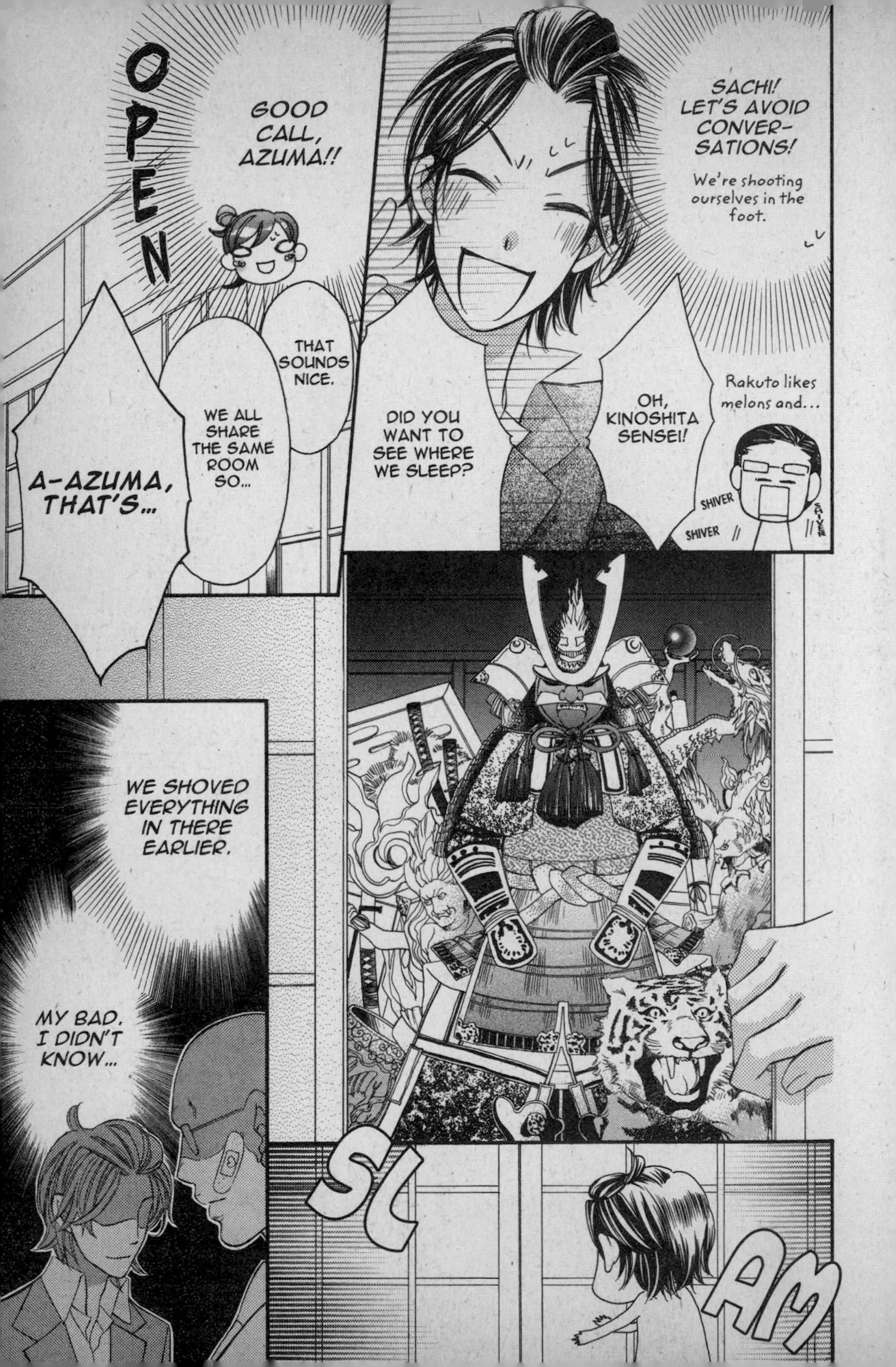
SACHI! LET'S AVOID CONVER-SATIONS!
We're shooting ourselves in the foot.
Rakuto likes melons and...
SHIVER
SHIVER
SHIVER
OH, KINOSHITA SENSEI!
DID YOU WANT TO SEE WHERE WE SLEEP?
GOOD CALL, AZUMA!!
OPEN
THAT SOUNDS NICE.
WE ALL SHARE THE SAME ROOM SO...
A-AZUMA, THAT'S...
WE SHOVED EVERYTHING IN THERE EARLIER.
MY BAD. I DIDN'T KNOW...
SL
AM

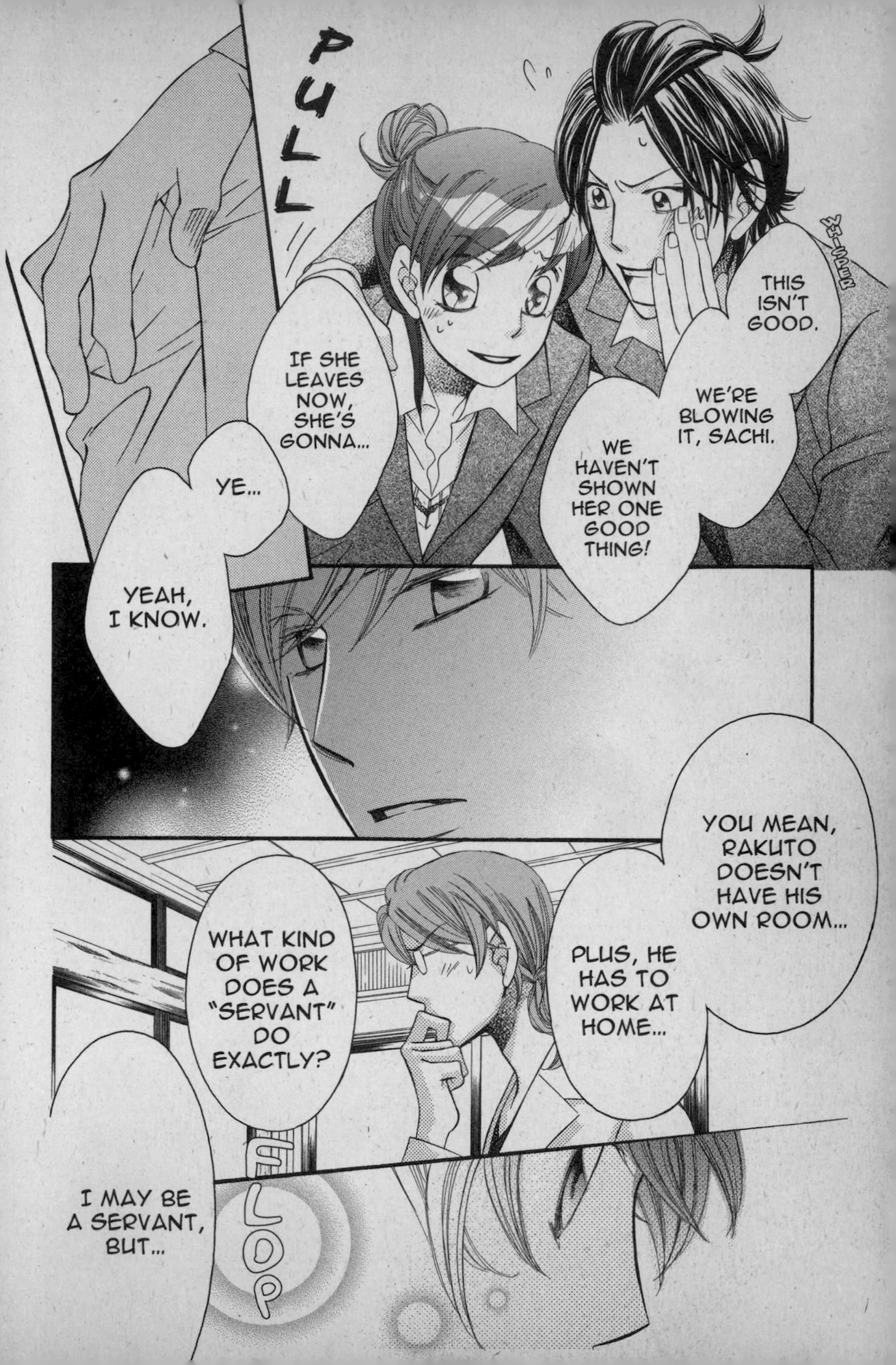
PULL
THIS ISN'T GOOD.
WE'RE BLOWING IT, SACHI.
WE HAVEN'T SHOWN HER ONE GOOD THING!
IF SHE LEAVES NOW, SHE'S GONNA...
YE...
YEAH, I KNOW.
YOU MEAN, RAKUTO DOESN'T HAVE HIS OWN ROOM...
PLUS, HE HAS TO WORK AT HOME...
WHAT KIND OF WORK DOES A "SERVANT" DO EXACTLY?
FLOP
I MAY BE A SERVANT, BUT...

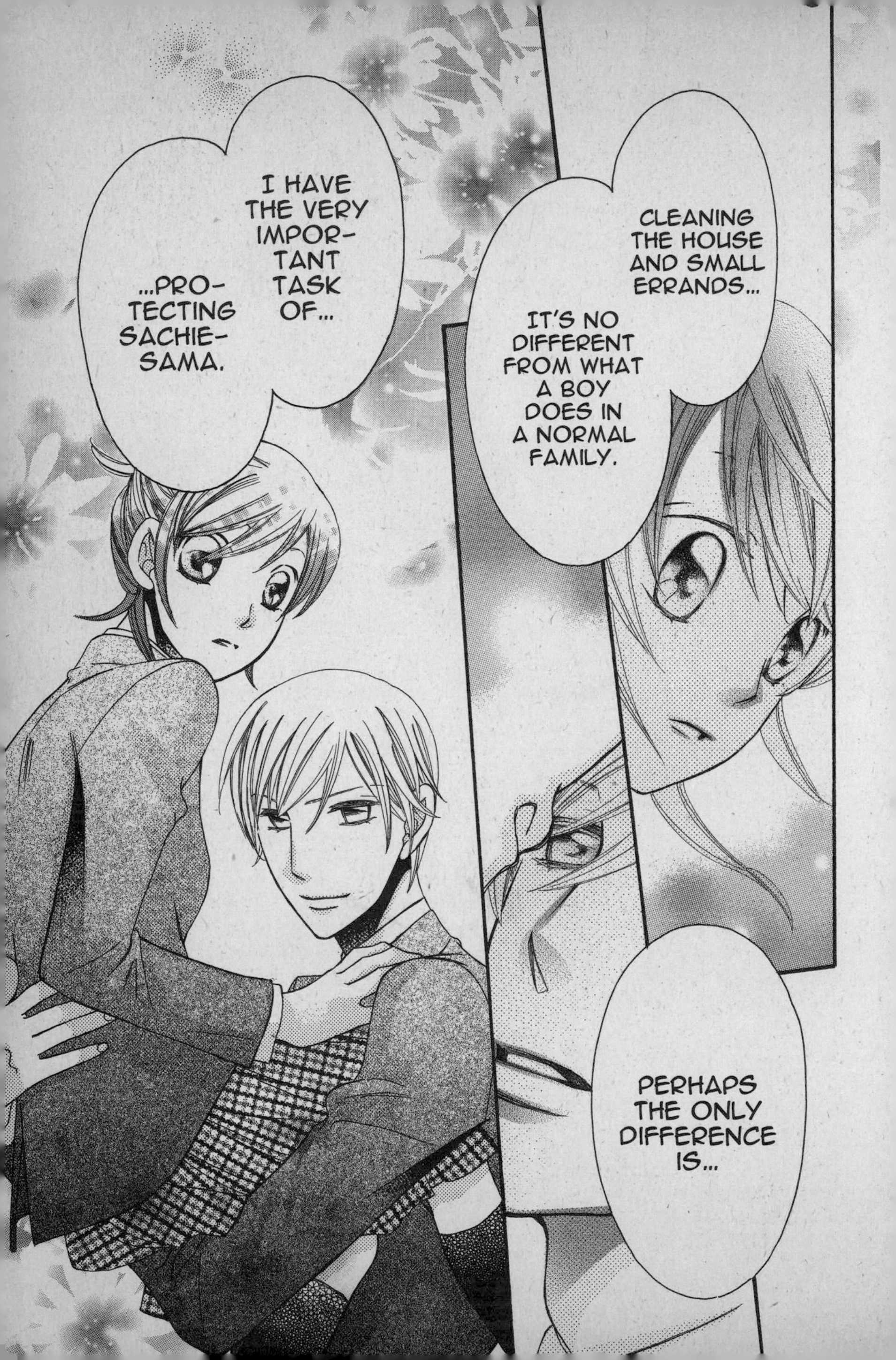

CLEANING THE HOUSE AND SMALL ERRANDS...
IT'S NO DIFFERENT FROM WHAT A BOY DOES IN A NORMAL FAMILY.
PERHAPS THE ONLY DIFFERENCE IS...
I HAVE THE VERY IMPORTANT TASK OF...
...PROTECTING SACHIE-SAMA.

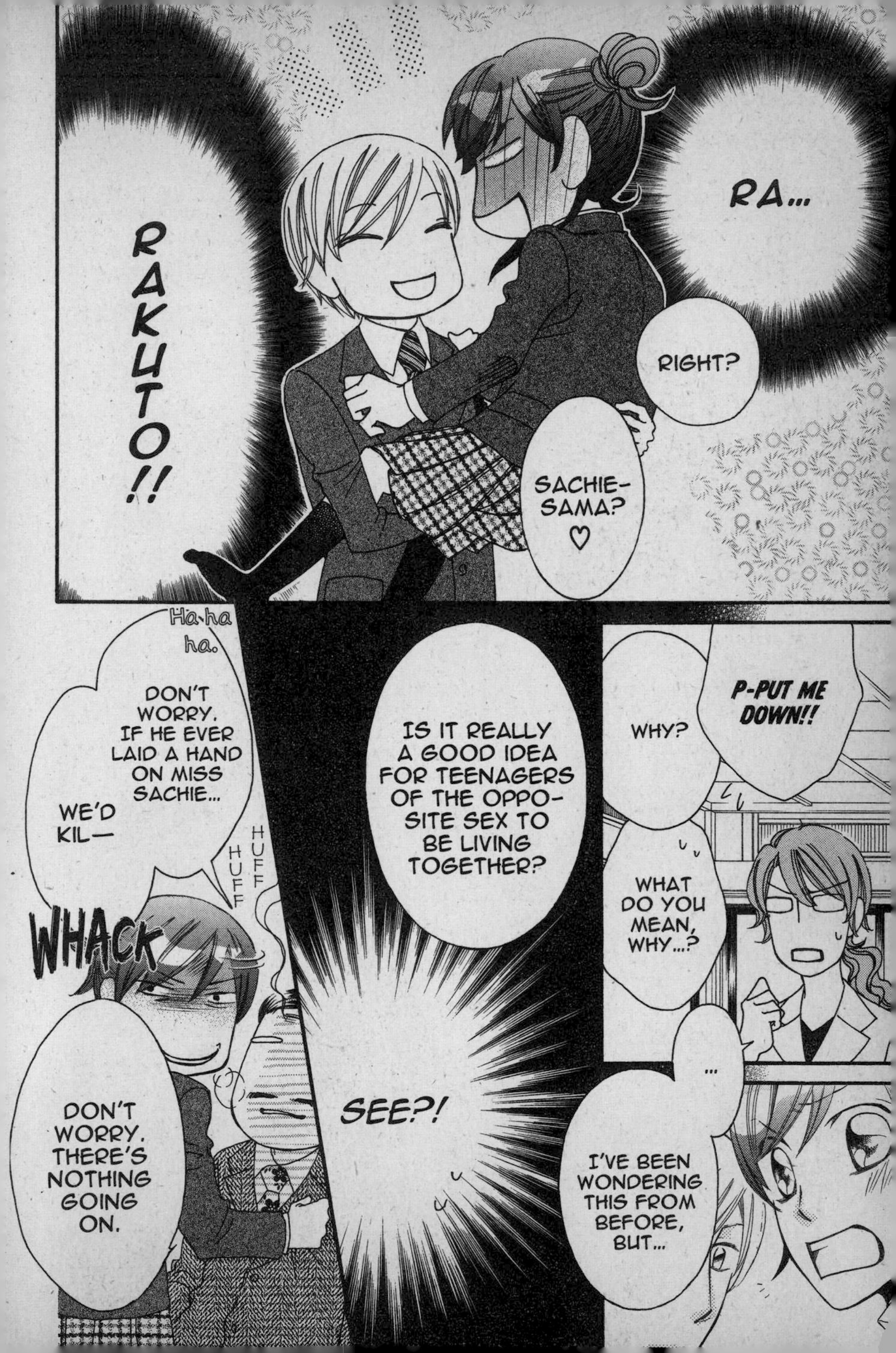
RA...
RIGHT?
SACHIE-SAMA? ♡
RAKUTO!!
P-PUT ME DOWN!!
WHY?
WHAT DO YOU MEAN, WHY...?
...
I'VE BEEN WONDERING THIS FROM BEFORE, BUT...
IS IT REALLY A GOOD IDEA FOR TEENAGERS OF THE OPPOSITE SEX TO BE LIVING TOGETHER?
SEE?!
Ha ha ha.
DON'T WORRY. IF HE EVER LAID A HAND ON MISS SACHIE...
WE'D KIL—
HUFF HUFF
WHACK
DON'T WORRY. THERE'S NOTHING GOING ON.

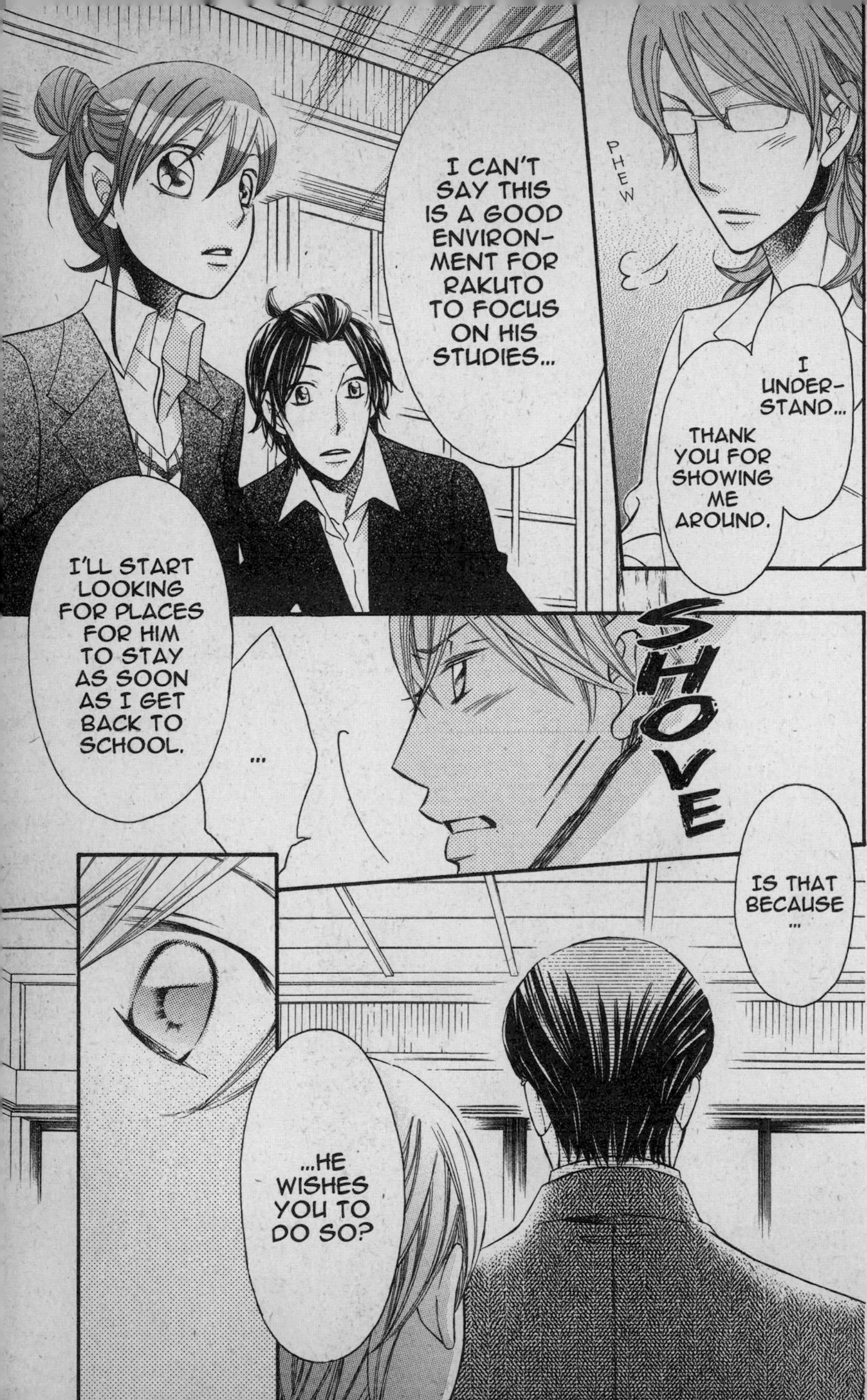
I CAN'T SAY THIS IS A GOOD ENVIRON-MENT FOR RAKUTO TO FOCUS ON HIS STUDIES...
PHEW
I UNDER-STAND...
THANK YOU FOR SHOWING ME AROUND.
I'LL START LOOKING FOR PLACES FOR HIM TO STAY AS SOON AS I GET BACK TO SCHOOL.
...
SHOVE
IS THAT BECAUSE ...
...HE WISHES YOU TO DO SO?

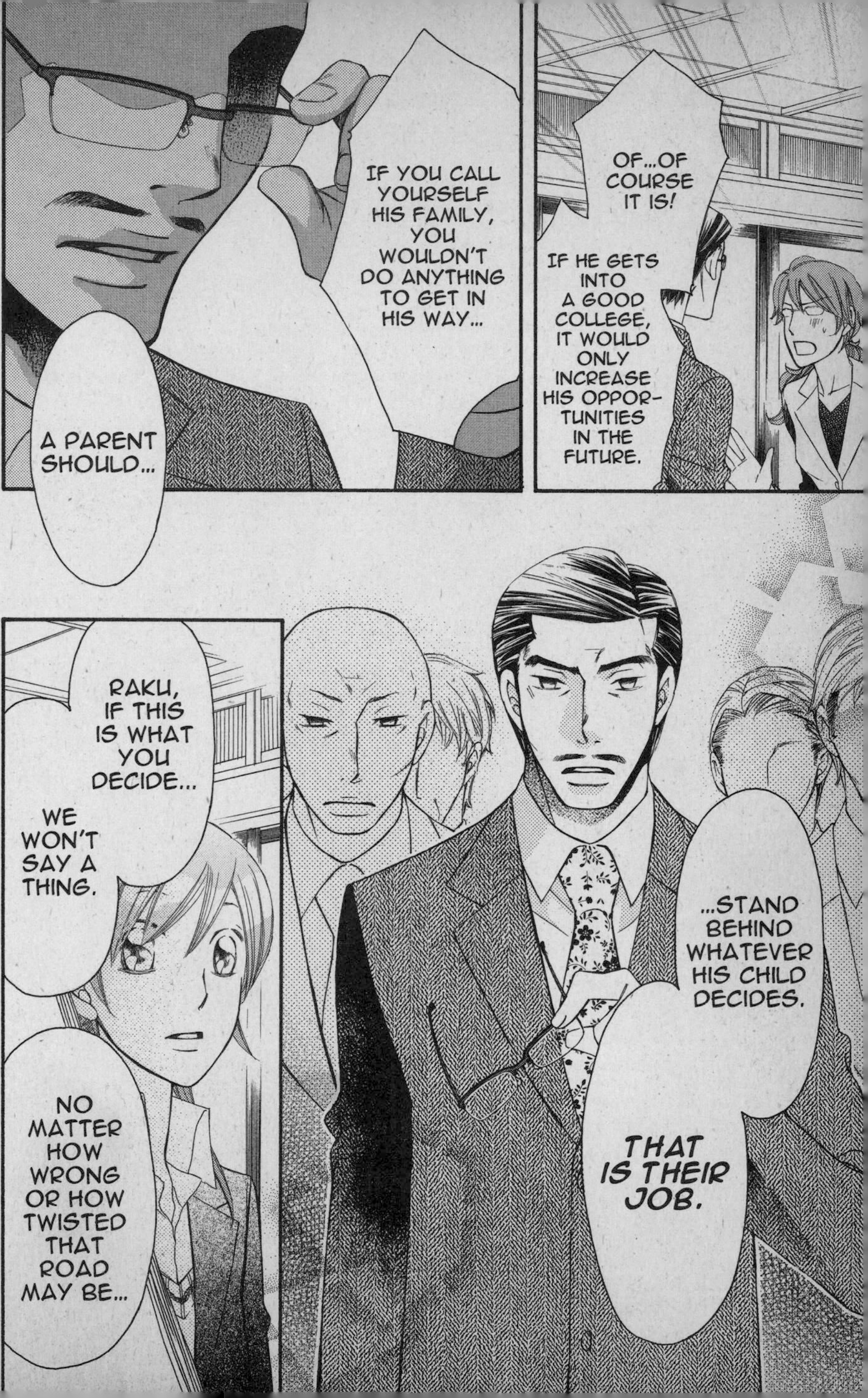
OF...OF COURSE IT IS!
IF HE GETS INTO A GOOD COLLEGE, IT WOULD ONLY INCREASE HIS OPPOR-TUNITIES IN THE FUTURE.
IF YOU CALL YOURSELF HIS FAMILY, YOU WOULDN'T DO ANYTHING TO GET IN HIS WAY...
A PARENT SHOULD...
...STAND BEHIND WHATEVER HIS CHILD DECIDES.
THAT IS THEIR JOB.
RAKU, IF THIS IS WHAT YOU DECIDE...
WE WON'T SAY A THING.
NO MATTER HOW WRONG OR HOW TWISTED THAT ROAD MAY BE...

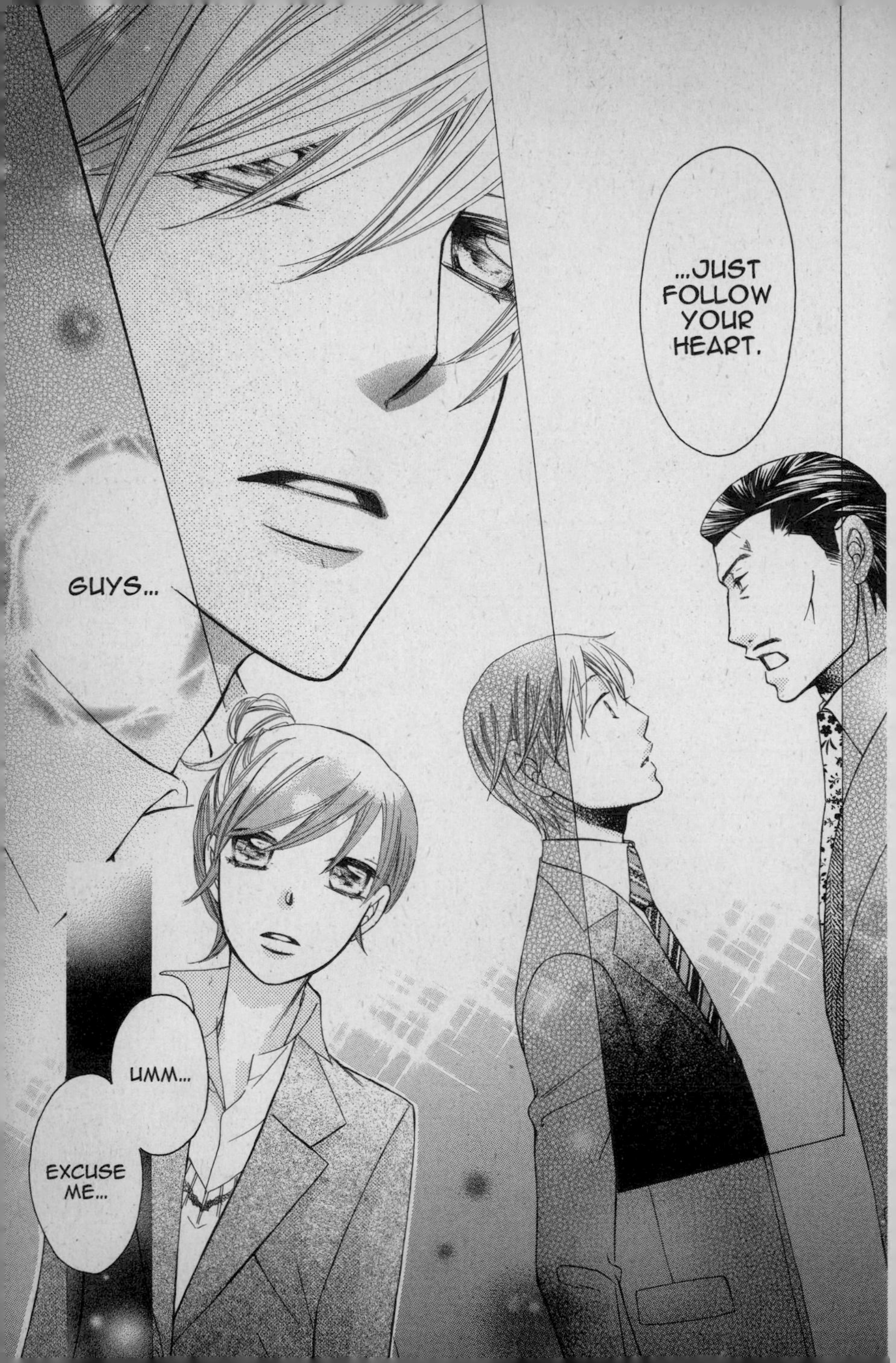
...JUST FOLLOW YOUR HEART.
GUYS...
UMM...
EXCUSE ME...

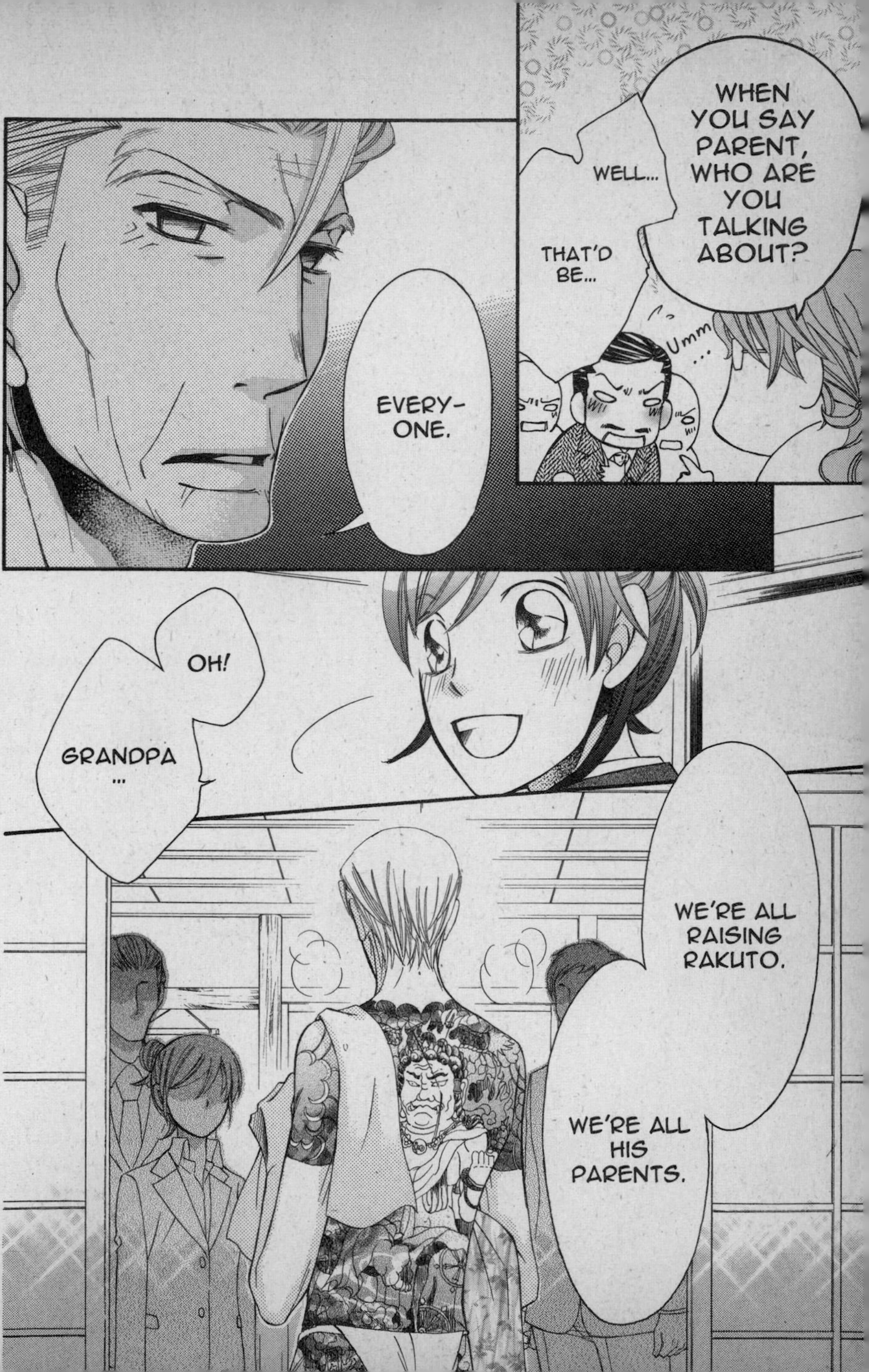
WHEN YOU SAY PARENT, WHO ARE YOU TALKING ABOUT?
WELL...
THAT'D BE...
Umm...
EVERY-ONE.
OH!
GRANDPA...
WE'RE ALL RAISING RAKUTO.
WE'RE ALL HIS PARENTS.

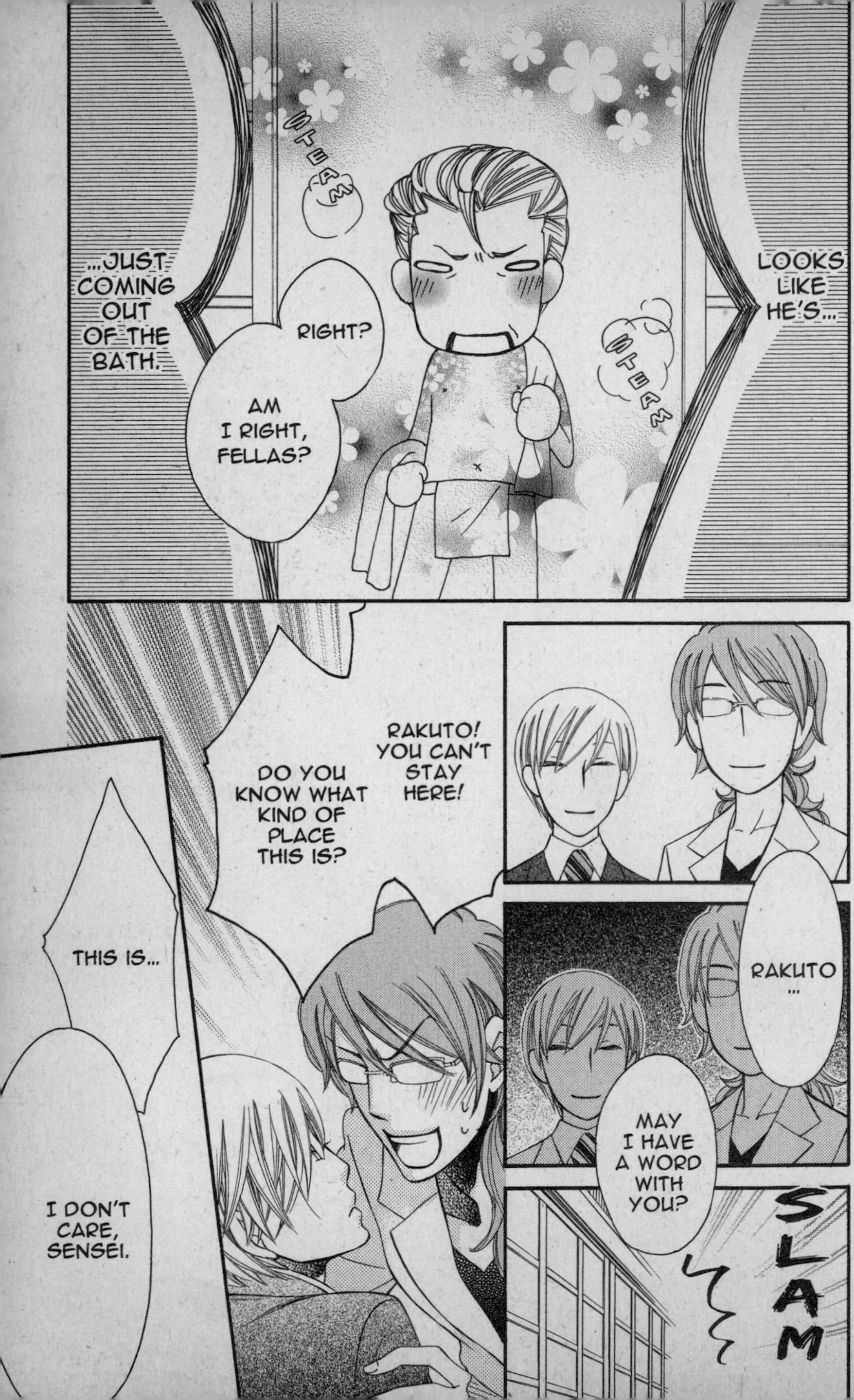
LOOKS LIKE HE'S...
STEAM
STEAM
RIGHT?
AM I RIGHT, FELLAS?
...JUST COMING OUT OF THE BATH.
RAKUTO ...
MAY I HAVE A WORD WITH YOU?
SLAM
RAKUTO! YOU CAN'T STAY HERE!
DO YOU KNOW WHAT KIND OF PLACE THIS IS?
THIS IS...
I DON'T CARE, SENSEI.

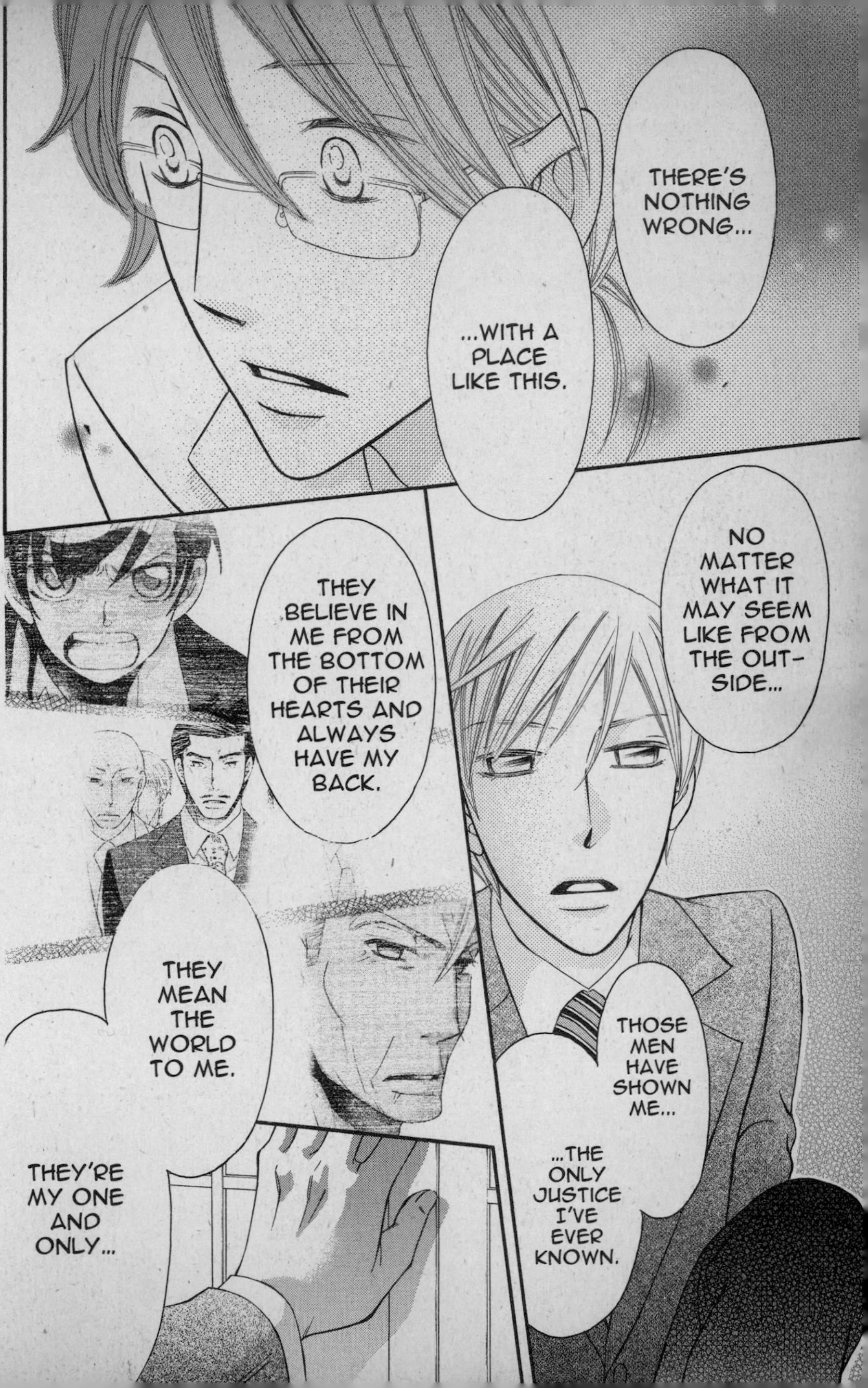
THERE'S NOTHING WRONG...
...WITH A PLACE LIKE THIS.
NO MATTER WHAT IT MAY SEEM LIKE FROM THE OUT-SIDE...
THOSE MEN HAVE SHOWN ME...
...THE ONLY JUSTICE I'VE EVER KNOWN.
THEY BELIEVE IN ME FROM THE BOTTOM OF THEIR HEARTS AND ALWAYS HAVE MY BACK.
THEY MEAN THE WORLD TO ME.
THEY'RE MY ONE AND ONLY...

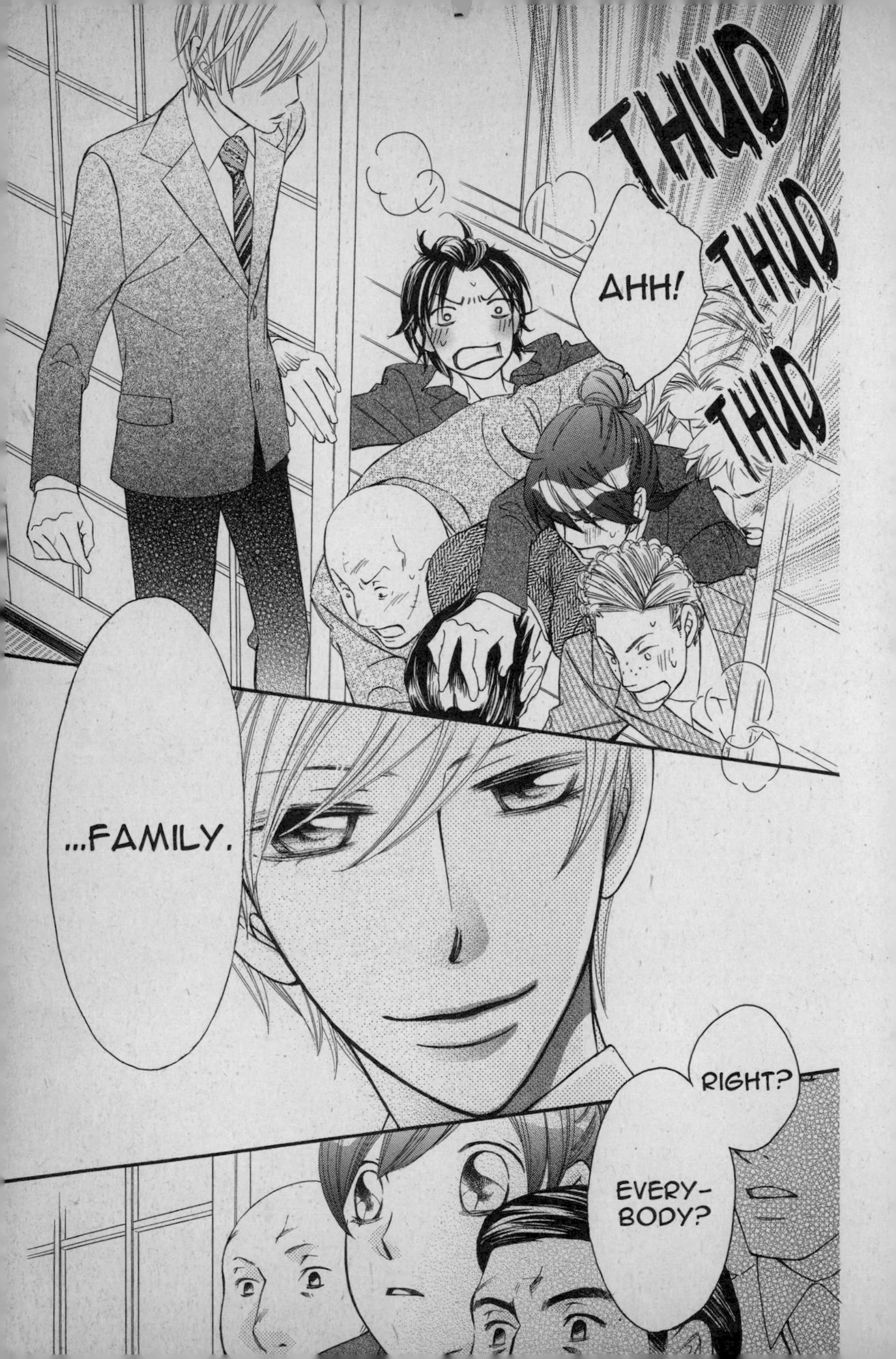
THUD THUD THUD
AHH!
...FAMILY.
RIGHT?
EVERY-BODY?

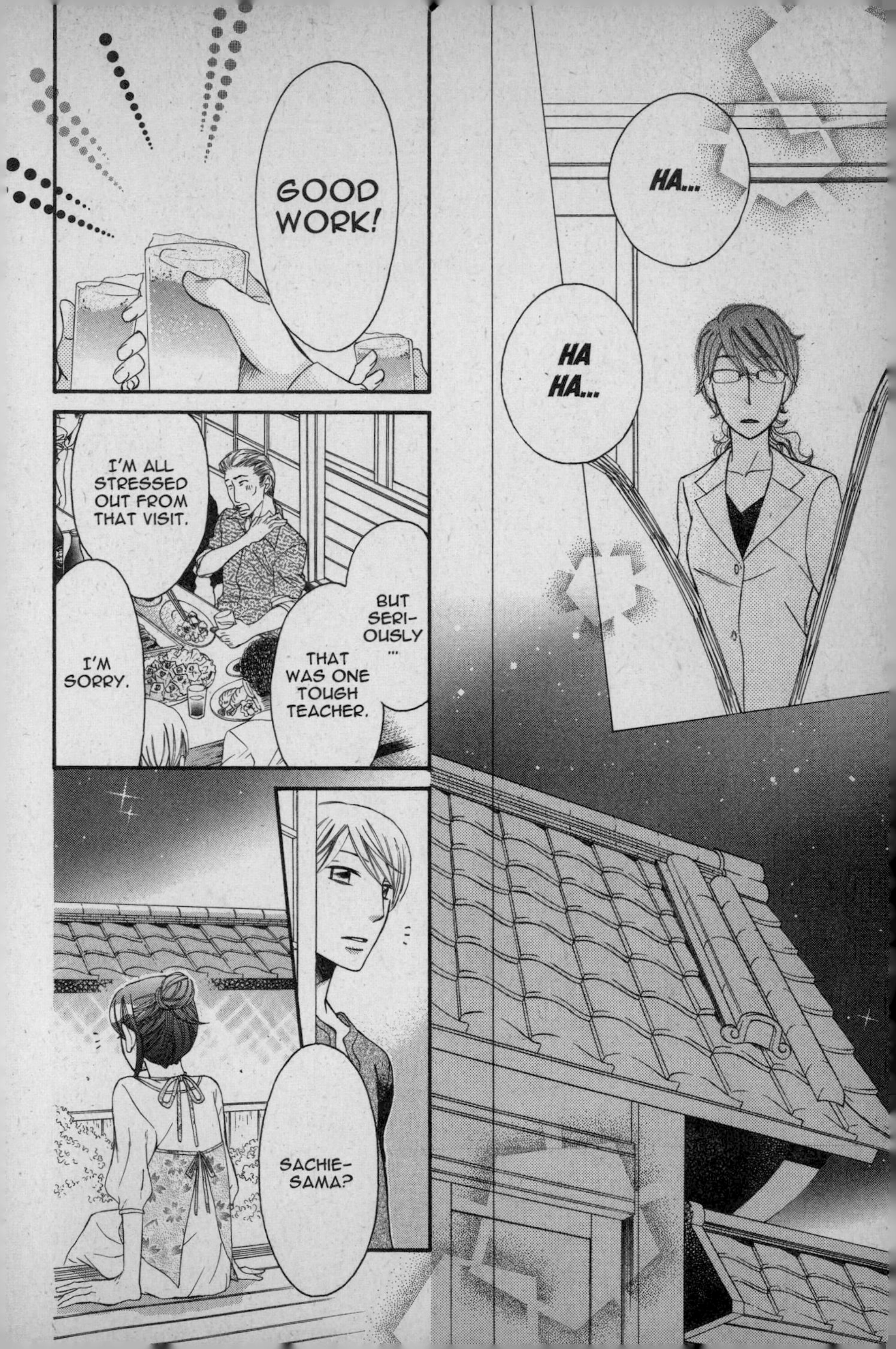
HA...
HA HA...
GOOD WORK!
I'M ALL STRESSED OUT FROM THAT VISIT.
BUT SERI-OUSLY... THAT WAS ONE TOUGH TEACHER.
I'M SORRY.
SACHIE-SAMA?

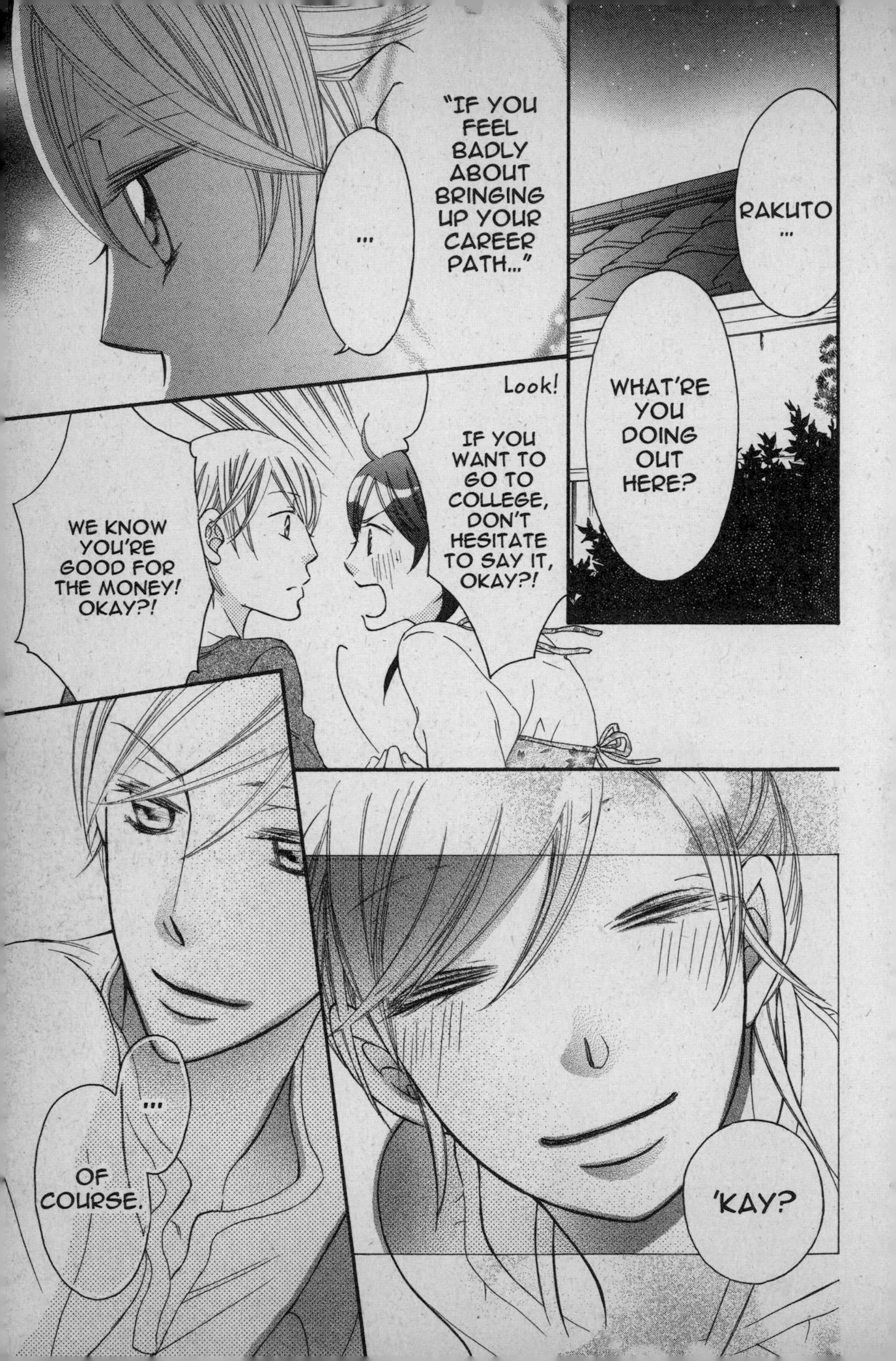
RAKUTO ...
WHAT'RE YOU DOING OUT HERE?
"IF YOU FEEL BADLY ABOUT BRINGING UP YOUR CAREER PATH..."
...
Look!
IF YOU WANT TO GO TO COLLEGE, DON'T HESITATE TO SAY IT, OKAY?!
WE KNOW YOU'RE GOOD FOR THE MONEY! OKAY?!
'KAY?
...
OF COURSE.

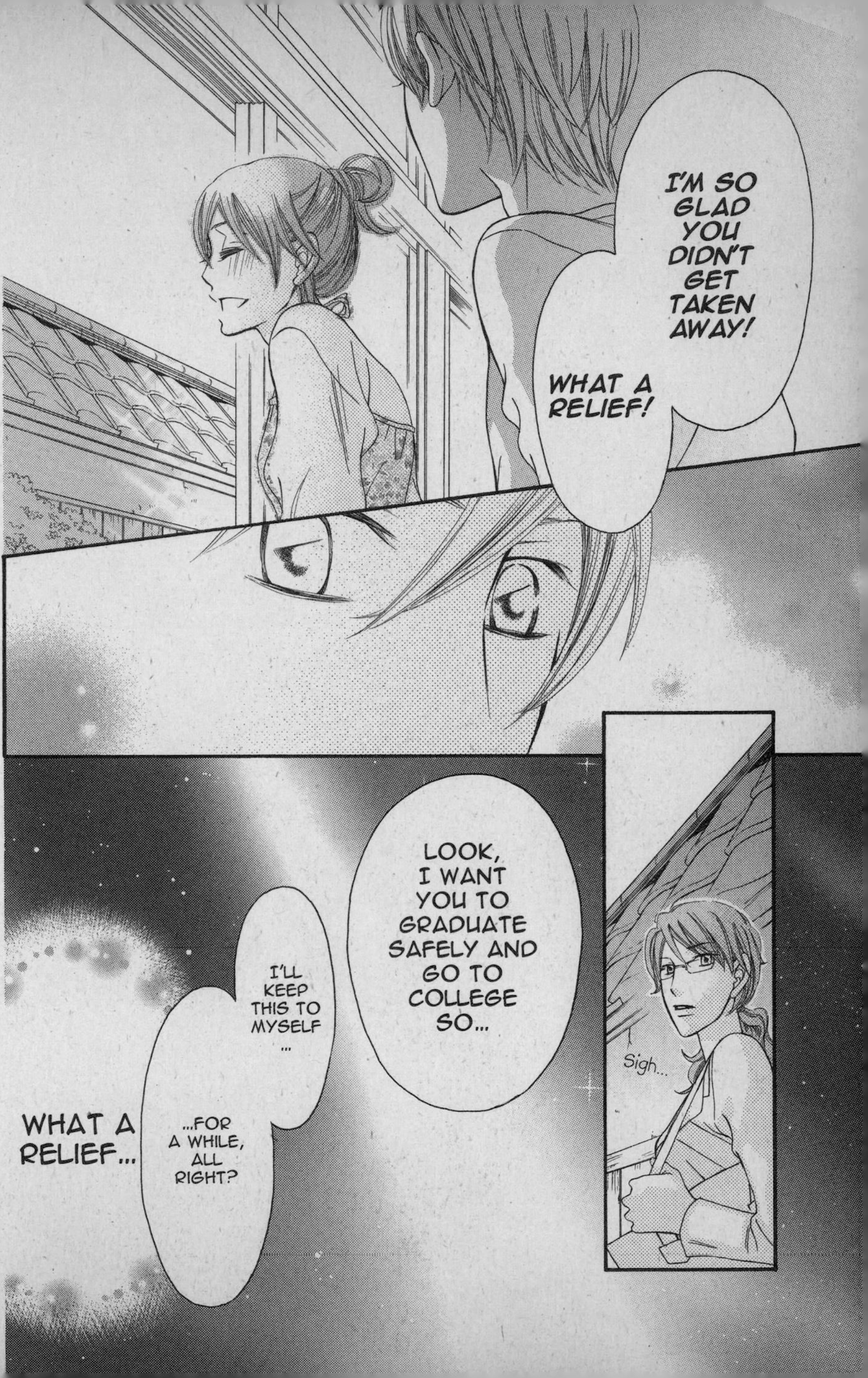
I'M SO GLAD YOU DIDN'T GET TAKEN AWAY!
WHAT A RELIEF!
Sigh...
LOOK, I WANT YOU TO GRADUATE SAFELY AND GO TO COLLEGE SO...
I'LL KEEP THIS TO MYSELF ...
...FOR A WHILE, ALL RIGHT?
WHAT A RELIEF...

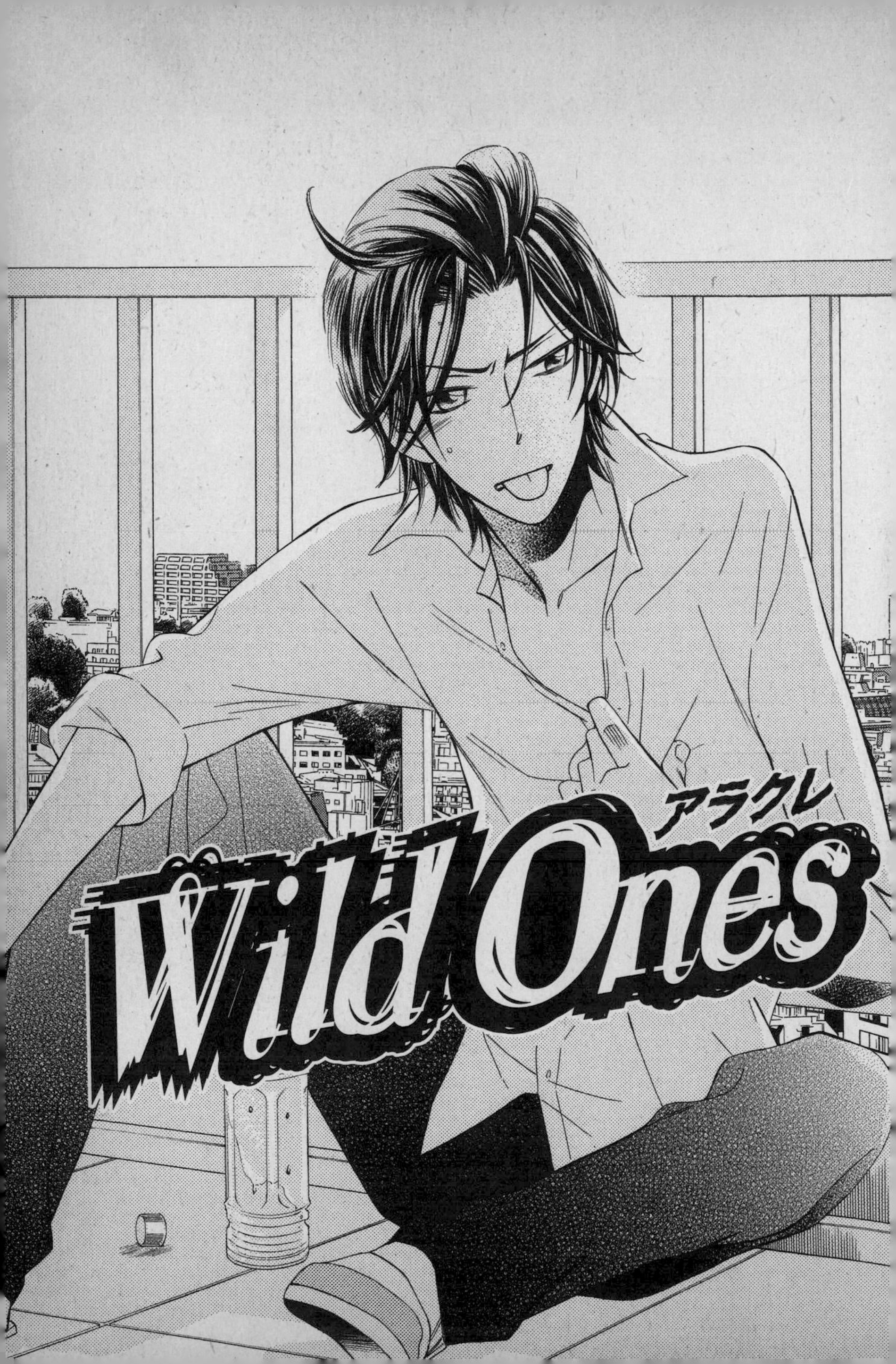
アラクレ
Wild Ones

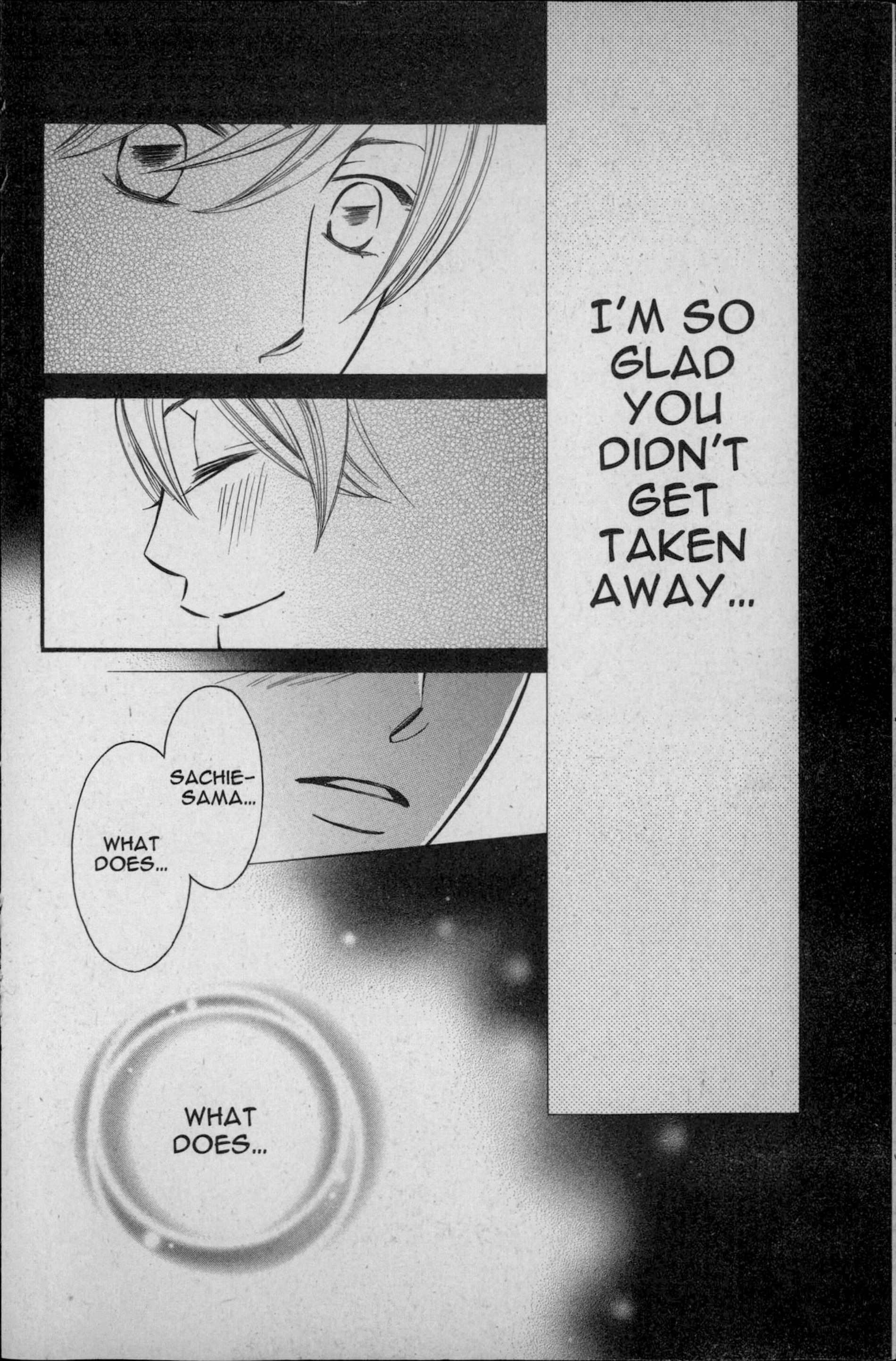
I'M SO GLAD YOU DIDN'T GET TAKEN AWAY...
SACHIE-SAMA...
WHAT DOES...
WHAT DOES...

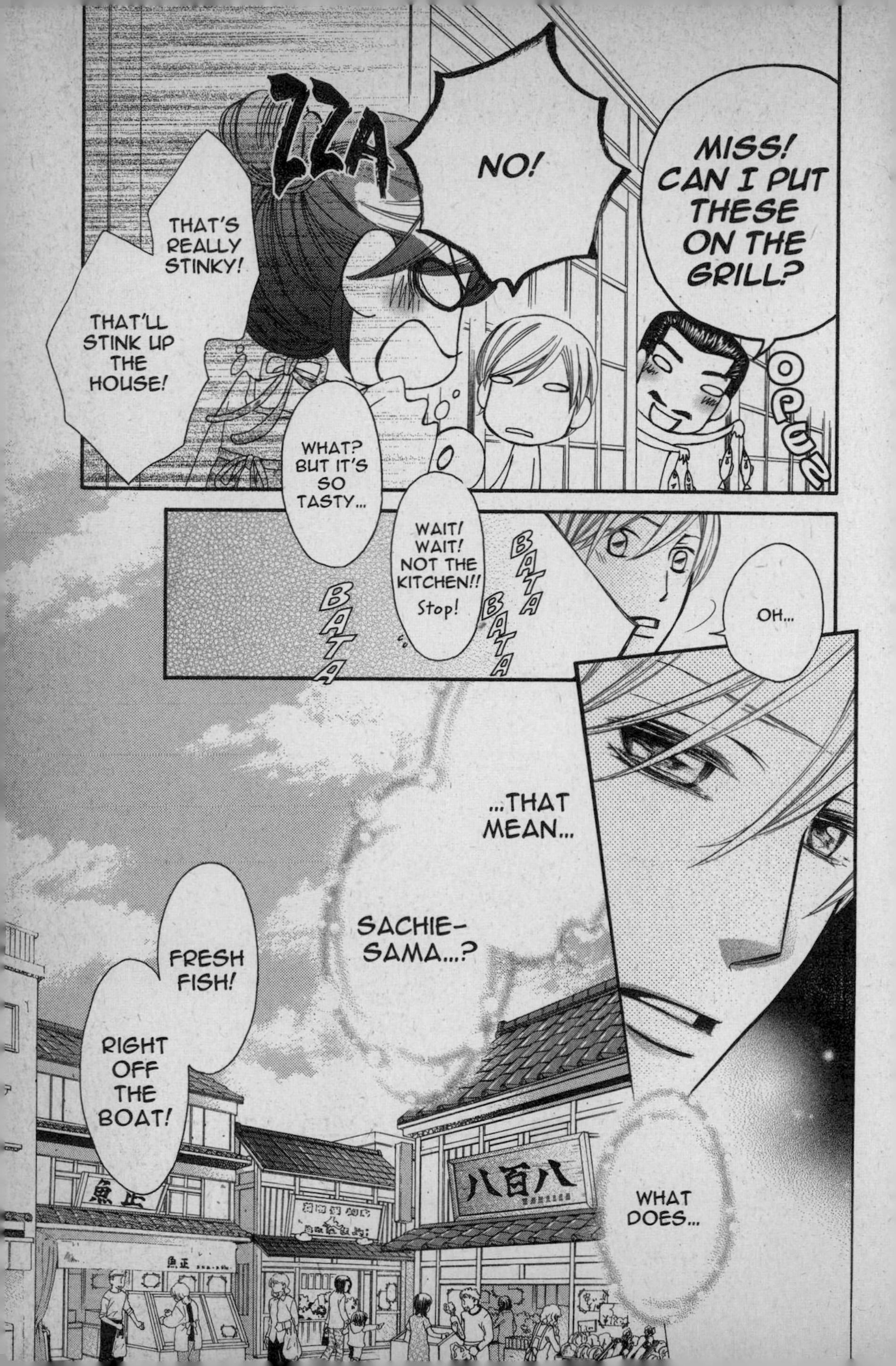

MISS! CAN I PUT THESE ON THE GRILL?
OPEN
NO!
ZZA
THAT'S REALLY STINKY!
THAT'LL STINK UP THE HOUSE!
WHAT? BUT IT'S SO TASTY...
OH...
BATA
BATA
WAIT! WAIT! NOT THE KITCHEN!! Stop!
BATA
BATA
WHAT DOES...
...THAT MEAN...
SACHIE-SAMA...?
八百八
魚正
FRESH FISH!
RIGHT OFF THE BOAT!

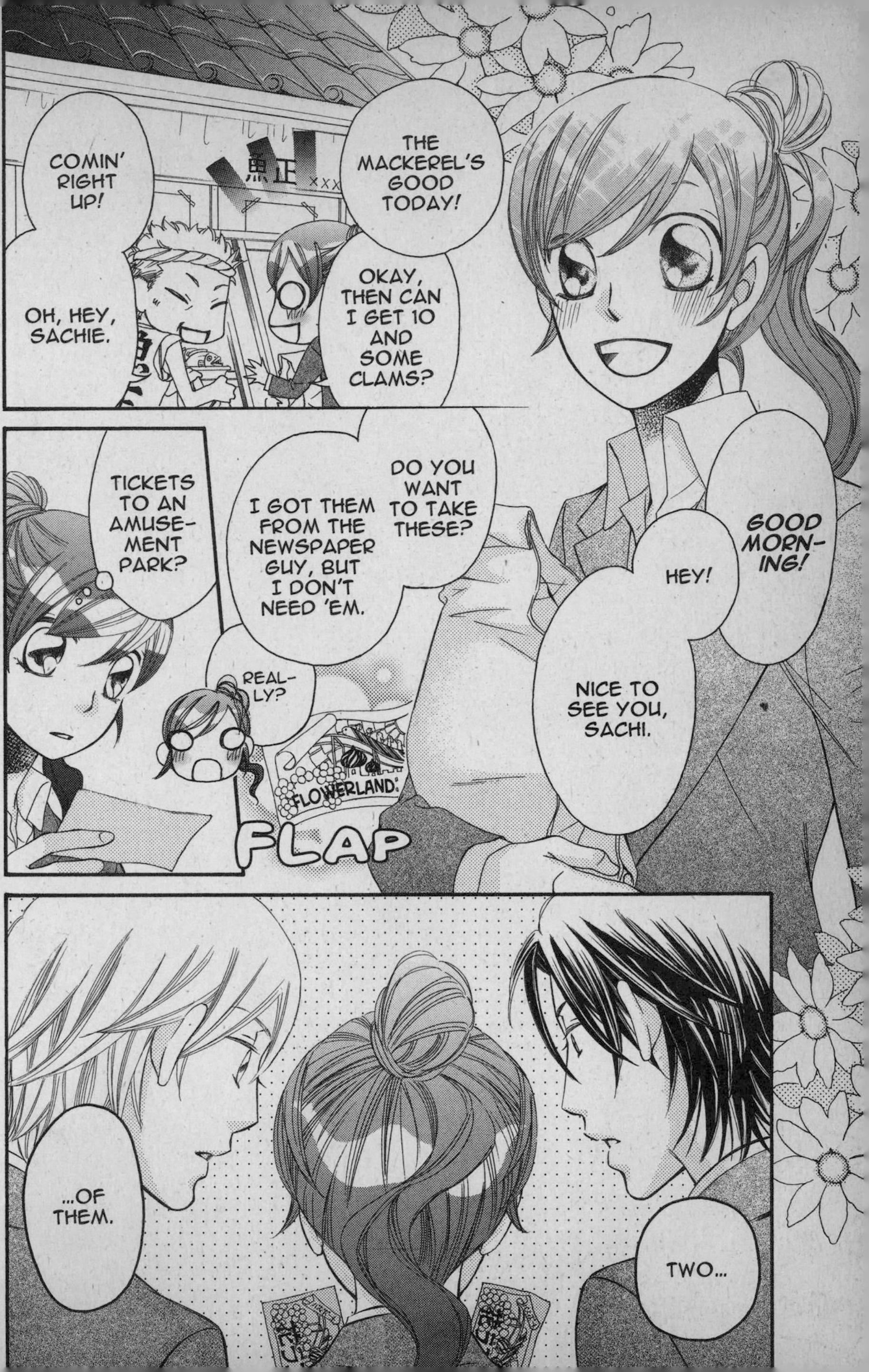
GOOD MORNING!
HEY!
NICE TO SEE YOU, SACHI.
THE MACKEREL'S GOOD TODAY!
OKAY, THEN CAN I GET 10 AND SOME CLAMS?
COMIN' RIGHT UP!
OH, HEY, SACHIE.
DO YOU WANT TO TAKE THESE?
I GOT THEM FROM THE NEWSPAPER GUY, BUT I DON'T NEED 'EM.
REAL-LY?
TICKETS TO AN AMUSE-MENT PARK?
FLOWERLAND
FLAP
TWO...
...OF THEM.

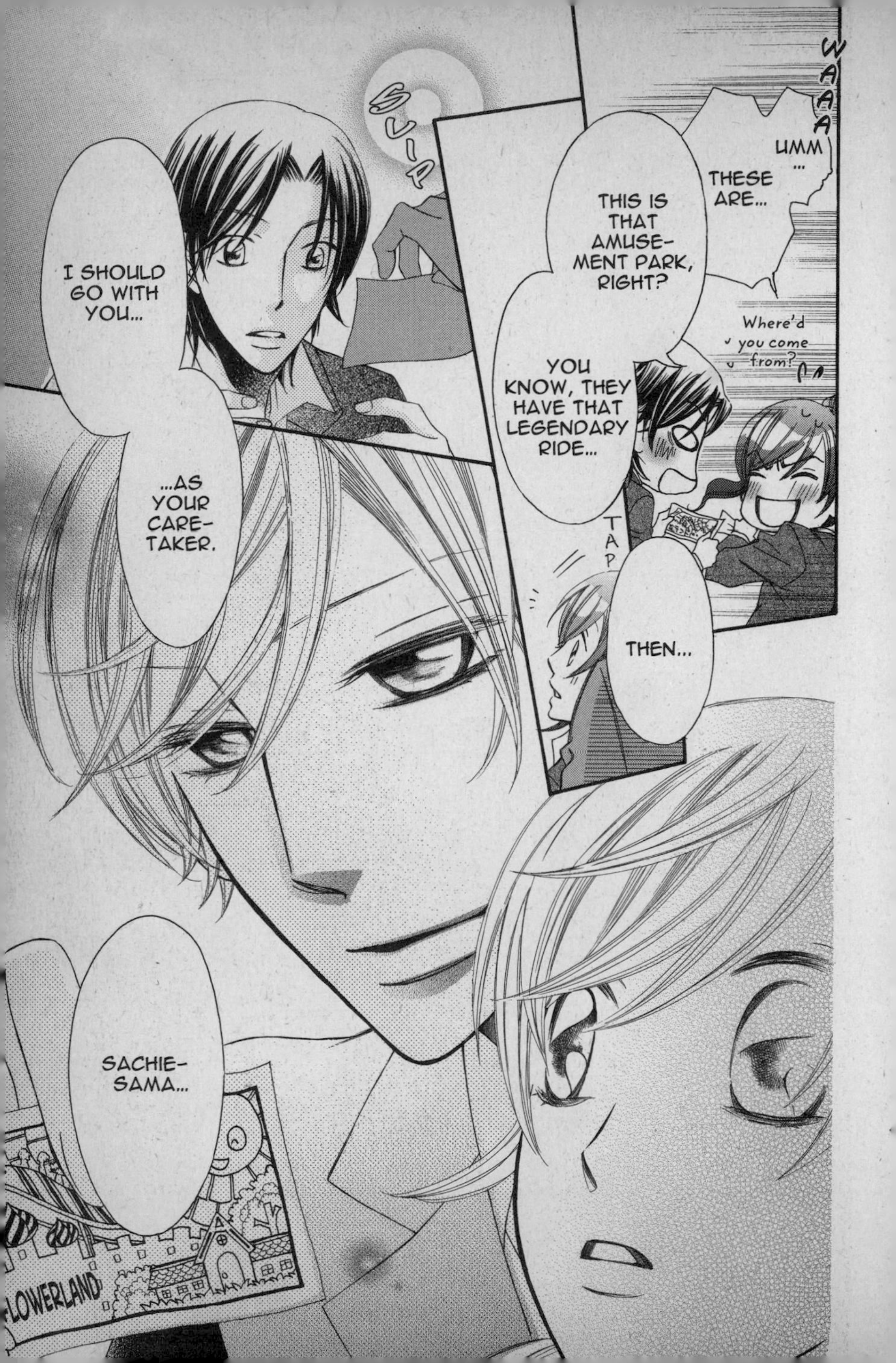
WAAAA
UMM...
THESE ARE...
Where'd you come from?
THIS IS THAT AMUSEMENT PARK, RIGHT?
YOU KNOW, THEY HAVE THAT LEGENDARY RIDE...
TAP
THEN...
SLIP
I SHOULD GO WITH YOU...
...AS YOUR CARE-TAKER.
SACHIE-SAMA...
LOWERLAND

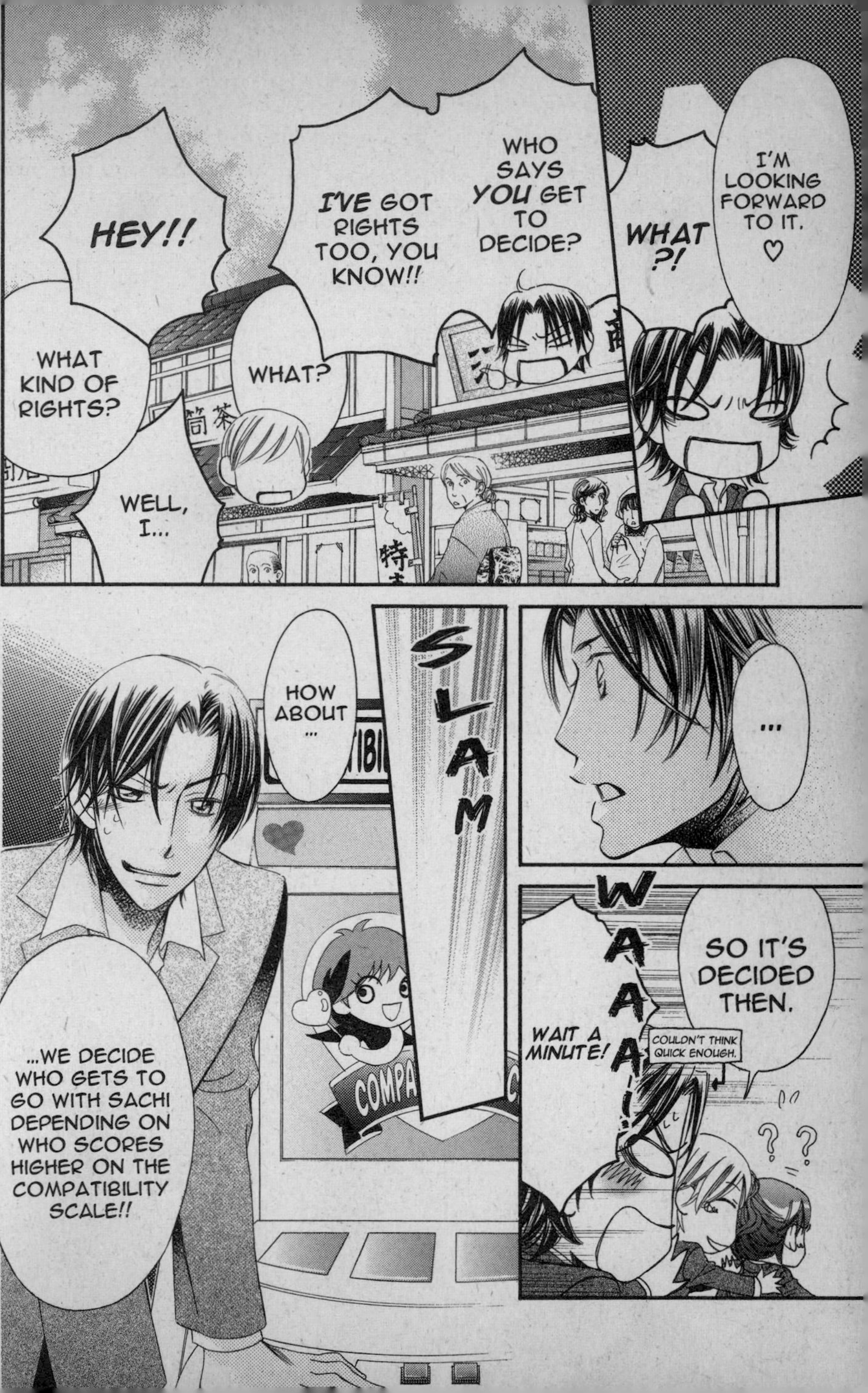
I'M LOOKING FORWARD TO IT. ♡
WHAT ?!
WHO SAYS YOU GET TO DECIDE?
I'VE GOT RIGHTS TOO, YOU KNOW!!
HEY!!
WHAT?
WHAT KIND OF RIGHTS?
WELL, I...
...
SO IT'S DECIDED THEN.
WAAAAI!
COULDN'T THINK QUICK ENOUGH.
WAIT A MINUTE!
SLAM
HOW ABOUT ...
...WE DECIDE WHO GETS TO GO WITH SACHI DEPENDING ON WHO SCORES HIGHER ON THE COMPATIBILITY SCALE!!

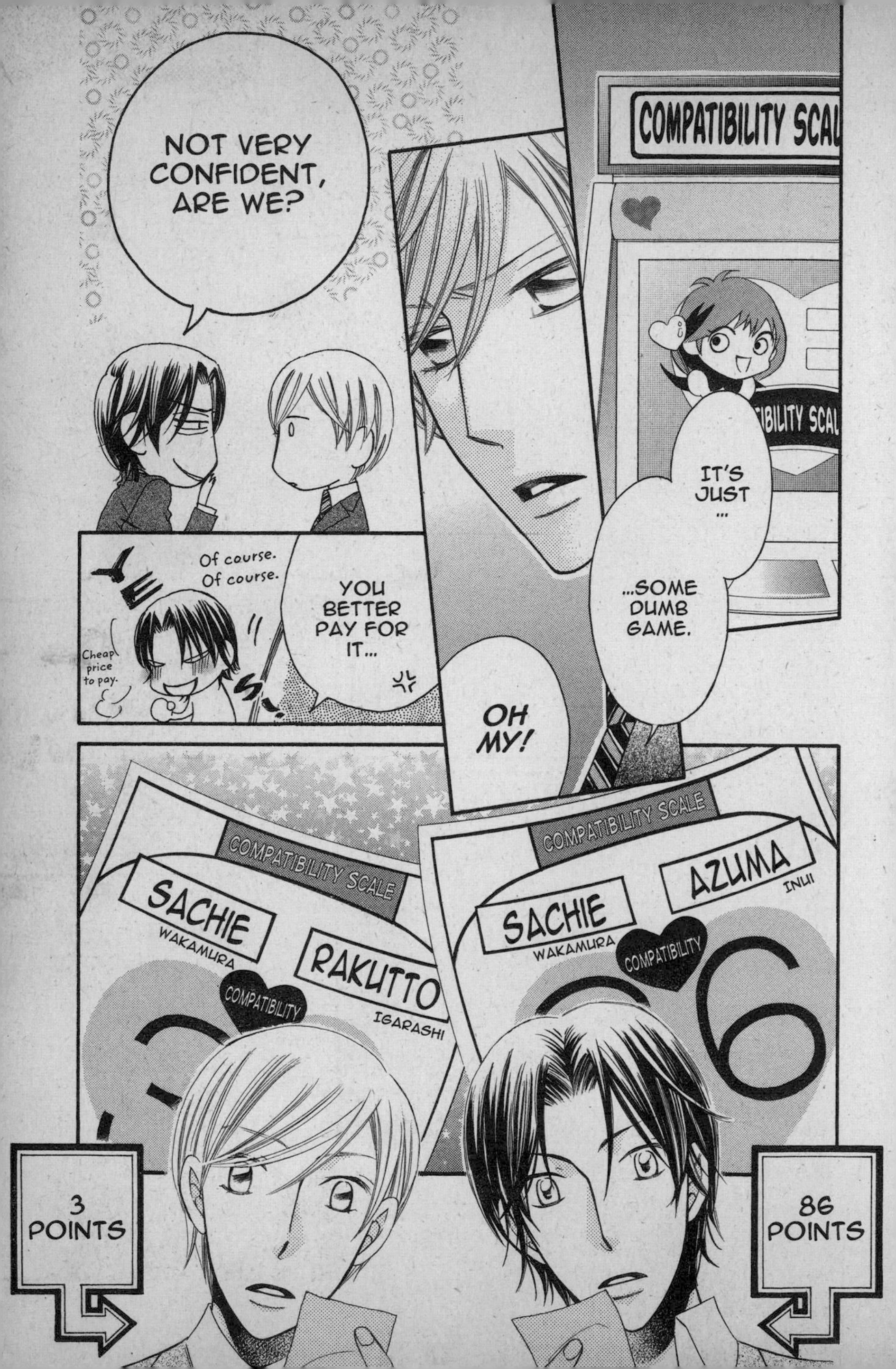
COMPATIBILITY SCAL
TIBILITY SCAL
IT'S JUST ...
...SOME DUMB GAME.
OH MY!
NOT VERY CONFIDENT, ARE WE?
YOU BETTER PAY FOR IT...
Of course. Of course.
Cheap price to pay.
COMPATIBILITY SCALE
SACHIE WAKAMURA
AZUMA INUI
COMPATIBILITY
86 POINTS
COMPATIBILITY SCALE
SACHIE WAKAMURA
RAKUTTO IGARASHI
COMPATIBILITY
3 POINTS

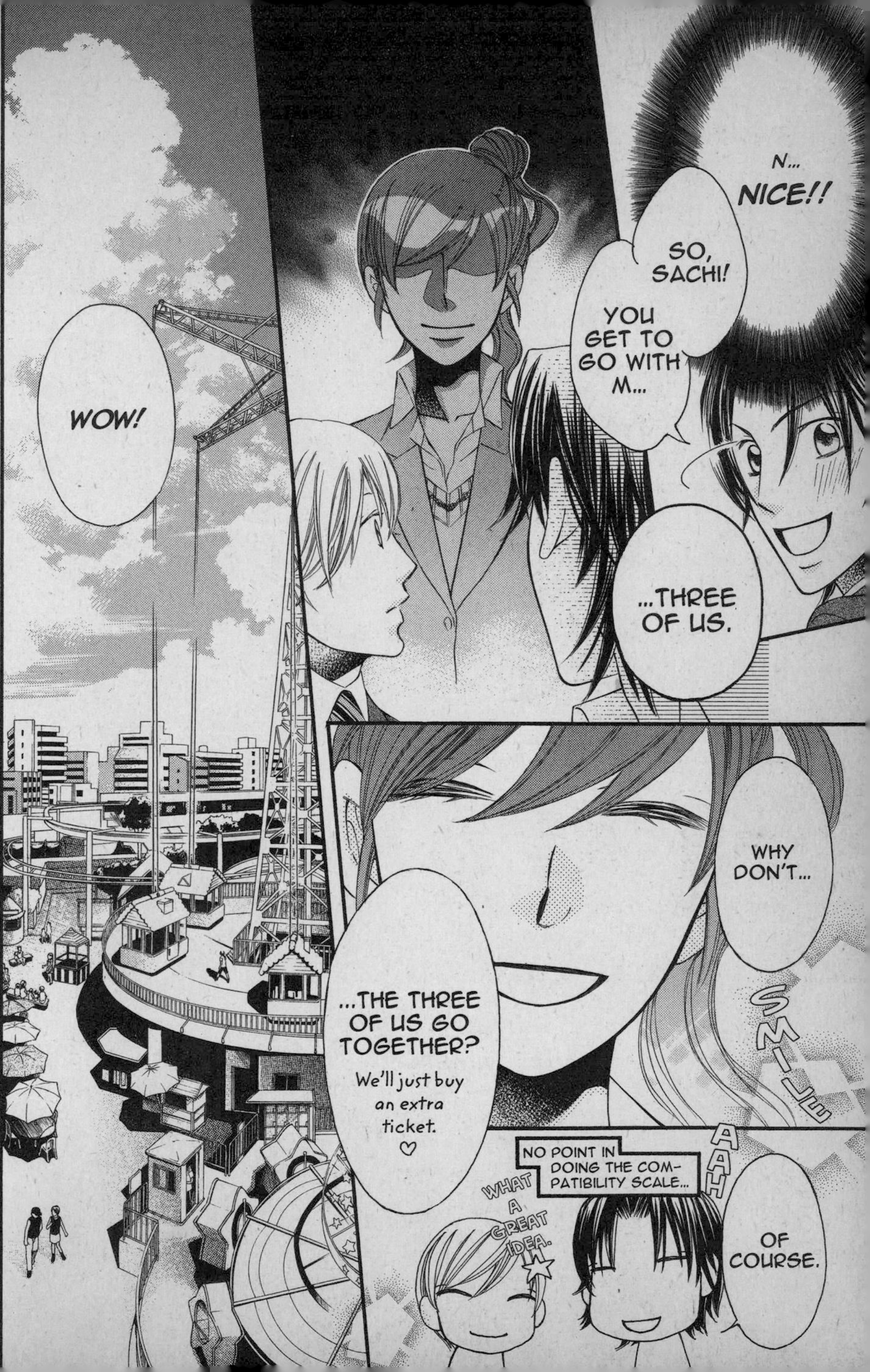
N... NICE!!
SO, SACHI!
YOU GET TO GO WITH M...
...THREE OF US.
WHY DON'T...
...THE THREE OF US GO TOGETHER?
We'll just buy an extra ticket. ♡
SMILE
OF COURSE.
AAAH
NO POINT IN DOING THE COM-PATIBILITY SCALE...
WHAT A GREAT IDEA.
WOW!

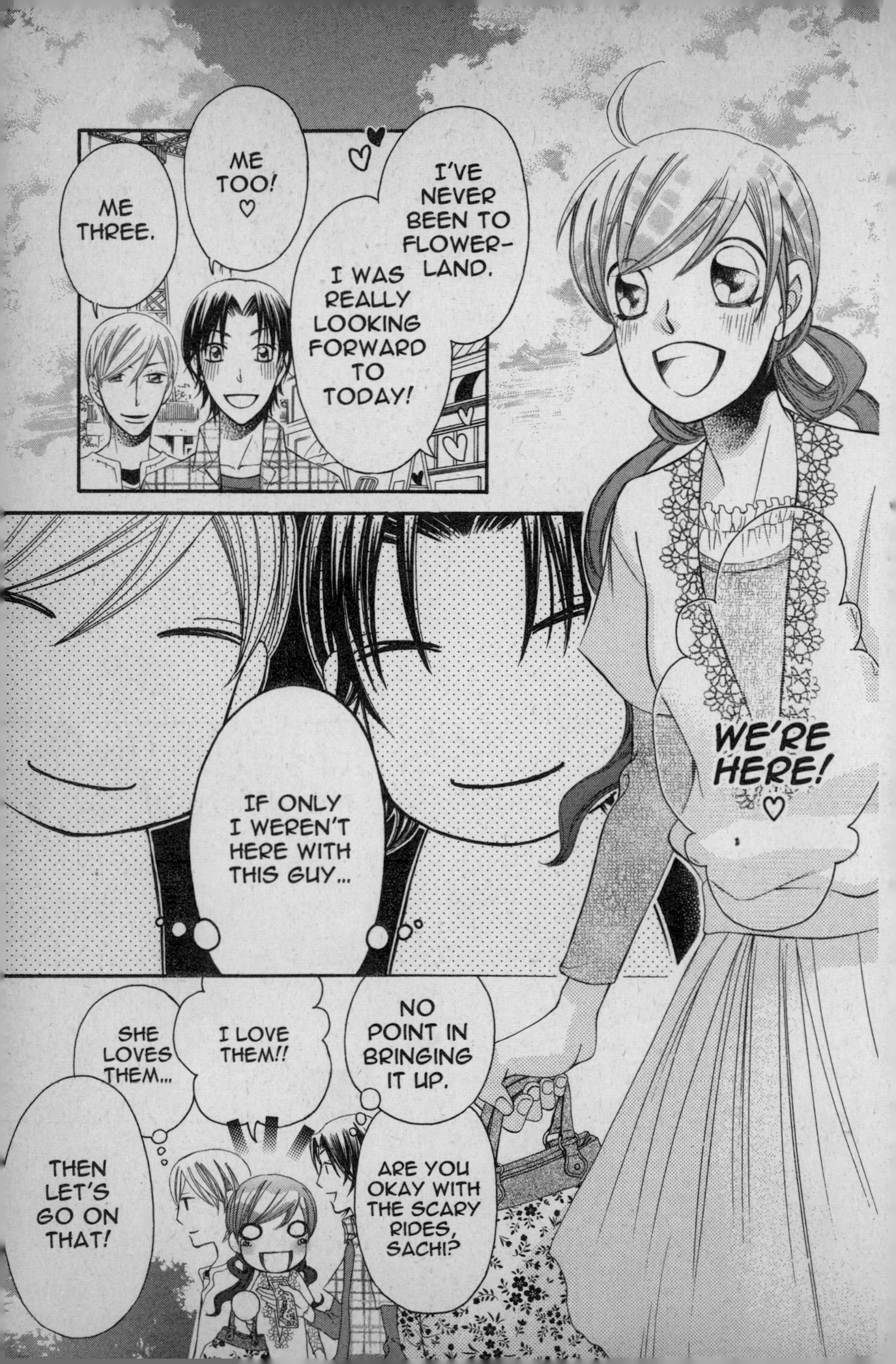
WE'RE HERE!
I'VE NEVER BEEN TO FLOWER-LAND.
I WAS REALLY LOOKING FORWARD TO TODAY!
ME TOO!
ME THREE.
IF ONLY I WEREN'T HERE WITH THIS GUY...
NO POINT IN BRINGING IT UP.
ARE YOU OKAY WITH THE SCARY RIDES, SACHI?
I LOVE THEM!!
SHE LOVES THEM...
THEN LET'S GO ON THAT!

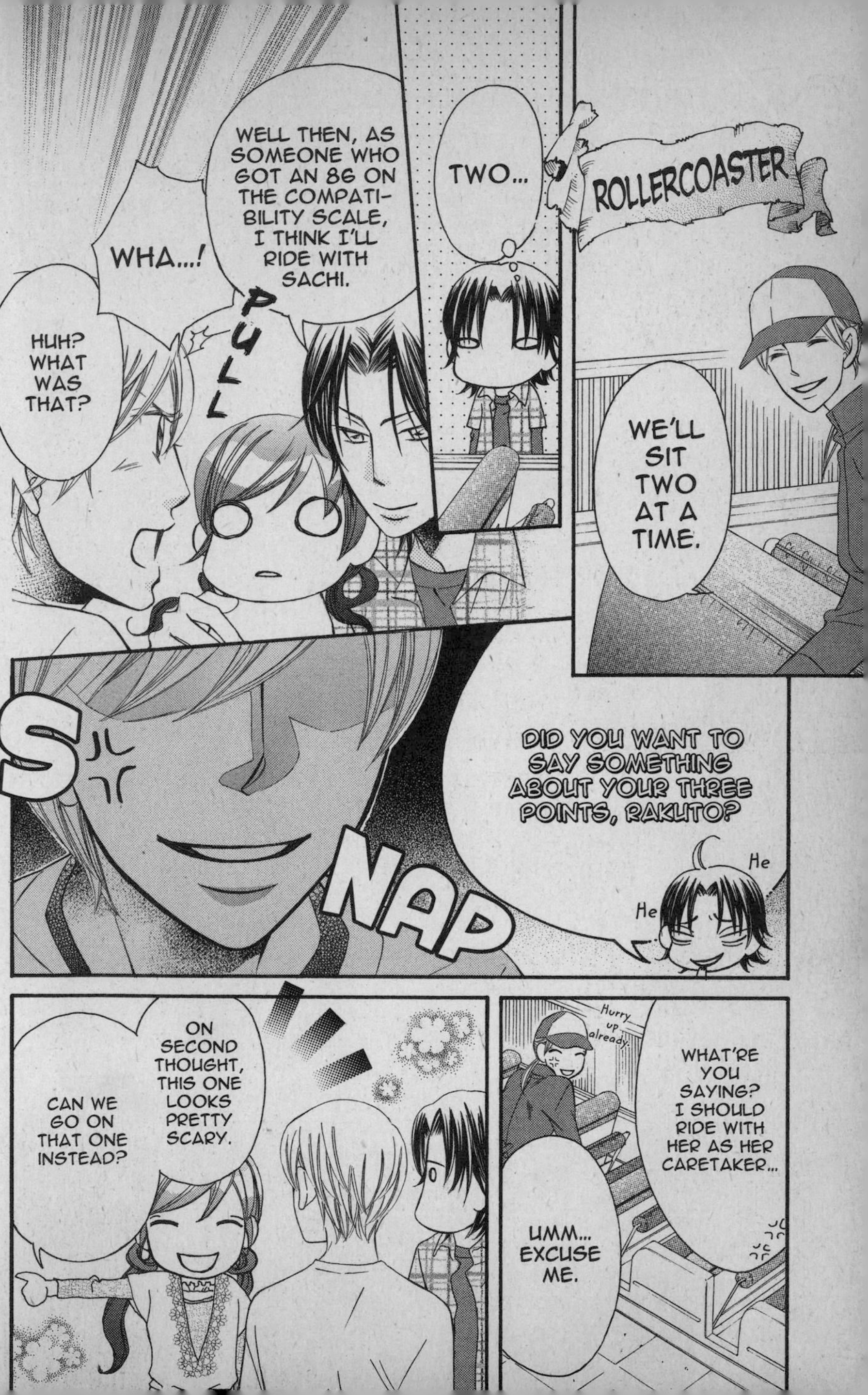
ROLLERCOASTER
WE'LL SIT TWO AT A TIME.
TWO...
WELL THEN, AS SOMEONE WHO GOT AN 86 ON THE COMPATIBILITY SCALE, I THINK I'LL RIDE WITH SACHI.
PULL
WHA...!
HUH? WHAT WAS THAT?
DID YOU WANT TO SAY SOMETHING ABOUT YOUR THREE POINTS, RAKUTO?
He
He
SNAP
Hurry up already.
WHAT'RE YOU SAYING? I SHOULD RIDE WITH HER AS HER CARETAKER...
UMM... EXCUSE ME.
ON SECOND THOUGHT, THIS ONE LOOKS PRETTY SCARY.
CAN WE GO ON THAT ONE INSTEAD?

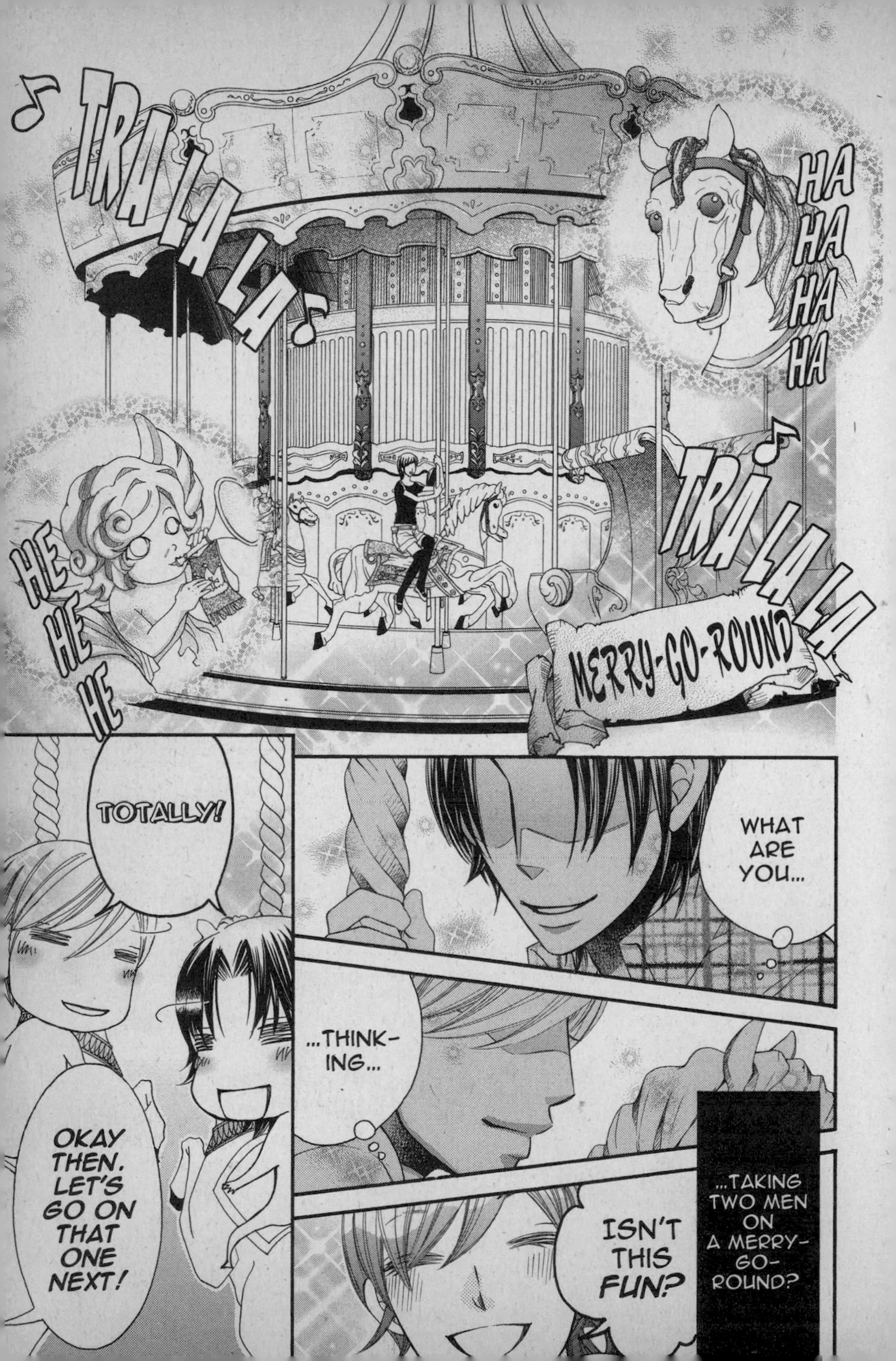

HA HA HA HA
TRA LA LA LA
MERRY-GO-ROUND
TRA LA LA LA
HE HE HE HE
WHAT ARE YOU...
...THINKING-ING...
...TAKING TWO MEN ON A MERRY-GO-ROUND?
ISN'T THIS FUN?
TOTALLY!
OKAY THEN. LET'S GO ON THAT ONE NEXT!

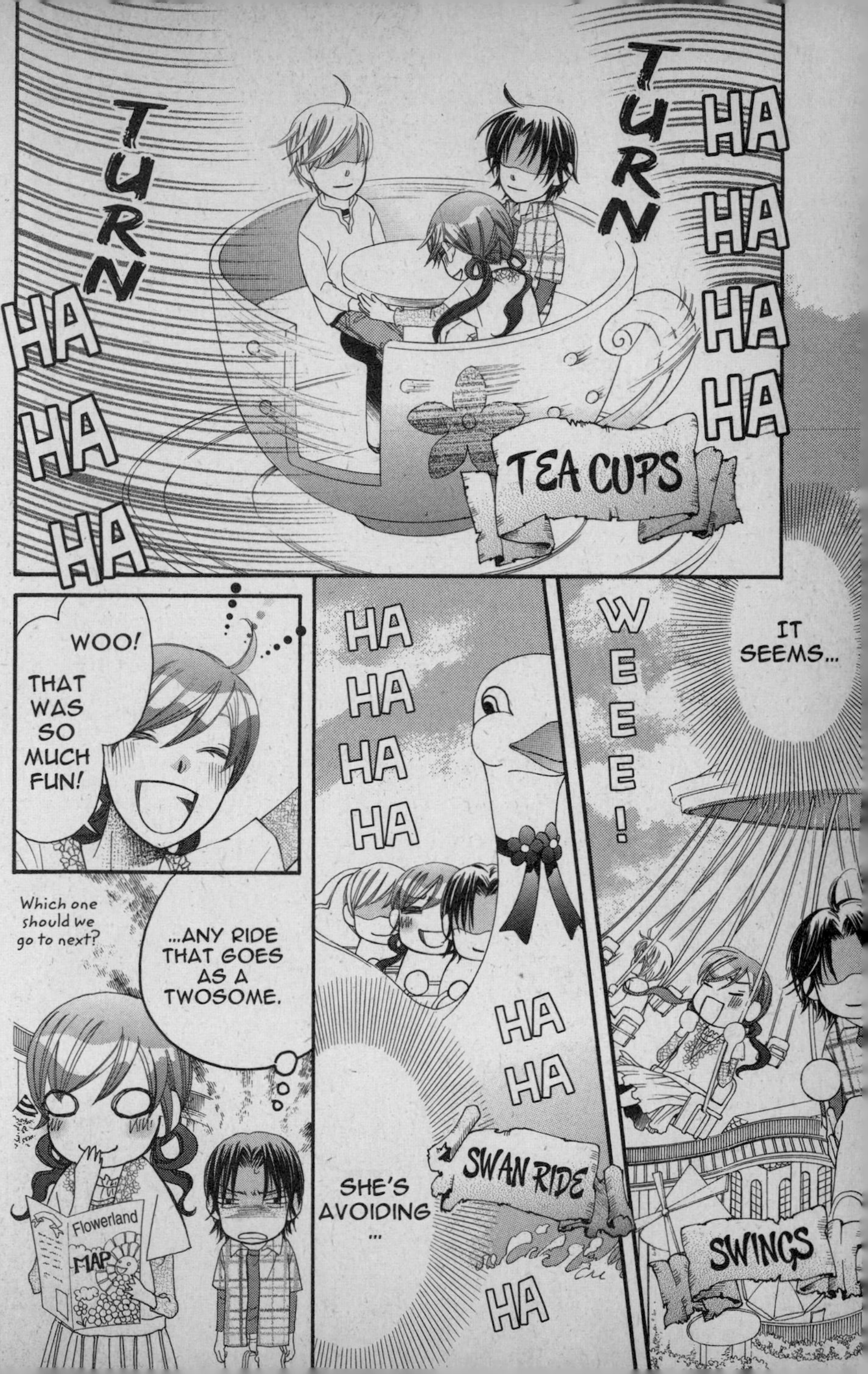
TURN
HA HA HA HA
TURN
HA HA HA
TEA CUPS
IT SEEMS...
WEEE!
SWINGS
HA HA HA HA
HA HA HA
SWAN RIDE
SHE'S AVOIDING ...
WOO!
THAT WAS SO MUCH FUN!
...ANY RIDE THAT GOES AS A TWOSOME.
Which one should we go to next?
Flowerland MAP

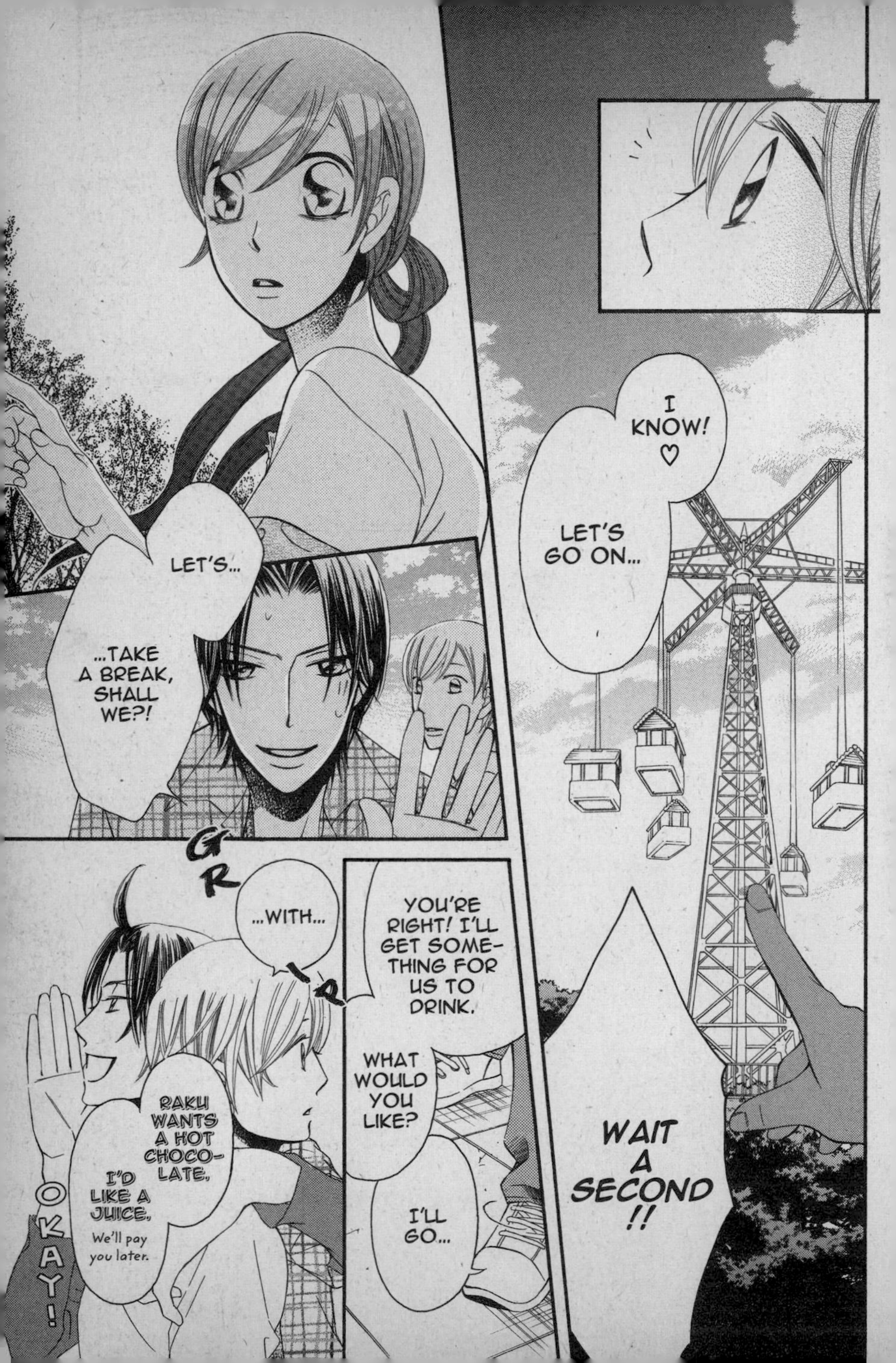
I KNOW! ♡
LET'S GO ON...
WAIT A SECOND!!
LET'S...
...TAKE A BREAK, SHALL WE?!
YOU'RE RIGHT! I'LL GET SOMETHING FOR US TO DRINK.
WHAT WOULD YOU LIKE?
I'LL GO...
GRIP
...WITH...
RAKU WANTS A HOT CHOCOLATE.
I'D LIKE A JUICE.
We'll pay you later.
OKAY!

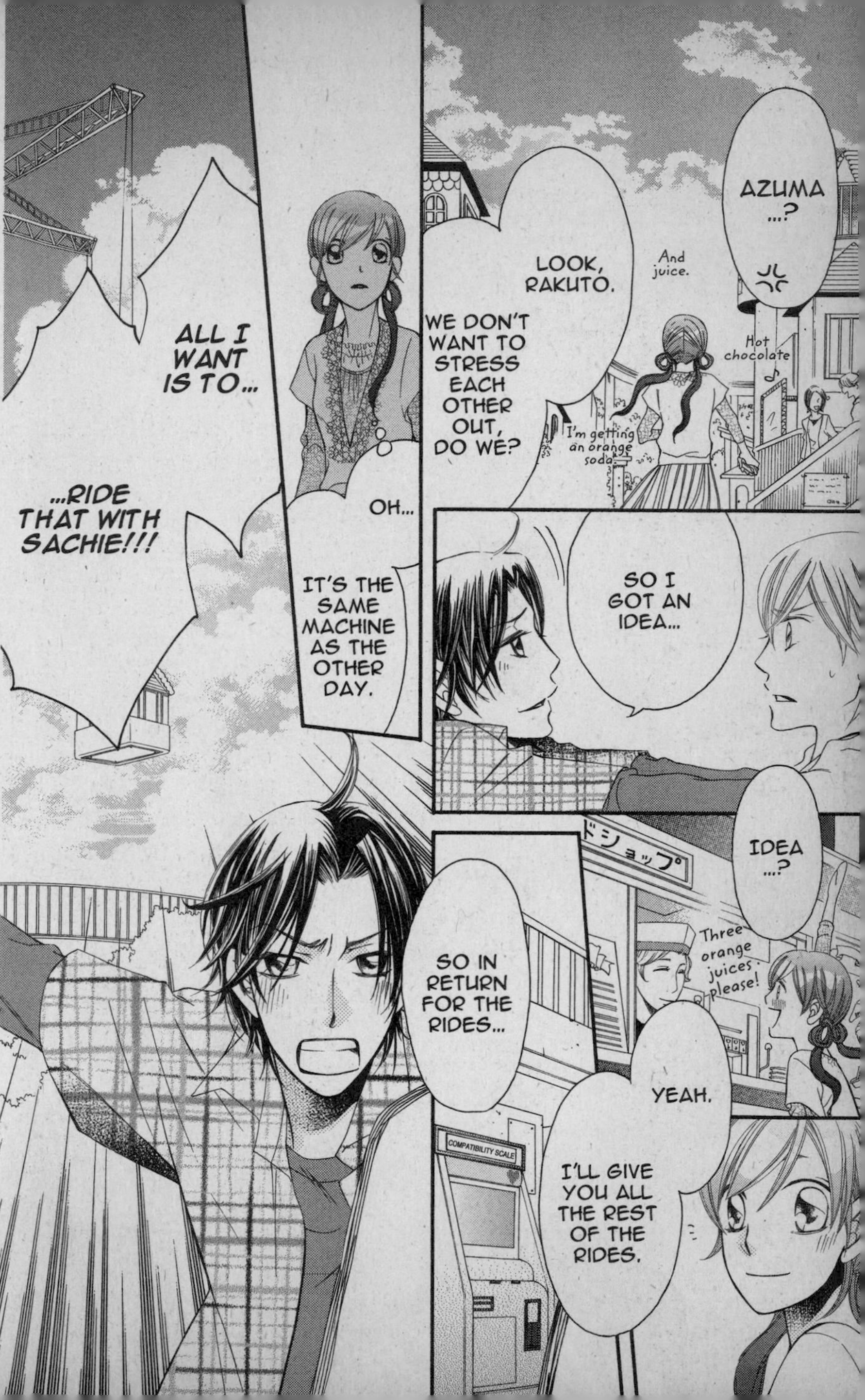
AZUMA ...?
Hot chocolate ♪
And juice.
LOOK, RAKUTO.
WE DON'T WANT TO STRESS EACH OTHER OUT, DO WE?
I'm getting an orange soda.
SO I GOT AN IDEA...
IDEA ...?
ドショップ
Three orange juices please!
YEAH.
SO IN RETURN FOR THE RIDES...
I'LL GIVE YOU ALL THE REST OF THE RIDES.
COMPATIBILITY SCALE
OH...
IT'S THE SAME MACHINE AS THE OTHER DAY.
ALL I WANT IS TO...
...RIDE THAT WITH SACHIE!!!

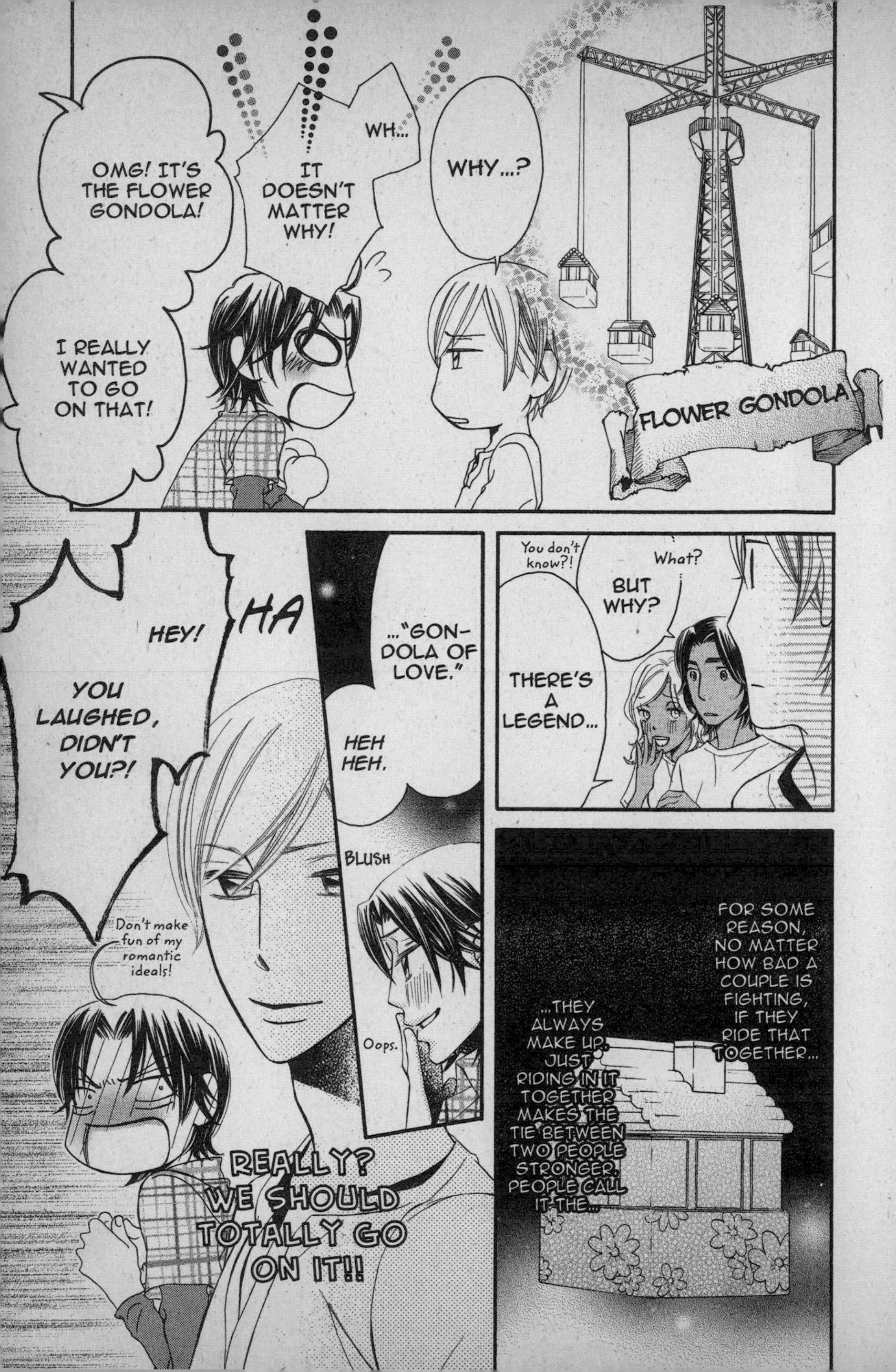
FLOWER GONDOLA
WHY...?
WH...
IT DOESN'T MATTER WHY!
OMG! IT'S THE FLOWER GONDOLA!
I REALLY WANTED TO GO ON THAT!
What?
BUT WHY?
You don't know?!
THERE'S A LEGEND...
FOR SOME REASON, NO MATTER HOW BAD A COUPLE IS FIGHTING, IF THEY RIDE THAT TOGETHER...
...THEY ALWAYS MAKE UP. JUST RIDING IN IT TOGETHER MAKES THE TIE BETWEEN TWO PEOPLE STRONGER. PEOPLE CALL IT THE...
..."GONDOLA OF LOVE."
HEH HEH.
BLUSH
Oops.
HA
HEY!
YOU LAUGHED, DIDN'T YOU?!
Don't make fun of my romantic ideals!
REALLY? WE SHOULD TOTALLY GO ON IT!!

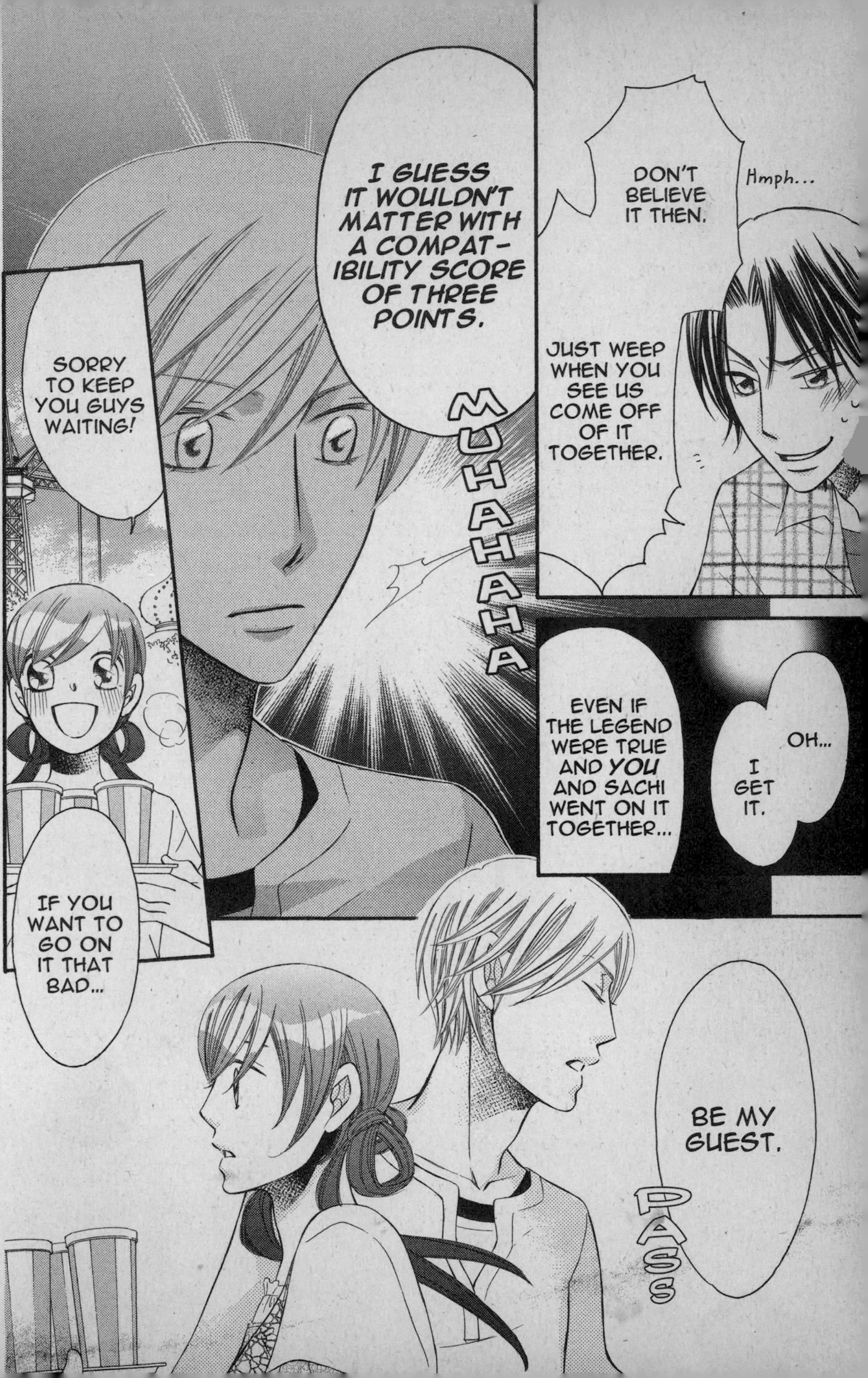
Hmph...
DON'T BELIEVE IT THEN.
JUST WEEP WHEN YOU SEE US COME OFF OF IT TOGETHER.
OH... I GET IT.
EVEN IF THE LEGEND WERE TRUE AND *YOU* AND SACHI WENT ON IT TOGETHER...
I GUESS IT WOULDN'T MATTER WITH A COMPAT-IBILITY SCORE OF THREE POINTS.
MUHAHAHA
SORRY TO KEEP YOU GUYS WAITING!
IF YOU WANT TO GO ON IT THAT BAD...
BE MY GUEST.
PASS

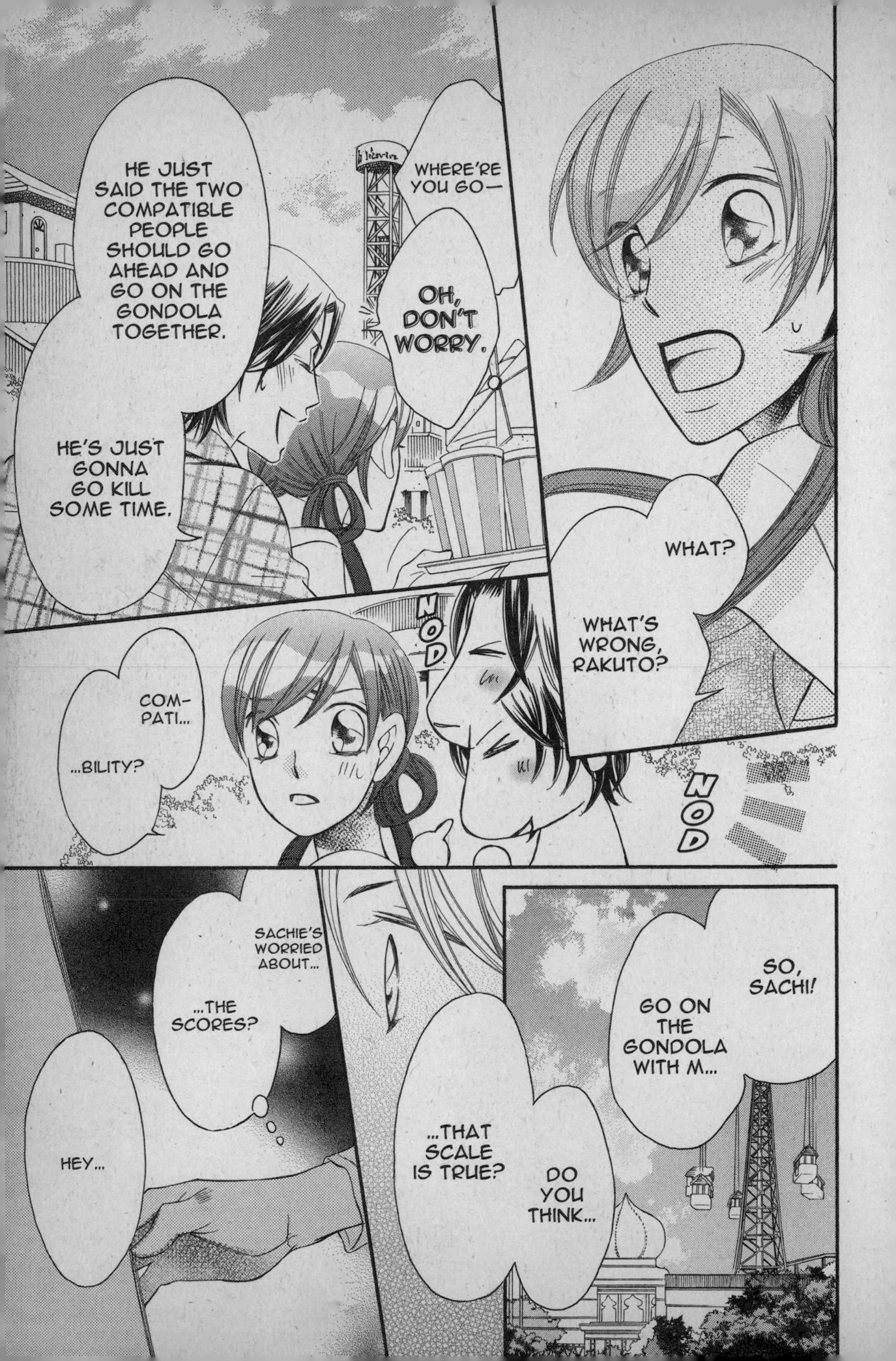
WHAT?
WHAT'S WRONG, RAKUTO?
WHERE'RE YOU GO—
OH, DON'T WORRY.
HE JUST SAID THE TWO COMPATIBLE PEOPLE SHOULD GO AHEAD AND GO ON THE GONDOLA TOGETHER.
HE'S JUST GONNA GO KILL SOME TIME.
NOD
NOD
COMPATI...
...BILITY?
SO, SACHI!
GO ON THE GONDOLA WITH M...
DO YOU THINK...
...THAT SCALE IS TRUE?
SACHIE'S WORRIED ABOUT...
...THE SCORES?
HEY...

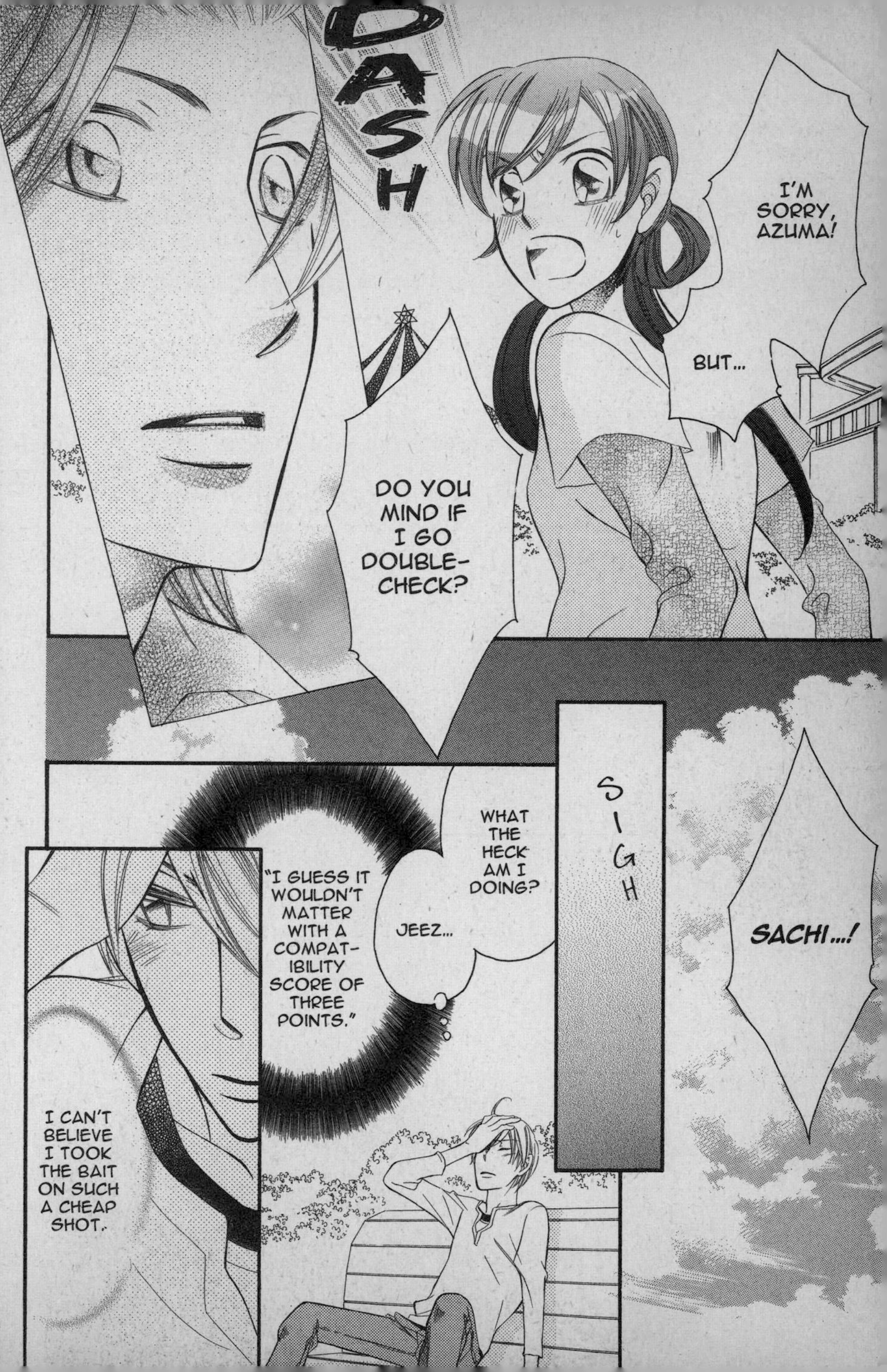
I'M SORRY, AZUMA!
BUT...
DASH
DO YOU MIND IF I GO DOUBLE-CHECK?
SACHI...!
SIGH
WHAT THE HECK AM I DOING?
JEEZ...
"I GUESS IT WOULDN'T MATTER WITH A COMPAT-IBILITY SCORE OF THREE POINTS."
I CAN'T BELIEVE I TOOK THE BAIT ON SUCH A CHEAP SHOT.

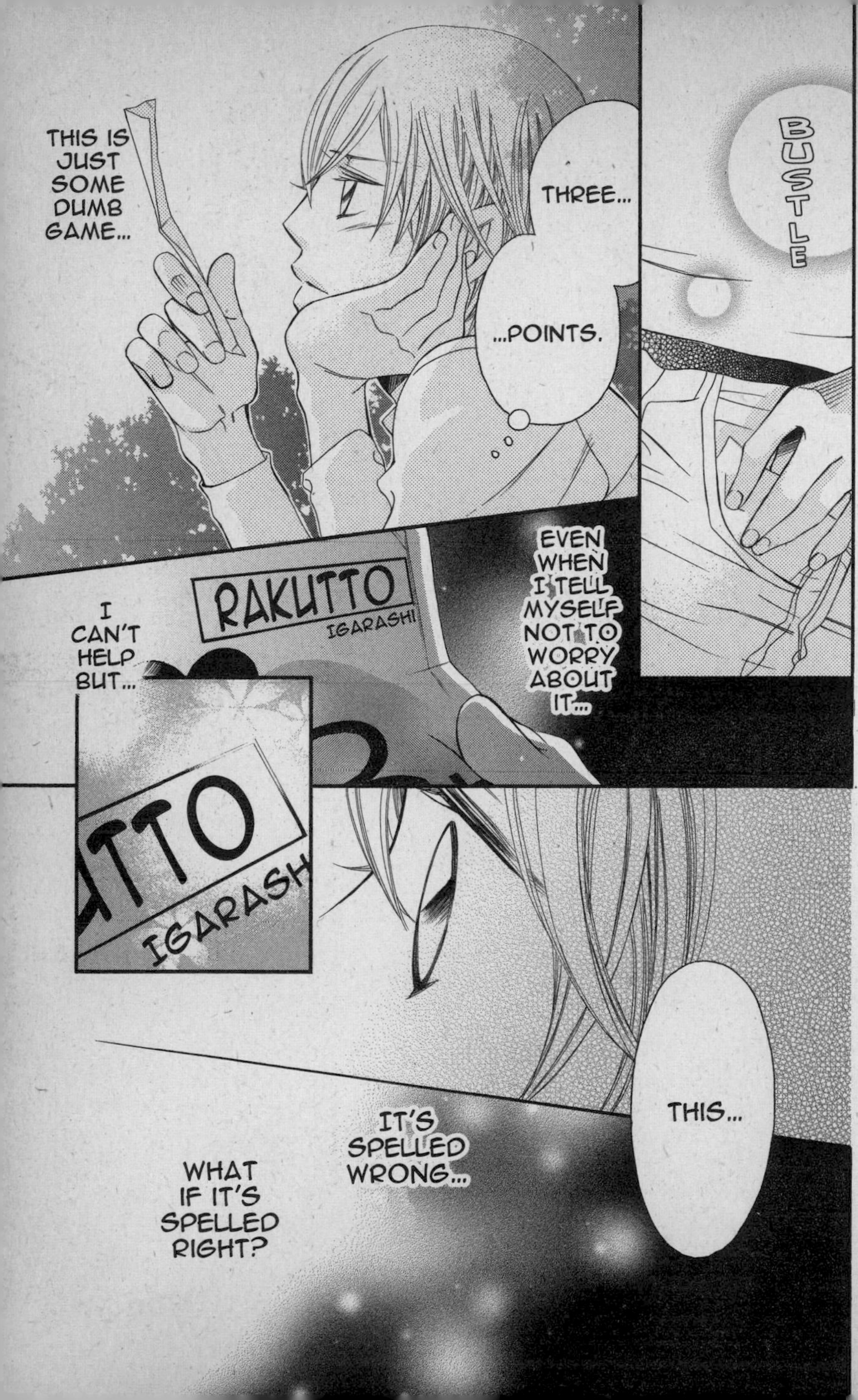
BUSTLE
THREE...
...POINTS.
THIS IS JUST SOME DUMB GAME...
EVEN WHEN I TELL MYSELF NOT TO WORRY ABOUT IT...
RAKUTTO
IGARASHI
I CAN'T HELP BUT...
TTO
IGARASH
THIS...
IT'S SPELLED WRONG...
WHAT IF IT'S SPELLED RIGHT?

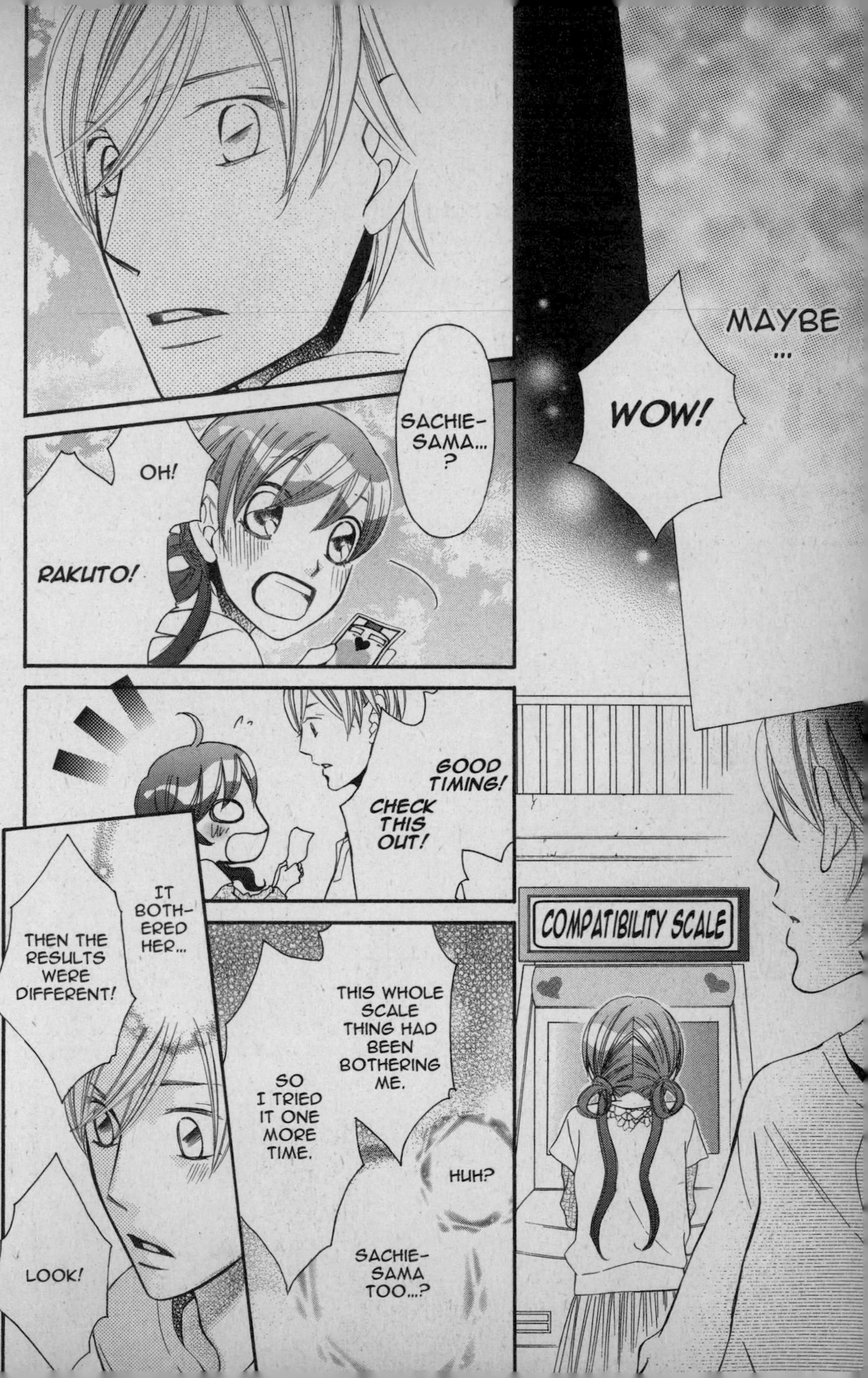
MAYBE ...
WOW!
COMPATIBILITY SCALE
SACHIE-SAMA...?
OH!
RAKUTO!
GOOD TIMING!
CHECK THIS OUT!
THIS WHOLE SCALE THING HAD BEEN BOTHERING ME.
SO I TRIED IT ONE MORE TIME.
HUH?
SACHIE-SAMA TOO...?
IT BOTHERED HER...
THEN THE RESULTS WERE DIFFERENT!
LOOK!

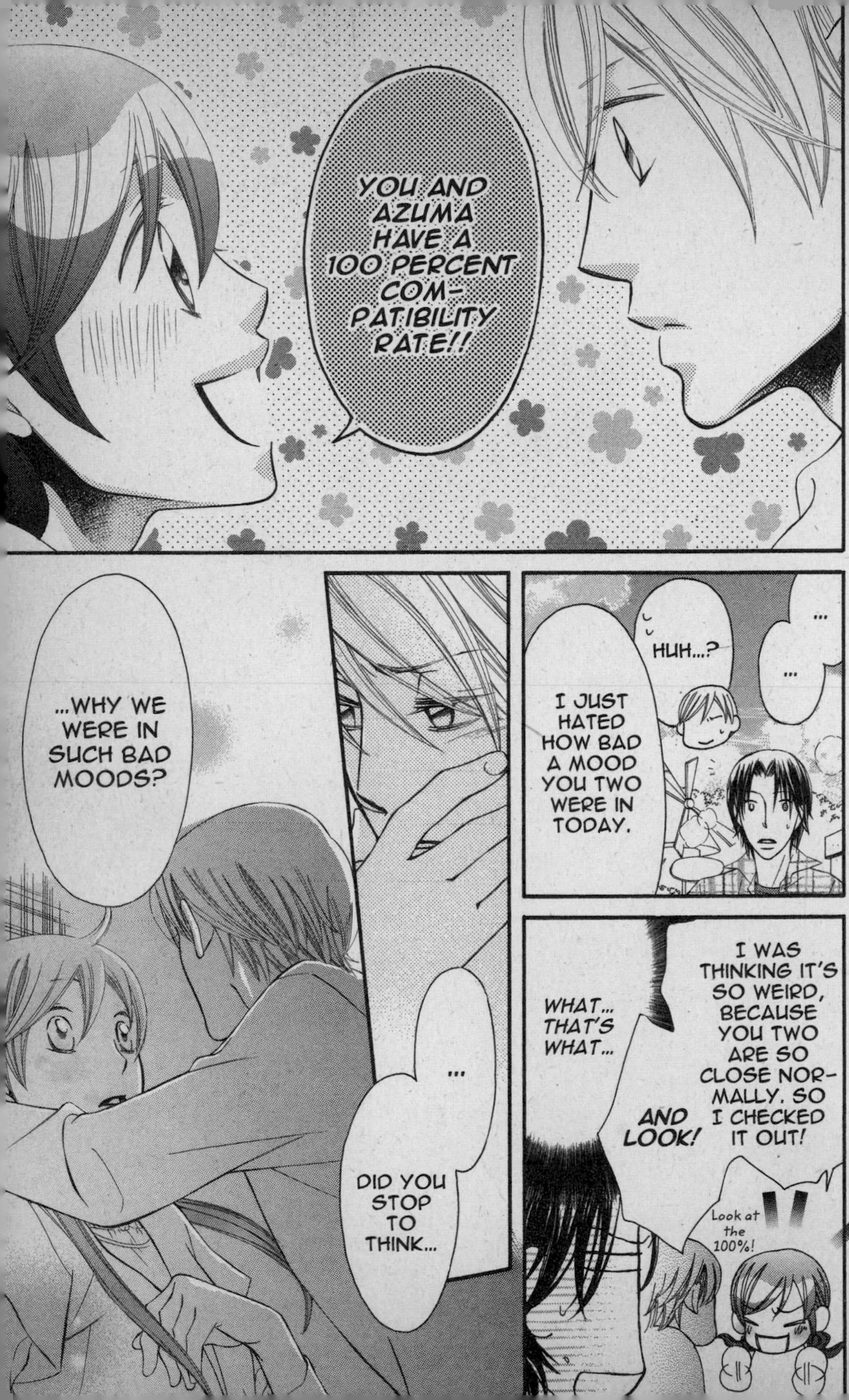
YOU AND AZUMA HAVE A 100 PERCENT COM-PATIBILITY RATE!!
...
...
HUH...?
I JUST HATED HOW BAD A MOOD YOU TWO WERE IN TODAY.
I WAS THINKING IT'S SO WEIRD, BECAUSE YOU TWO ARE SO CLOSE NOR-MALLY. SO I CHECKED IT OUT!
WHAT... THAT'S WHAT...
AND LOOK!
Look at the 100%!
...
DID YOU STOP TO THINK...
...WHY WE WERE IN SUCH BAD MOODS?

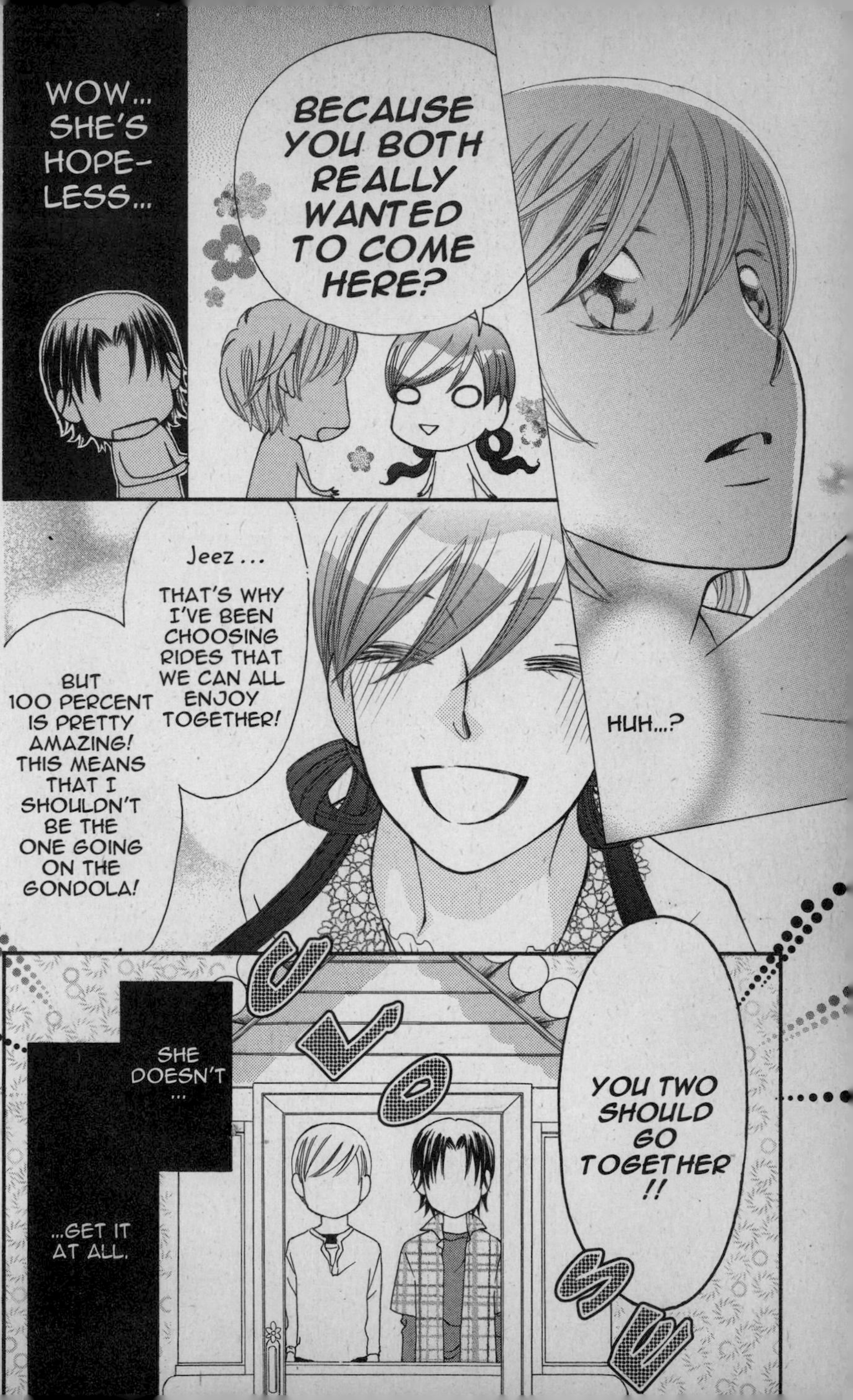
HUH...?
BECAUSE YOU BOTH REALLY WANTED TO COME HERE?
WOW... SHE'S HOPE-LESS...
Jeez...
THAT'S WHY I'VE BEEN CHOOSING RIDES THAT WE CAN ALL ENJOY TOGETHER!
BUT 100 PERCENT IS PRETTY AMAZING! THIS MEANS THAT I SHOULDN'T BE THE ONE GOING ON THE GONDOLA!
YOU TWO SHOULD GO TOGETHER!!
SHE DOESN'T...
...GET IT AT ALL.

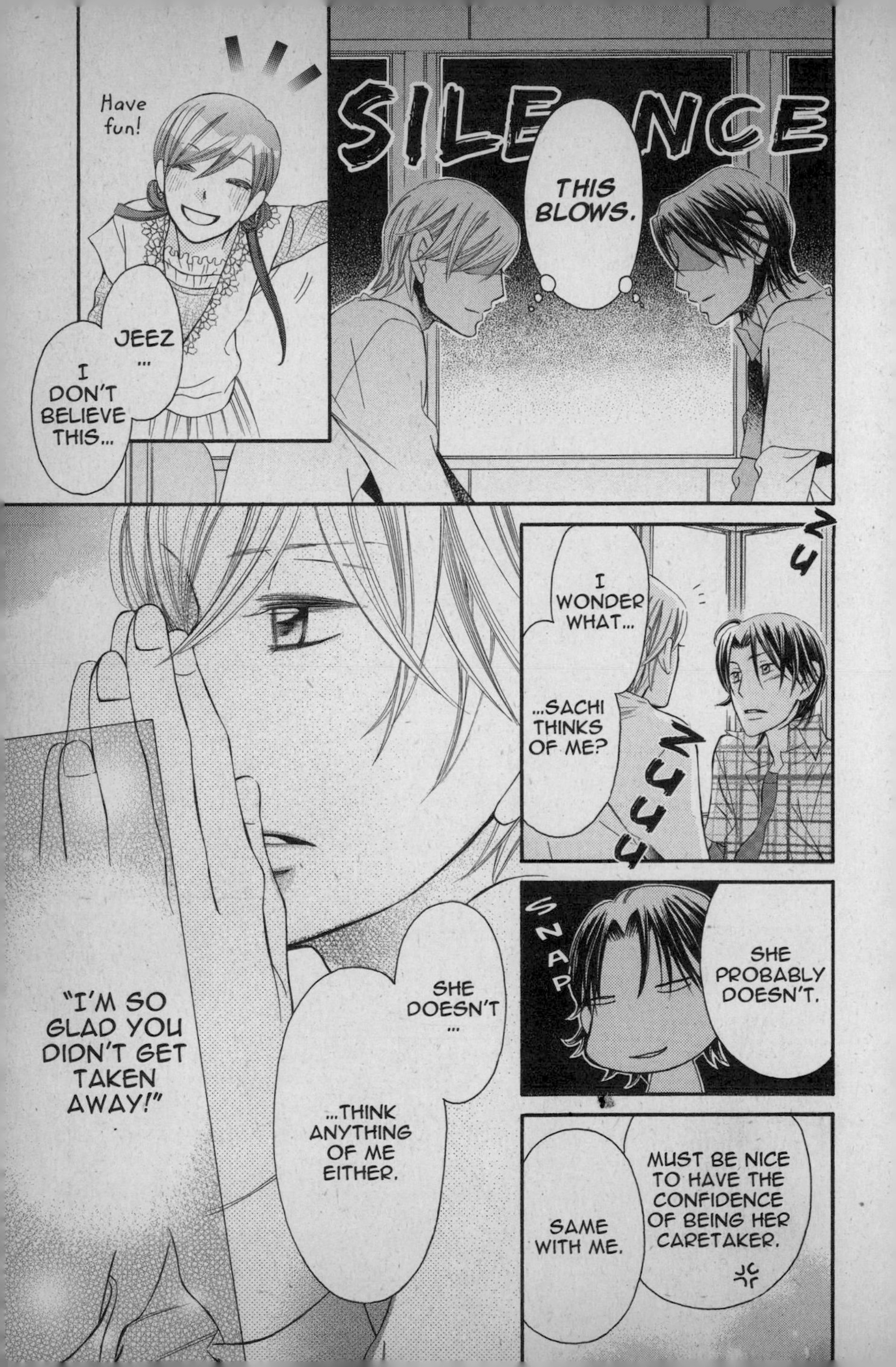
SILENCE
THIS BLOWS.
Have fun!
JEEZ...
I DON'T BELIEVE THIS...
I WONDER WHAT...
...SACHI THINKS OF ME?
ZUUUU
SNAP
SHE PROBABLY DOESN'T.
MUST BE NICE TO HAVE THE CONFIDENCE OF BEING HER CARETAKER.
SAME WITH ME.
SHE DOESN'T...
...THINK ANYTHING OF ME EITHER.
"I'M SO GLAD YOU DIDN'T GET TAKEN AWAY!"

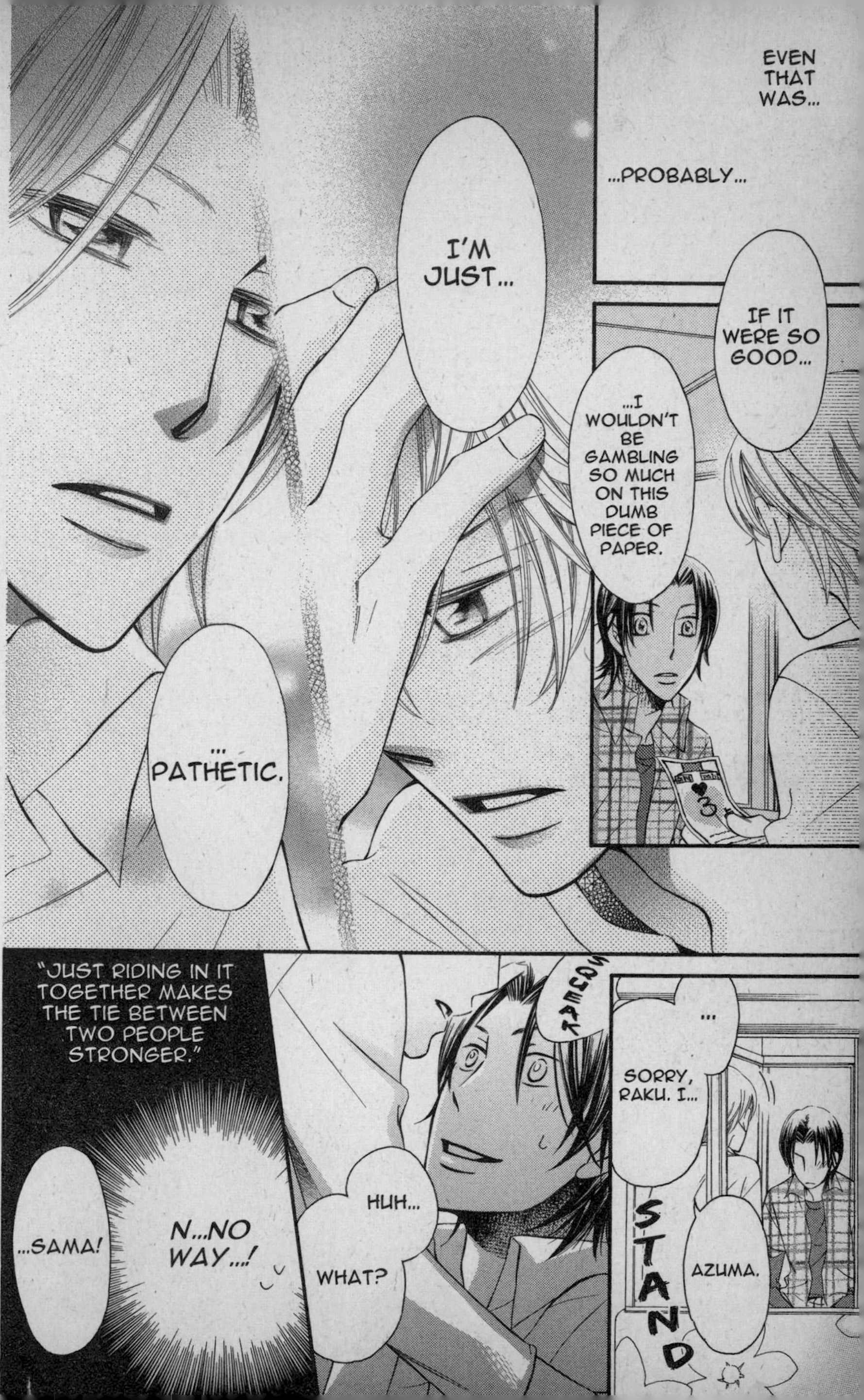
EVEN THAT WAS...
...PROBABLY...
IF IT WERE SO GOOD...
...I WOULDN'T BE GAMBLING SO MUCH ON THIS DUMB PIECE OF PAPER.
I'M JUST...
... PATHETIC.
...
SORRY, RAKU. I...
STAND
AZUMA.
SQUEAK
HUH...
WHAT?
"JUST RIDING IN IT TOGETHER MAKES THE TIE BETWEEN TWO PEOPLE STRONGER."
N...NO WAY...!
...SAMA!

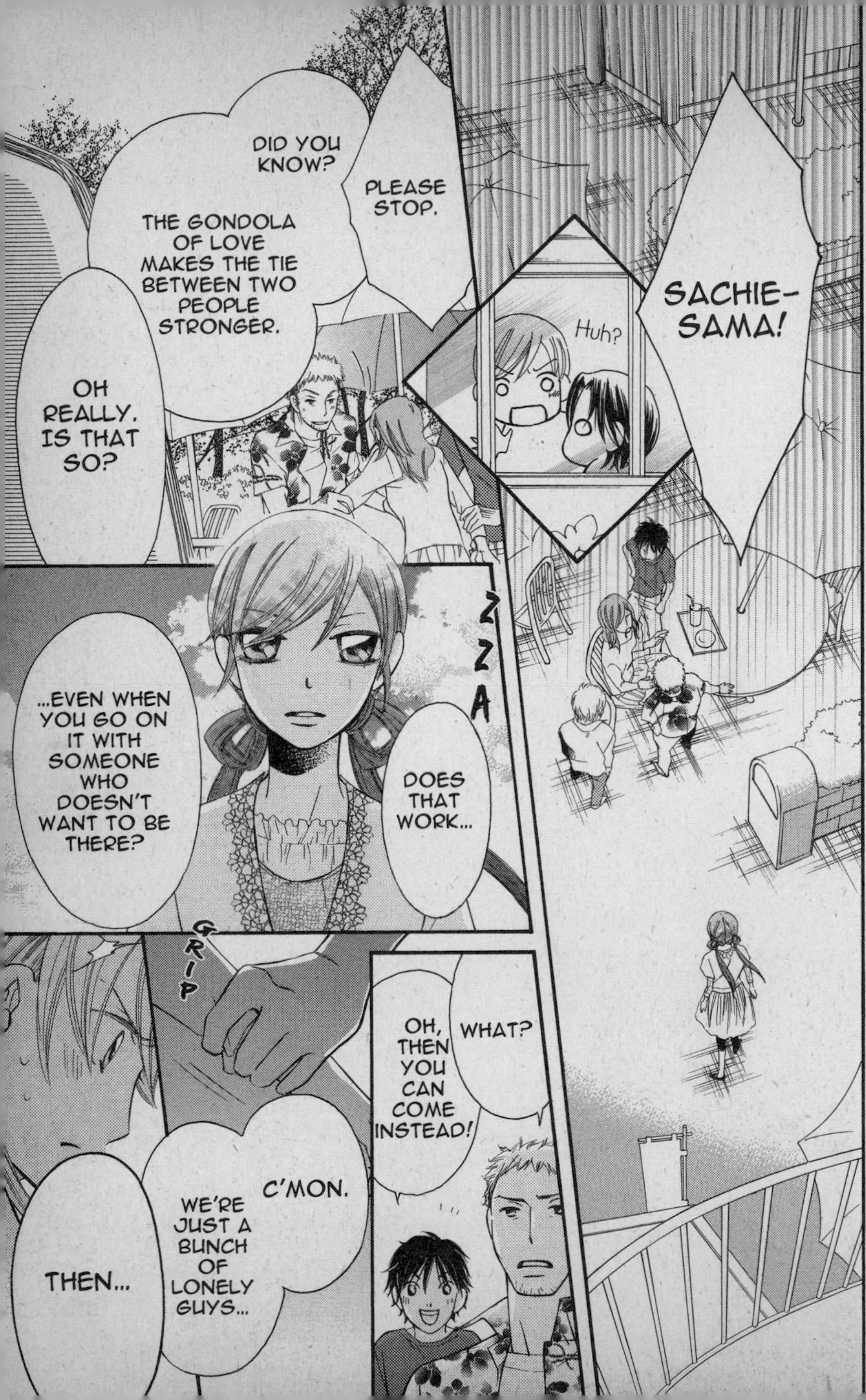
SACHIE-SAMA!
Huh?
DID YOU KNOW? THE GONDOLA OF LOVE MAKES THE TIE BETWEEN TWO PEOPLE STRONGER.
PLEASE STOP.
OH REALLY. IS THAT SO?
ZZZA
DOES THAT WORK...
...EVEN WHEN YOU GO ON IT WITH SOMEONE WHO DOESN'T WANT TO BE THERE?
WHAT?
OH, THEN YOU CAN COME INSTEAD!
GRIP
C'MON. WE'RE JUST A BUNCH OF LONELY GUYS...
THEN...

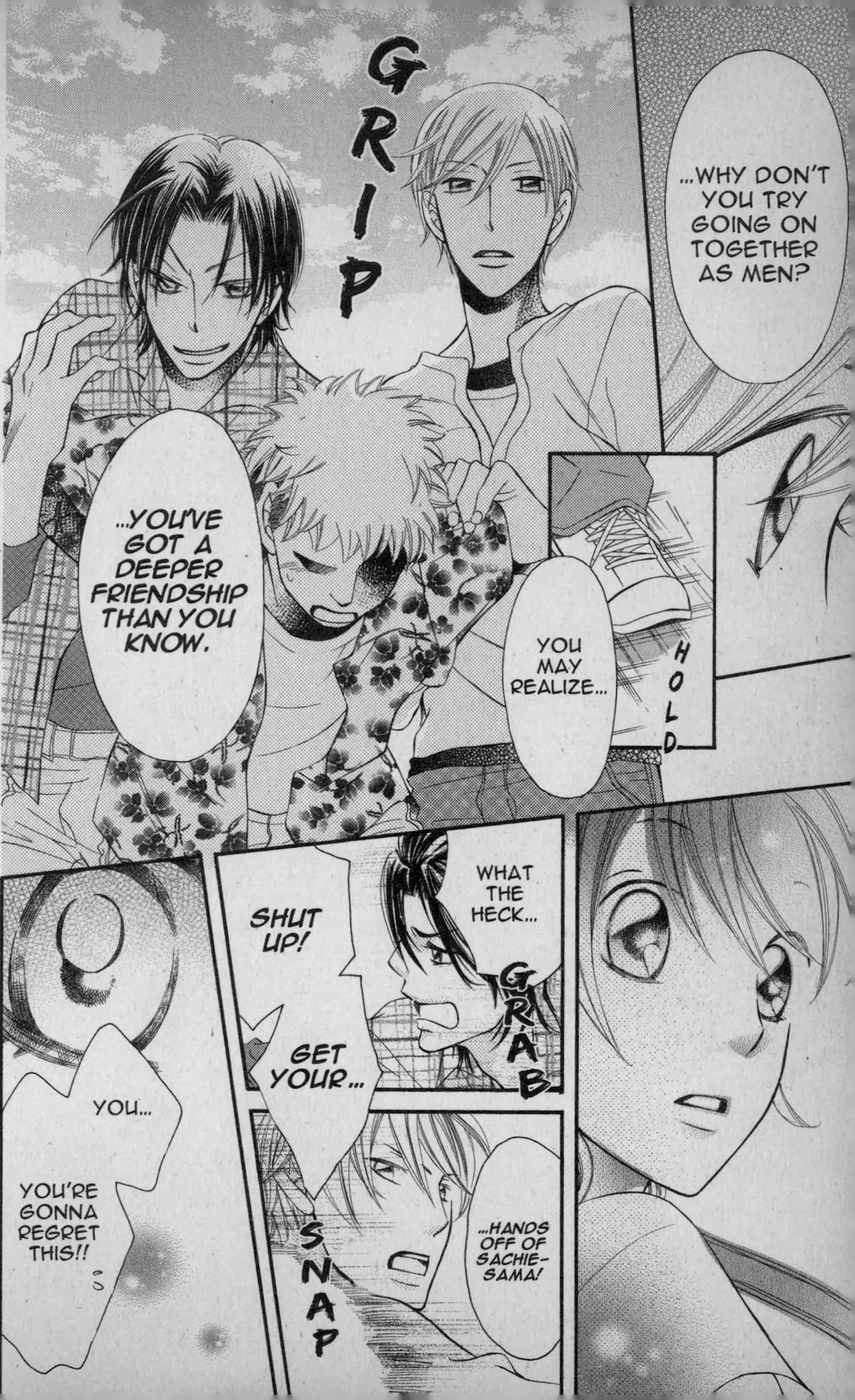

...WHY DON'T YOU TRY GOING ON TOGETHER AS MEN?
HOLD
YOU MAY REALIZE...
GRIP
...YOU'VE GOT A DEEPER FRIENDSHIP THAN YOU KNOW.
WHAT THE HECK...
SHUT UP!
GRAB
GET YOUR...
...HANDS OFF OF SACHIE-SAMA!
SNAP
YOU...
YOU'RE GONNA REGRET THIS!!

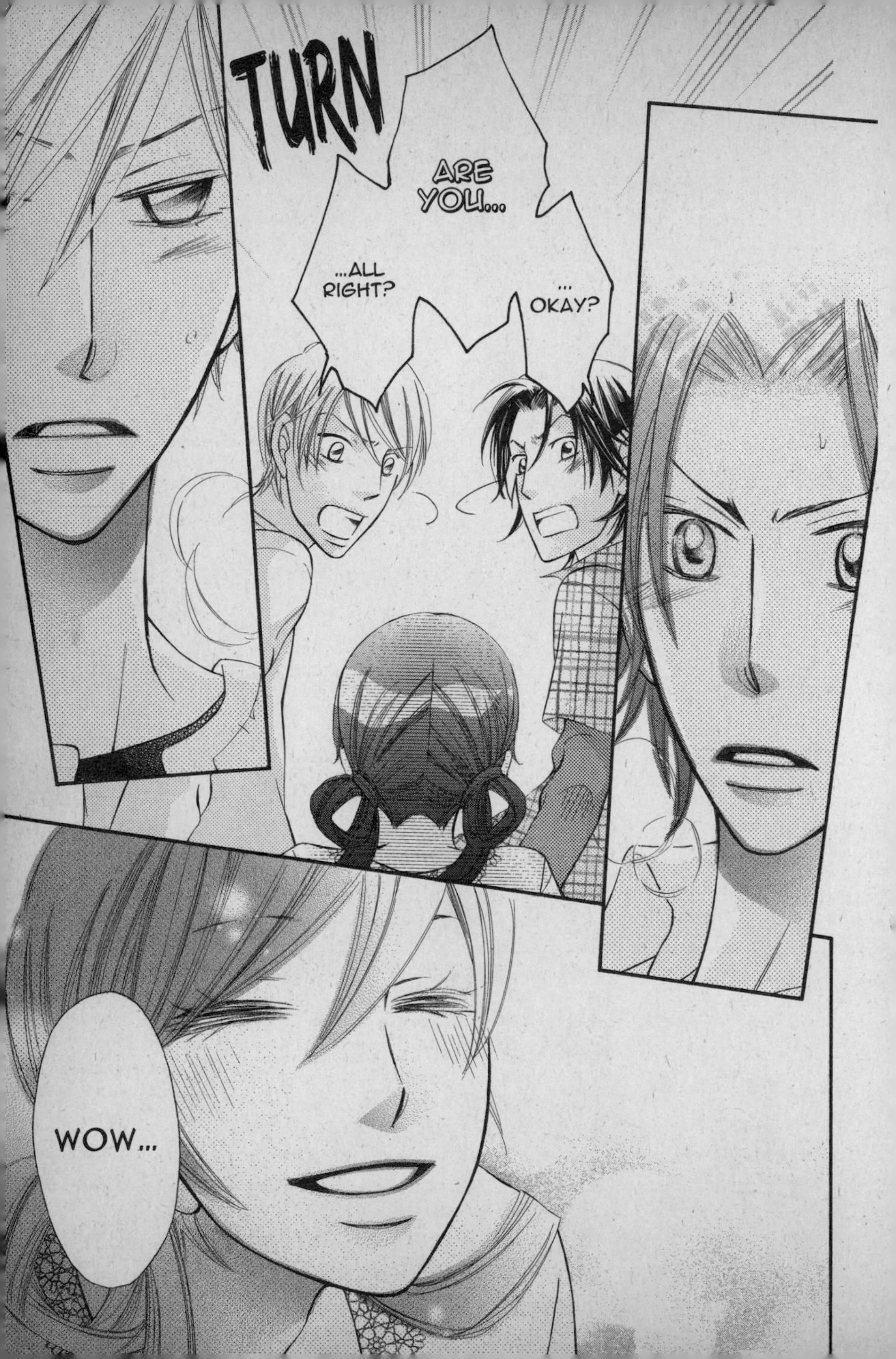
TURN
ARE YOU...
...ALL RIGHT?
... OKAY?
WOW...

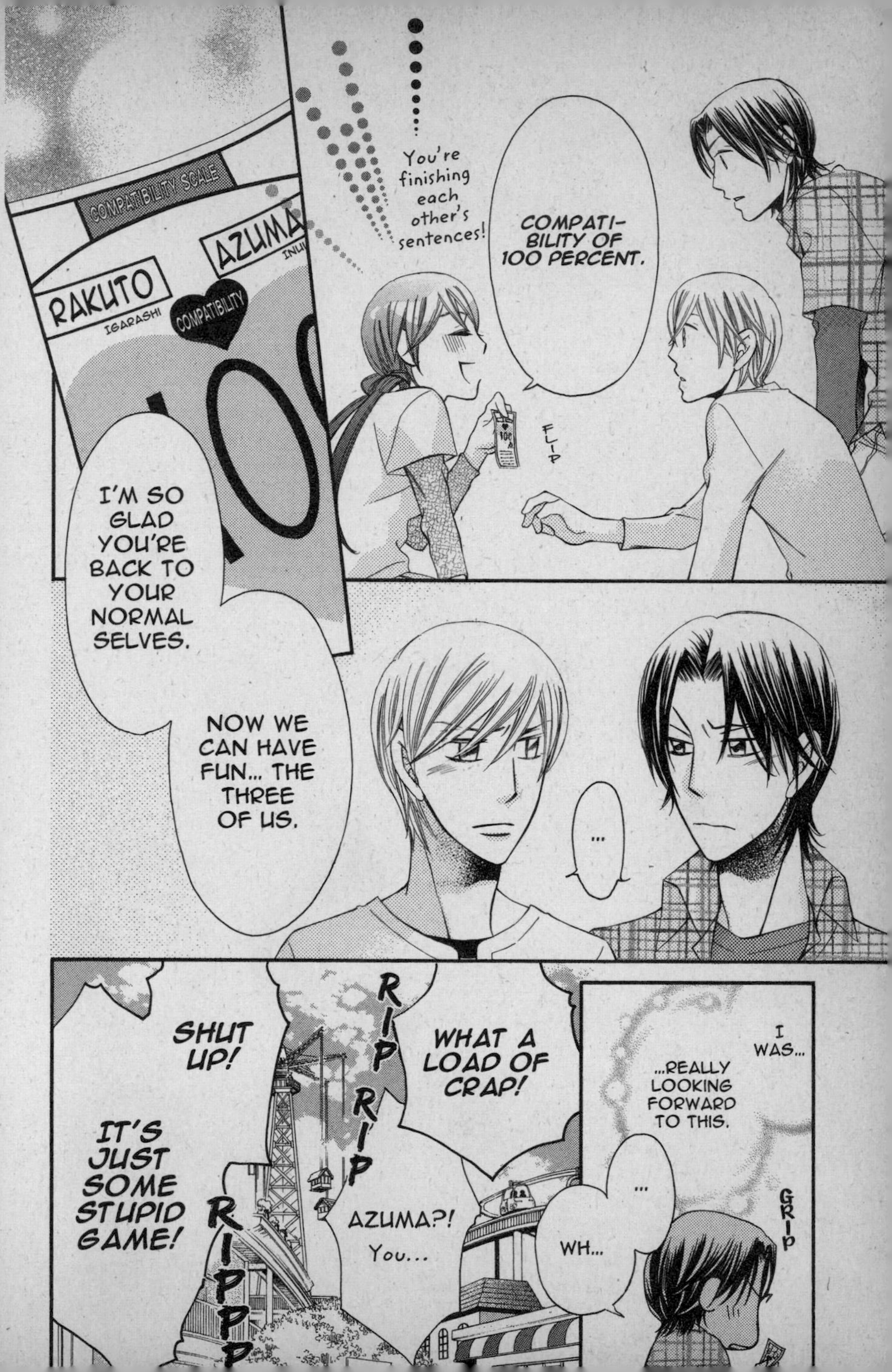
COMPATI-BILITY OF 100 PERCENT.
FLIP
You're finishing each other's sentences!
COMPATIBILITY SCALE
AZUMA
INUI
RAKUTO
IGARASHI
COMPATIBILITY
I'M SO GLAD YOU'RE BACK TO YOUR NORMAL SELVES.
NOW WE CAN HAVE FUN... THE THREE OF US.
...
I WAS...
...REALLY LOOKING FORWARD TO THIS.
GRIP
...
WH...
WHAT A LOAD OF CRAP!
RIP RIP
AZUMA?!
You...
SHUT UP!
IT'S JUST SOME STUPID GAME!
RIPP

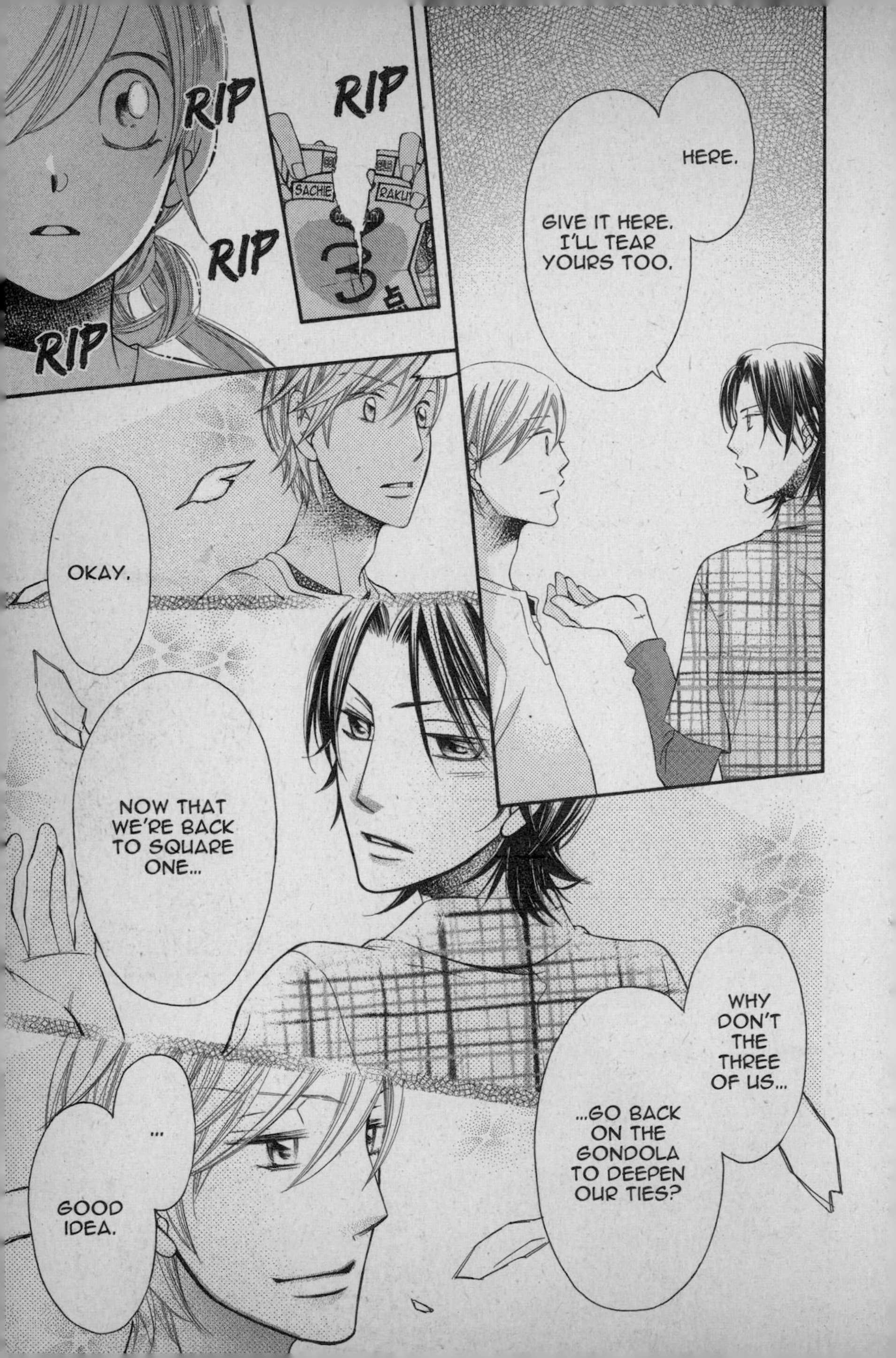
HERE.
GIVE IT HERE. I'LL TEAR YOURS TOO.
RIP
SACHIE
RIP
RIP
RIP
OKAY.
NOW THAT WE'RE BACK TO SQUARE ONE...
WHY DON'T THE THREE OF US...
...GO BACK ON THE GONDOLA TO DEEPEN OUR TIES?
...
GOOD IDEA.

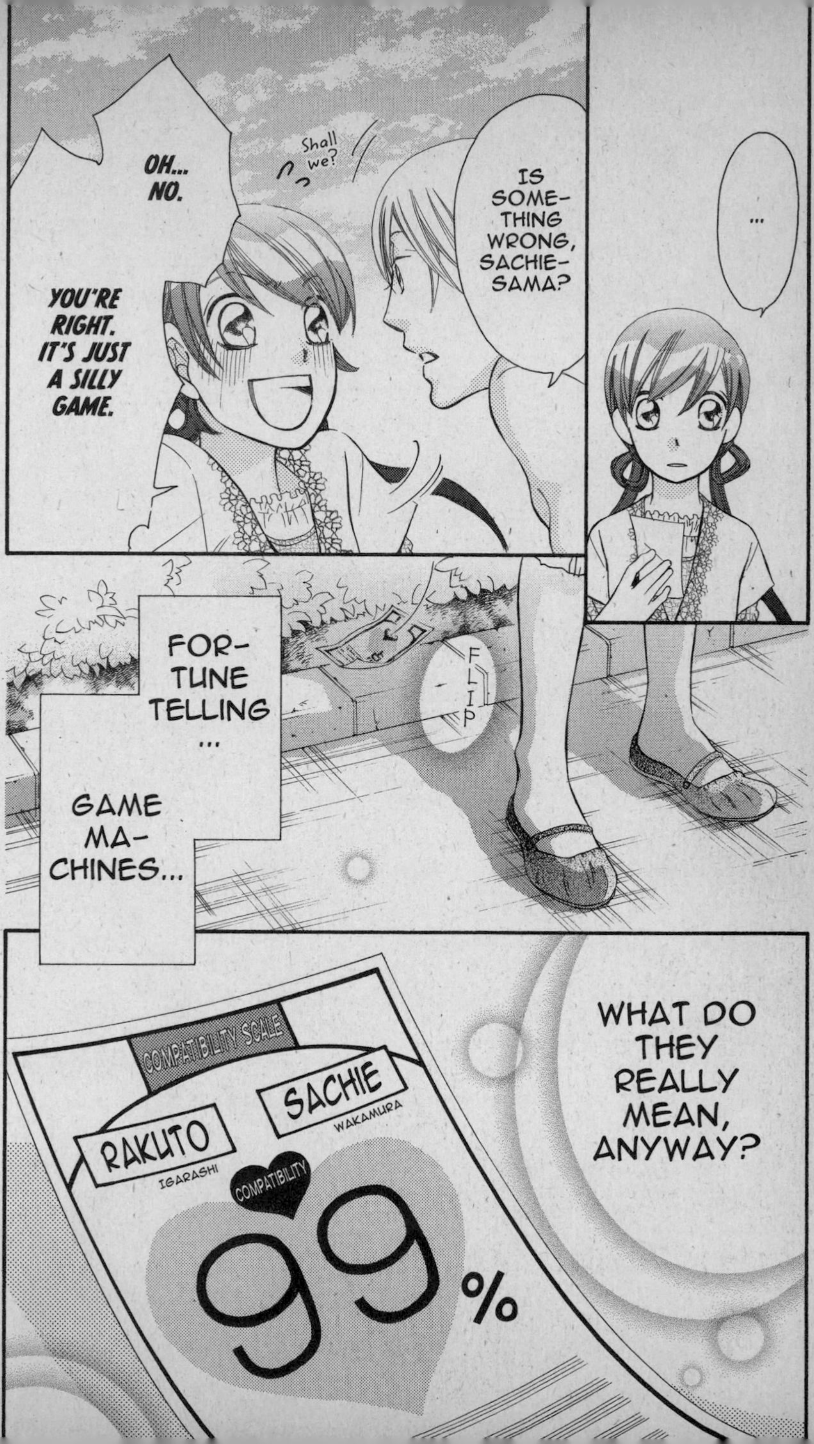
...
IS SOMETHING-WRONG, SACHIE-SAMA?
Shall we?
OH... NO.
YOU'RE RIGHT. IT'S JUST A SILLY GAME.
FLIP
FORTUNE TELLING...
GAME MACHINES...
WHAT DO THEY REALLY MEAN, ANYWAY?
COMPATIBILITY SCALE
SACHIE
WAKAMURA
RAKUTO
IGARASHI
COMPATIBILITY
99%

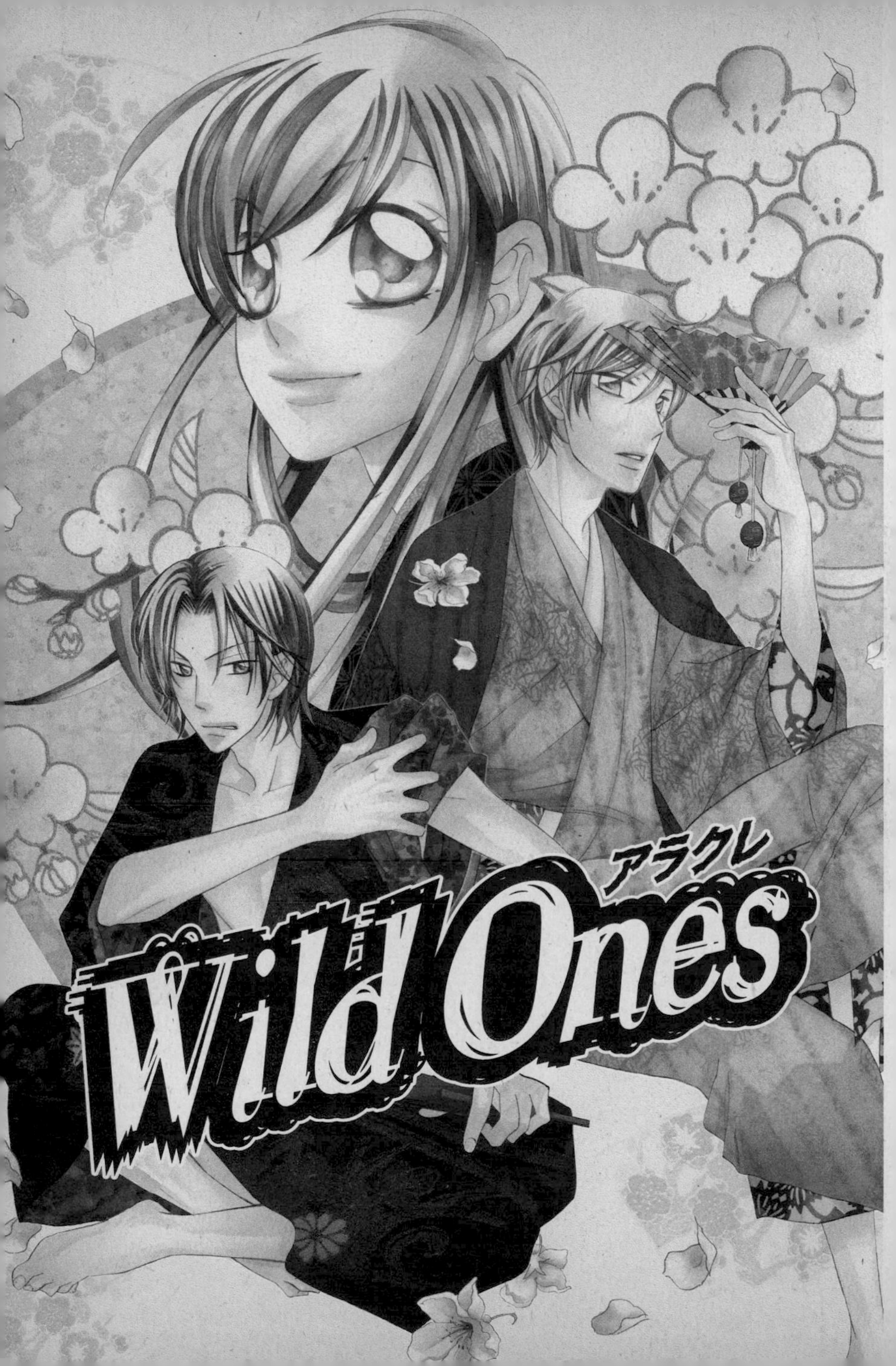

アラクレ
Wild Ones

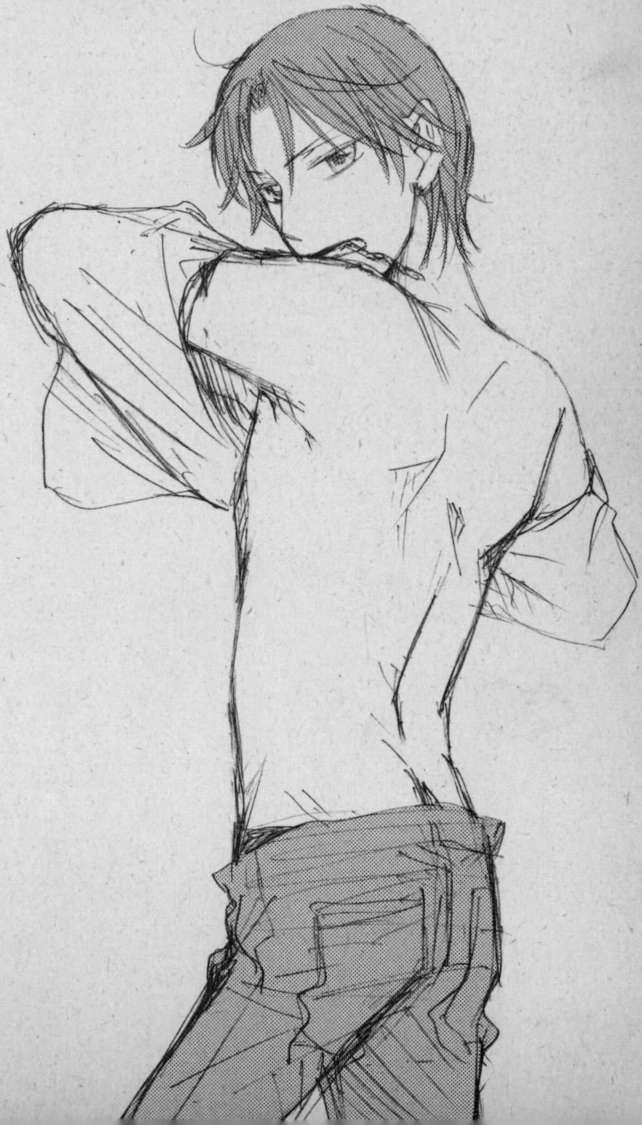

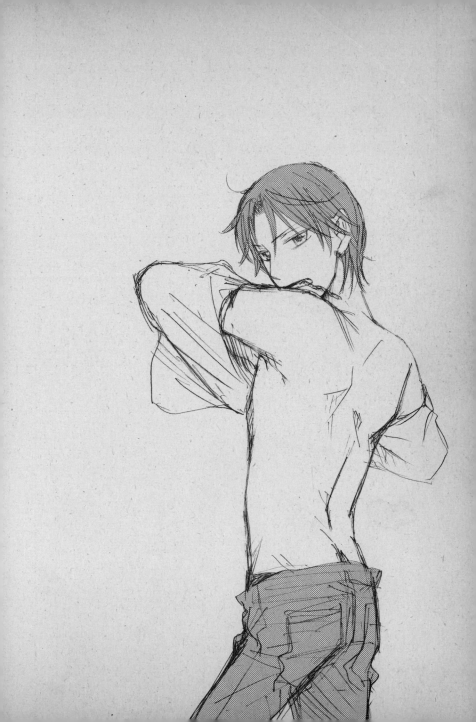

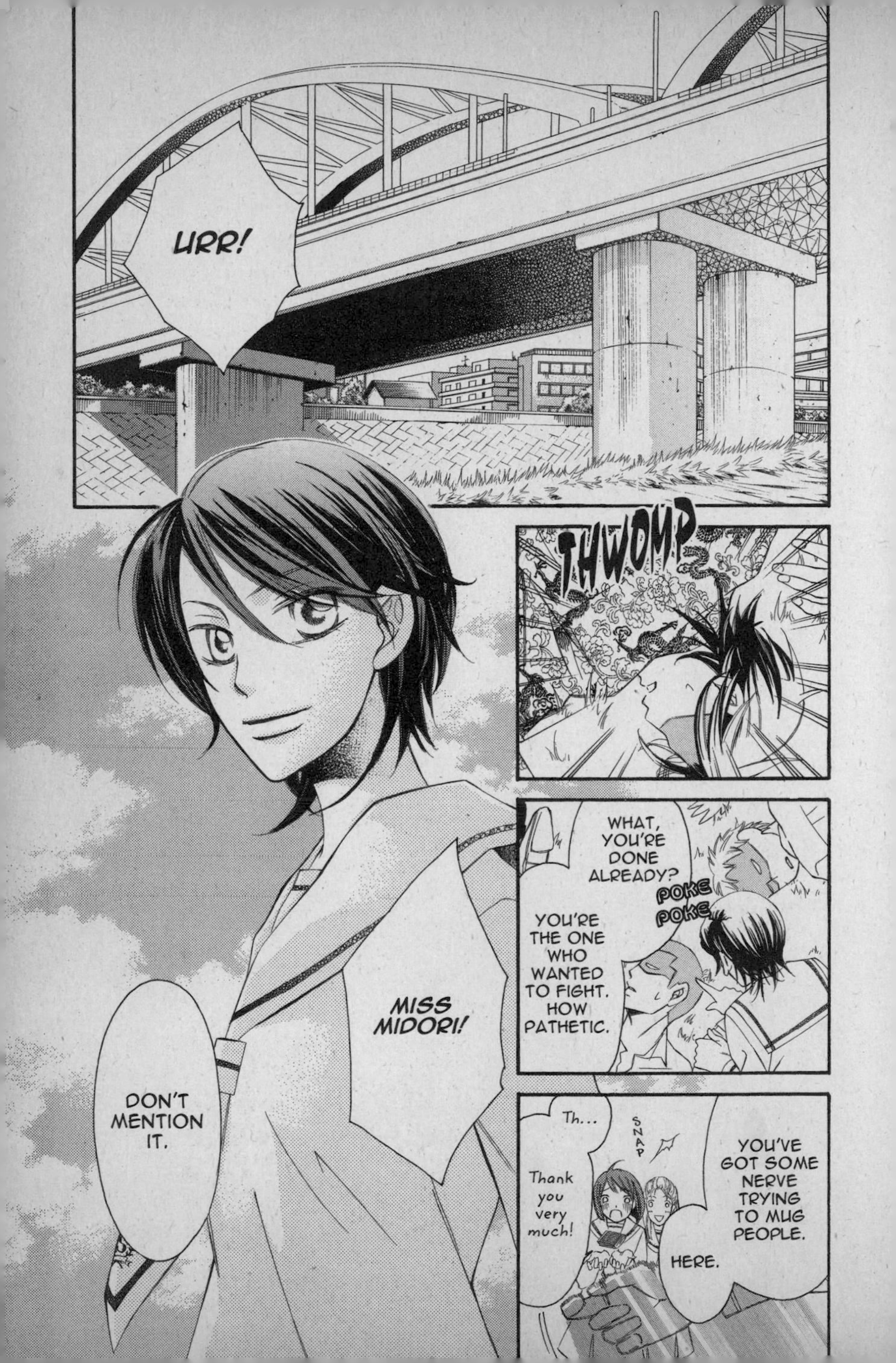
URR!
THWOMP
WHAT, YOU'RE DONE ALREADY?
POKE POKE
YOU'RE THE ONE WHO WANTED TO FIGHT. HOW PATHETIC.
YOU'VE GOT SOME NERVE TRYING TO MUG PEOPLE.
HERE.
SNAP
Th...
Thank you very much!
MISS MIDORI!
DON'T MENTION IT.

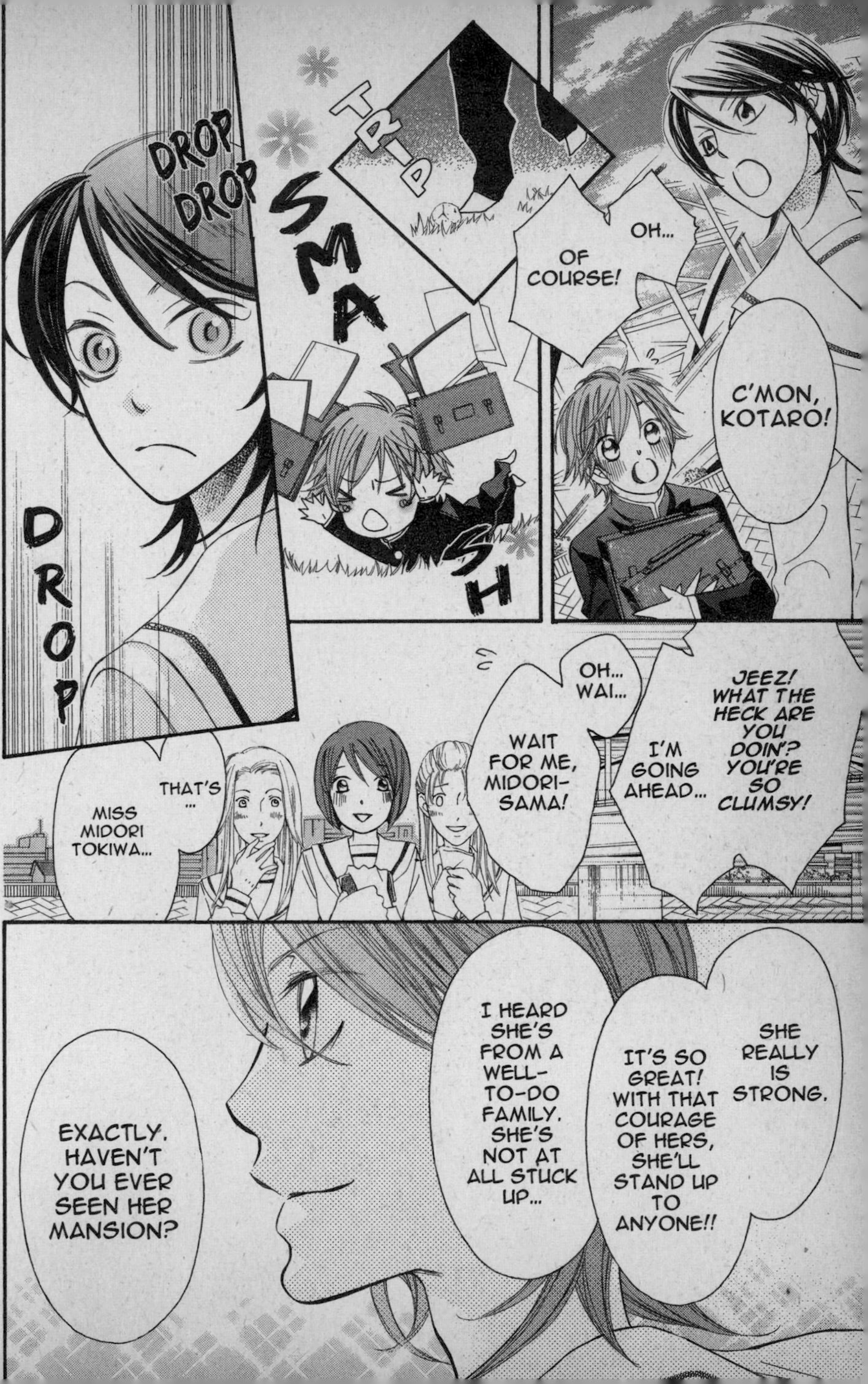

C'MON, KOTARO!
OH... OF COURSE!
TRIP
SMASH
DROP DROP
DROP
JEEZ! WHAT THE HECK ARE YOU DOIN'? YOU'RE SO CLUMSY!
I'M GOING AHEAD...
OH... WAI... WAIT FOR ME, MIDORI-SAMA!
THAT'S ... MISS MIDORI TOKIWA...
SHE REALLY IS STRONG.
IT'S SO GREAT! WITH THAT COURAGE OF HERS, SHE'LL STAND UP TO ANYONE!!
I HEARD SHE'S FROM A WELL-TO-DO FAMILY. SHE'S NOT AT ALL STUCK UP...
EXACTLY. HAVEN'T YOU EVER SEEN HER MANSION?

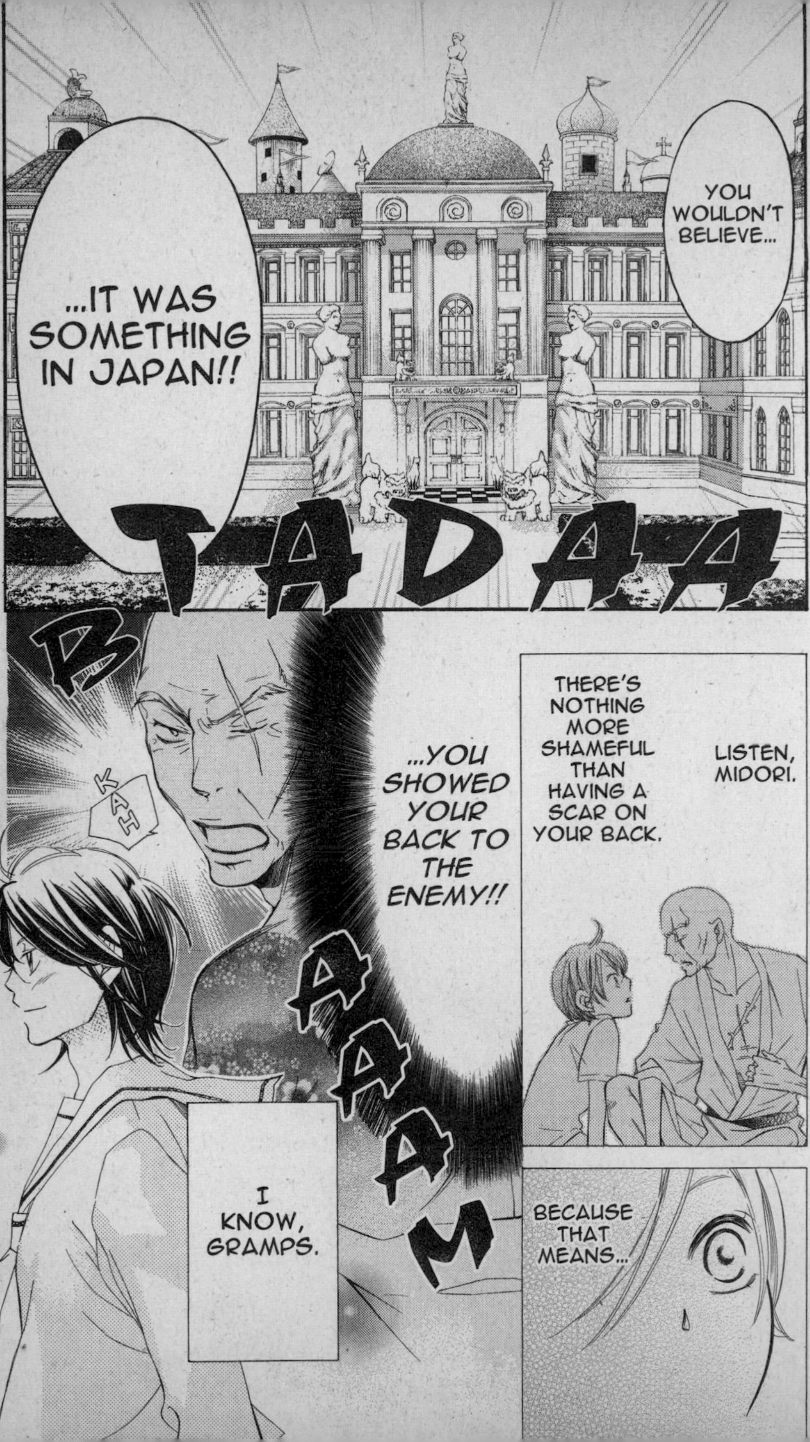
YOU WOULDN'T BELIEVE...
...IT WAS SOMETHING IN JAPAN!!
TADAA
LISTEN, MIDORI.
THERE'S NOTHING MORE SHAMEFUL THAN HAVING A SCAR ON YOUR BACK.
BECAUSE THAT MEANS...
...YOU SHOWED YOUR BACK TO THE ENEMY!!
BAAAAM
KAH
I KNOW, GRAMPS.

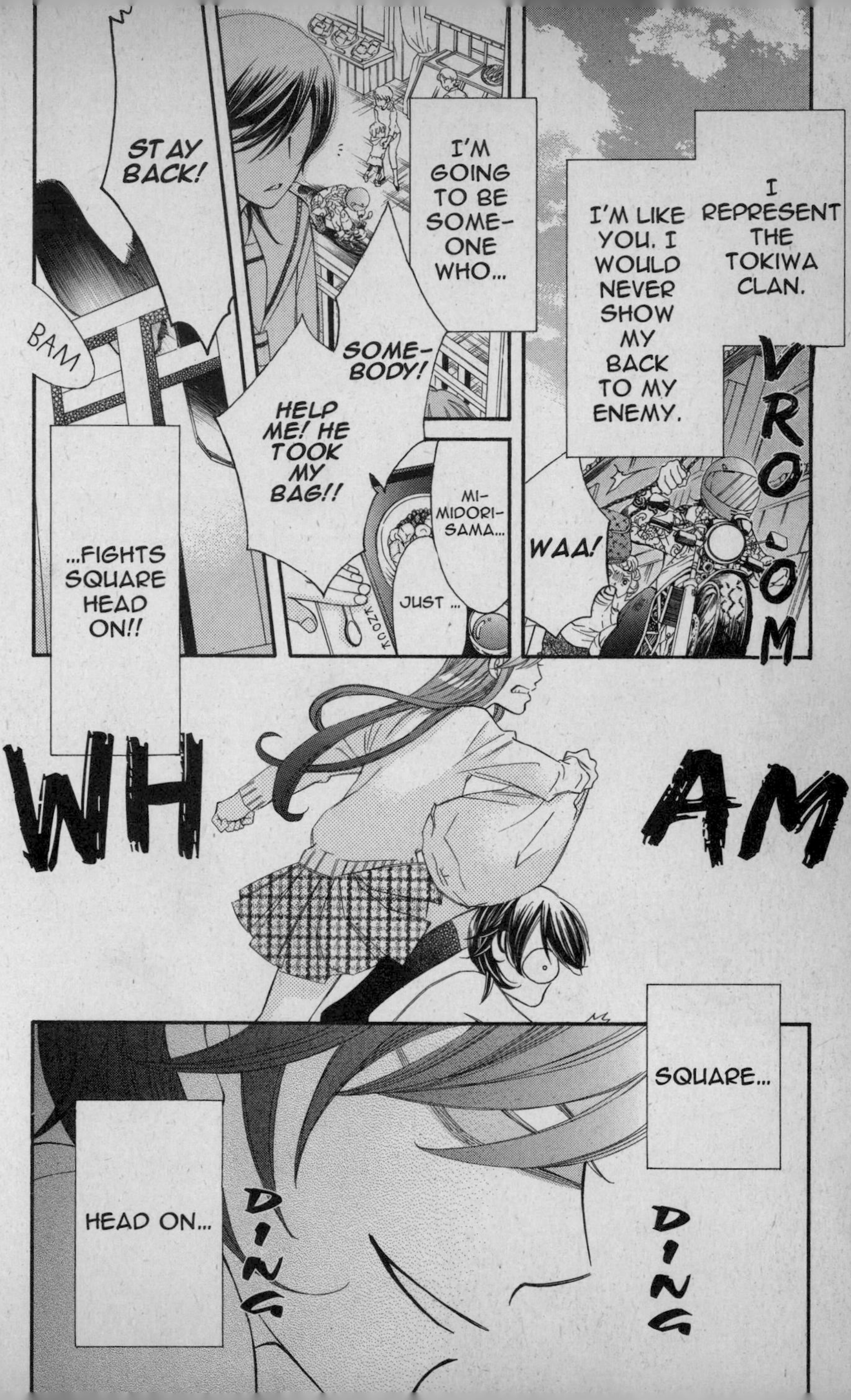
I REPRESENT THE TOKIWA CLAN.
I'M LIKE YOU. I WOULD NEVER SHOW MY BACK TO MY ENEMY.
VROOM
WAA!
I'M GOING TO BE SOME-ONE WHO...
SOME-BODY!
HELP ME! HE TOOK MY BAG!!
MI-MIDORI-SAMA...
JUST ...
STAY BACK!
BAM
...FIGHTS SQUARE HEAD ON!!
WH AM
SQUARE...
HEAD ON...
DING
DING

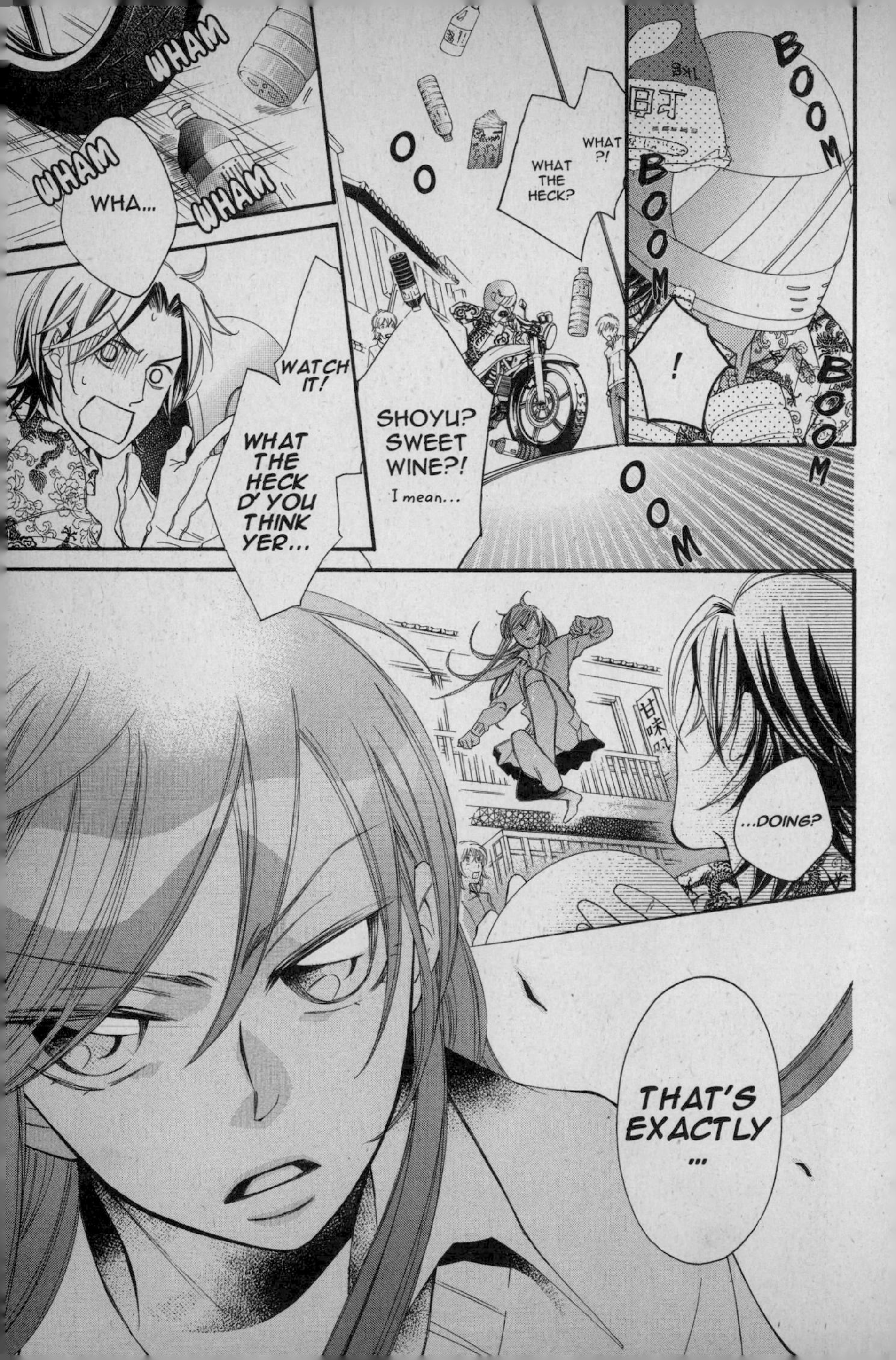

BOOM
BOOM
BOOM
BOOM
!
BOOM
WHAT ?!
WHAT THE HECK?
O O
O O
SHOYU? SWEET WINE?!
I mean...
WHAM
WHAM
WHAM
WHA...
WATCH IT!
WHAT THE HECK D' YOU THINK YER...
...DOING?
THAT'S EXACTLY ...

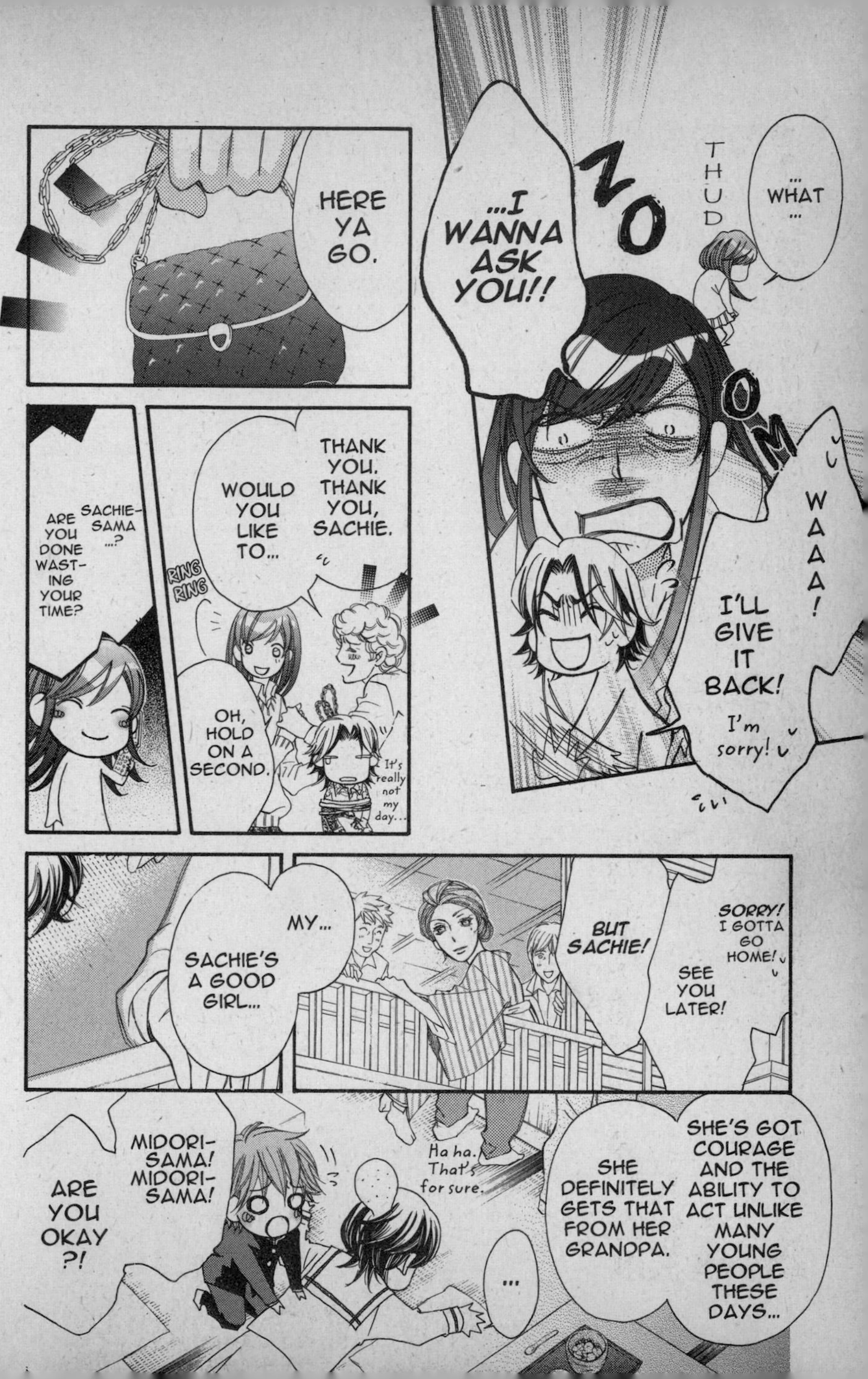
...WHAT...
THUD
ZOOM
...I WANNA ASK YOU!!
WAAAA!
I'LL GIVE IT BACK!
I'm sorry!
HERE YA GO.
THANK YOU. THANK YOU, SACHIE.
WOULD YOU LIKE TO...
RING RING
OH, HOLD ON A SECOND.
It's really not my day...
SACHIE-SAMA ...?
ARE YOU DONE WASTING YOUR TIME?
SORRY! I GOTTA GO HOME!
SEE YOU LATER!
BUT SACHIE!
MY...
SACHIE'S A GOOD GIRL...
SHE'S GOT COURAGE AND THE ABILITY TO ACT UNLIKE MANY YOUNG PEOPLE THESE DAYS...
SHE DEFINITELY GETS THAT FROM HER GRANDPA.
...
Ha ha. That's for sure.
MIDORI-SAMA! MIDORI-SAMA!
ARE YOU OKAY?!

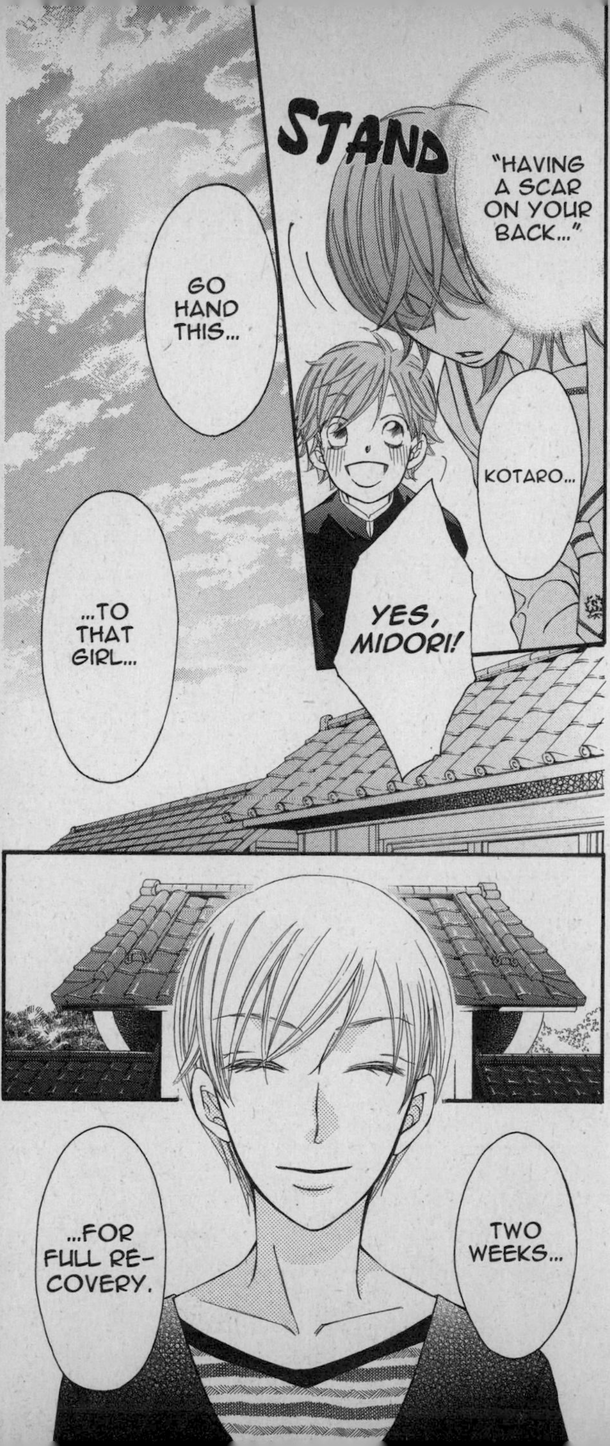
STAND
"HAVING A SCAR ON YOUR BACK..."
KOTARO...
YES, MIDORI!
GO HAND THIS...
...TO THAT GIRL...
TWO WEEKS...
...FOR FULL RE-COVERY.

...IT SAID, "PLEASE WAIT...!" I SEE... IT'S JUST SO SAD... I GUESS YOU COULD SEE IT THAT WAY... I'M SO IMPRESSED WITH MY EDITOR WHO CAN DECIPHER MY CODE! LAYOUTS DON'T EVEN HAVE DRAWINGS... THANK YOU SO MUCH. MY EDITOR ACTUALLY MADE THE VOLUME ENDING FOR ME!! HEE HEE! I'M SO HAPPY! THIS WAS THE FIRST TIME THAT MY EDITOR WAS INVOLVED LIKE THIS, SO I WAS PARTICULARLY THRILLED. I HOPE YOU ENJOY IT! THANK YOU, KURACHI-SAN!

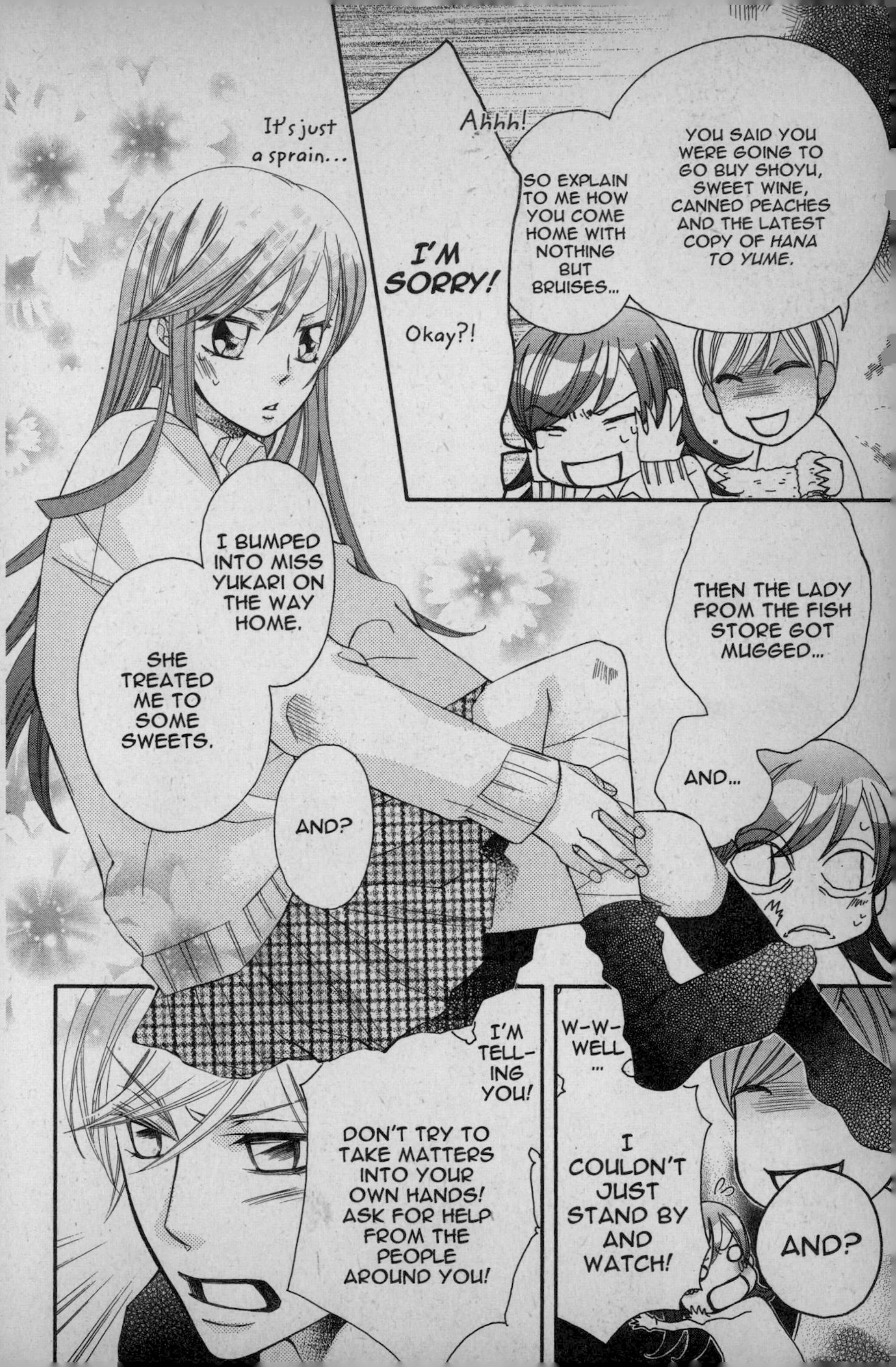
YOU SAID YOU WERE GOING TO GO BUY SHOYU, SWEET WINE, CANNED PEACHES AND THE LATEST COPY OF *HANA TO YUME*.
SO EXPLAIN TO ME HOW YOU COME HOME WITH NOTHING BUT BRUISES...
Ahhh!
I'M SORRY!
Okay?!
It's just a sprain...
I BUMPED INTO MISS YUKARI ON THE WAY HOME.
SHE TREATED ME TO SOME SWEETS.
AND?
THEN THE LADY FROM THE FISH STORE GOT MUGGED...
AND...
W-W-WELL...
I COULDN'T JUST STAND BY AND WATCH!
AND?
I'M TELL-ING YOU!
DON'T TRY TO TAKE MATTERS INTO YOUR OWN HANDS! ASK FOR HELP FROM THE PEOPLE AROUND YOU!

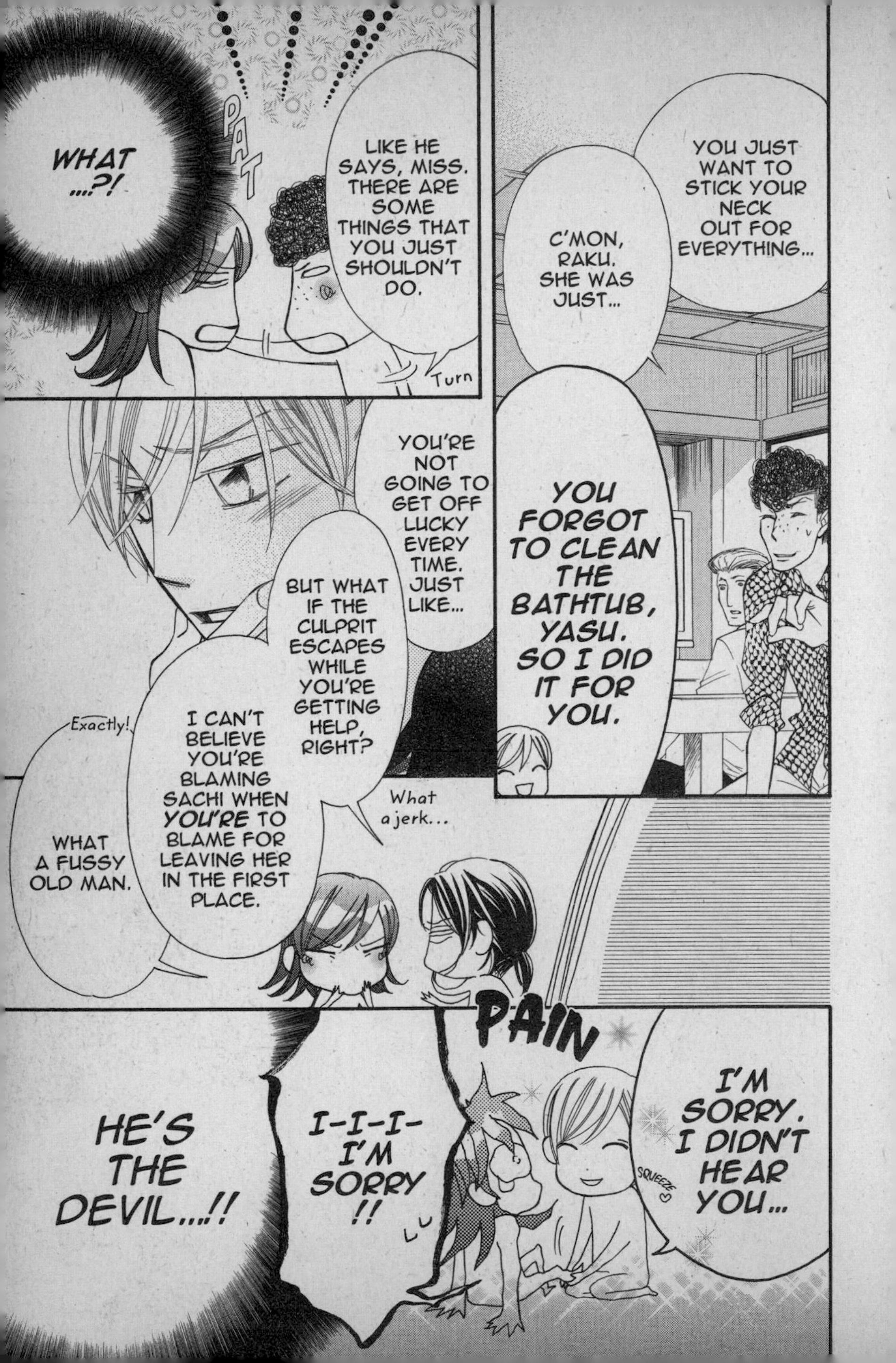

YOU JUST WANT TO STICK YOUR NECK OUT FOR EVERYTHING...
C'MON, RAKU. SHE WAS JUST...
YOU FORGOT TO CLEAN THE BATHTUB, YASU. SO I DID IT FOR YOU.
LIKE HE SAYS, MISS. THERE ARE SOME THINGS THAT YOU JUST SHOULDN'T DO.
PAT
Turn
WHAT ...?!
YOU'RE NOT GOING TO GET OFF LUCKY EVERY TIME. JUST LIKE...
BUT WHAT IF THE CULPRIT ESCAPES WHILE YOU'RE GETTING HELP, RIGHT?
What a jerk...
I CAN'T BELIEVE YOU'RE BLAMING SACHI WHEN YOU'RE TO BLAME FOR LEAVING HER IN THE FIRST PLACE.
Exactly!
WHAT A FUSSY OLD MAN.
PAIN
I'M SORRY. I DIDN'T HEAR YOU...
SQUEEZE
I-I-I-I'M SORRY!!
HE'S THE DEVIL...!!

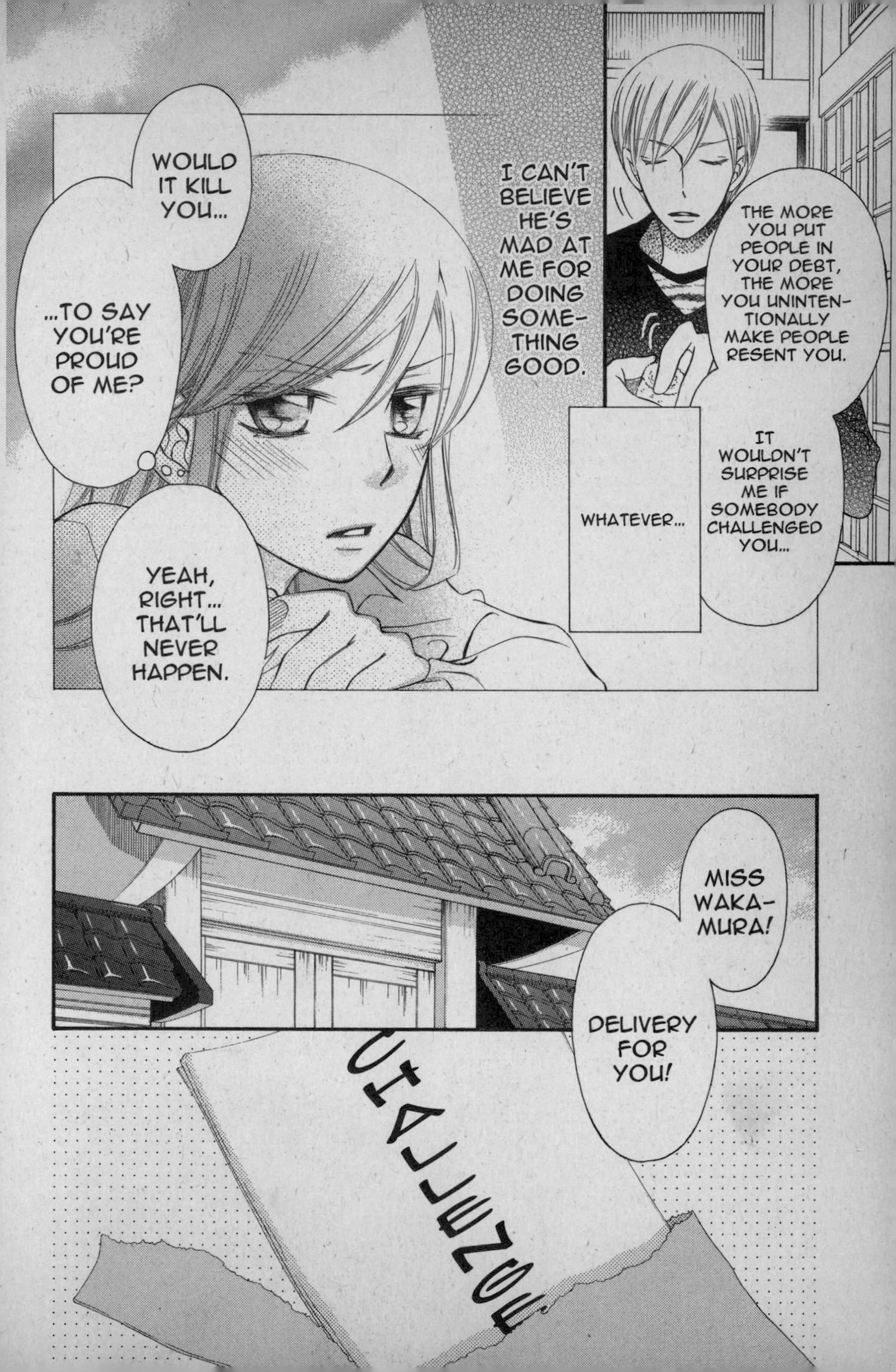
THE MORE YOU PUT PEOPLE IN YOUR DEBT, THE MORE YOU UNINTEN-TIONALLY MAKE PEOPLE RESENT YOU.
IT WOULDN'T SURPRISE ME IF SOMEBODY CHALLENGED YOU...
WHATEVER...
I CAN'T BELIEVE HE'S MAD AT ME FOR DOING SOME-THING GOOD.
WOULD IT KILL YOU...
...TO SAY YOU'RE PROUD OF ME?
YEAH, RIGHT... THAT'LL NEVER HAPPEN.
MISS WAKA-MURA!
DELIVERY FOR YOU!

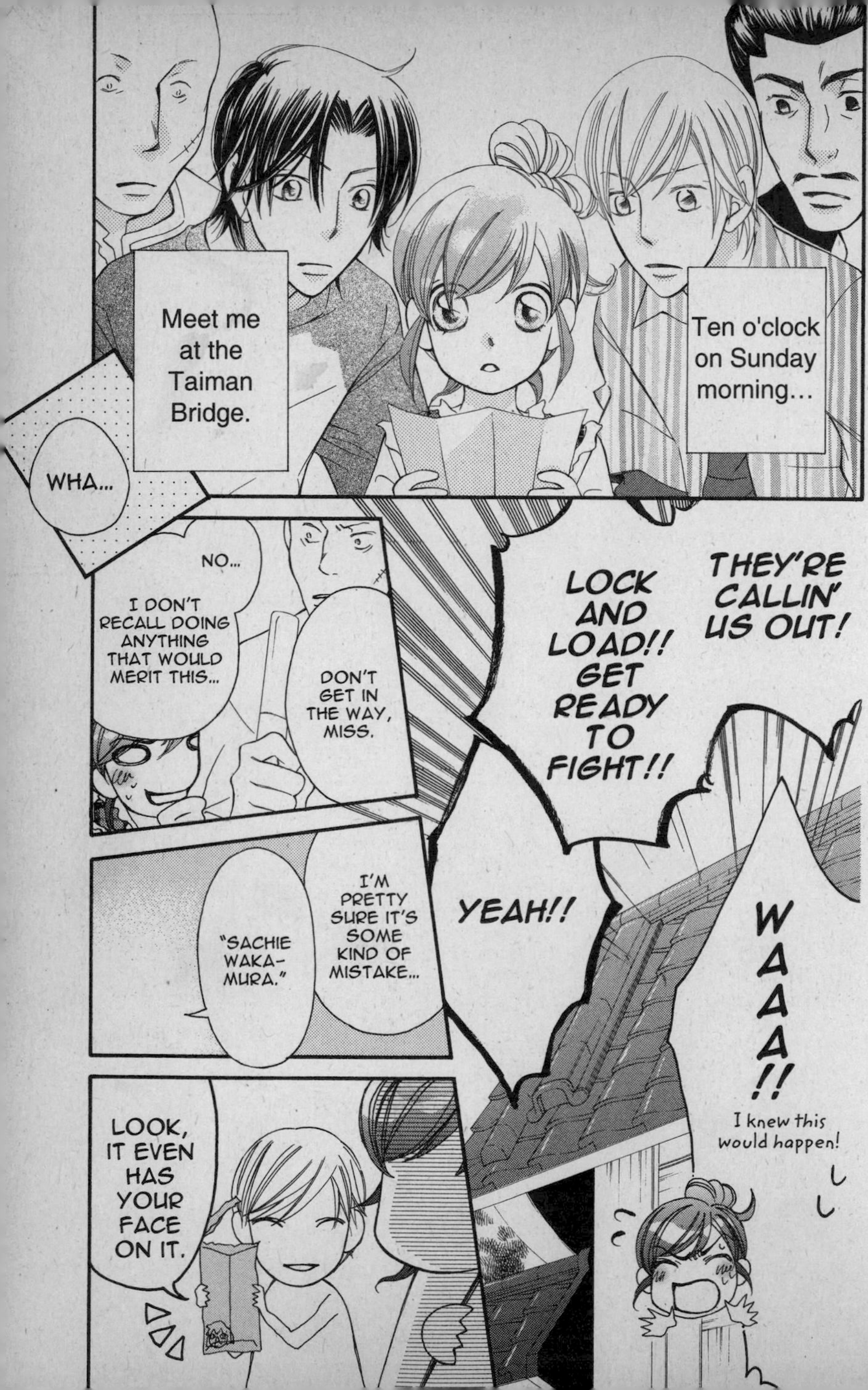
Ten o'clock on Sunday morning…
Meet me at the Taiman Bridge.
WHA...
THEY'RE CALLIN' US OUT!
LOCK AND LOAD!! GET READY TO FIGHT!!
YEAH!!
WAAAA!!
I knew this would happen!
DON'T GET IN THE WAY, MISS.
NO... I DON'T RECALL DOING ANYTHING THAT WOULD MERIT THIS...
I'M PRETTY SURE IT'S SOME KIND OF MISTAKE...
"SACHIE WAKAMURA."
LOOK, IT EVEN HAS YOUR FACE ON IT.

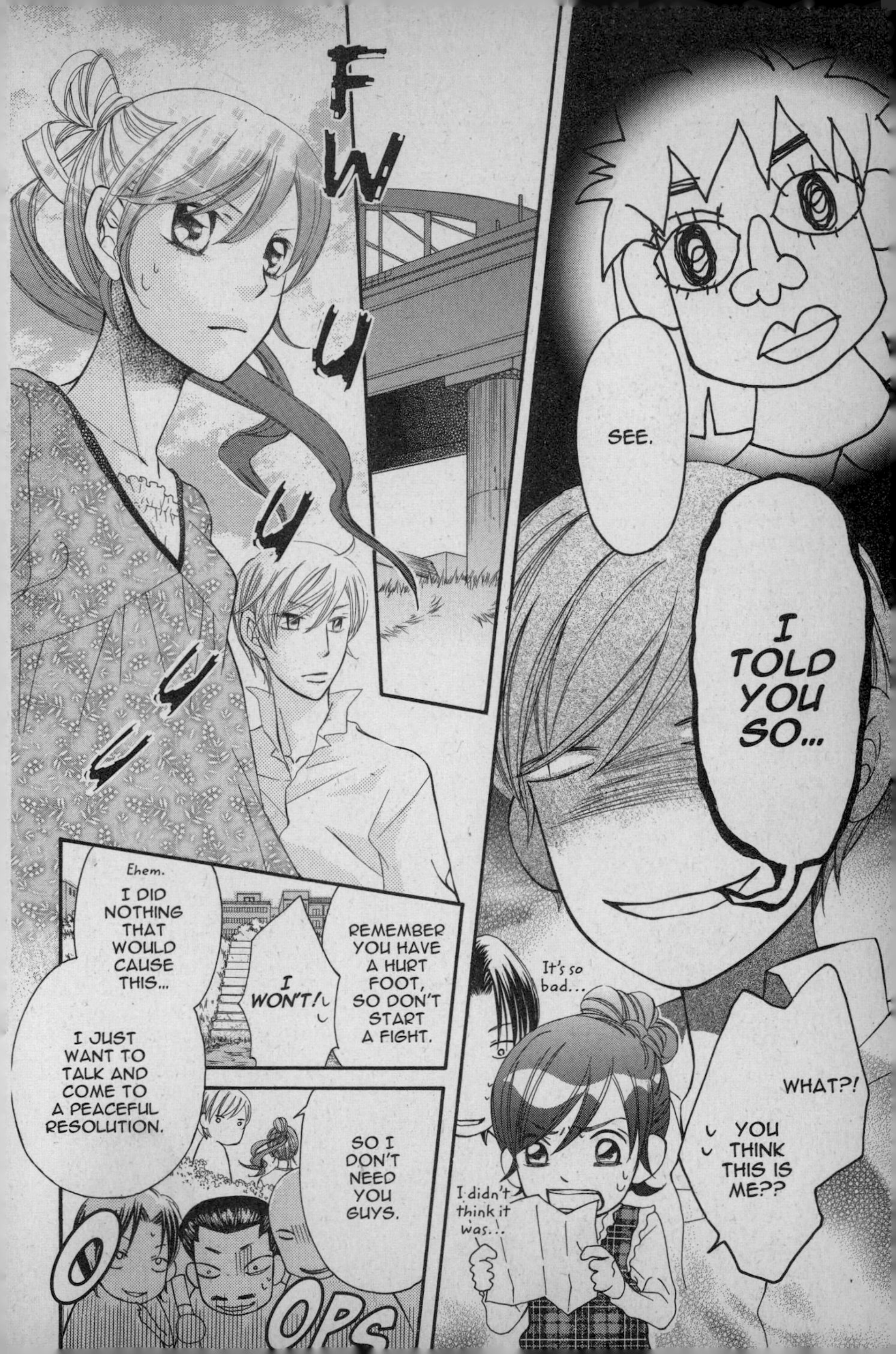
SEE.
I TOLD YOU SO...
WHAT?!
YOU THINK THIS IS ME??
It's so bad...
I didn't think it was...!
FWUUUU
REMEMBER YOU HAVE A HURT FOOT, SO DON'T START A FIGHT.
I WON'T!
Ehem.
I DID NOTHING THAT WOULD CAUSE THIS...
I JUST WANT TO TALK AND COME TO A PEACEFUL RESOLUTION.
SO I DON'T NEED YOU GUYS.
OOPS

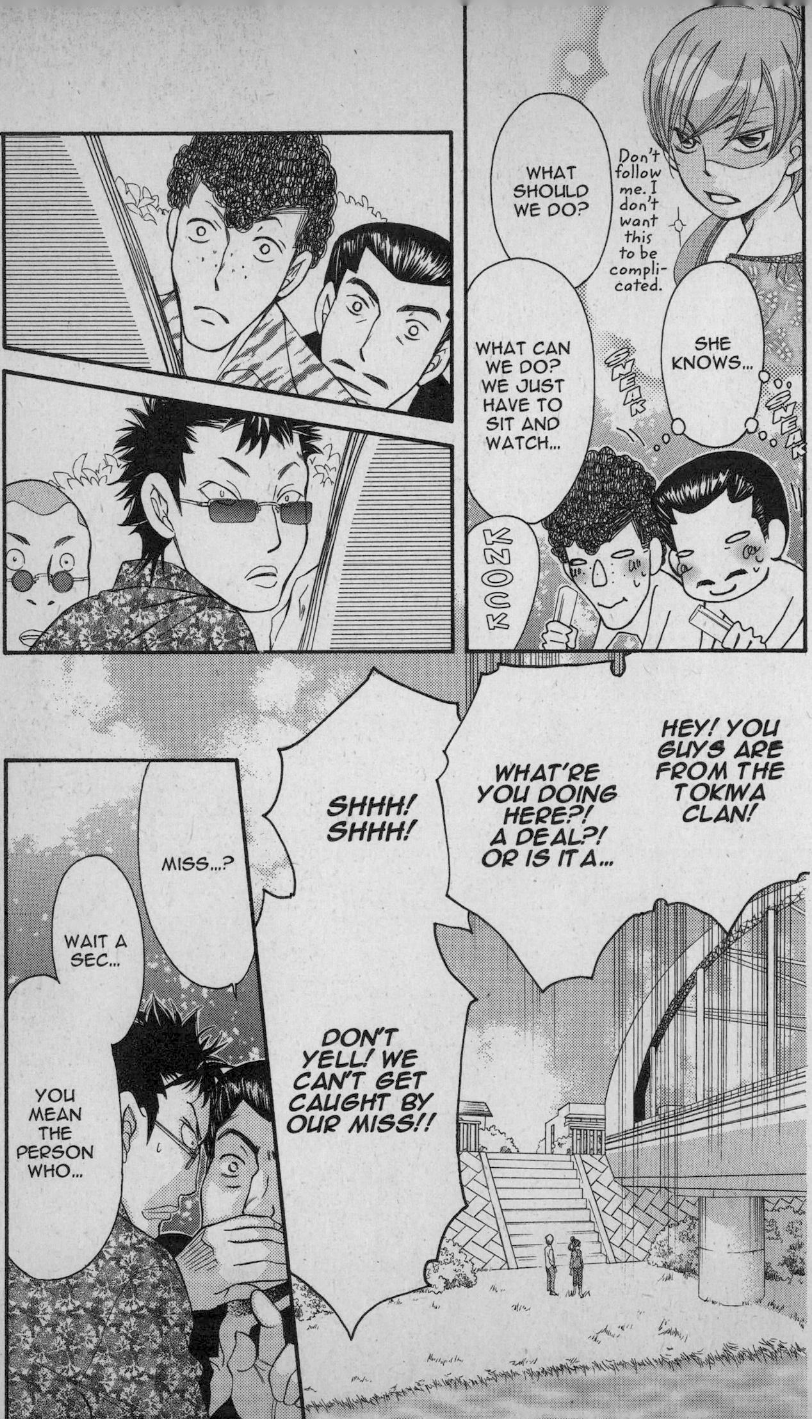
Don't follow me. I don't want this to be complicated.
WHAT SHOULD WE DO?
SHE KNOWS...
SNEAK
SNEAK
WHAT CAN WE DO? WE JUST HAVE TO SIT AND WATCH...
KNOCK
HEY! YOU GUYS ARE FROM THE TOKIWA CLAN!
WHAT'RE YOU DOING HERE?! A DEAL?! OR IS IT A...
SHHH! SHHH!
MISS...?
WAIT A SEC...
DON'T YELL! WE CAN'T GET CAUGHT BY OUR MISS!!
YOU MEAN THE PERSON WHO...

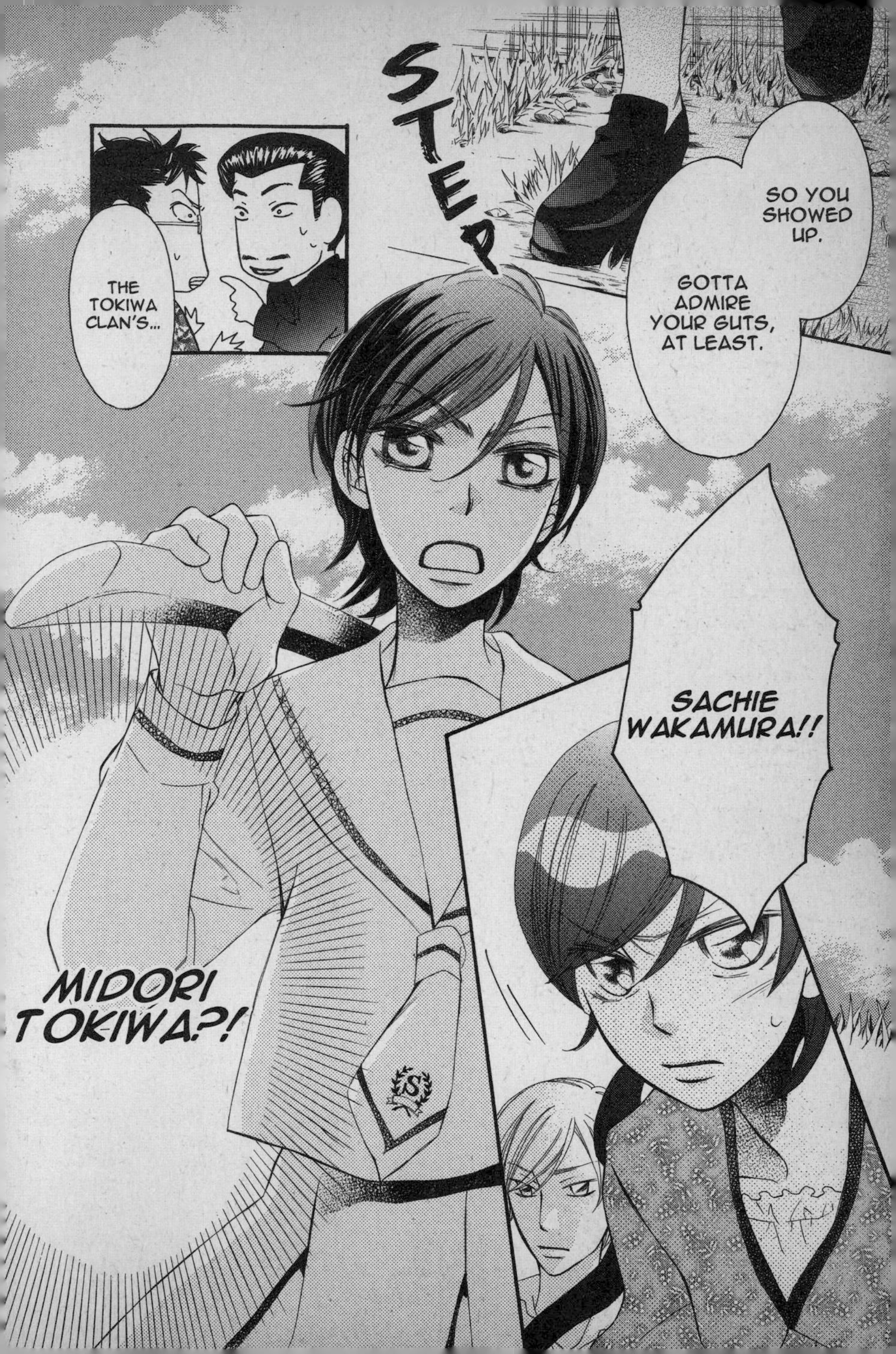
STEP
SO YOU SHOWED UP.
GOTTA ADMIRE YOUR GUTS, AT LEAST.
THE TOKIWA CLAN'S...
SACHIE WAKAMURA!!
MIDORI TOKIWA?!

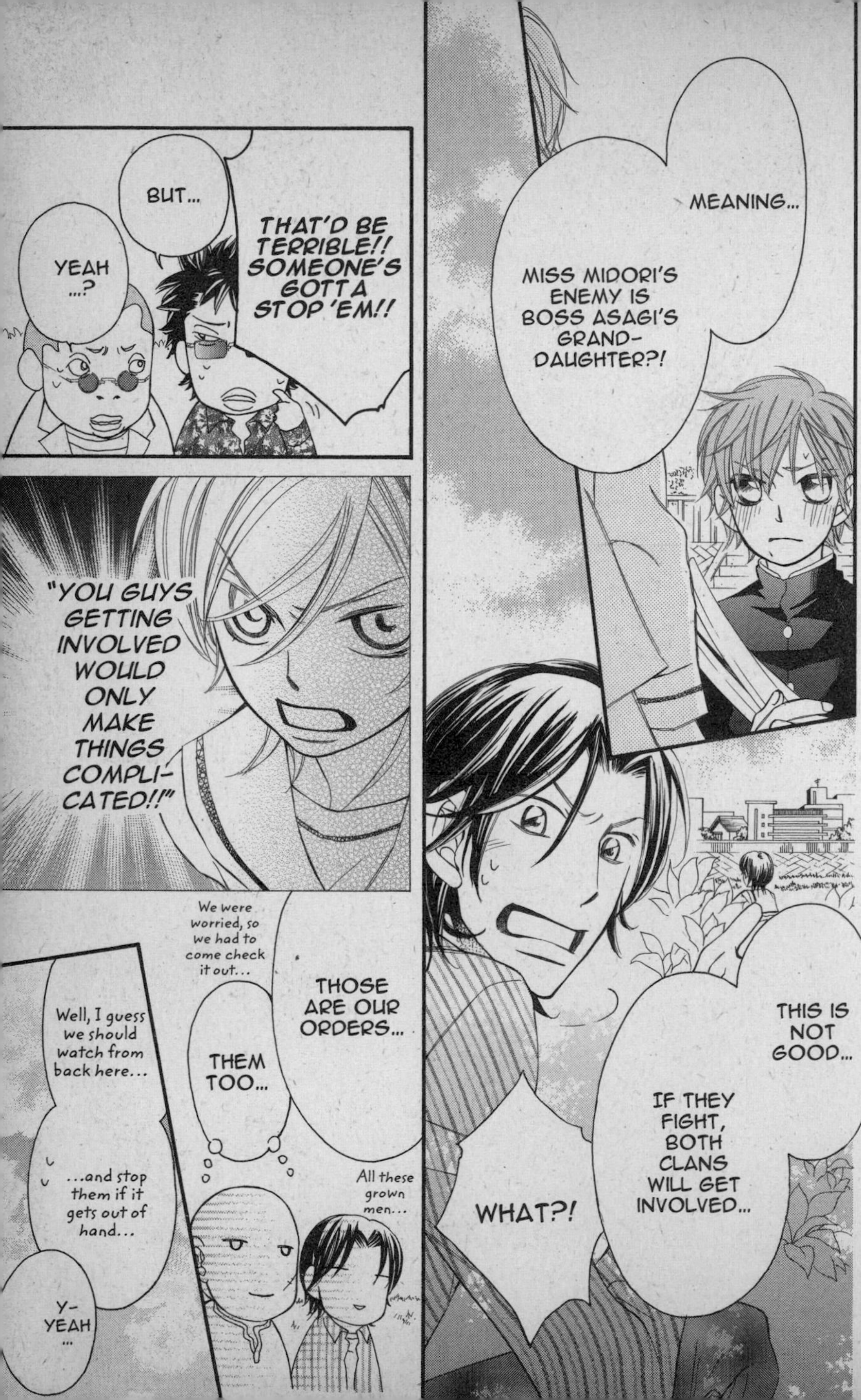

MEANING...
MISS MIDORI'S ENEMY IS BOSS ASAGI'S GRAND-DAUGHTER?!
THIS IS NOT GOOD...
IF THEY FIGHT, BOTH CLANS WILL GET INVOLVED...
WHAT?!
THAT'D BE TERRIBLE!! SOMEONE'S GOTTA STOP 'EM!!
BUT...
YEAH ...?
"YOU GUYS GETTING INVOLVED WOULD ONLY MAKE THINGS COMPLI-CATED!!"
THOSE ARE OUR ORDERS...
We were worried, so we had to come check it out...
THEM TOO...
All these grown men...
Well, I guess we should watch from back here...
...and stop them if it gets out of hand...
Y-YEAH ...

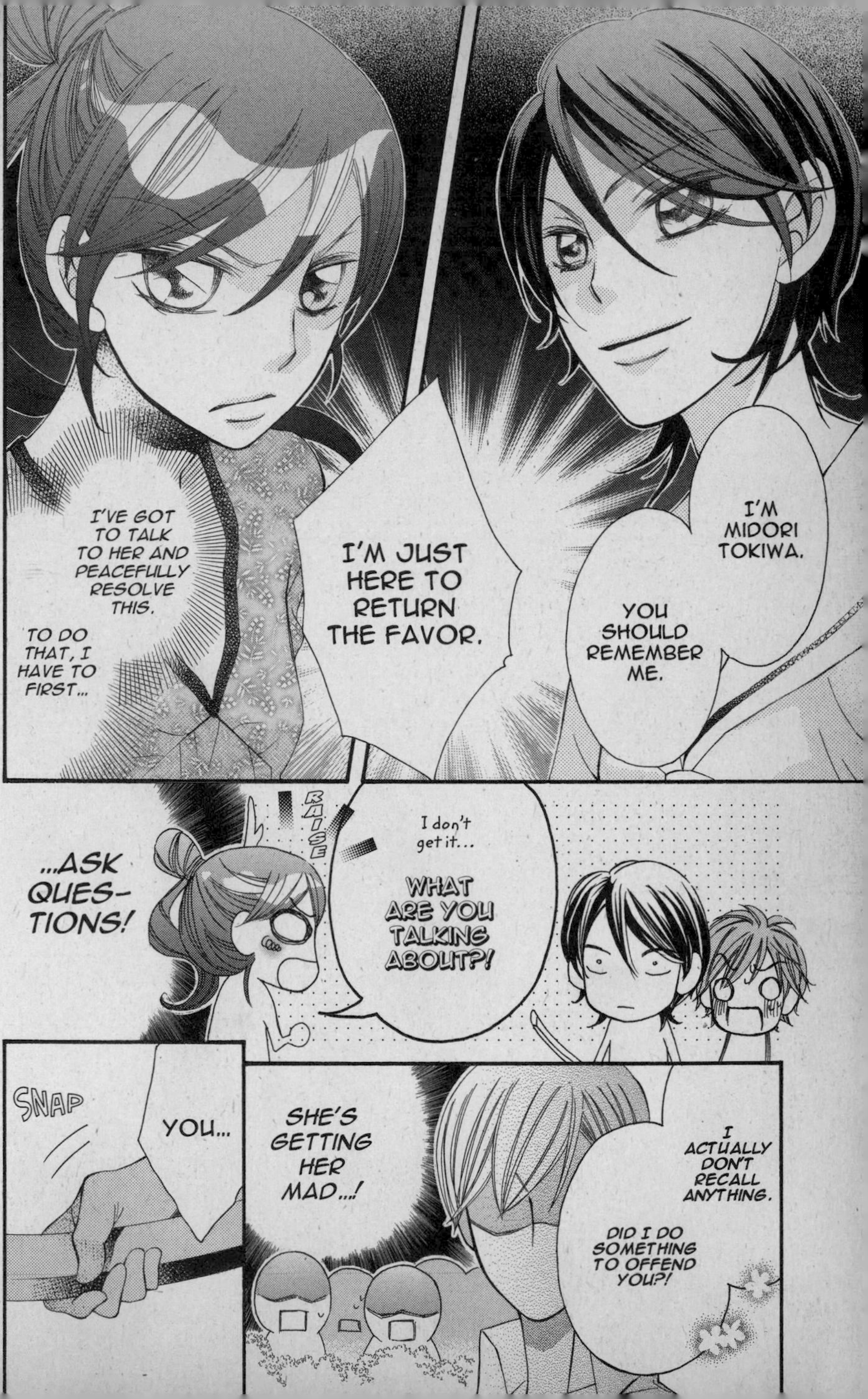
I'M MIDORI TOKIWA.
YOU SHOULD REMEMBER ME.
I'M JUST HERE TO RETURN THE FAVOR.
I'VE GOT TO TALK TO HER AND PEACEFULLY RESOLVE THIS.
TO DO THAT, I HAVE TO FIRST...
I don't get it...
WHAT ARE YOU TALKING ABOUT?!
RAISE
...ASK QUES-TIONS!
I ACTUALLY DON'T RECALL ANYTHING.
DID I DO SOMETHING TO OFFEND YOU?!
SHE'S GETTING HER MAD...!
YOU...
SNAP

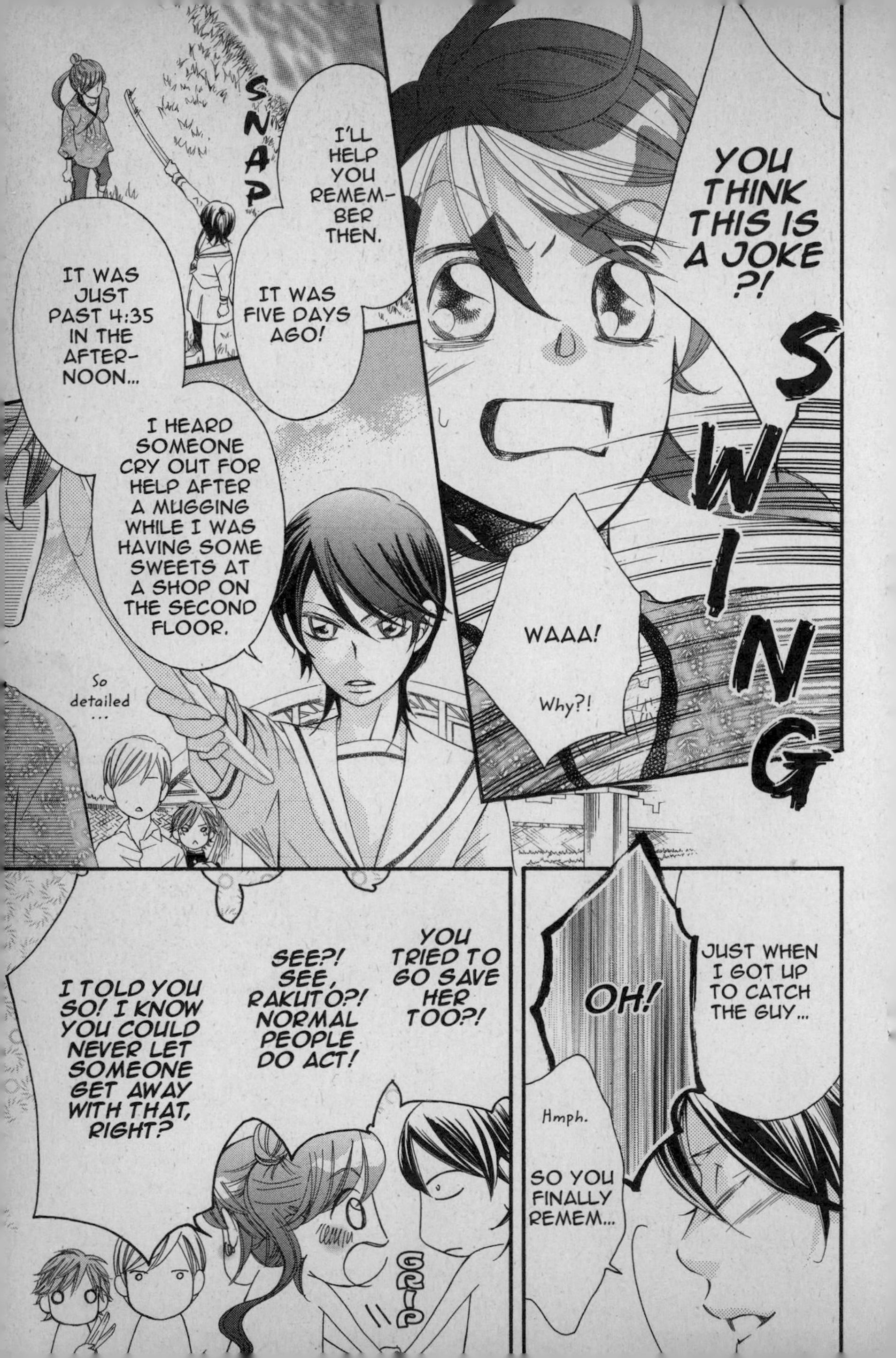
YOU THINK THIS IS A JOKE ?!
SWING
WAAA!
Why?!
I'LL HELP YOU REMEM-BER THEN.
SNAP
IT WAS FIVE DAYS AGO!
IT WAS JUST PAST 4:35 IN THE AFTER-NOON...
I HEARD SOMEONE CRY OUT FOR HELP AFTER A MUGGING WHILE I WAS HAVING SOME SWEETS AT A SHOP ON THE SECOND FLOOR.
So detailed ...
JUST WHEN I GOT UP TO CATCH THE GUY...
OH!
SO YOU FINALLY REMEM...
Hmph.
YOU TRIED TO GO SAVE HER TOO?!
SEE?! SEE, RAKUTO?! NORMAL PEOPLE DO ACT!
I TOLD YOU SO! I KNOW YOU COULD NEVER LET SOMEONE GET AWAY WITH THAT, RIGHT?
GRIP

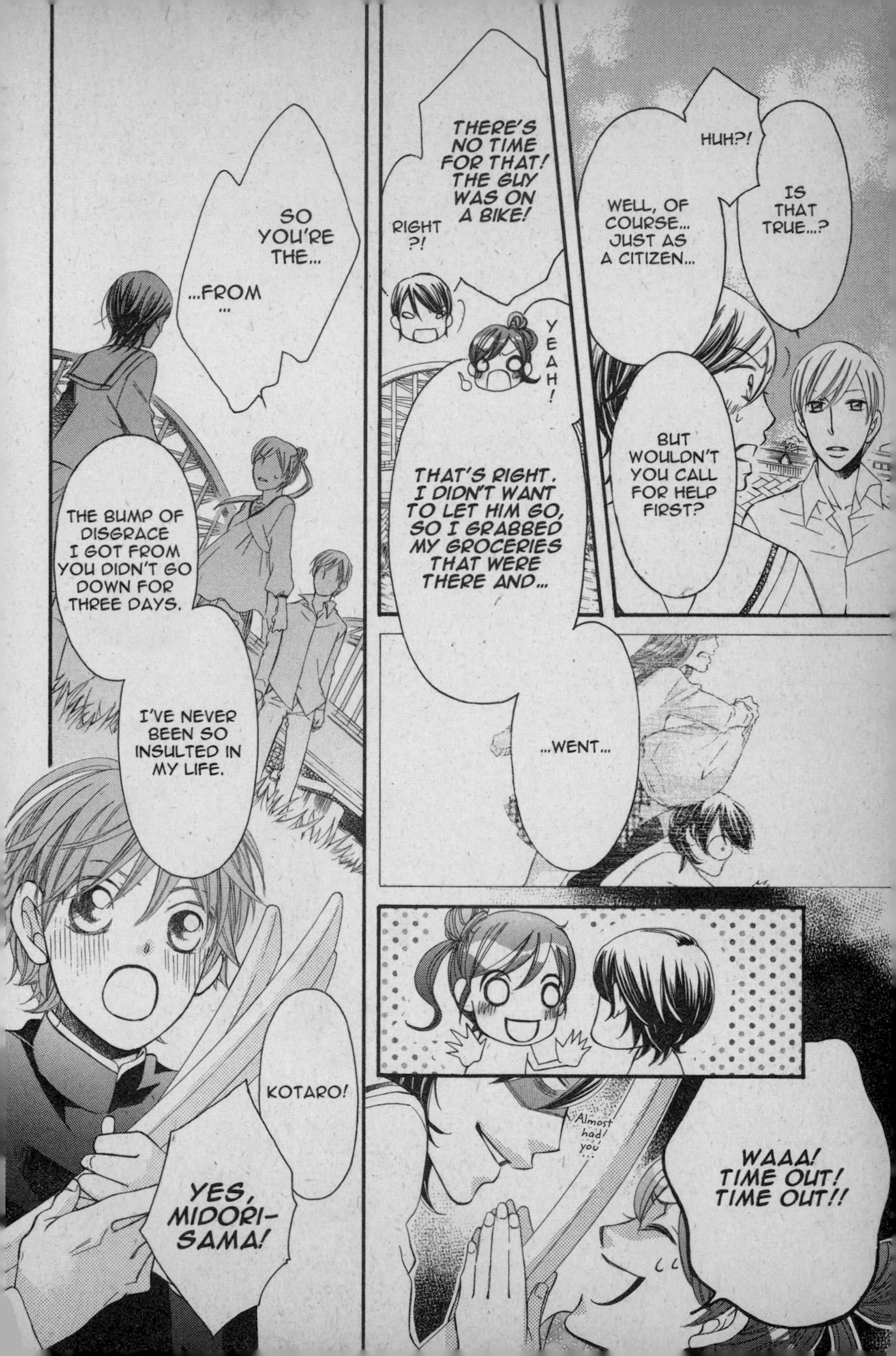
HUH?!
IS THAT TRUE...?
WELL, OF COURSE... JUST AS A CITIZEN...
BUT WOULDN'T YOU CALL FOR HELP FIRST?
THERE'S NO TIME FOR THAT! THE GUY WAS ON A BIKE!
RIGHT?!
YEAH!
THAT'S RIGHT. I DIDN'T WANT TO LET HIM GO, SO I GRABBED MY GROCERIES THAT WERE THERE AND...
...WENT...
WAAA! TIME OUT! TIME OUT!!
Almost had you...
SO YOU'RE THE...
...FROM...
THE BUMP OF DISGRACE I GOT FROM YOU DIDN'T GO DOWN FOR THREE DAYS.
I'VE NEVER BEEN SO INSULTED IN MY LIFE.
KOTARO!
YES, MIDORI-SAMA!

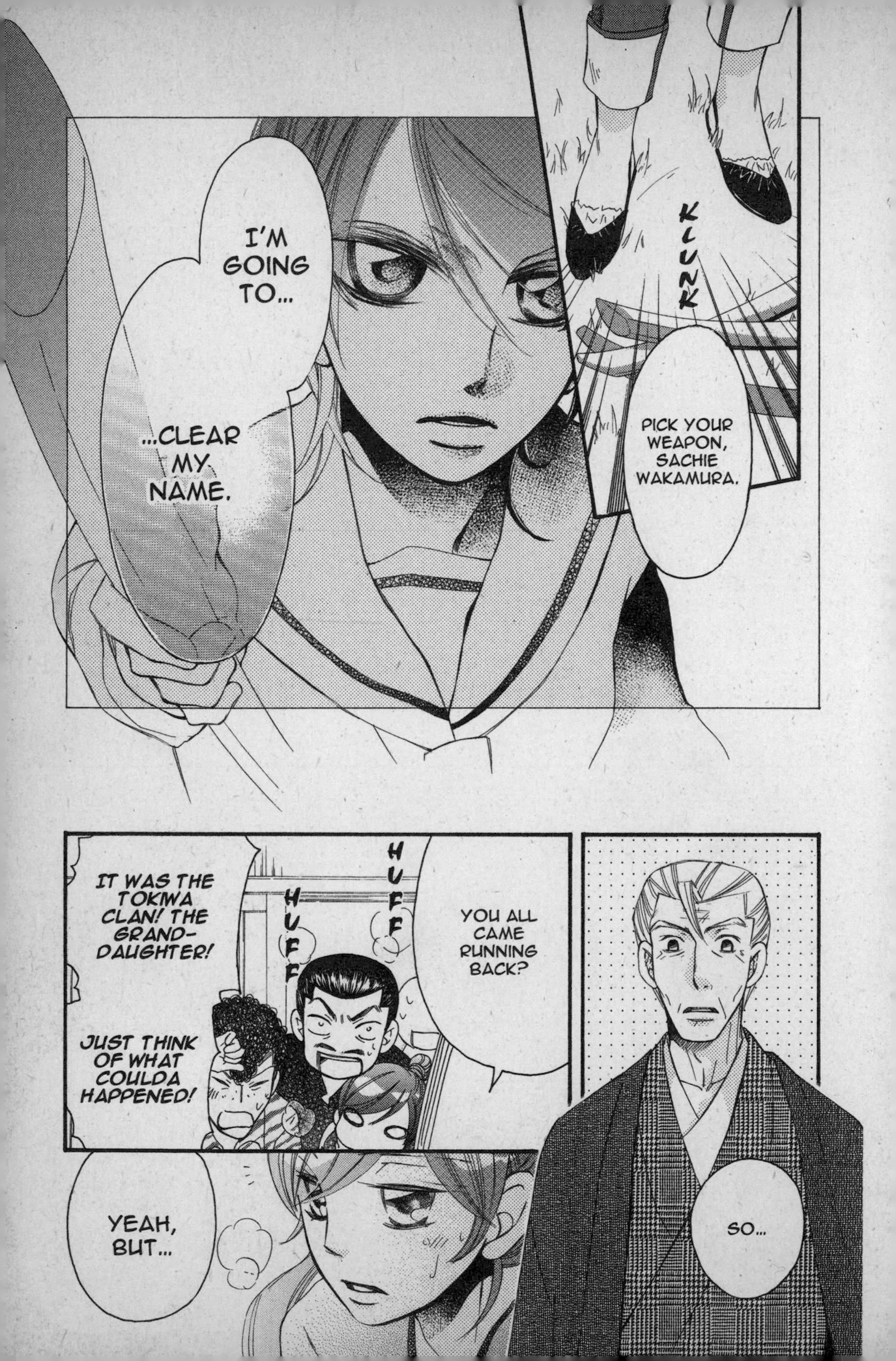
KLUNK
PICK YOUR WEAPON, SACHIE WAKAMURA.
I'M GOING TO...
...CLEAR MY NAME.
YOU ALL CAME RUNNING BACK?
HUFF
HUFF
IT WAS THE TOKIWA CLAN! THE GRAND-DAUGHTER!
JUST THINK OF WHAT COULDA HAPPENED!
SO...
YEAH, BUT...

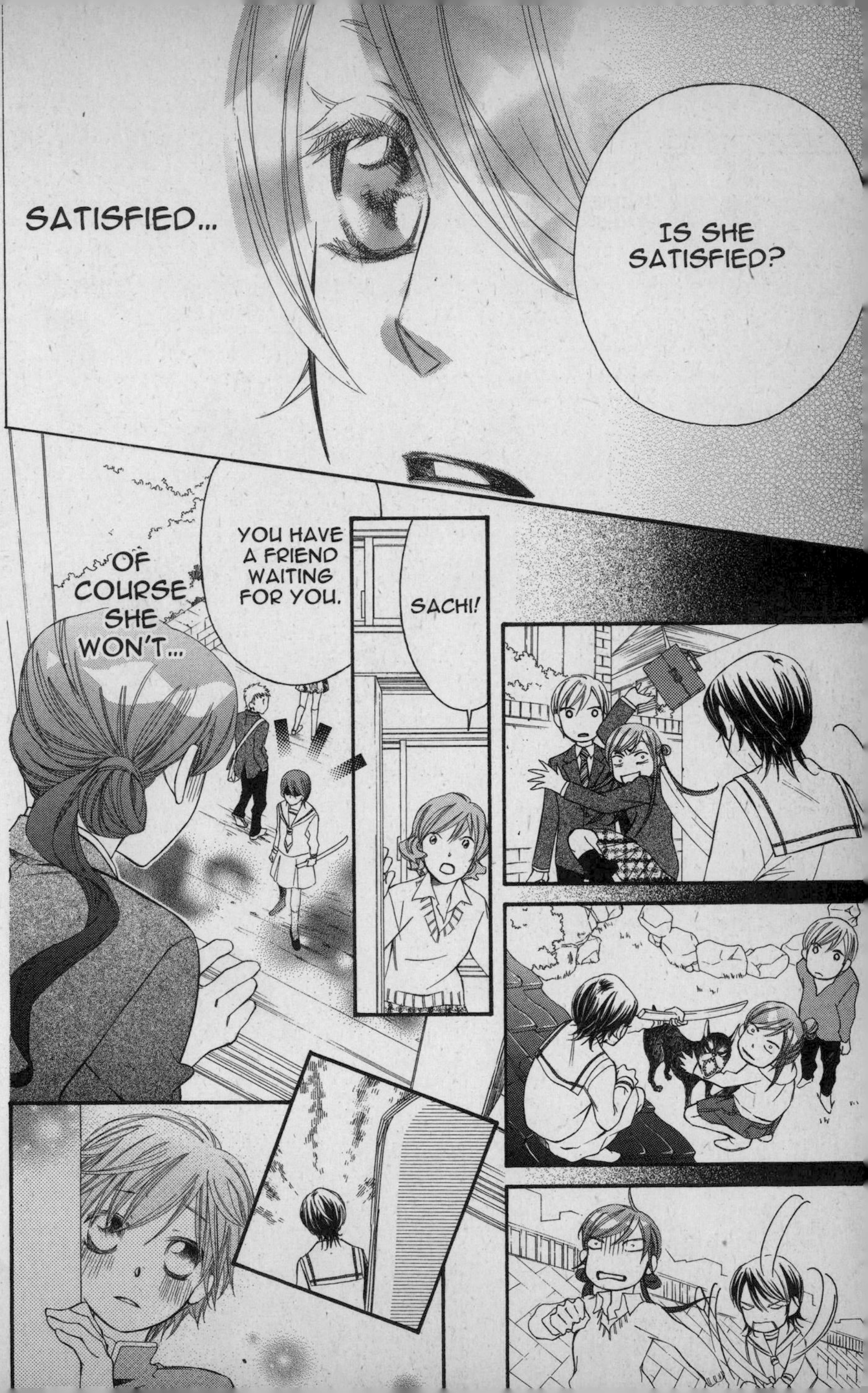
IS SHE SATISFIED?
SATISFIED...
SACHI!
YOU HAVE A FRIEND WAITING FOR YOU.
OF COURSE SHE WON'T...

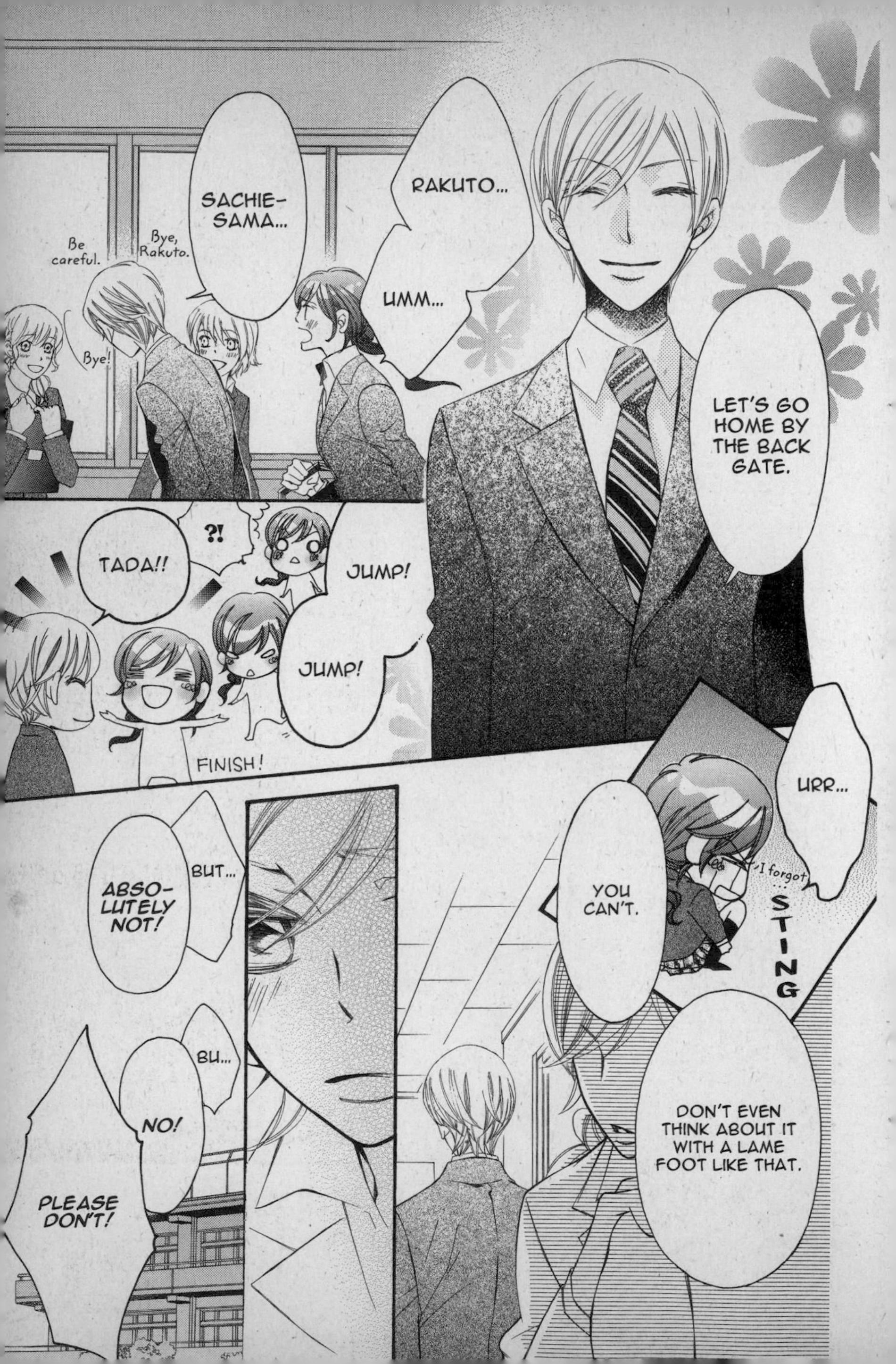
RAKUTO...
UMM...
LET'S GO HOME BY THE BACK GATE.
SACHIE-SAMA...
Bye, Rakuto.
Be careful.
Bye!
JUMP!
JUMP!
FINISH!
?!
TADA!!
URR...
I forgot...
STING
YOU CAN'T.
DON'T EVEN THINK ABOUT IT WITH A LAME FOOT LIKE THAT.
BUT...
ABSOLUTELY NOT!
BU...
NO!
PLEASE DON'T!

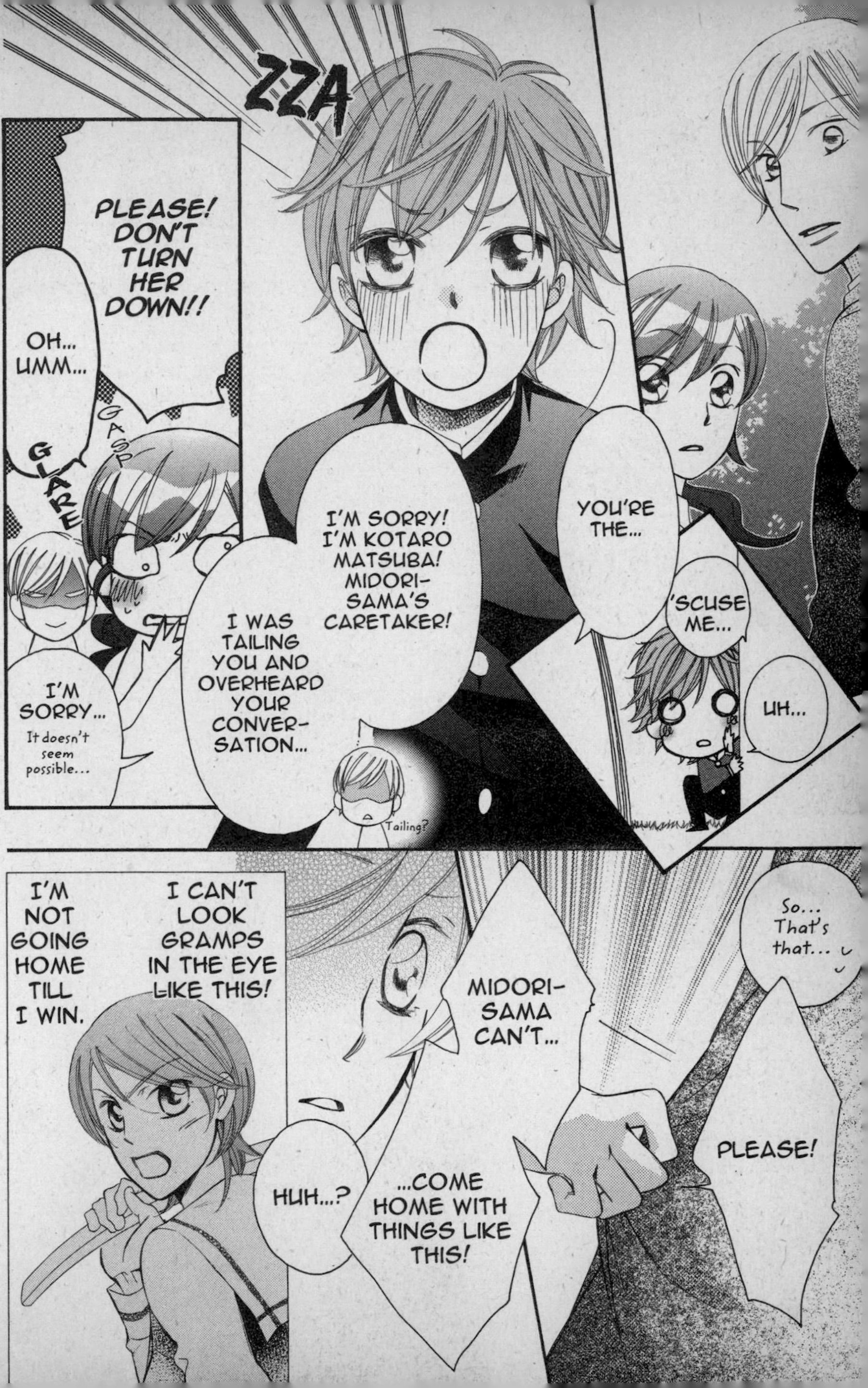

YOU'RE THE...
'SCUSE ME...
UH...
ZZA
I'M SORRY! I'M KOTARO MATSUBA! MIDORI-SAMA'S CARETAKER!
I WAS TAILING YOU AND OVERHEARD YOUR CONVERSATION...
Tailing?
PLEASE! DON'T TURN HER DOWN!!
OH... UMM...
GASP
GLARE
I'M SORRY...
It doesn't seem possible...
So... That's that...
PLEASE!
MIDORI-SAMA CAN'T...
...COME HOME WITH THINGS LIKE THIS!
HUH...?
I CAN'T LOOK GRAMPS IN THE EYE LIKE THIS!
I'M NOT GOING HOME TILL I WIN.

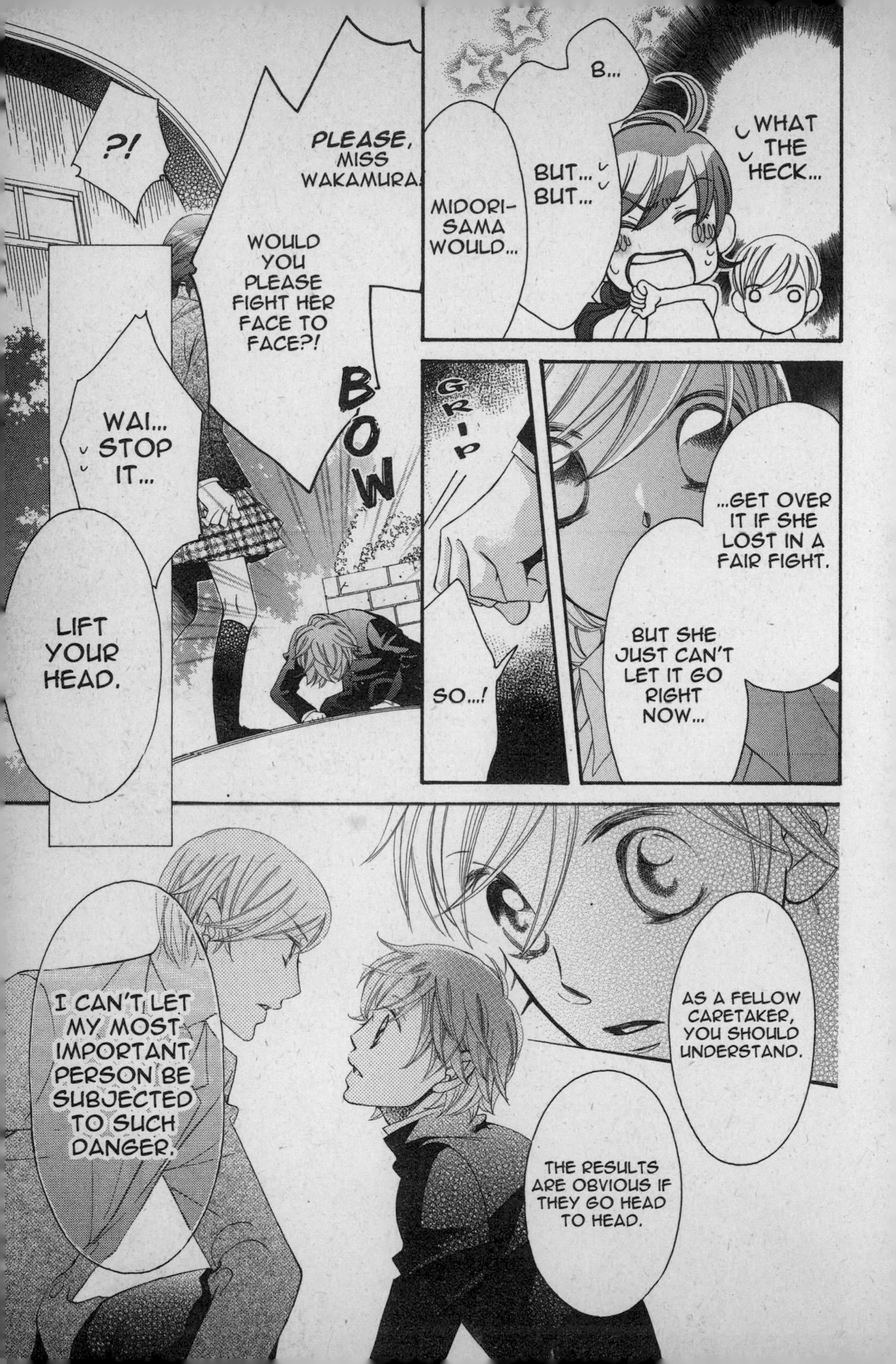
WHAT THE HECK...
B...
BUT... BUT...
MIDORI-SAMA WOULD...
...GET OVER IT IF SHE LOST IN A FAIR FIGHT.
BUT SHE JUST CAN'T LET IT GO RIGHT NOW...
GRIP
SO...!
?!
PLEASE, MISS WAKAMURA!
WOULD YOU PLEASE FIGHT HER FACE TO FACE?!
BOW
WAI... STOP IT...
LIFT YOUR HEAD.
AS A FELLOW CARETAKER, YOU SHOULD UNDERSTAND.
THE RESULTS ARE OBVIOUS IF THEY GO HEAD TO HEAD.
I CAN'T LET MY MOST IMPORTANT PERSON BE SUBJECTED TO SUCH DANGER.

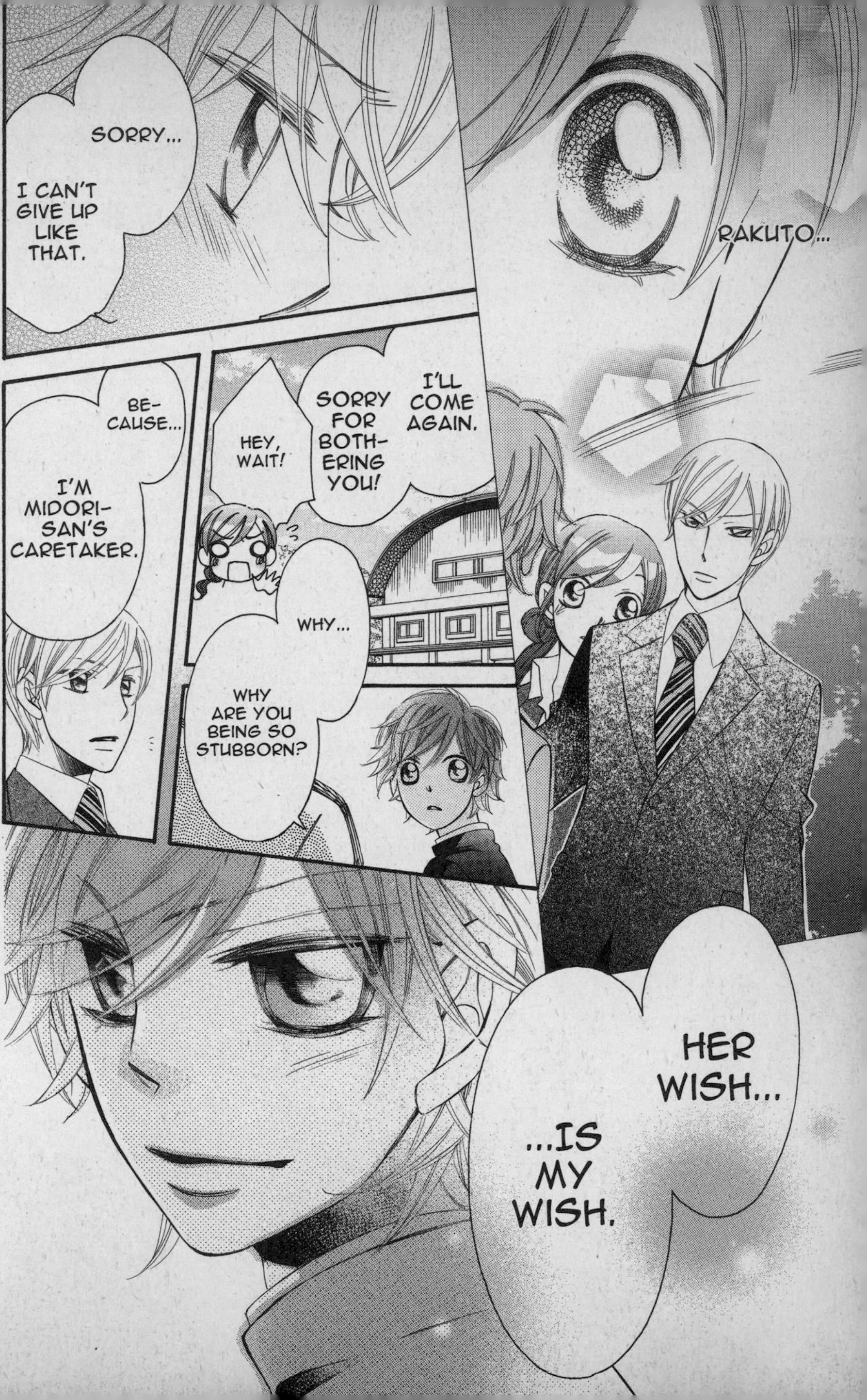
RAKUTO...
SORRY...
I CAN'T GIVE UP LIKE THAT.
I'LL COME AGAIN.
SORRY FOR BOTHERING YOU!
HEY, WAIT!
WHY...
WHY ARE YOU BEING SO STUBBORN?
BECAUSE...
I'M MIDORI-SAN'S CARETAKER.
HER WISH...
...IS MY WISH.

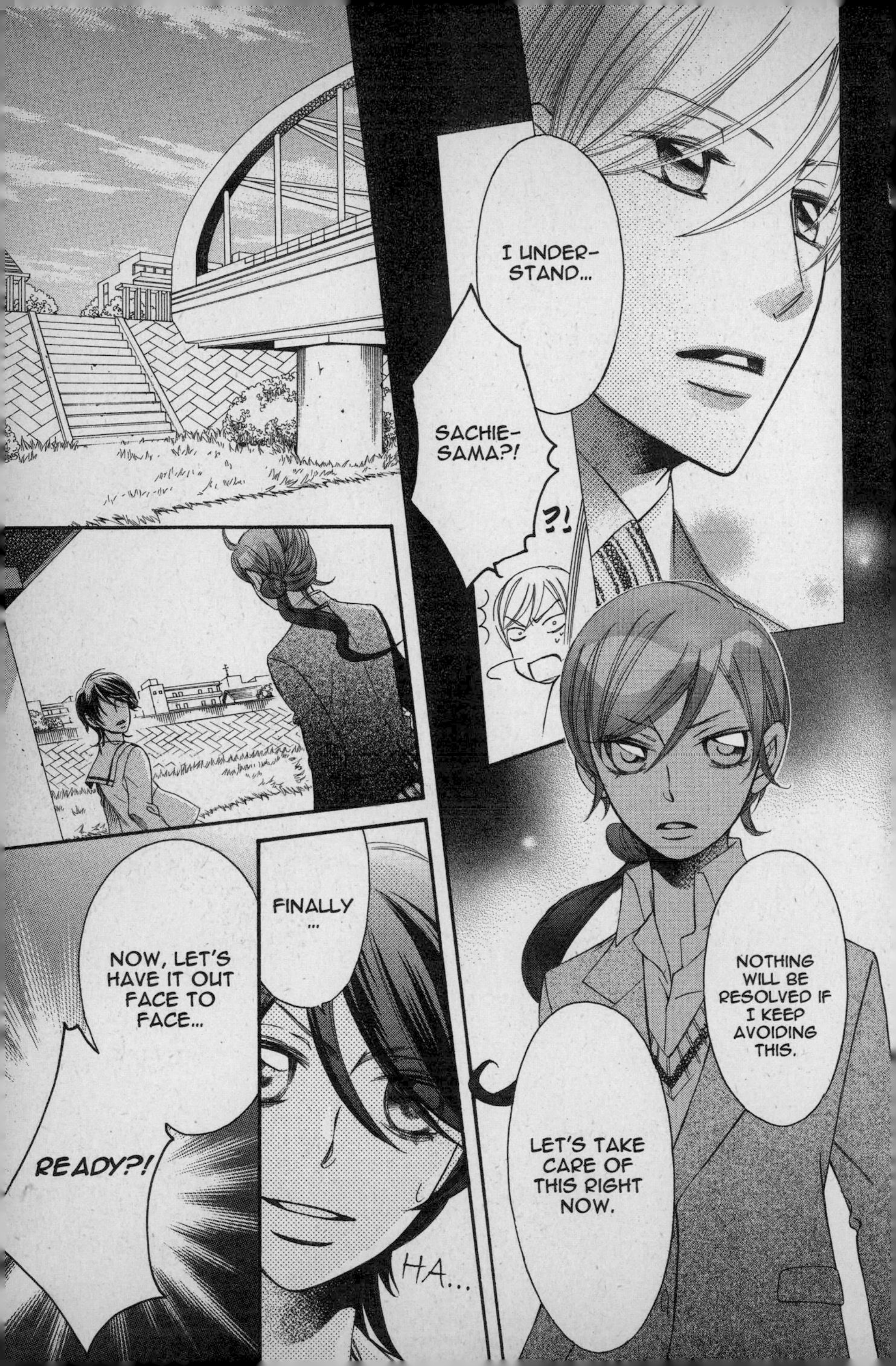
I UNDER-
STAND...
SACHIE-
SAMA?!
?!
NOTHING WILL BE RESOLVED IF I KEEP AVOIDING THIS.
LET'S TAKE CARE OF THIS RIGHT NOW.
FINALLY ...
NOW, LET'S HAVE IT OUT FACE TO FACE...
READY?!
HA...

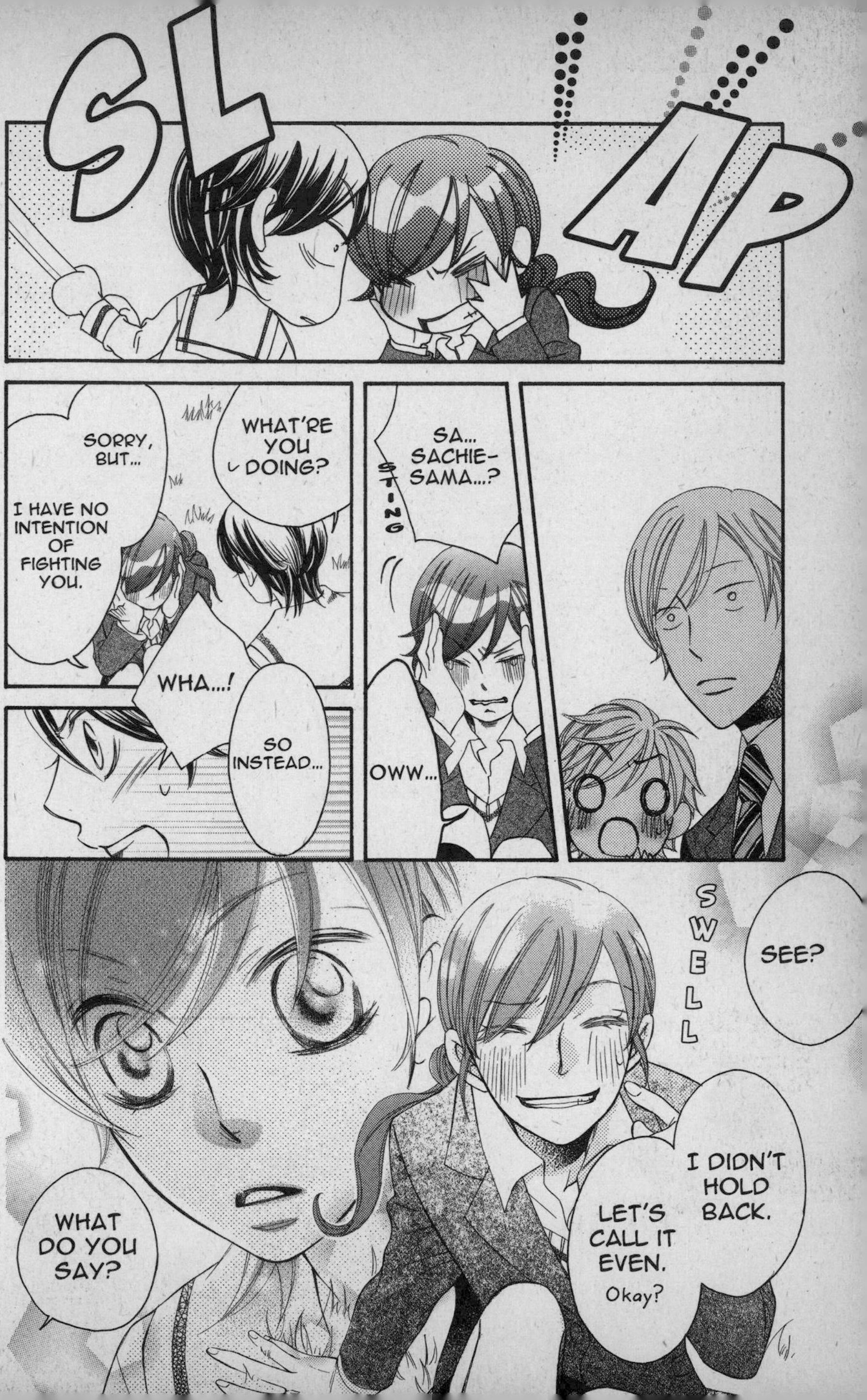
SLAP
SA... SACHIE-SAMA...?
STING
OWW...
WHAT'RE YOU DOING?
SORRY, BUT...
I HAVE NO INTENTION OF FIGHTING YOU.
WHA...!
SO INSTEAD...
SEE?
SWELL
I DIDN'T HOLD BACK.
LET'S CALL IT EVEN.
Okay?
WHAT DO YOU SAY?

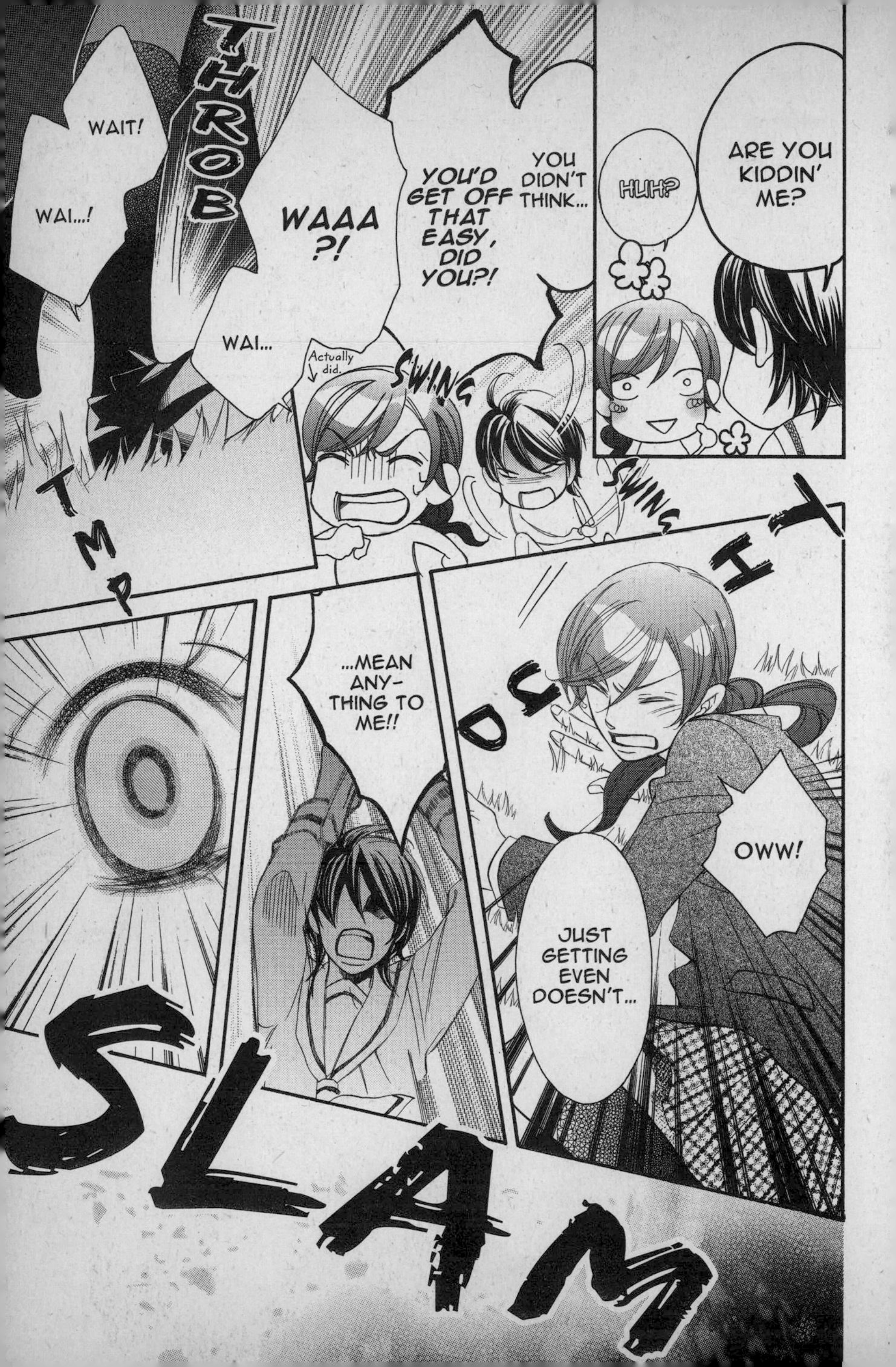
ARE YOU KIDDIN' ME?
HUH?
YOU DIDN'T THINK...
YOU'D GET OFF THAT EASY, DID YOU?!
SWING
SWING
Actually did.
WAAA ?!
WAI...
THROB
WAIT!
WAI...!
TMP
THUD
OWW!
JUST GETTING EVEN DOESN'T...
...MEAN ANY-THING TO ME!!
SLAM

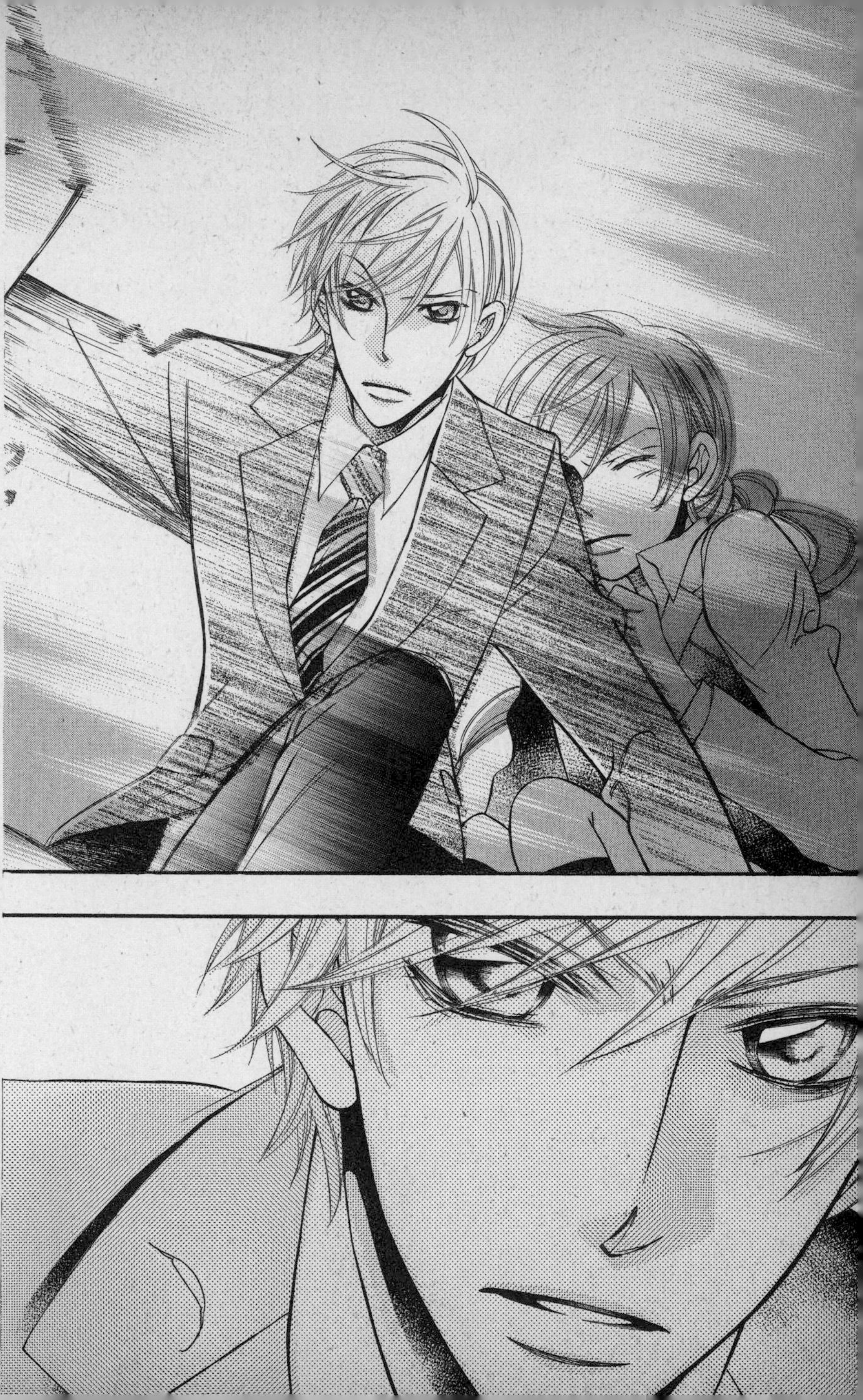

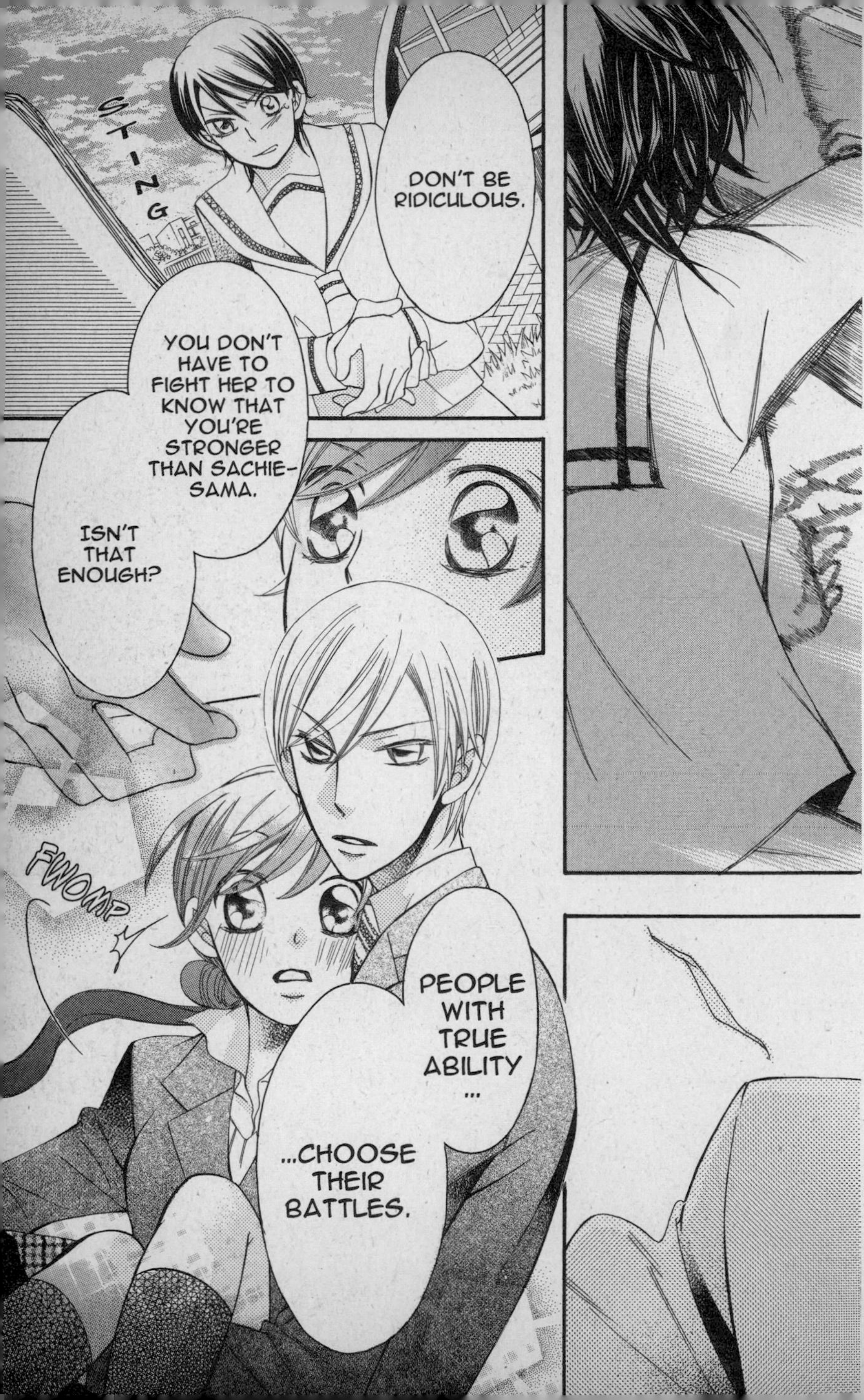
DON'T BE RIDICULOUS.
STING
YOU DON'T HAVE TO FIGHT HER TO KNOW THAT YOU'RE STRONGER THAN SACHIE-SAMA.
ISN'T THAT ENOUGH?
FWOMP
PEOPLE WITH TRUE ABILITY ...
...CHOOSE THEIR BATTLES.

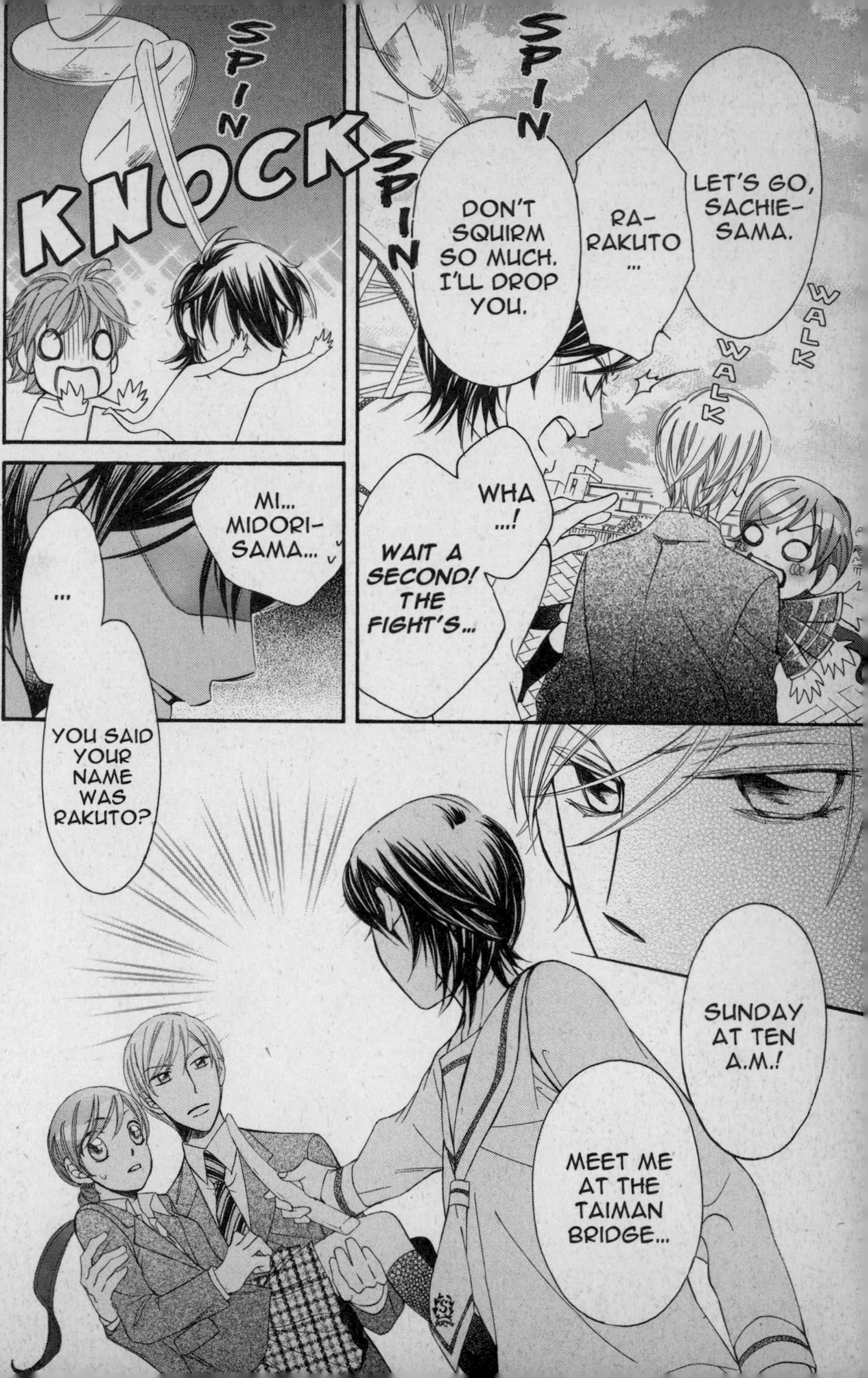
SPIN
LET'S GO, SACHIE-SAMA.
RA-RAKUTO ...
DON'T SQUIRM SO MUCH. I'LL DROP YOU.
SPIN
WALK
WALK
WHA ...!
WAIT A SECOND! THE FIGHT'S...
SPIN
KNOCK
MI... MIDORI-SAMA...
...
SUNDAY AT TEN A.M.!
MEET ME AT THE TAIMAN BRIDGE...
YOU SAID YOUR NAME WAS RAKUTO?

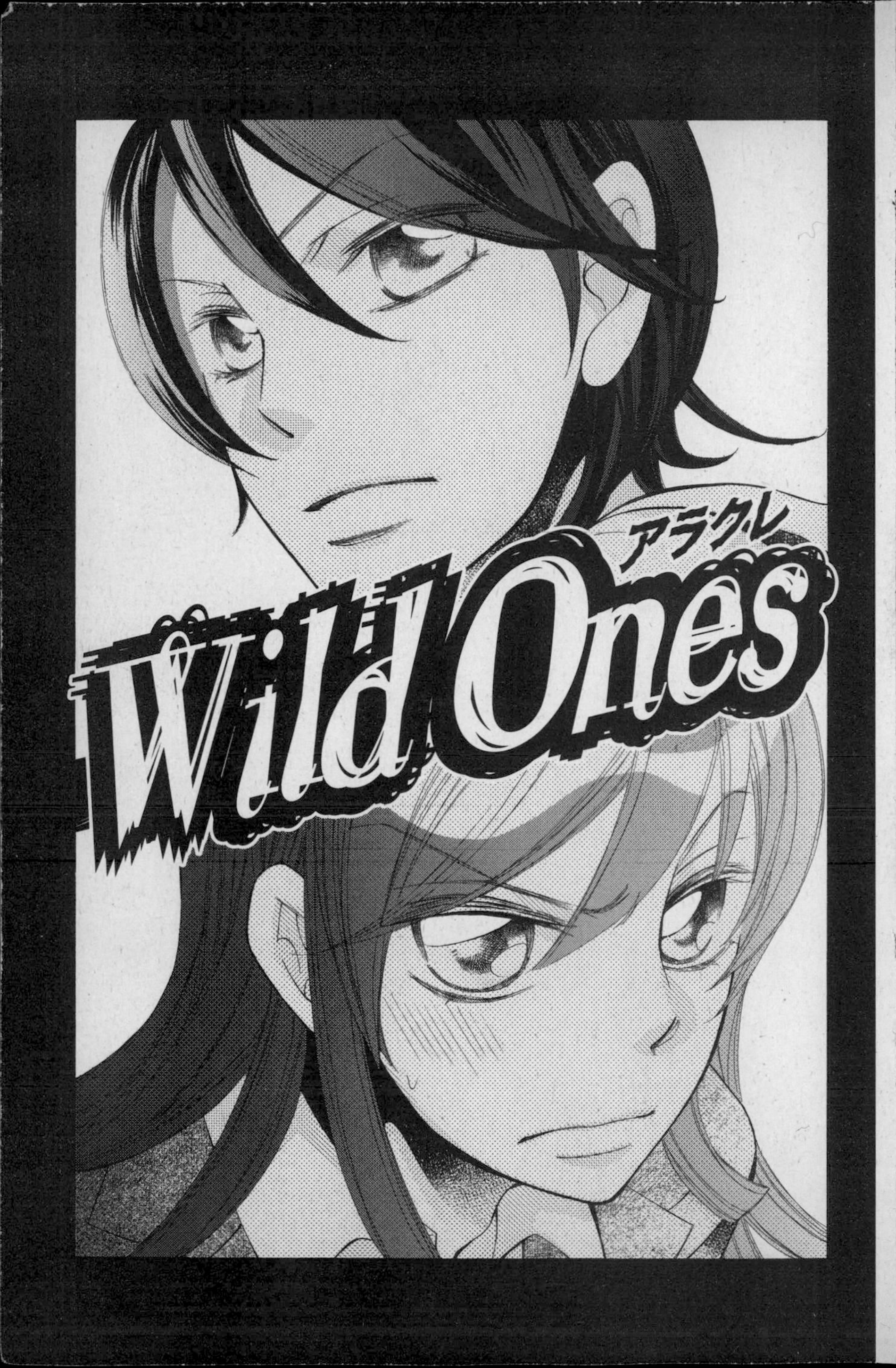
アラクレ
Wild Ones

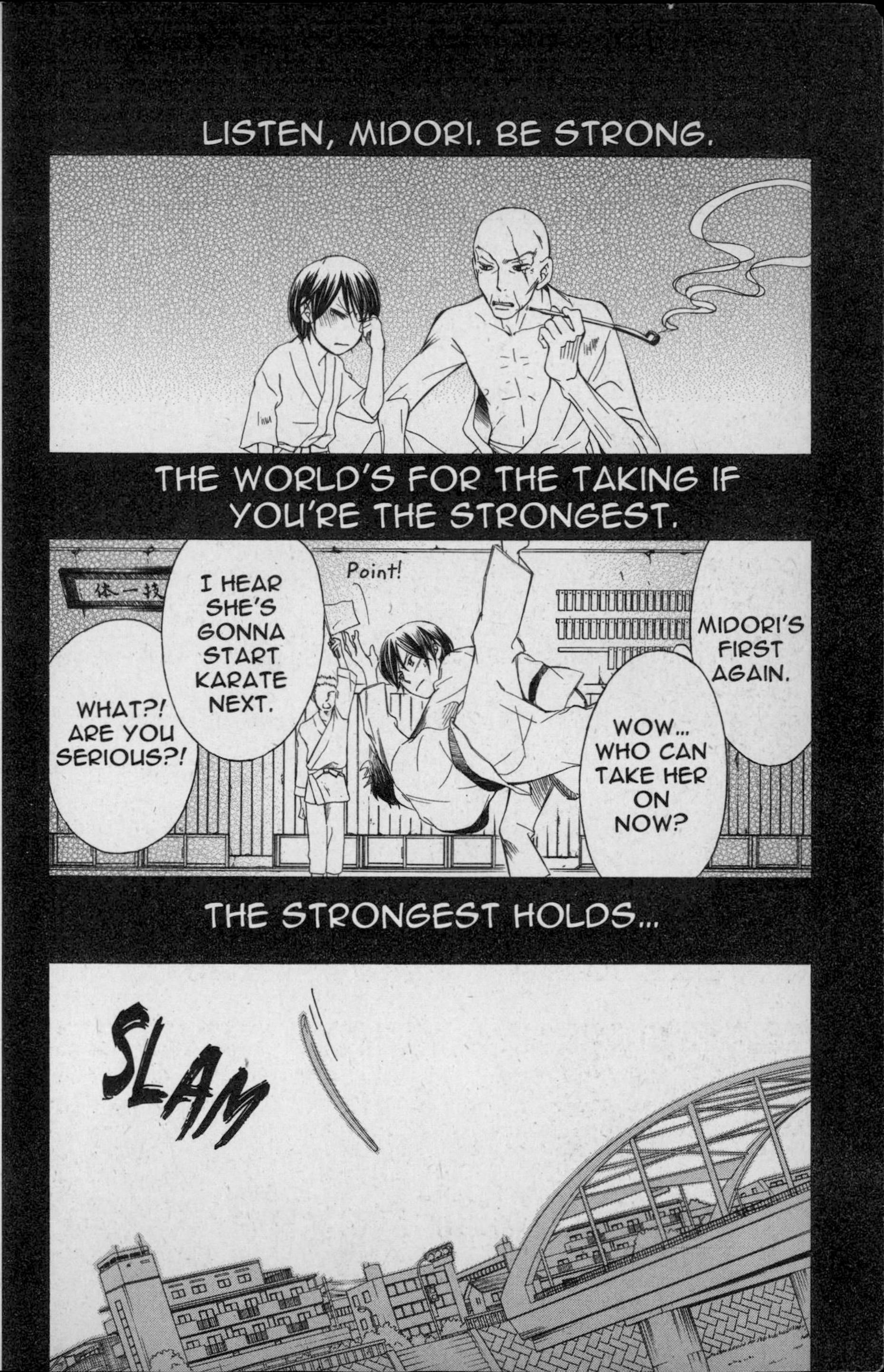
LISTEN, MIDORI. BE STRONG.
THE WORLD'S FOR THE TAKING IF YOU'RE THE STRONGEST.
MIDORI'S FIRST AGAIN.
WOW... WHO CAN TAKE HER ON NOW?
Point!
I HEAR SHE'S GONNA START KARATE NEXT.
WHAT?! ARE YOU SERIOUS?!
THE STRONGEST HOLDS...
SLAM

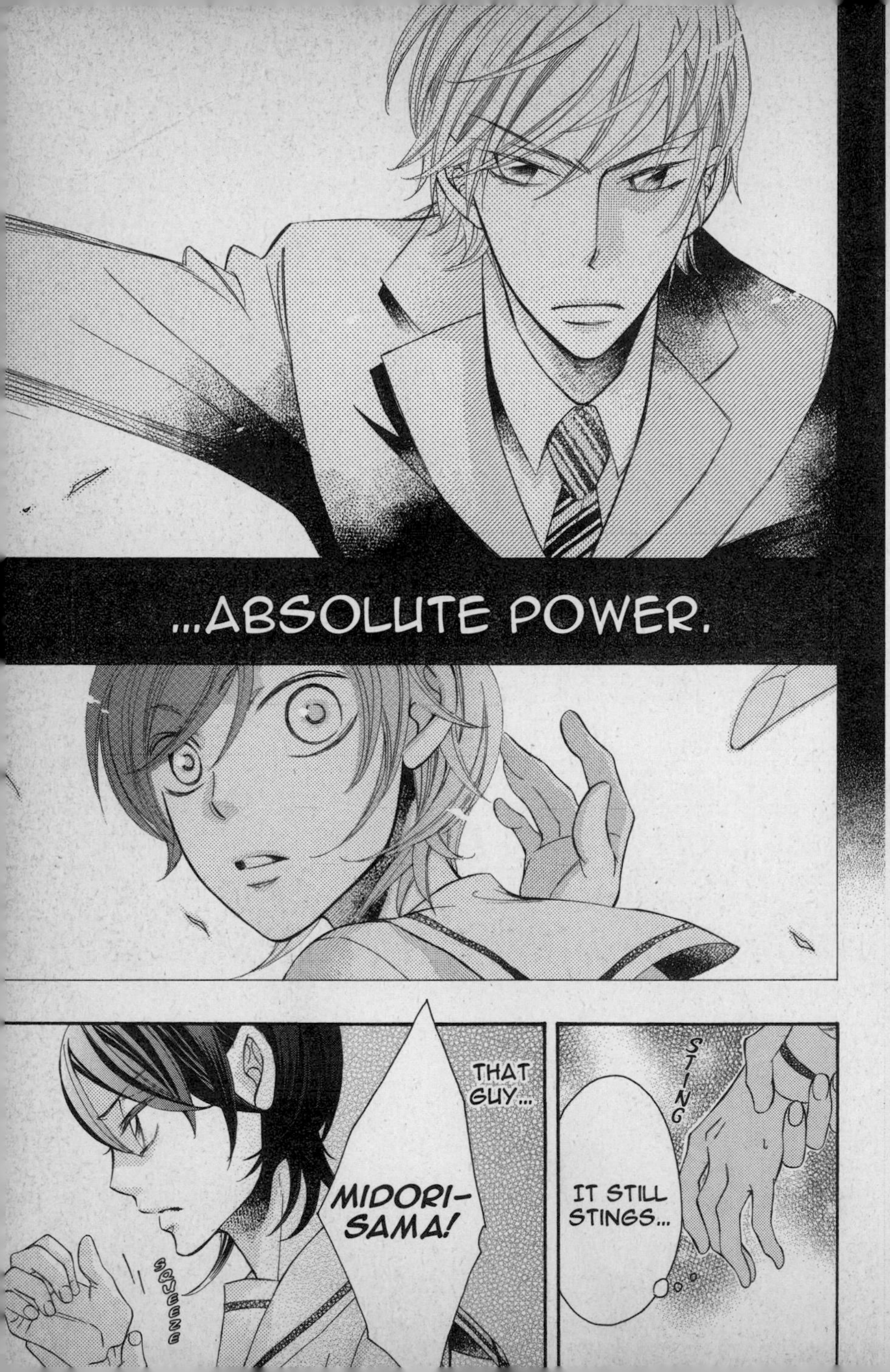
...ABSOLUTE POWER.
STING
IT STILL STINGS...
THAT GUY...
MIDORI-SAMA!
SQUEEZE

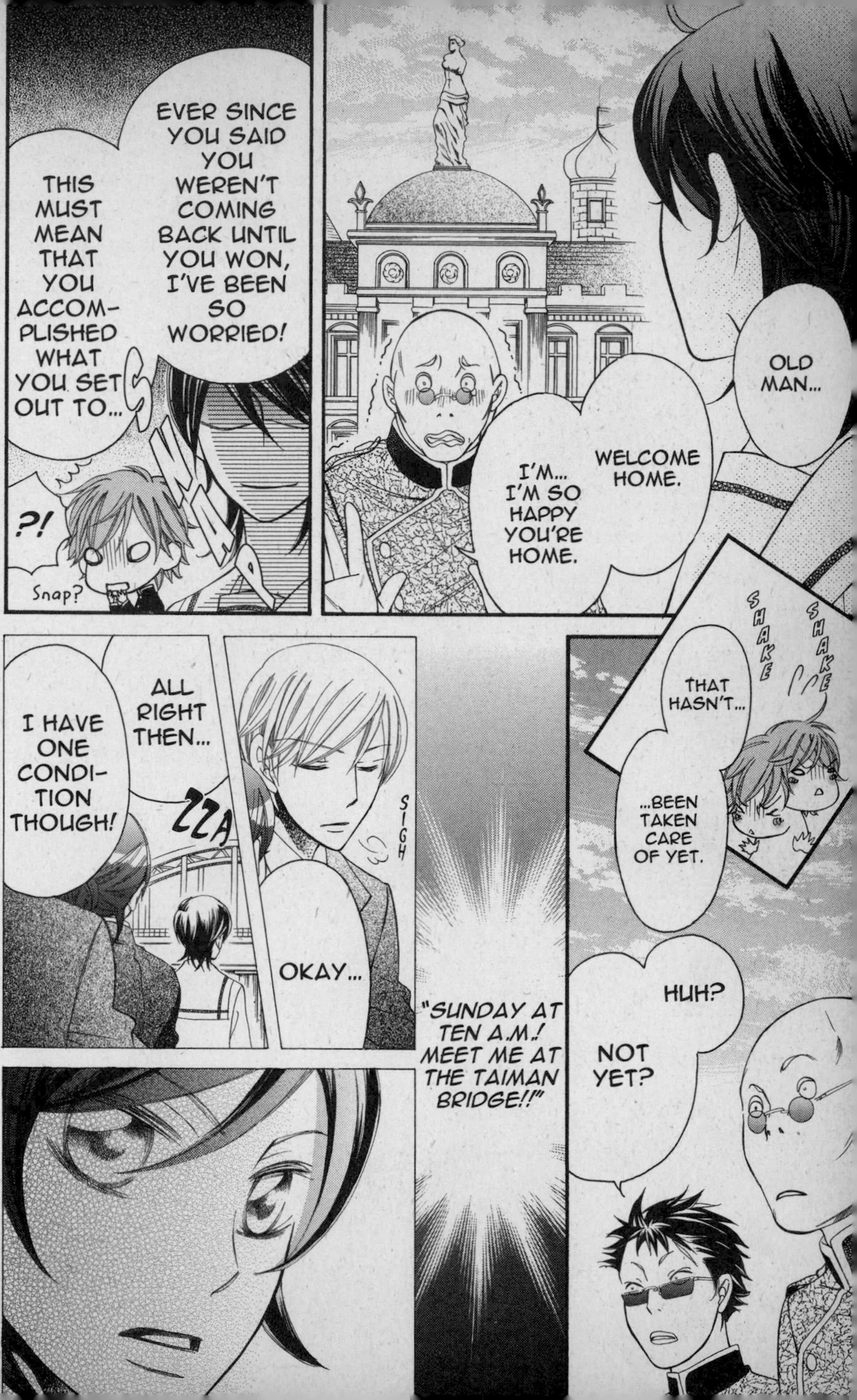
OLD MAN...
WELCOME HOME.
I'M... I'M SO HAPPY YOU'RE HOME.
EVER SINCE YOU SAID YOU WEREN'T COMING BACK UNTIL YOU WON, I'VE BEEN SO WORRIED!
THIS MUST MEAN THAT YOU ACCOMPLISHED WHAT YOU SET OUT TO...
?!
Snap?
SHAKE
SHAKE
THAT HASN'T...
...BEEN TAKEN CARE OF YET.
HUH?
NOT YET?
SIGH
OKAY...
ALL RIGHT THEN...
I HAVE ONE CONDITION THOUGH!
ZZA
"SUNDAY AT TEN A.M.! MEET ME AT THE TAIMAN BRIDGE!!"

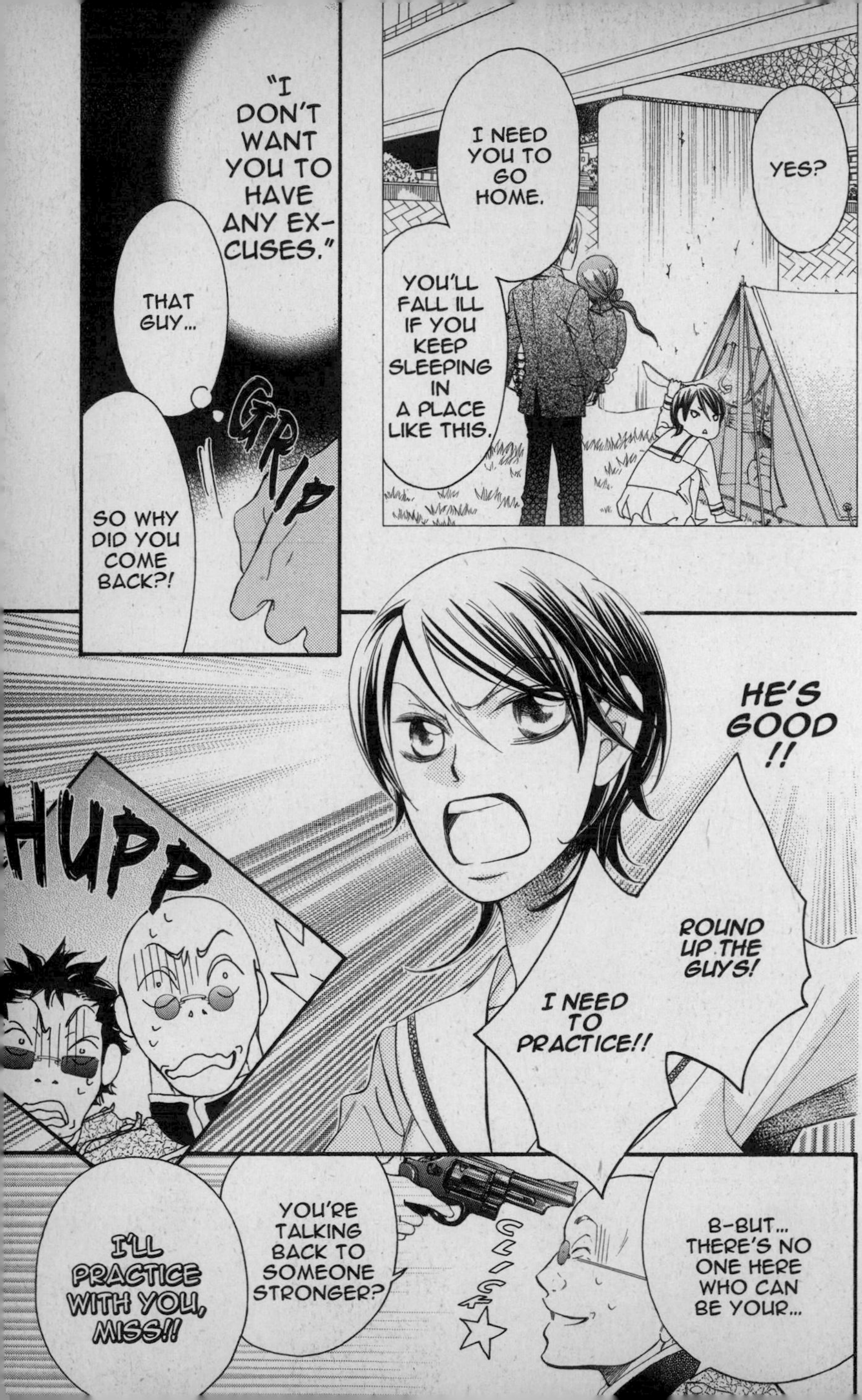
YES?
I NEED YOU TO GO HOME.
YOU'LL FALL ILL IF YOU KEEP SLEEPING IN A PLACE LIKE THIS.
"I DON'T WANT YOU TO HAVE ANY EX-CUSES."
THAT GUY...
GRIP
SO WHY DID YOU COME BACK?!
HE'S GOOD!!
ROUND UP THE GUYS!
I NEED TO PRACTICE!!
HUPP
B-BUT... THERE'S NO ONE HERE WHO CAN BE YOUR...
CLICK
YOU'RE TALKING BACK TO SOMEONE STRONGER?
I'LL PRACTICE WITH YOU, MISS!!

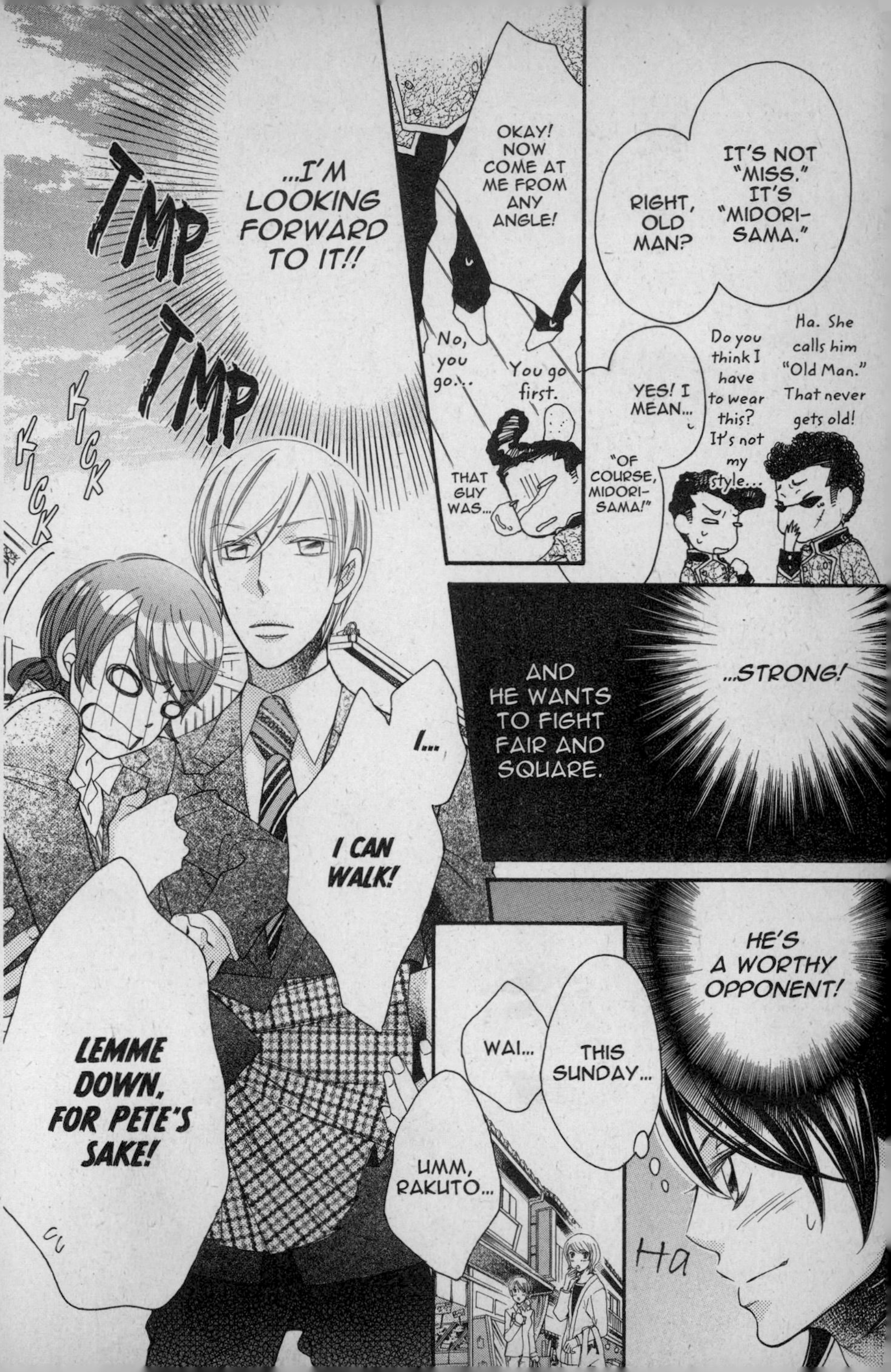
IT'S NOT "MISS." IT'S "MIDORI-SAMA."
RIGHT, OLD MAN?
YES! I MEAN...
"OF COURSE, MIDORI-SAMA!"
Ha. She calls him "Old Man." That never gets old!
Do you think I have to wear this? It's not my style...
OKAY! NOW COME AT ME FROM ANY ANGLE!
You go first.
No, you go...
THAT GUY WAS...
...STRONG!
AND HE WANTS TO FIGHT FAIR AND SQUARE.
HE'S A WORTHY OPPONENT!
Ha
THIS SUNDAY...
WAI...
UMM, RAKUTO...
...I'M LOOKING FORWARD TO IT!!
TMP TMP TMP
KICK KICK
I...
I CAN WALK!
LEMME DOWN, FOR PETE'S SAKE!

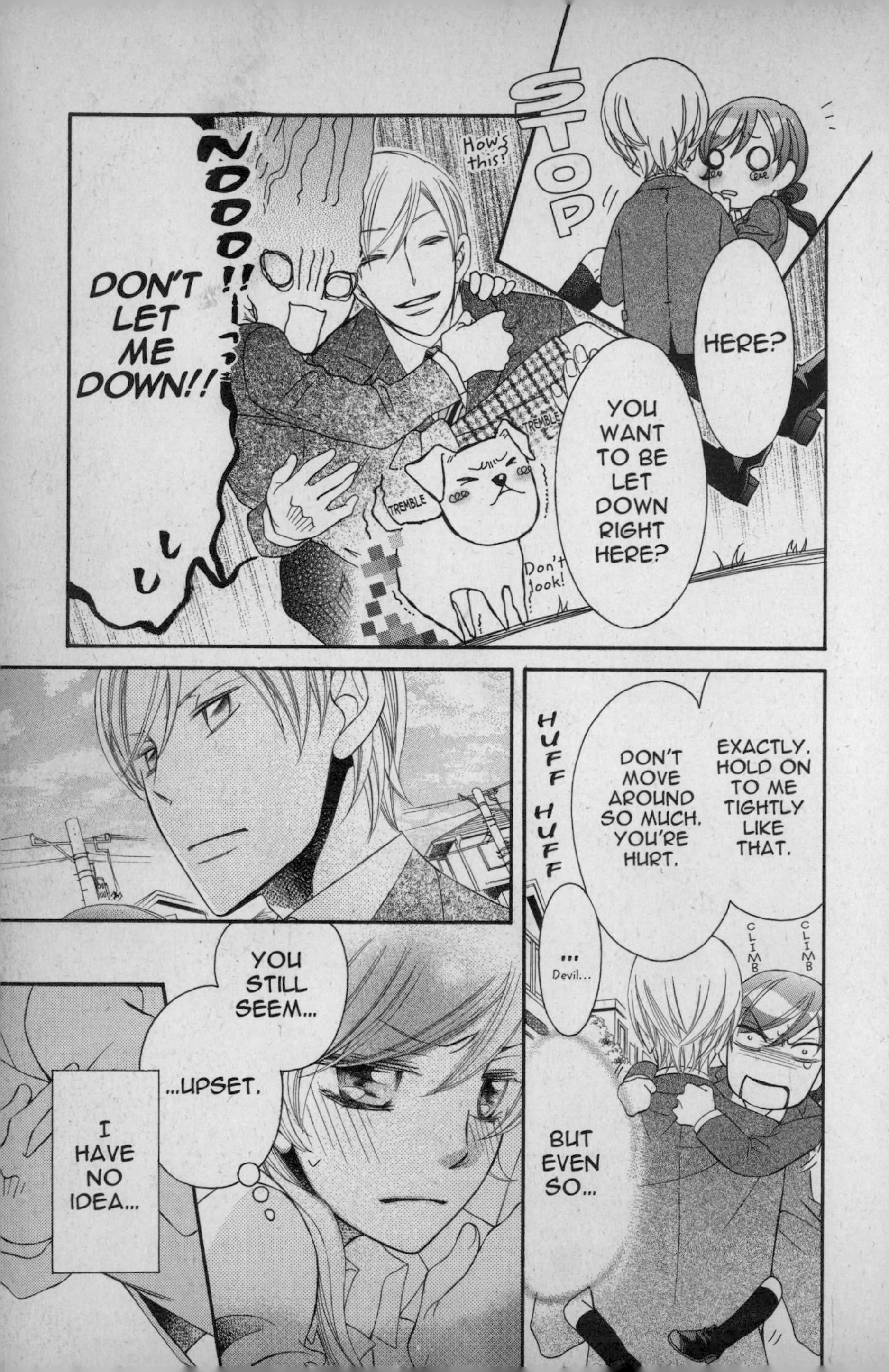
STOP
HERE?
YOU WANT TO BE LET DOWN RIGHT HERE?
How's this?
NOOOO!!
DON'T LET ME DOWN!!
TREMBLE
TREMBLE
Don't look!
HUFF HUFF
EXACTLY. HOLD ON TO ME TIGHTLY LIKE THAT.
DON'T MOVE AROUND SO MUCH. YOU'RE HURT.
... Devil...
CLIMB CLIMB
BUT EVEN SO...
YOU STILL SEEM...
...UPSET.
I HAVE NO IDEA...

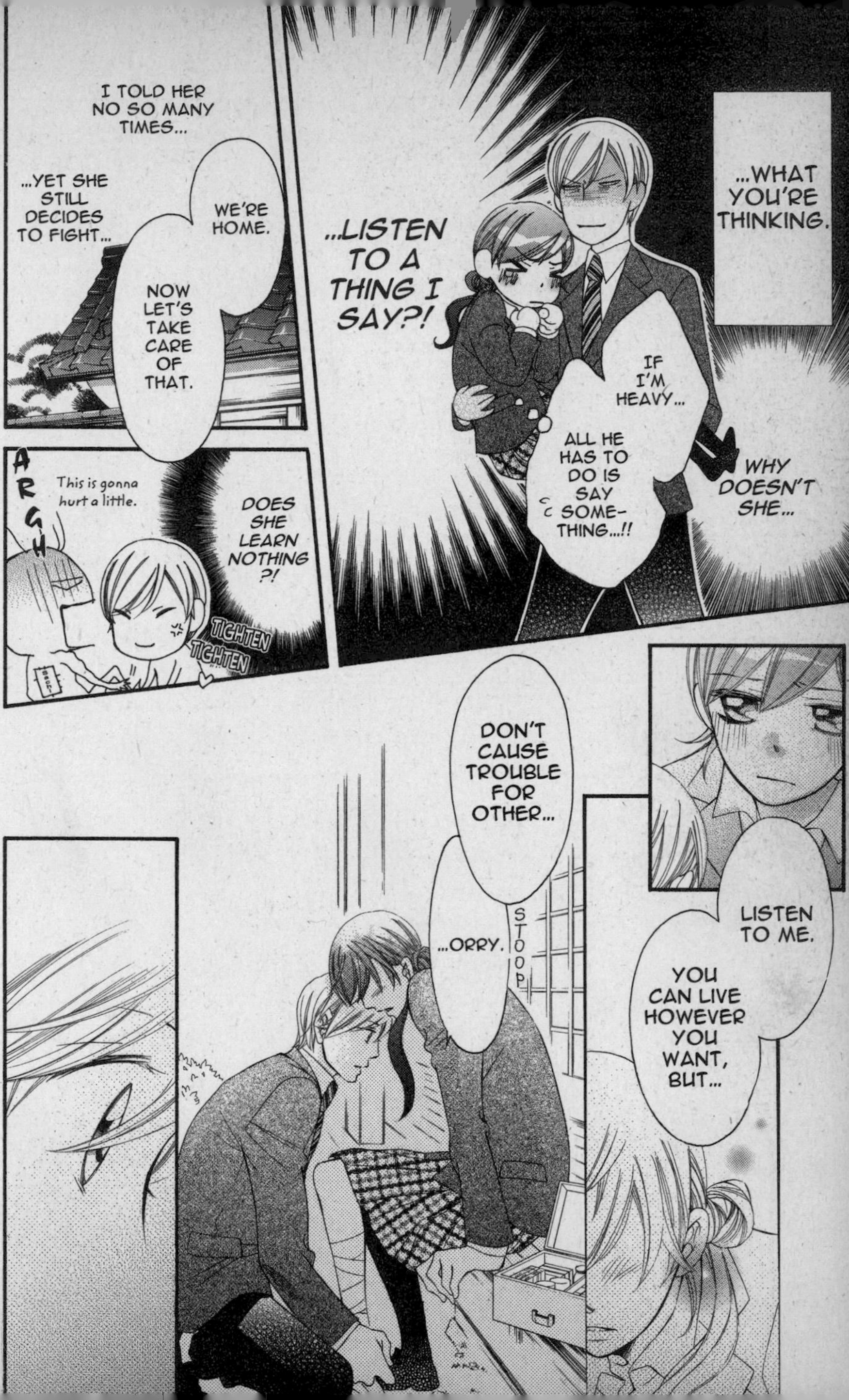
...WHAT YOU'RE THINKING.
...LISTEN TO A THING I SAY?!
IF I'M HEAVY...
ALL HE HAS TO DO IS SAY SOMETHING...!!
WHY DOESN'T SHE...
I TOLD HER NO SO MANY TIMES...
WE'RE HOME.
...YET SHE STILL DECIDES TO FIGHT...
NOW LET'S TAKE CARE OF THAT.
DOES SHE LEARN NOTHING?!
This is gonna hurt a little.
ARGH
TIGHTEN
TIGHTEN
LISTEN TO ME.
YOU CAN LIVE HOWEVER YOU WANT, BUT...
DON'T CAUSE TROUBLE FOR OTHER...
STOOP
...ORRY.

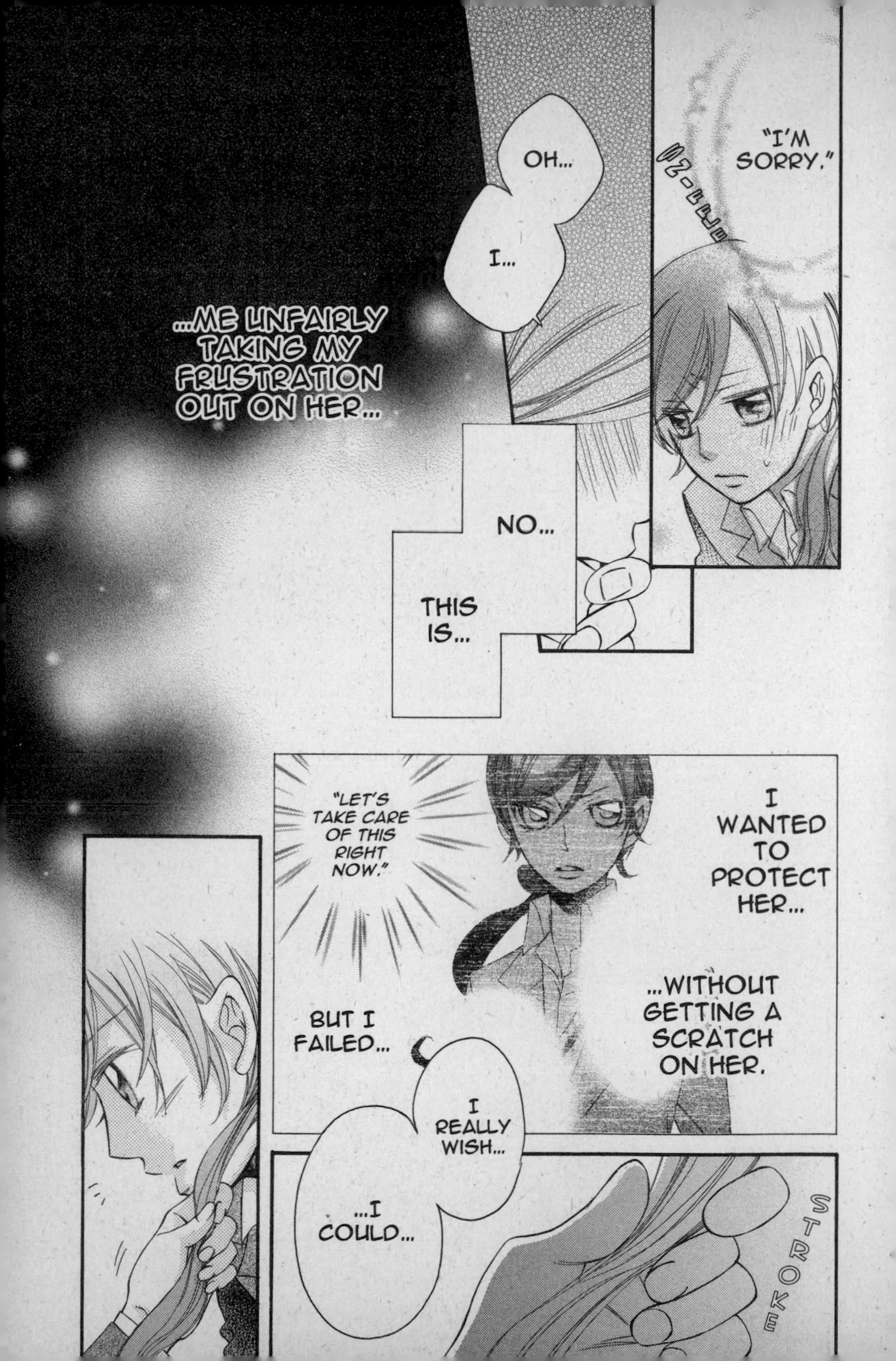
"I'M SORRY."
OH...
I...
NO...
THIS IS...
...ME UNFAIRLY TAKING MY FRUSTRATION OUT ON HER...
I WANTED TO PROTECT HER...
"LET'S TAKE CARE OF THIS RIGHT NOW."
...WITHOUT GETTING A SCRATCH ON HER.
BUT I FAILED...
I REALLY WISH...
...I COULD...
STROKE

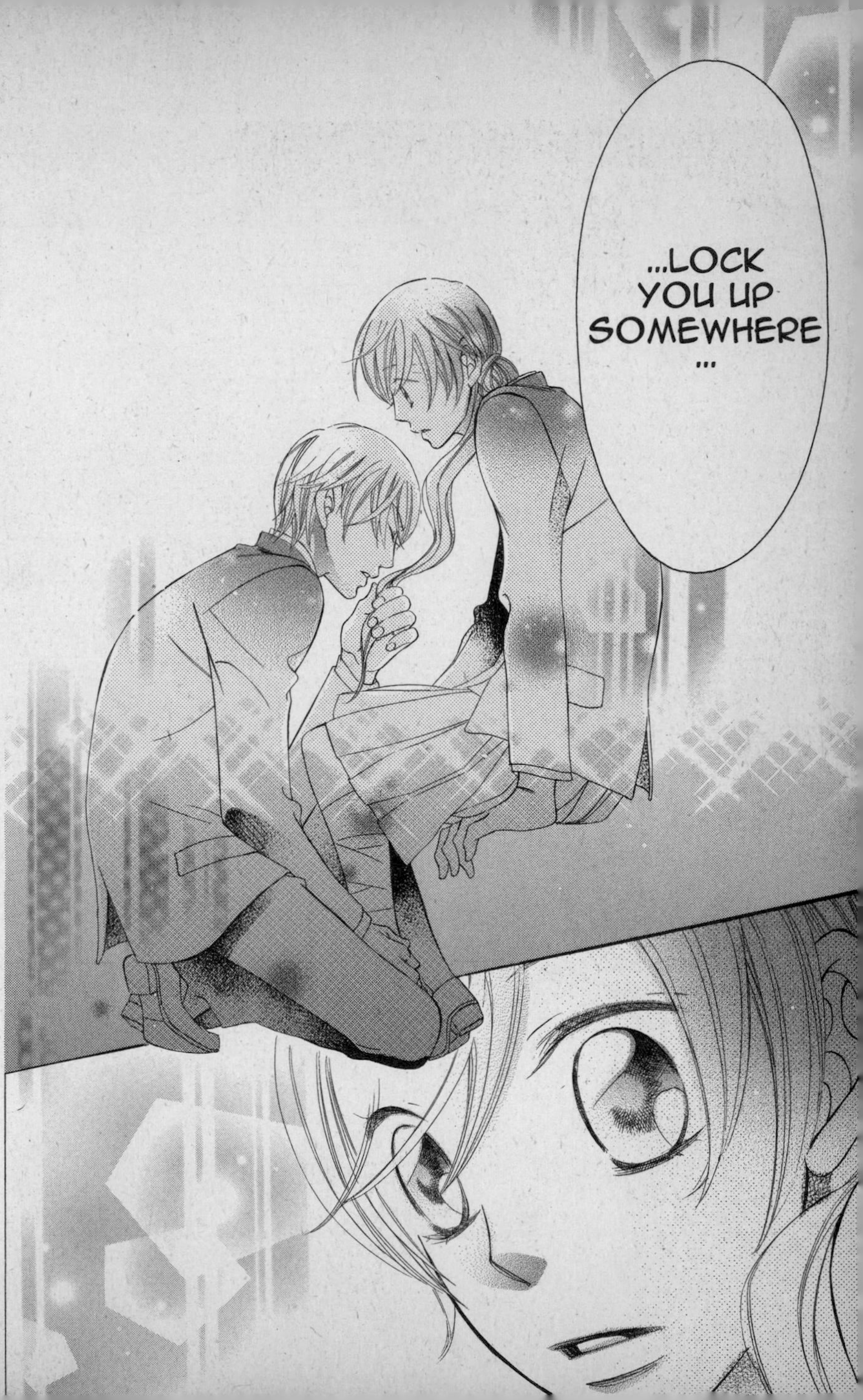
...LOCK YOU UP SOMEWHERE ...

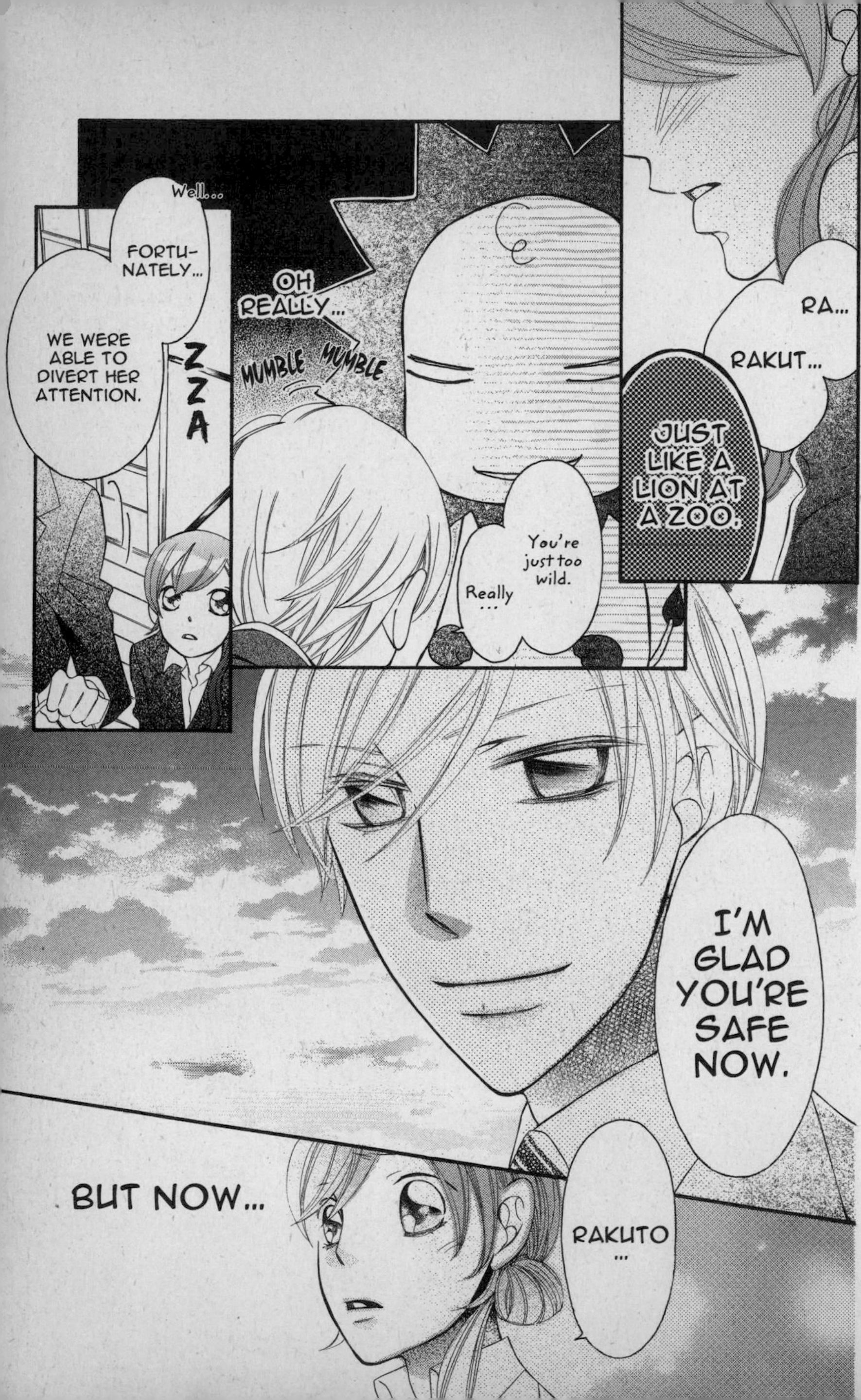
RA...
RAKUT...
JUST LIKE A LION AT A ZOO.
OH REALLY...
MUMBLE MUMBLE
You're just too wild.
Really...
Well...
FORTU-NATELY...
WE WERE ABLE TO DIVERT HER ATTENTION.
ZZA
I'M GLAD YOU'RE SAFE NOW.
RAKUTO...
BUT NOW...

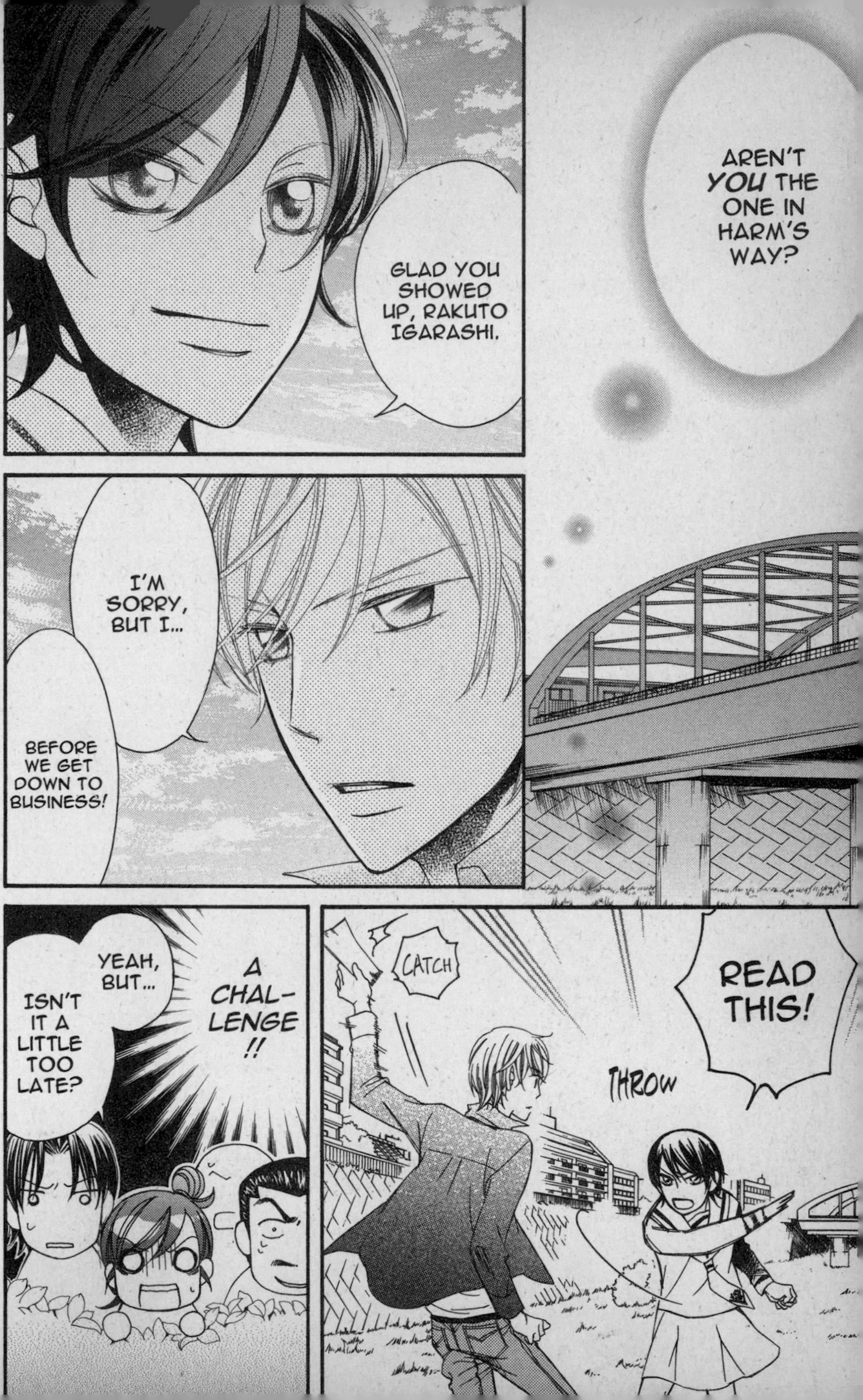
ARE'NT YOU THE ONE IN HARM'S WAY?
GLAD YOU SHOWED UP, RAKUTO IGARASHI.
I'M SORRY, BUT I...
BEFORE WE GET DOWN TO BUSINESS!
READ THIS!
THROW
CATCH
A CHAL-LENGE!!
YEAH, BUT...
ISN'T IT A LITTLE TOO LATE?

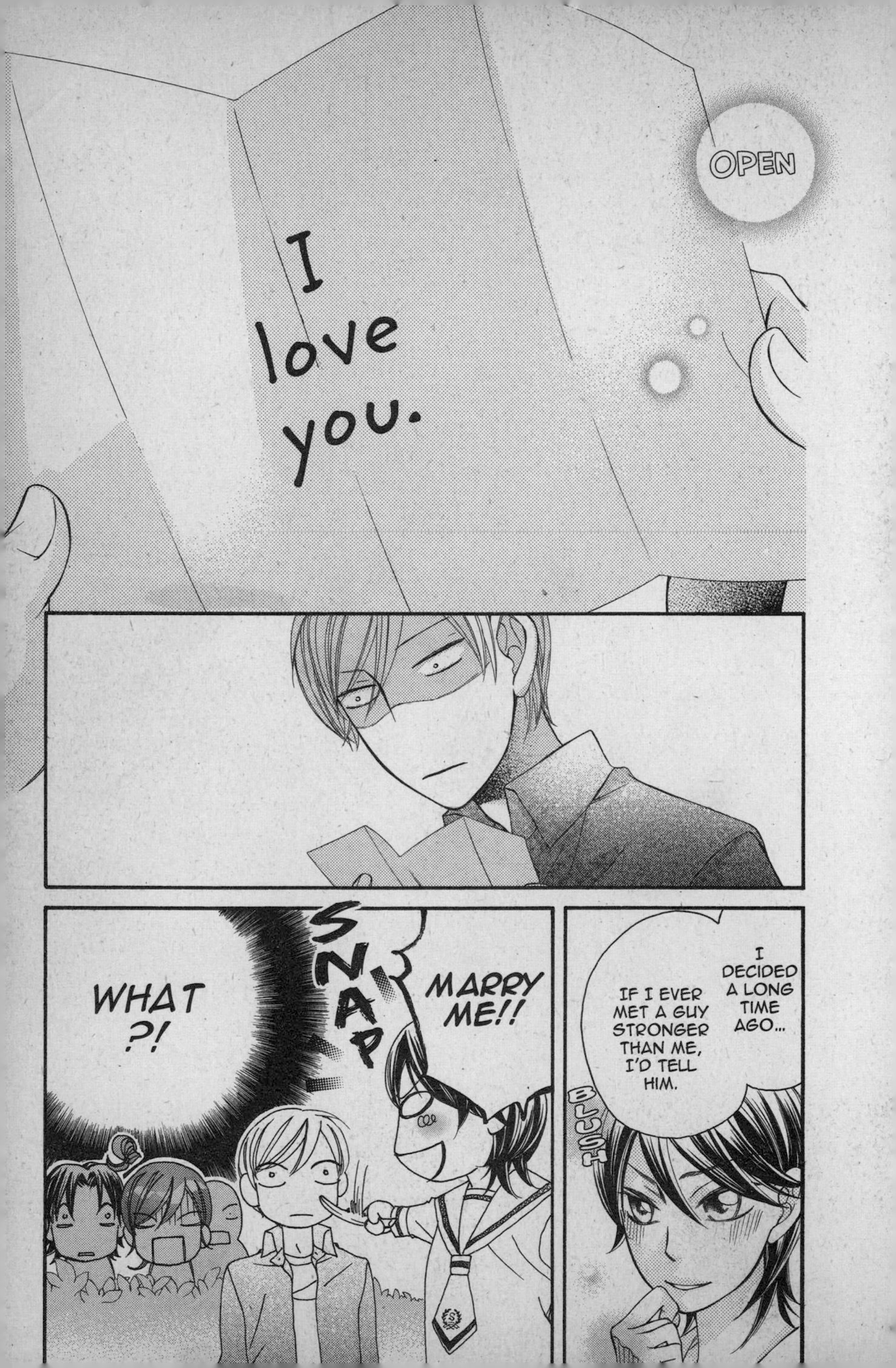
OPEN
I love you.
I DECIDED A LONG TIME AGO...
IF I EVER MET A GUY STRONGER THAN ME, I'D TELL HIM.
BLUSH
MARRY ME!!
SNAP
WHAT?!

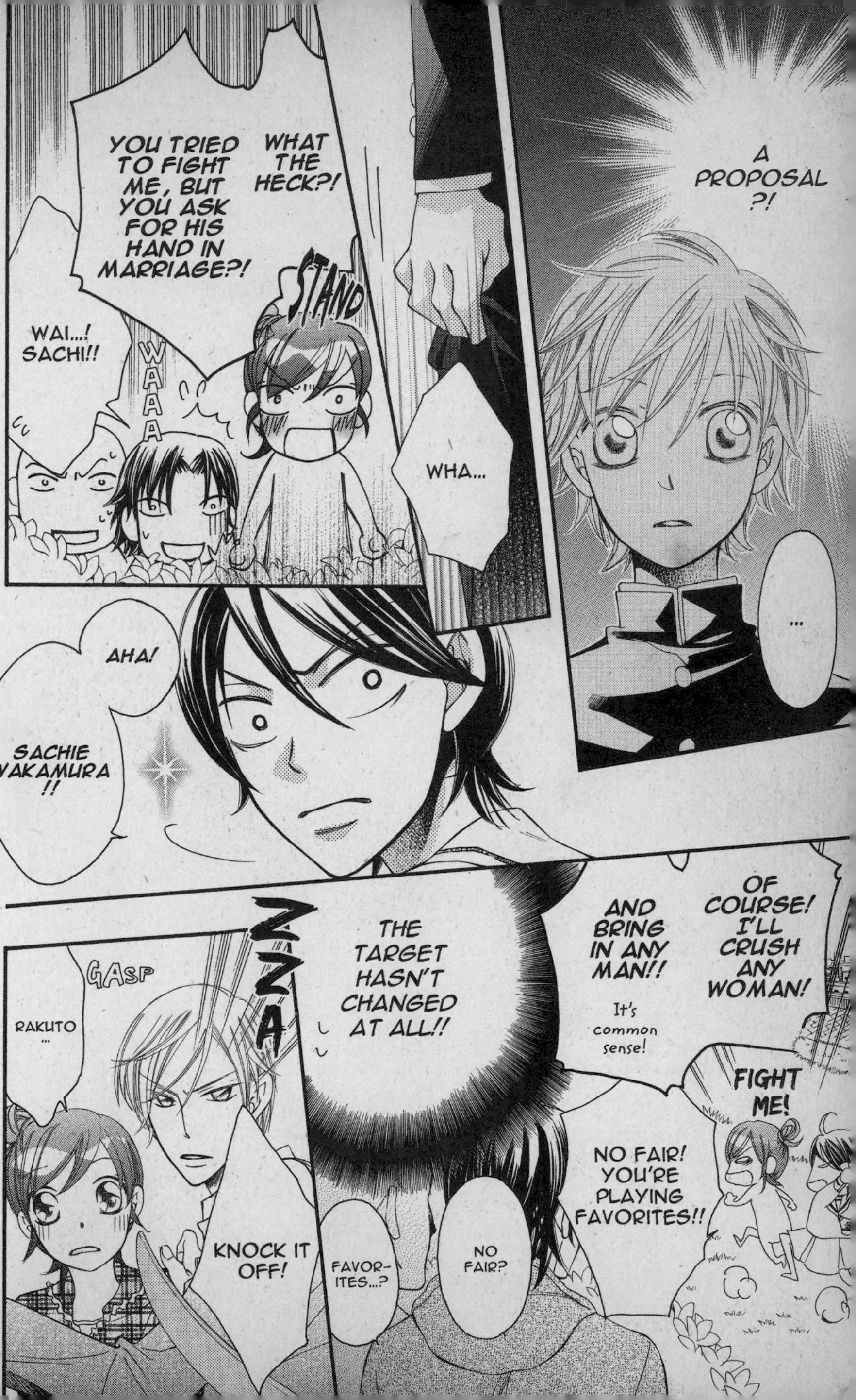
A PROPOSAL?!
...
WHA...
WHAT THE HECK?!
YOU TRIED TO FIGHT ME, BUT YOU ASK FOR HIS HAND IN MARRIAGE?!
STAND
WAI...! SACHI!!
WAAAA
AHA!
SACHIE WAKAMURA!!
OF COURSE! I'LL CRUSH ANY WOMAN!
AND BRING IN ANY MAN!!
It's common sense!
FIGHT ME!
NO FAIR! YOU'RE PLAYING FAVORITES!!
NO FAIR?
FAVOR-ITES...?
ZZZA
THE TARGET HASN'T CHANGED AT ALL!!
KNOCK IT OFF!
GASP
RAKUTO...

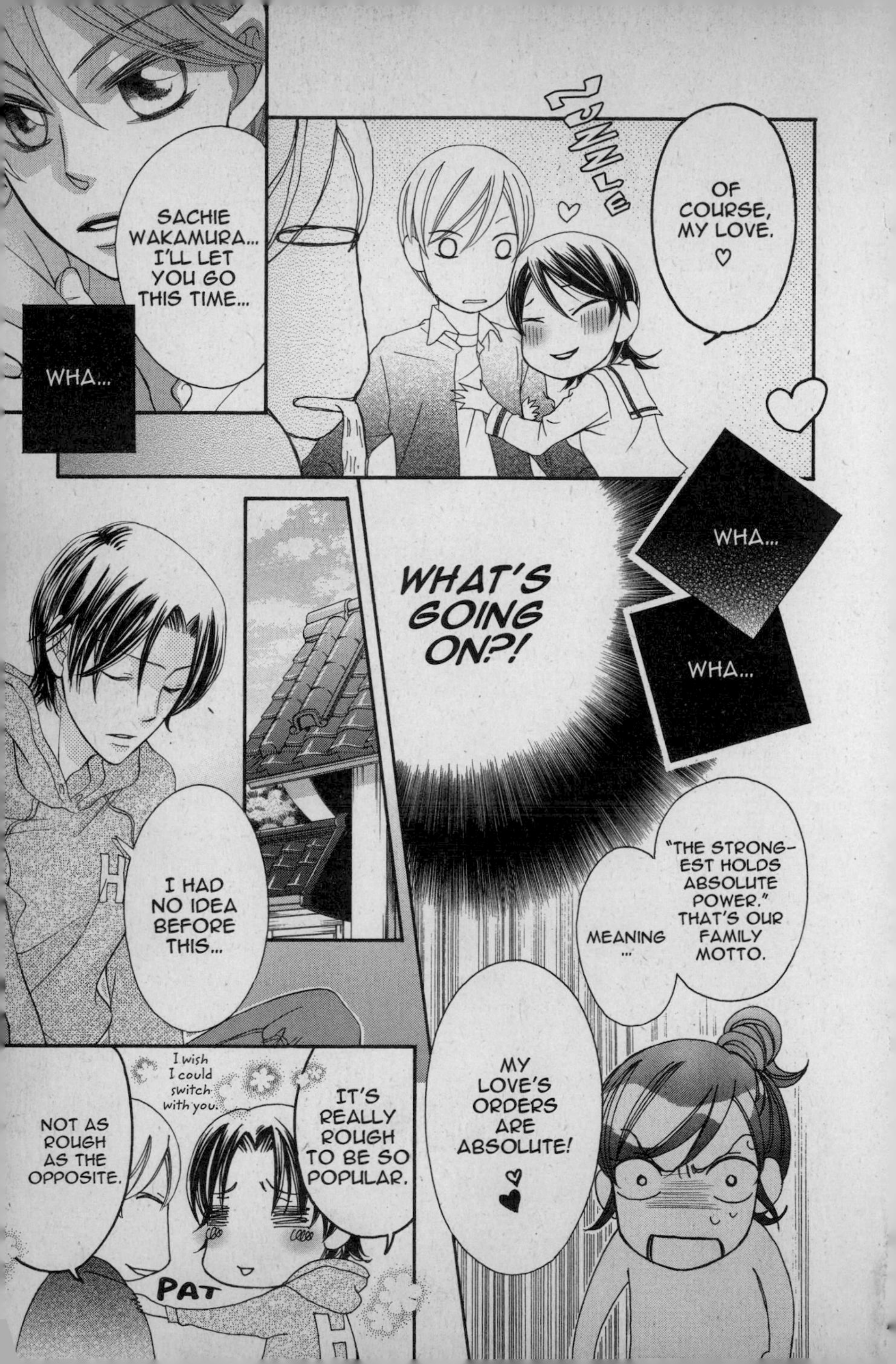
NUZZLE
OF COURSE, MY LOVE. ♡
SACHIE WAKAMURA... I'LL LET YOU GO THIS TIME...
WHA...
WHA...
WHA...
WHAT'S GOING ON?!
"THE STRONGEST HOLDS ABSOLUTE POWER." THAT'S OUR FAMILY MOTTO.
MEANING ...
MY LOVE'S ORDERS ARE ABSOLUTE! ♡
I HAD NO IDEA BEFORE THIS...
IT'S REALLY ROUGH TO BE SO POPULAR.
I wish I could switch with you.
NOT AS ROUGH AS THE OPPOSITE.
PAT

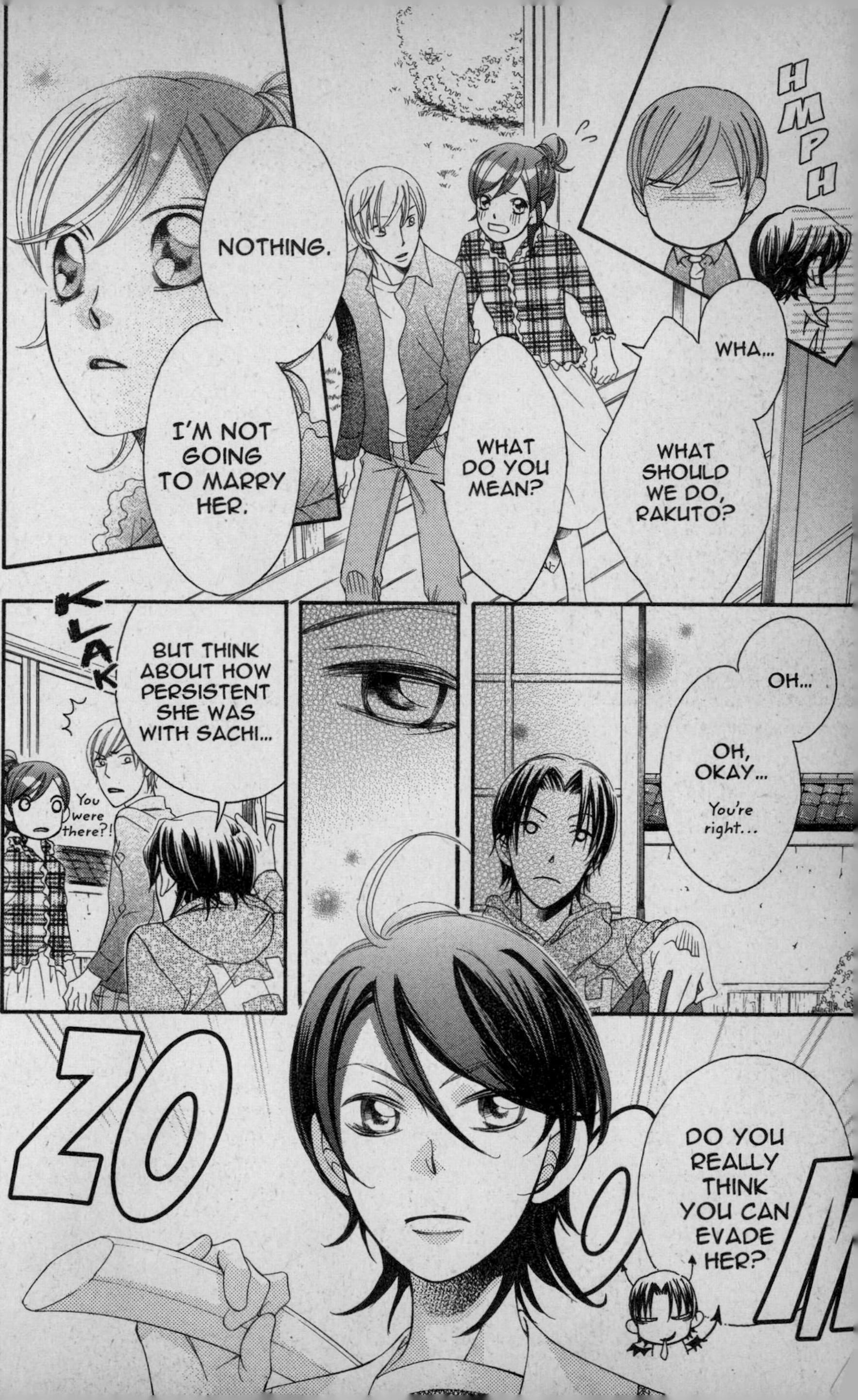
HMPH
WHA...
WHAT SHOULD WE DO, RAKUTO?
WHAT DO YOU MEAN?
NOTHING.
I'M NOT GOING TO MARRY HER.
OH...
OH, OKAY...
You're right...
KLAK
BUT THINK ABOUT HOW PERSISTENT SHE WAS WITH SACHI...
You were there?!
ZOOM
DO YOU REALLY THINK YOU CAN EVADE HER?

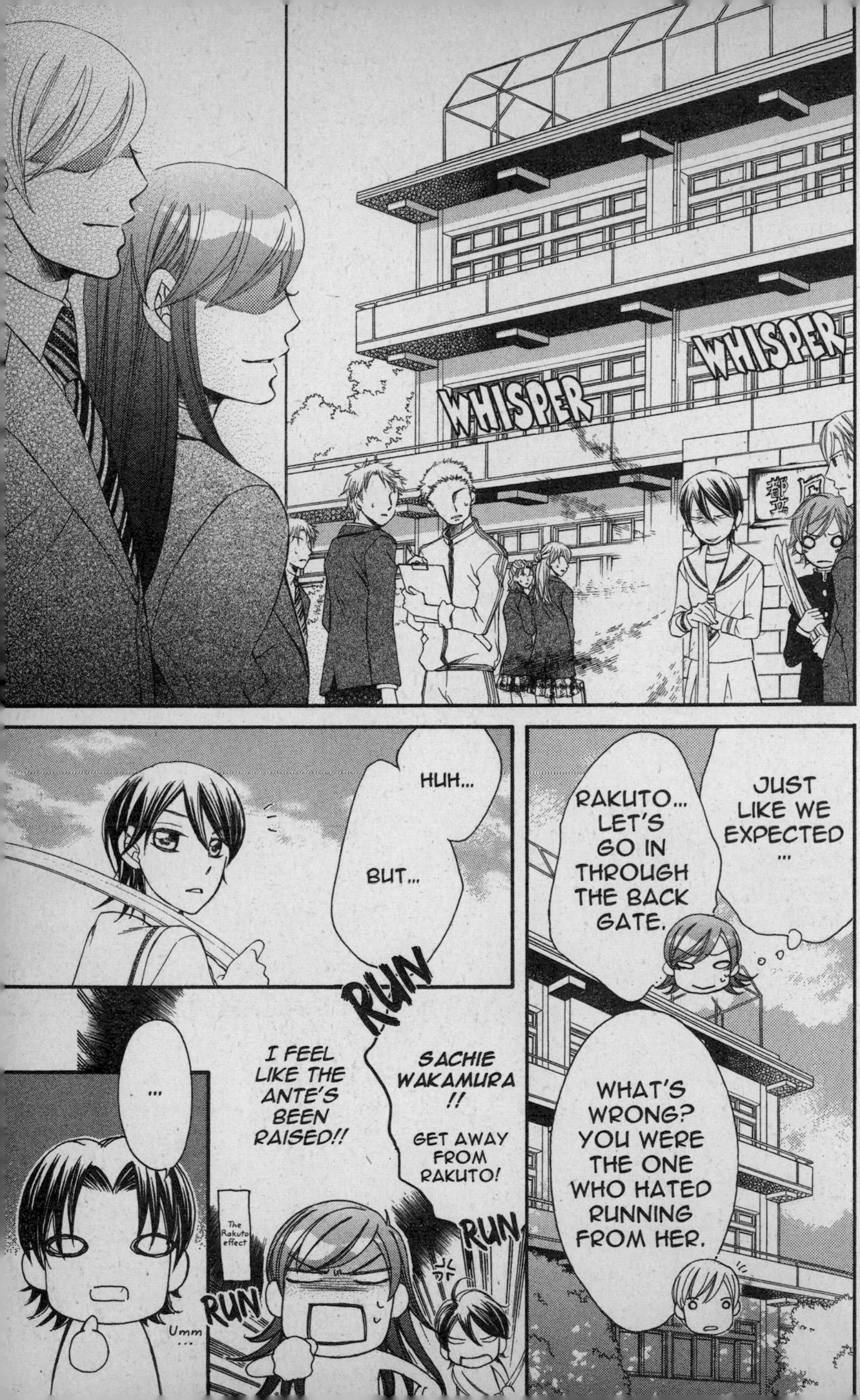
WHISPER
WHISPER
JUST LIKE WE EXPECTED ...
RAKUTO... LET'S GO IN THROUGH THE BACK GATE.
HUH...
BUT...
WHAT'S WRONG? YOU WERE THE ONE WHO HATED RUNNING FROM HER.
RUN
SACHIE WAKAMURA!!
GET AWAY FROM RAKUTO!
RUN
I FEEL LIKE THE ANTE'S BEEN RAISED!!
...
The Rakuto effect
RUN
Umm...

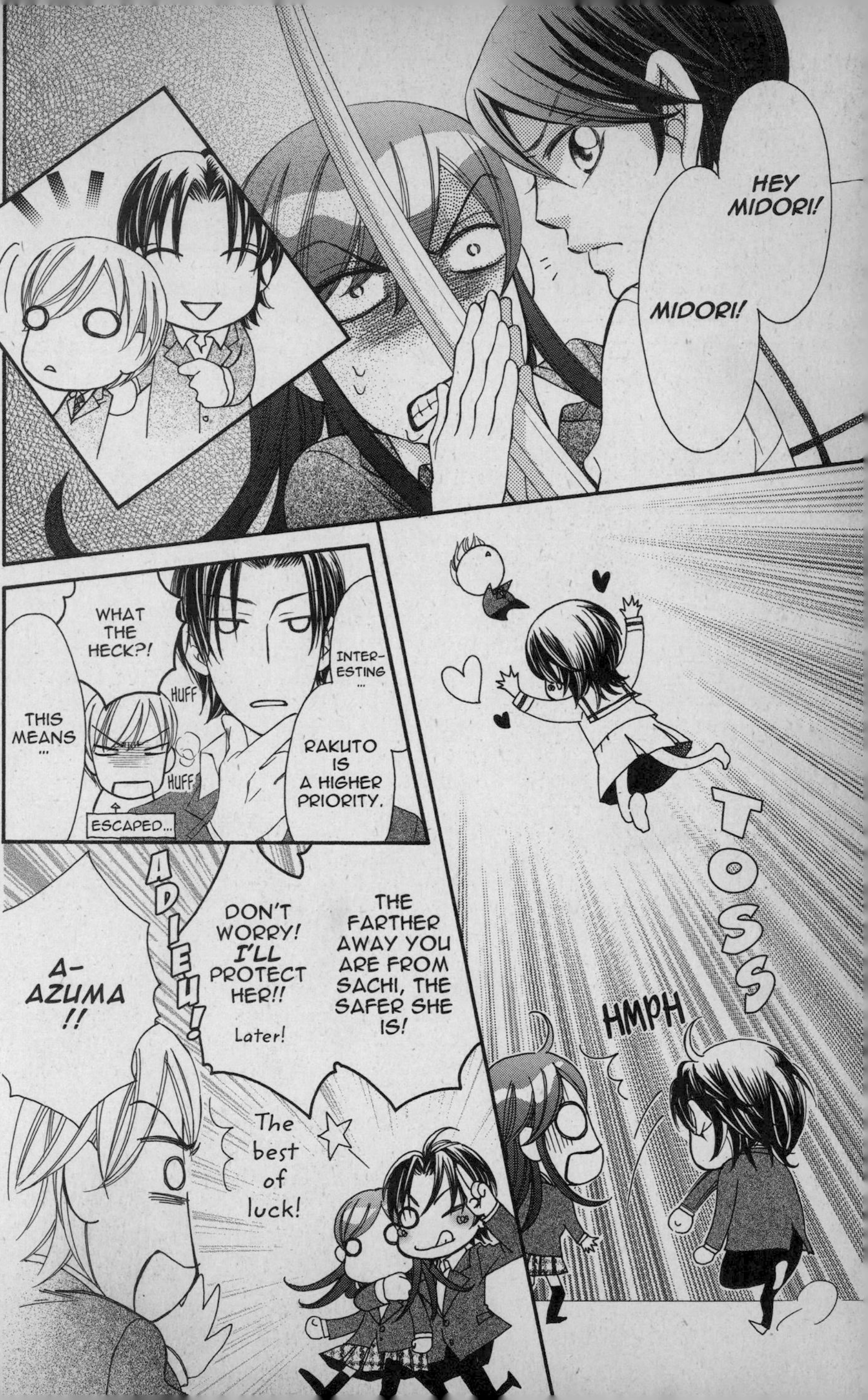
HEY MIDORI!
MIDORI!
TOSS
HMPH
INTER-ESTING ...
RAKUTO IS A HIGHER PRIORITY.
WHAT THE HECK?!
HUFF
HUFF
THIS MEANS ...
ESCAPED...
THE FARTHER AWAY YOU ARE FROM SACHI, THE SAFER SHE IS!
DON'T WORRY! I'LL PROTECT HER!!
Later!
ADIEU!
A-AZUMA!!
The best of luck!

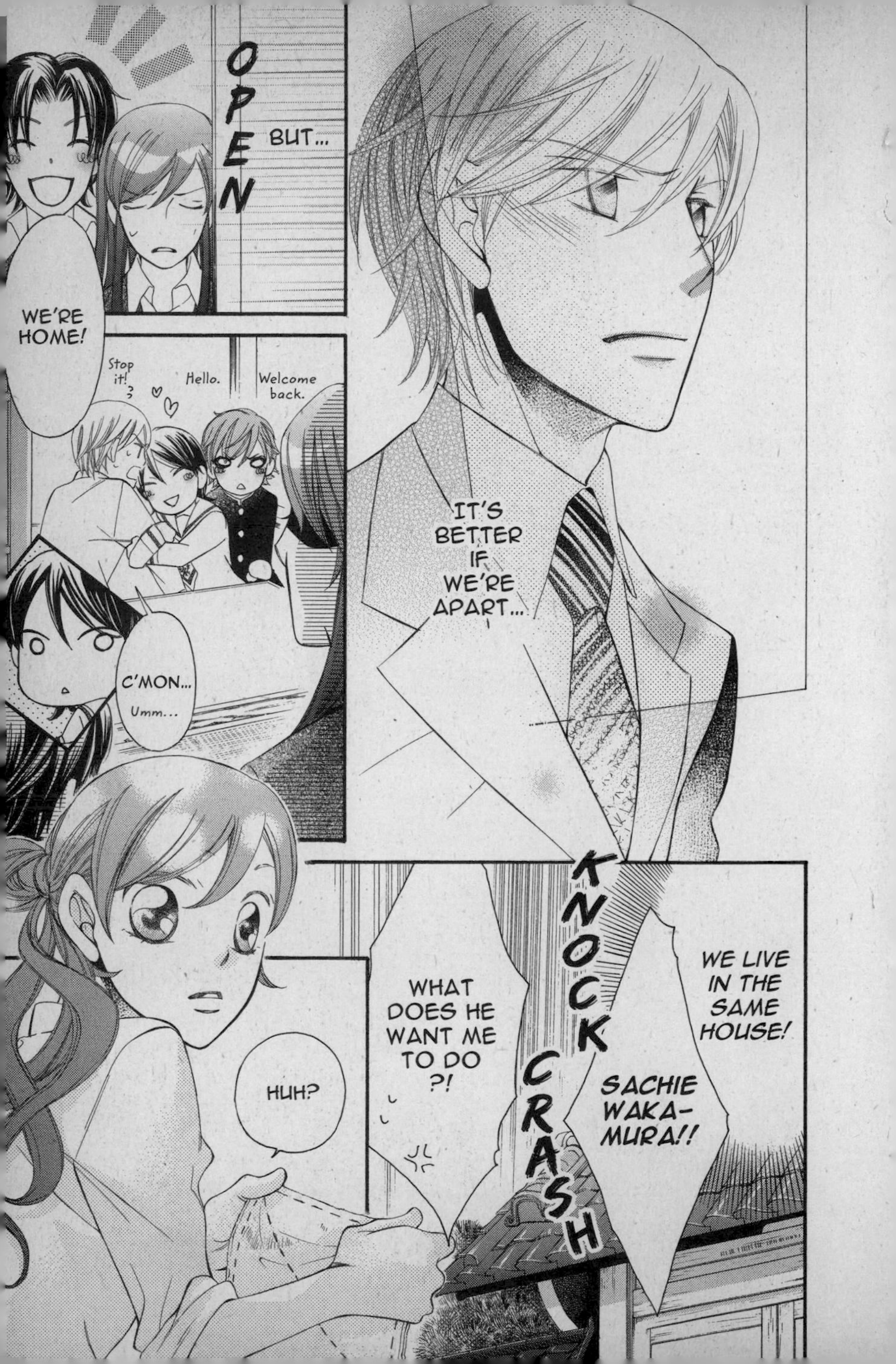
IT'S BETTER IF WE'RE APART...
OPEN
BUT...
WE'RE HOME!
Welcome back.
Hello.
Stop it!
C'MON...
Umm...
WE LIVE IN THE SAME HOUSE!
SACHIE WAKAMURA!!
KNOCK
CRASH
WHAT DOES HE WANT ME TO DO ?!
HUH?

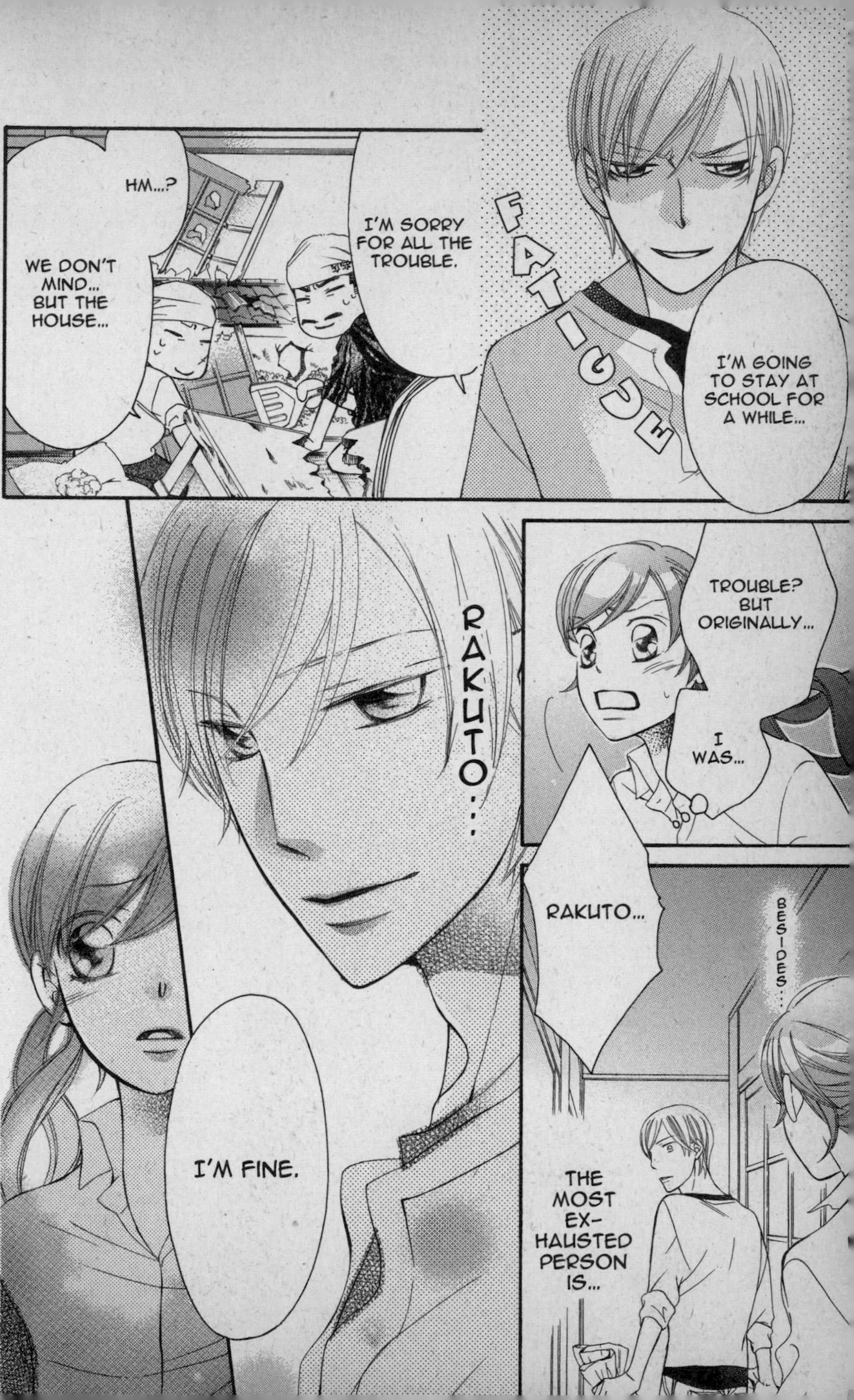
FATIGUE
I'M GOING TO STAY AT SCHOOL FOR A WHILE...
I'M SORRY FOR ALL THE TROUBLE.
HM...?
WE DON'T MIND... BUT THE HOUSE...
TROUBLE? BUT ORIGINALLY...
I WAS...
RAKUTO...
BESIDES...
THE MOST EX-HAUSTED PERSON IS...
RAKUTO...
I'M FINE.

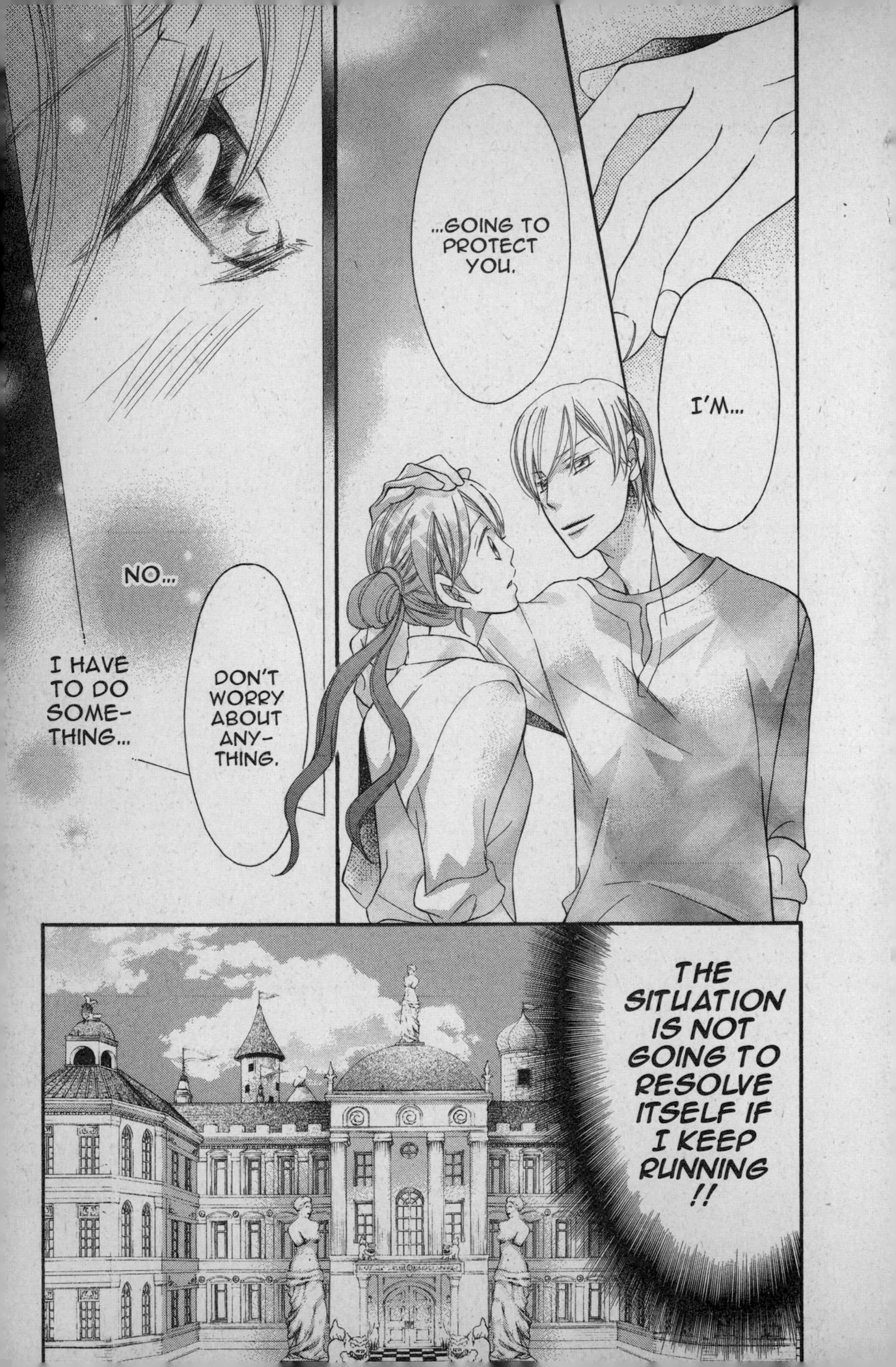
I'M...
...GOING TO PROTECT YOU.
DON'T WORRY ABOUT ANYTHING.
NO...
I HAVE TO DO SOMETHING...
THE SITUATION IS NOT GOING TO RESOLVE ITSELF IF I KEEP RUNNING!!

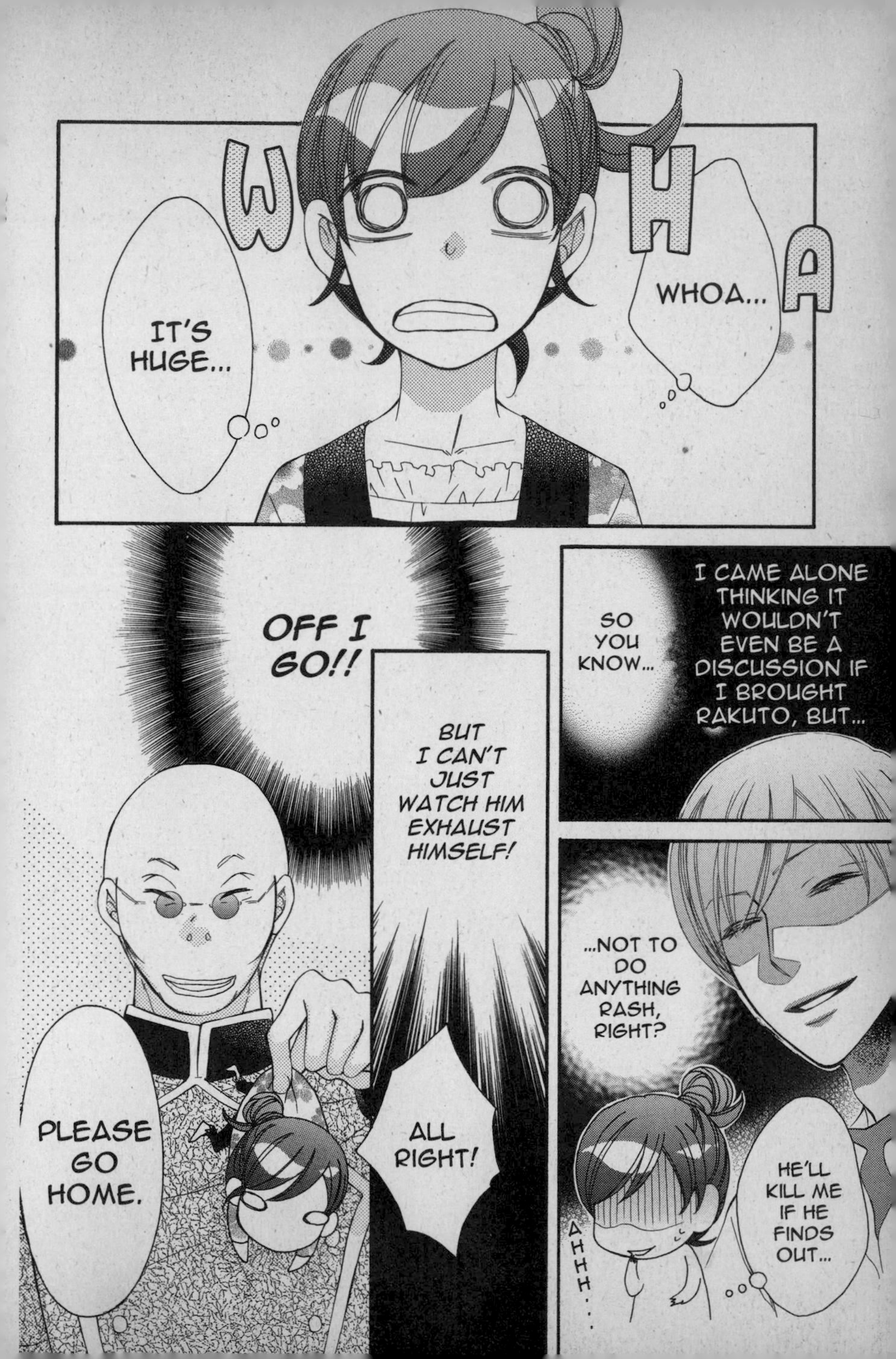
WHOA...
WHA
IT'S HUGE...
I CAME ALONE THINKING IT WOULDN'T EVEN BE A DISCUSSION IF I BROUGHT RAKUTO, BUT...
SO YOU KNOW...
...NOT TO DO ANYTHING RASH, RIGHT?
HE'LL KILL ME IF HE FINDS OUT...
AHHH...
OFF I GO!!
BUT I CAN'T JUST WATCH HIM EXHAUST HIMSELF!
ALL RIGHT!
PLEASE GO HOME.

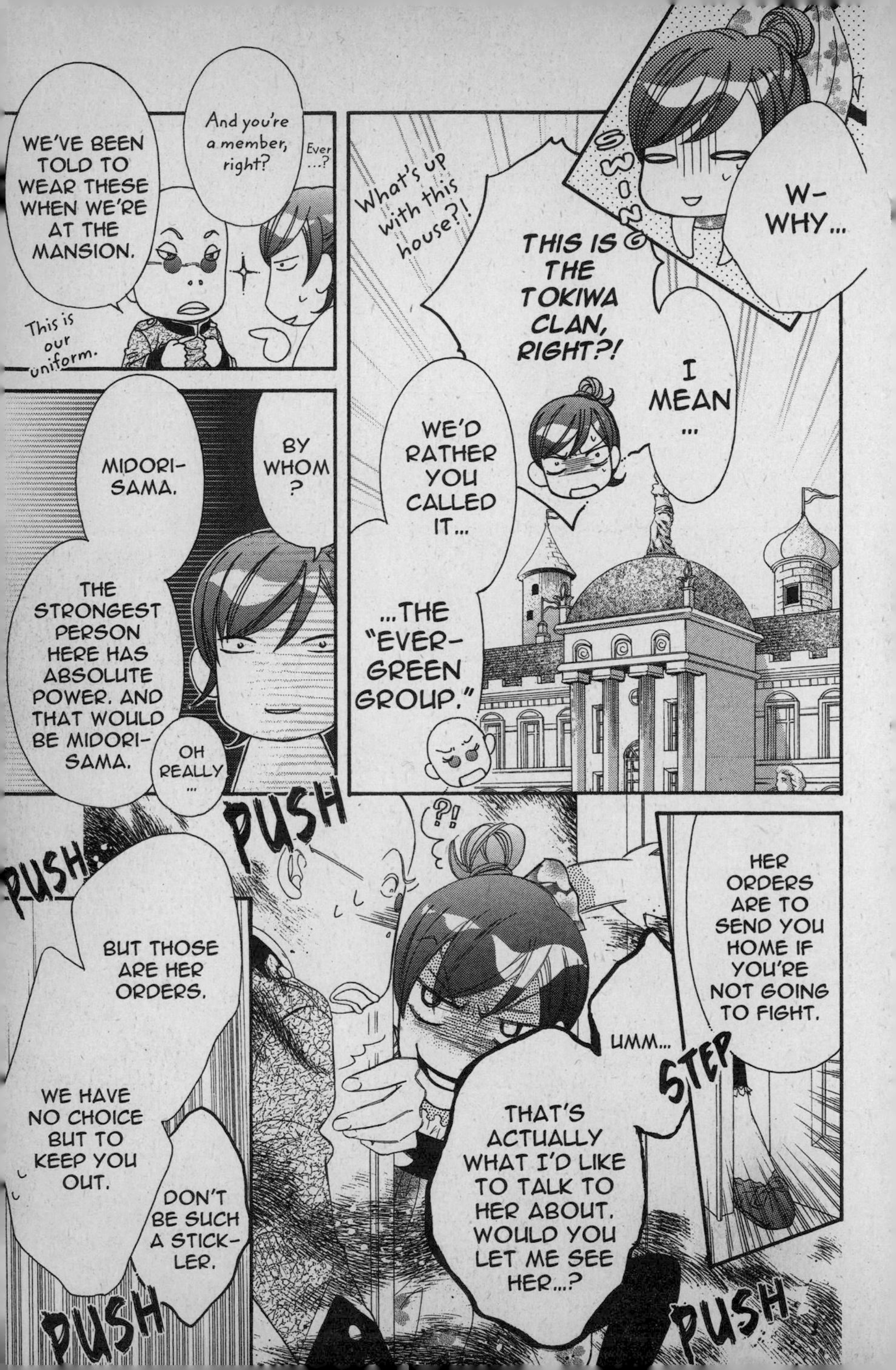
SWOON
W-WHY...
I MEAN...
THIS IS THE TOKIWA CLAN, RIGHT?!
What's up with this house?!
WE'D RATHER YOU CALLED IT...
...THE "EVER-GREEN GROUP."
And you're a member, right?
Ever...?
WE'VE BEEN TOLD TO WEAR THESE WHEN WE'RE AT THE MANSION.
This is our uniform.
BY WHOM?
MIDORI-SAMA.
THE STRONGEST PERSON HERE HAS ABSOLUTE POWER. AND THAT WOULD BE MIDORI-SAMA.
OH REALLY...
HER ORDERS ARE TO SEND YOU HOME IF YOU'RE NOT GOING TO FIGHT.
STEP
UMM...
THAT'S ACTUALLY WHAT I'D LIKE TO TALK TO HER ABOUT. WOULD YOU LET ME SEE HER...?
?!
PUSH
PUSH
PUSH
BUT THOSE ARE HER ORDERS.
WE HAVE NO CHOICE BUT TO KEEP YOU OUT.
DON'T BE SUCH A STICKLER.
PUSH

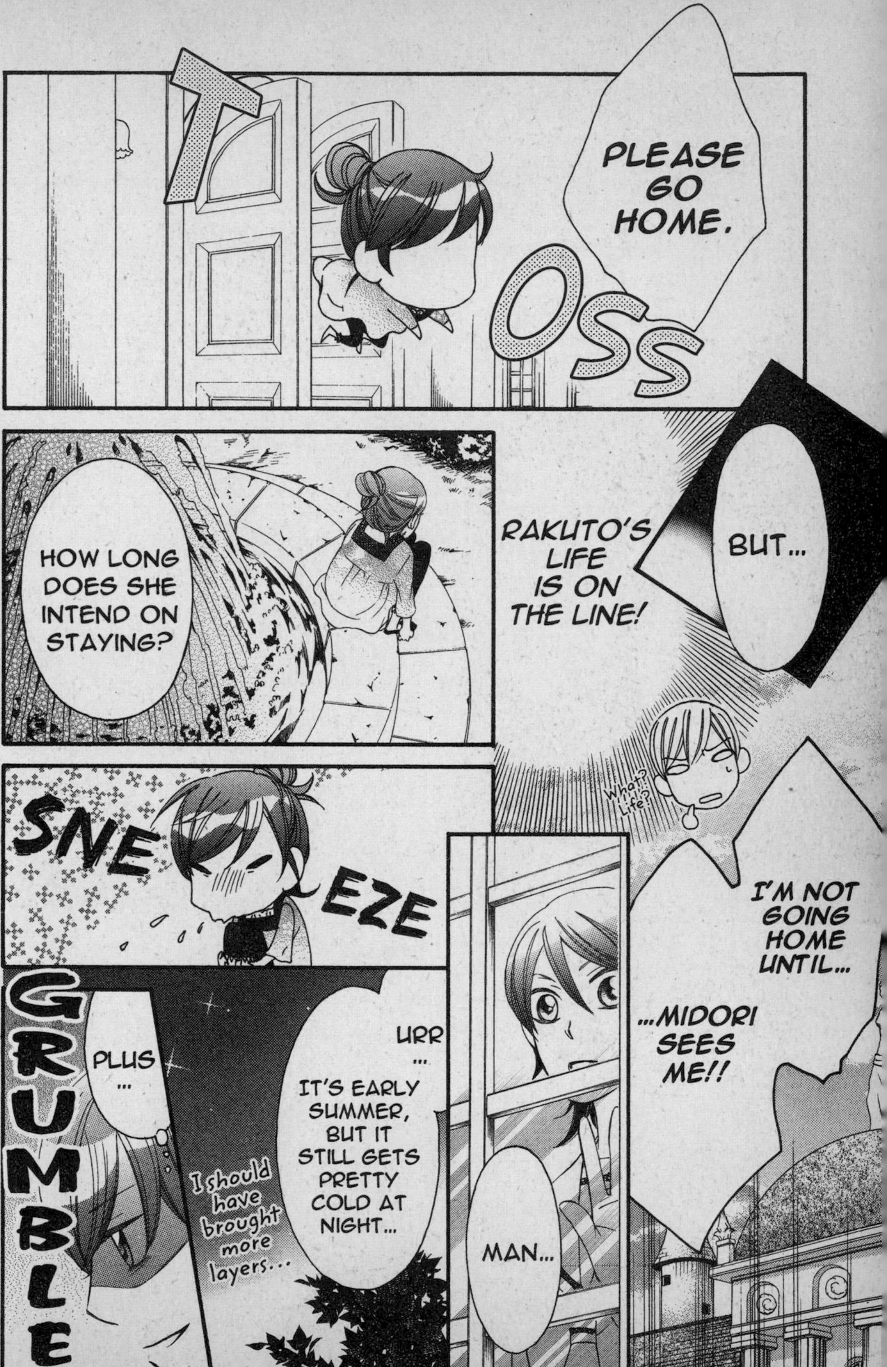
PLEASE GO HOME.
T
OSS
BUT...
RAKUTO'S LIFE IS ON THE LINE!
What? Life?
HOW LONG DOES SHE INTEND ON STAYING?
I'M NOT GOING HOME UNTIL...
...MIDORI SEES ME!!
MAN...
SNE
EZE
URR...
IT'S EARLY SUMMER, BUT IT STILL GETS PRETTY COLD AT NIGHT...
PLUS...
I should have brought more layers...
GRUMBLE

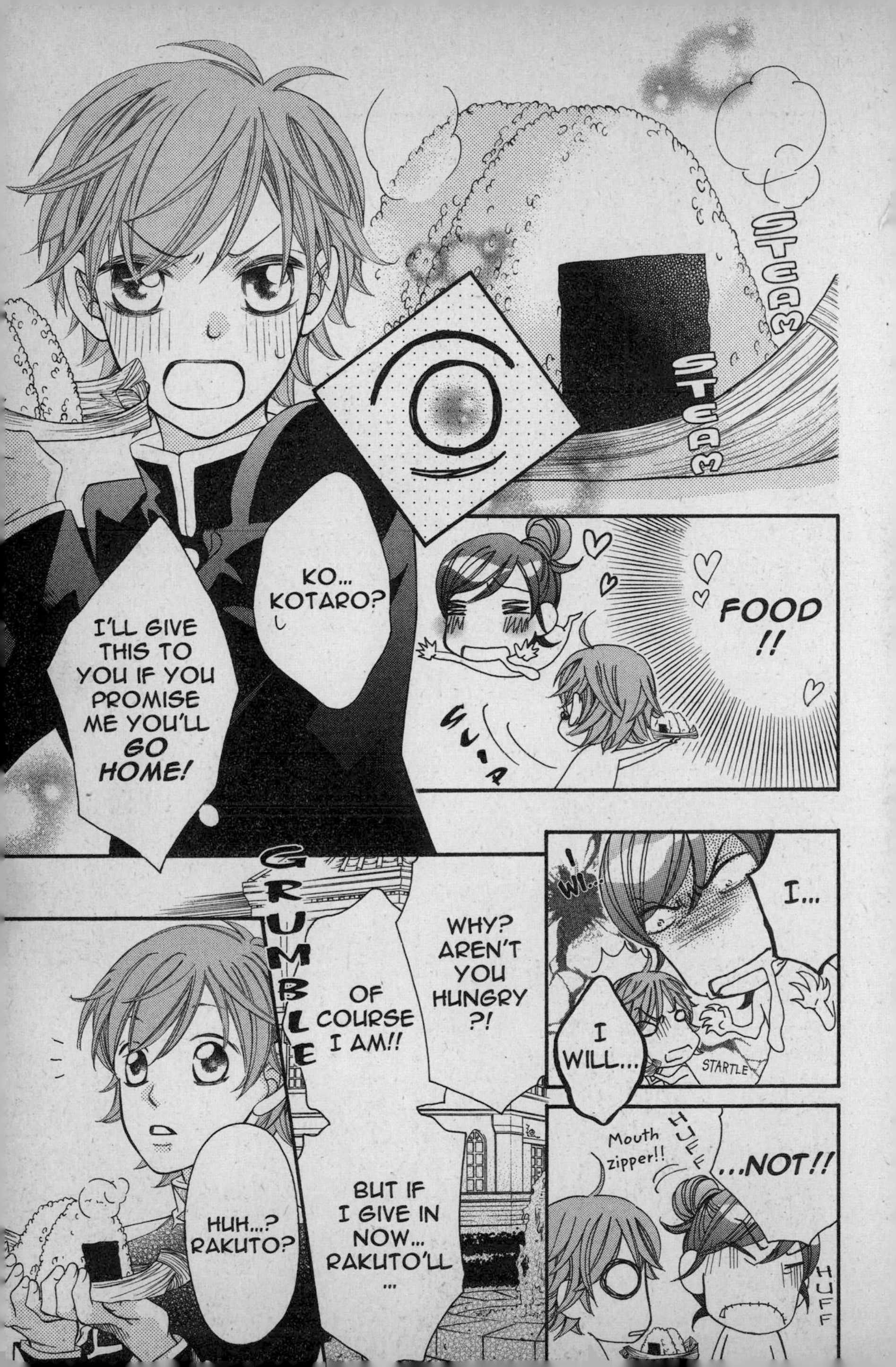
STEAM
STEAM
FOOD!!
KO... KOTARO?
I'LL GIVE THIS TO YOU IF YOU PROMISE ME YOU'LL GO HOME!
I...
I WI...
I WILL...
STARTLE
...NOT!!
Mouth zipper!!
HUFF
HUFF
WHY? AREN'T YOU HUNGRY?!
GRUMBLE
OF COURSE I AM!!
BUT IF I GIVE IN NOW... RAKUTO'LL...
HUH...? RAKUTO?

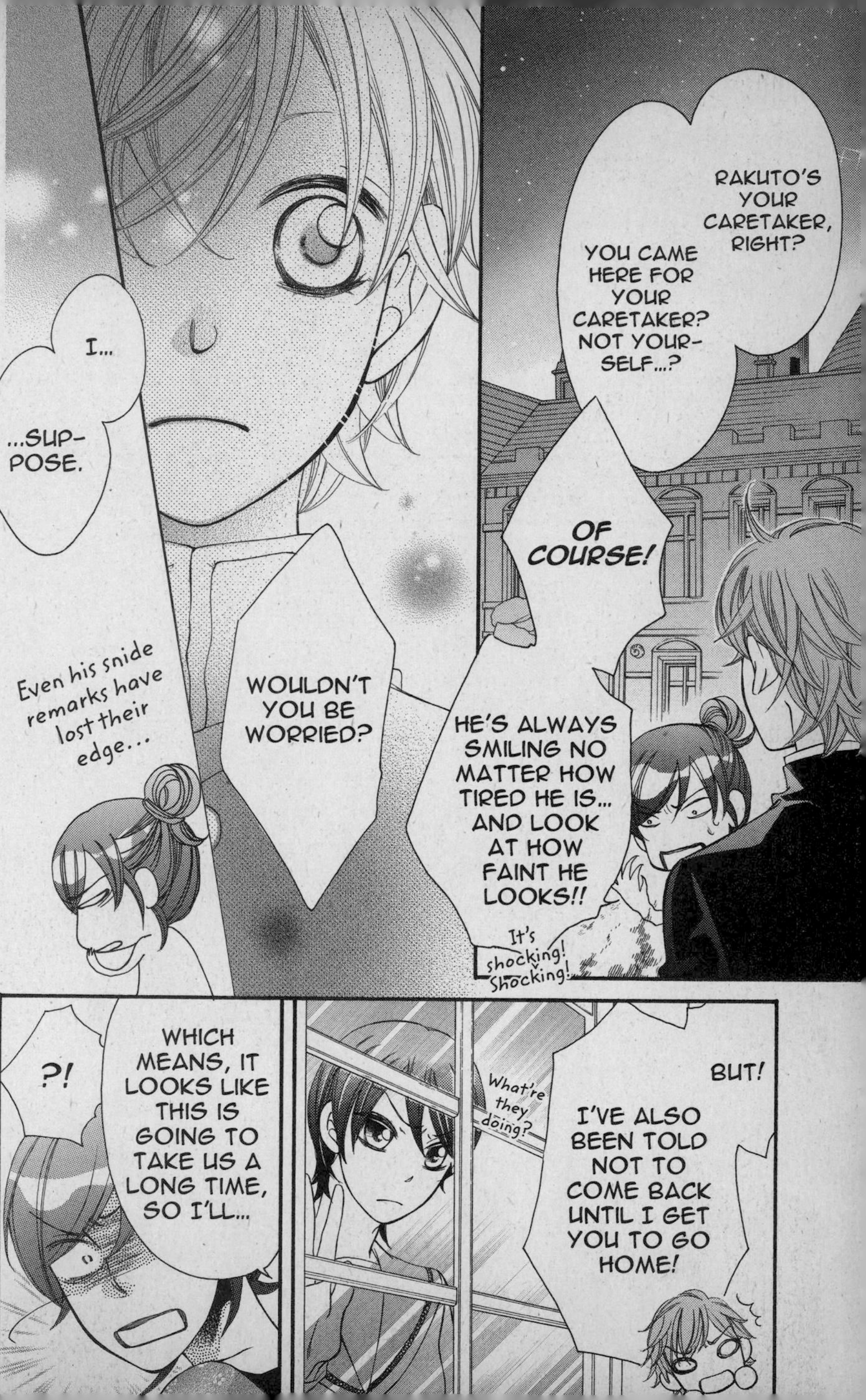

RAKUTO'S YOUR CARETAKER, RIGHT?
YOU CAME HERE FOR YOUR CARETAKER? NOT YOURSELF...?
OF COURSE!
HE'S ALWAYS SMILING NO MATTER HOW TIRED HE IS... AND LOOK AT HOW FAINT HE LOOKS!!
It's shocking! Shocking!
WOULDN'T YOU BE WORRIED?
I...
...SUP-POSE.
Even his snide remarks have lost their edge...
BUT!
I'VE ALSO BEEN TOLD NOT TO COME BACK UNTIL I GET YOU TO GO HOME!
What're they doing?
WHICH MEANS, IT LOOKS LIKE THIS IS GOING TO TAKE US A LONG TIME, SO I'LL...
?!

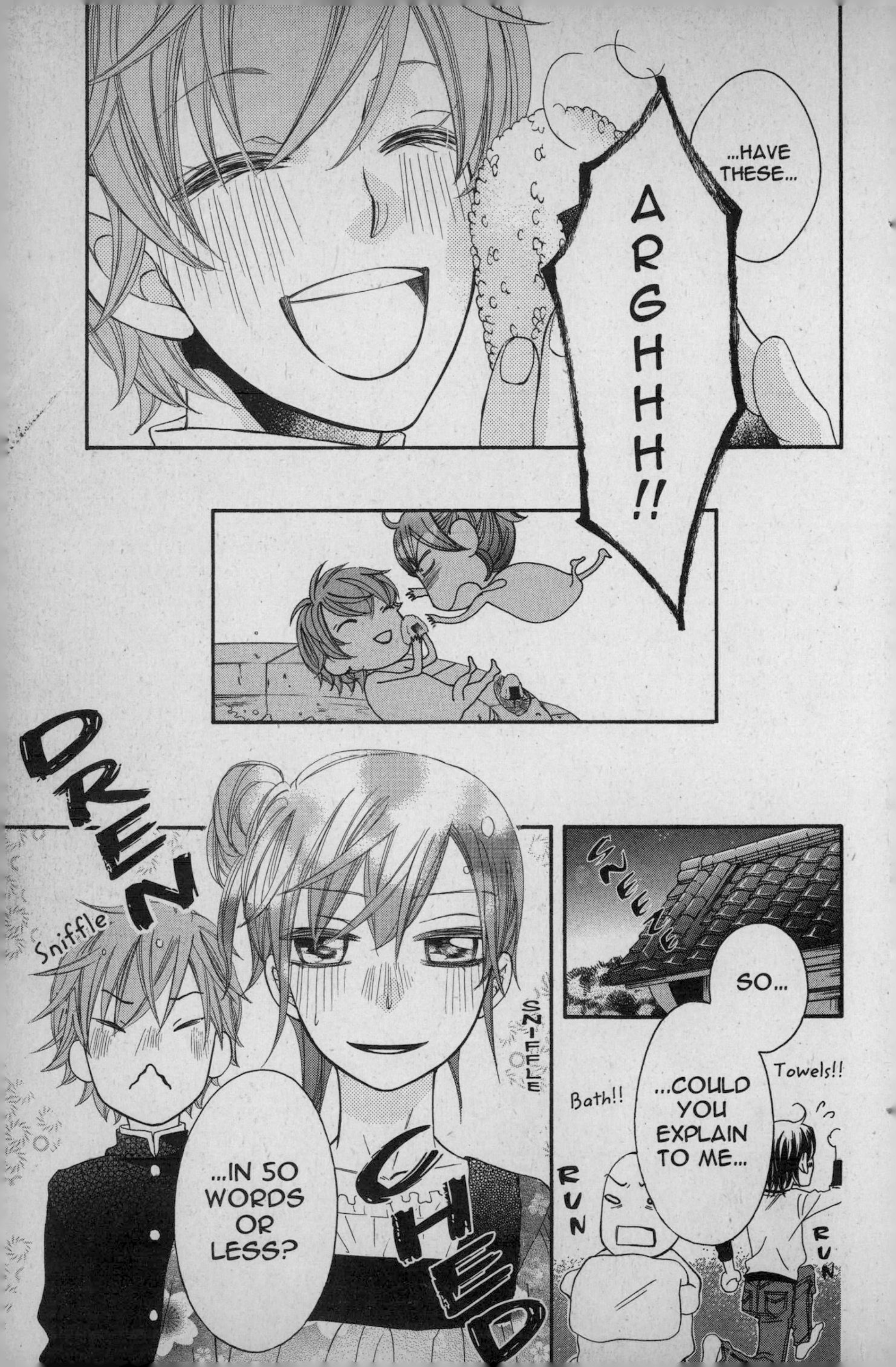
...HAVE THESE...
ARGHHH!!
SNEEZE
SO...
...COULD YOU EXPLAIN TO ME...
Towels!!
Bath!!
RUN
RUN
DRENCHED
SNIFFLE
Sniffle
...IN 50 WORDS OR LESS?

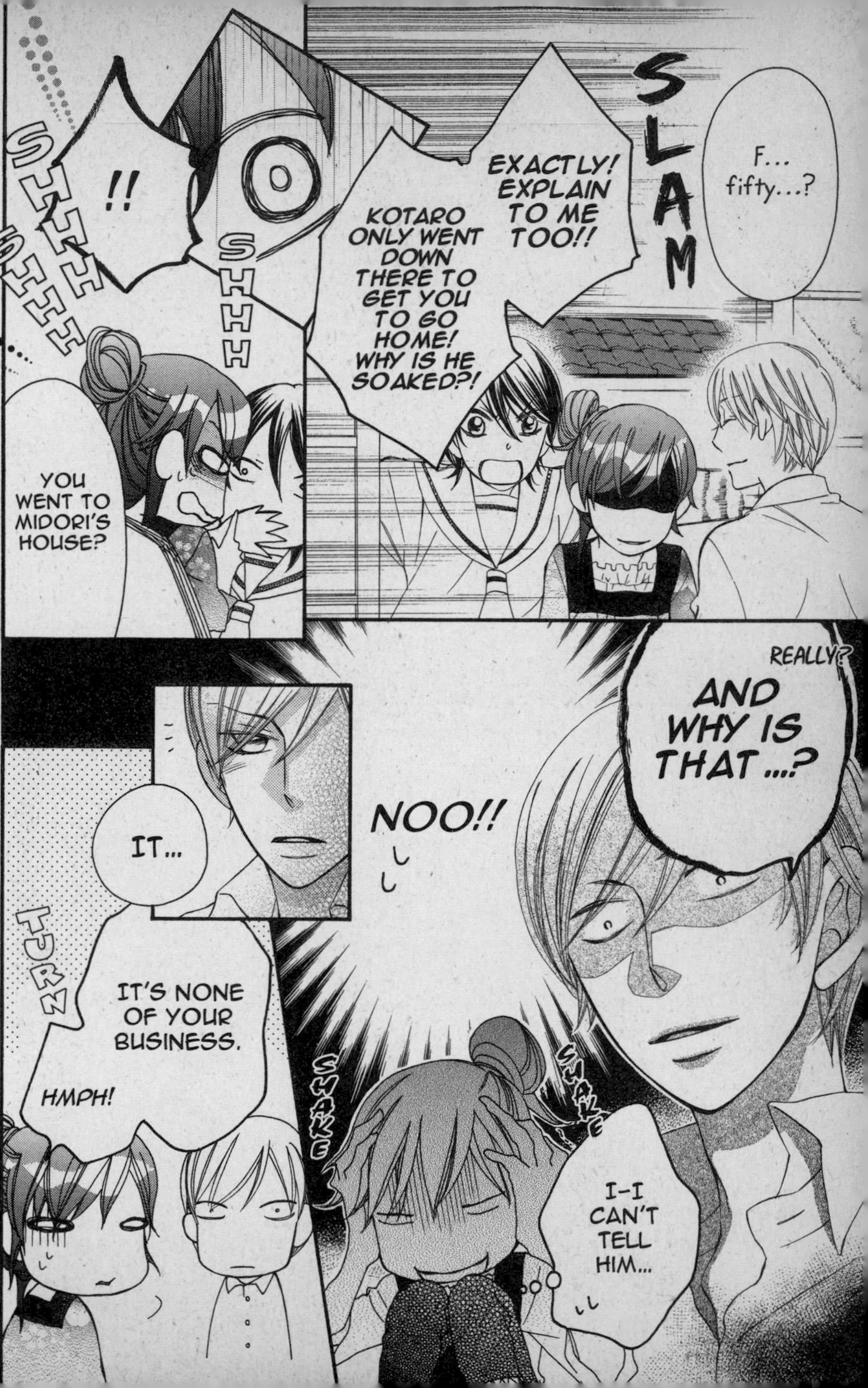
F... fifty...?
SLAM
EXACTLY! EXPLAIN TO ME TOO!!
KOTARO ONLY WENT DOWN THERE TO GET YOU TO GO HOME! WHY IS HE SOAKED?!
!!
SHHHH
SHHHH
SHHHH
YOU WENT TO MIDORI'S HOUSE?
REALLY?
AND WHY IS THAT...?
NOO!!
SHAKE
SHAKE
I-I CAN'T TELL HIM...
IT...
TURN
IT'S NONE OF YOUR BUSINESS.
HMPH!

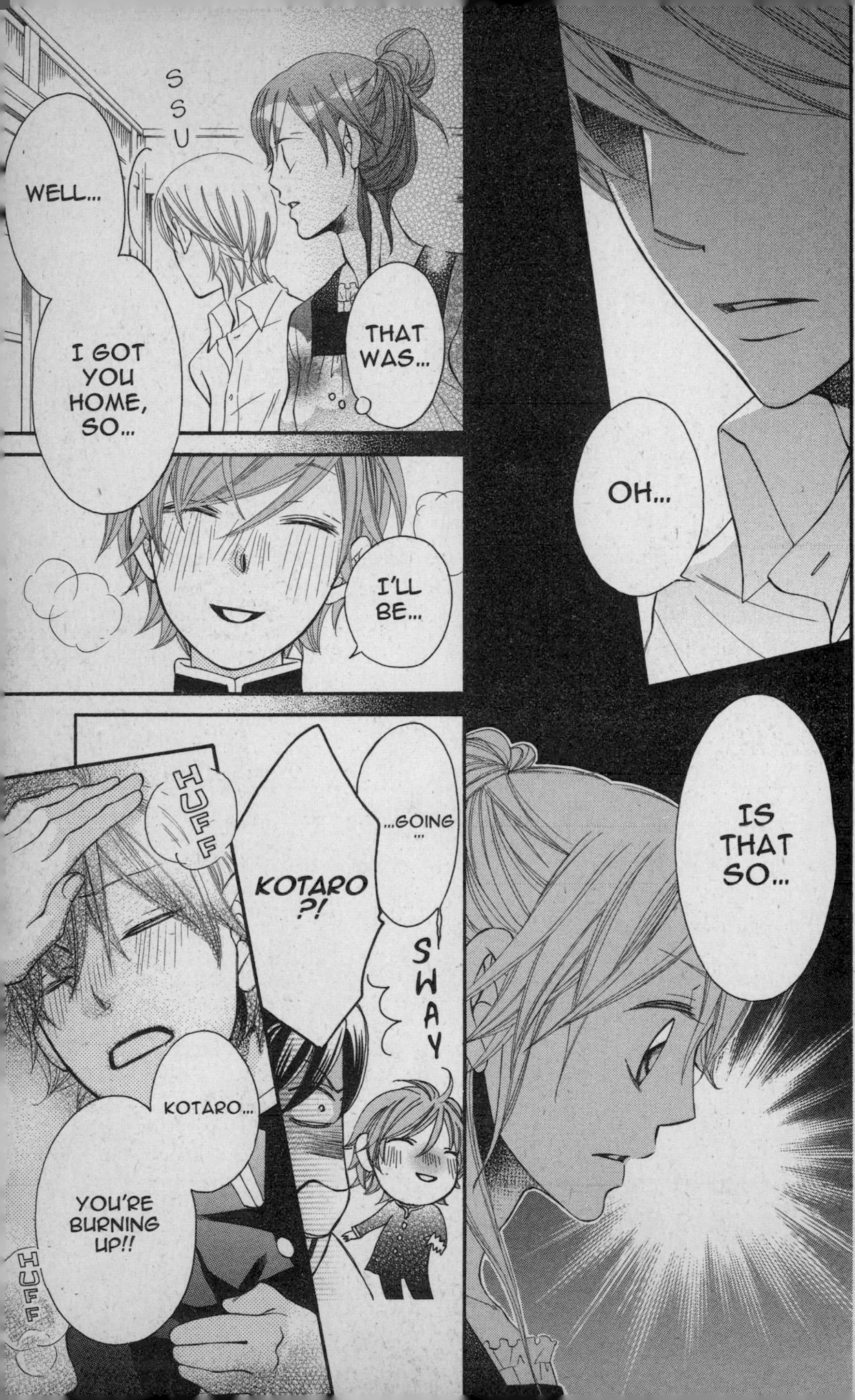

OH...
SSU
WELL...
I GOT YOU HOME, SO...
THAT WAS...
I'LL BE...
IS THAT SO...
...GOING...
HUFF
KOTARO?!
SWAY
KOTARO...
YOU'RE BURNING UP!!
HUFF

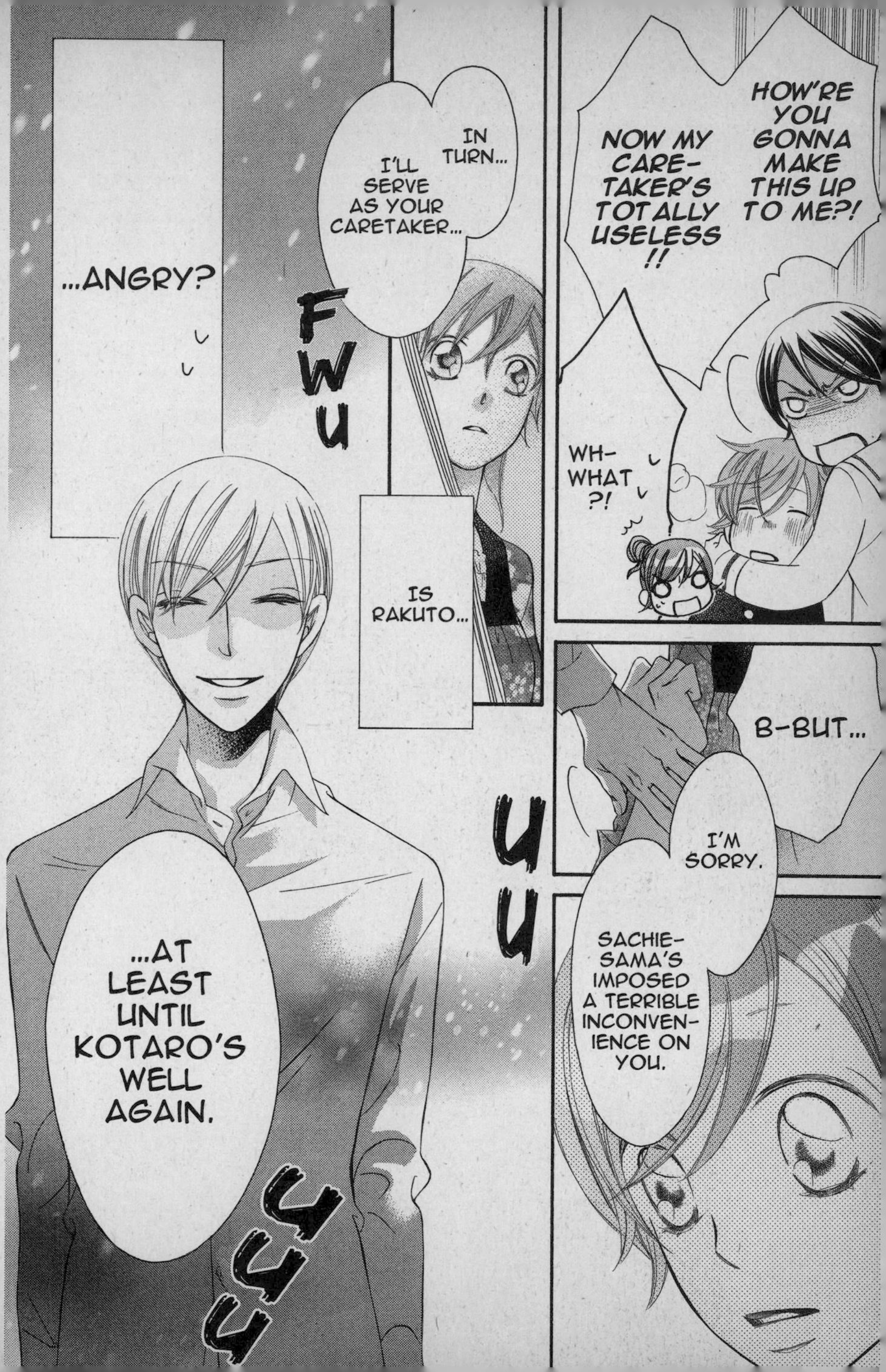
HOW'RE YOU GONNA MAKE THIS UP TO ME?!
NOW MY CARE-TAKER'S TOTALLY USELESS!!
WH-WHAT?!
B-BUT...
I'M SORRY.
SACHIE-SAMA'S IMPOSED A TERRIBLE INCONVEN-IENCE ON YOU.
IN TURN...
I'LL SERVE AS YOUR CARETAKER...
FWU
IS RAKUTO...
...ANGRY?
UU
...AT LEAST UNTIL KOTARO'S WELL AGAIN.
UUU

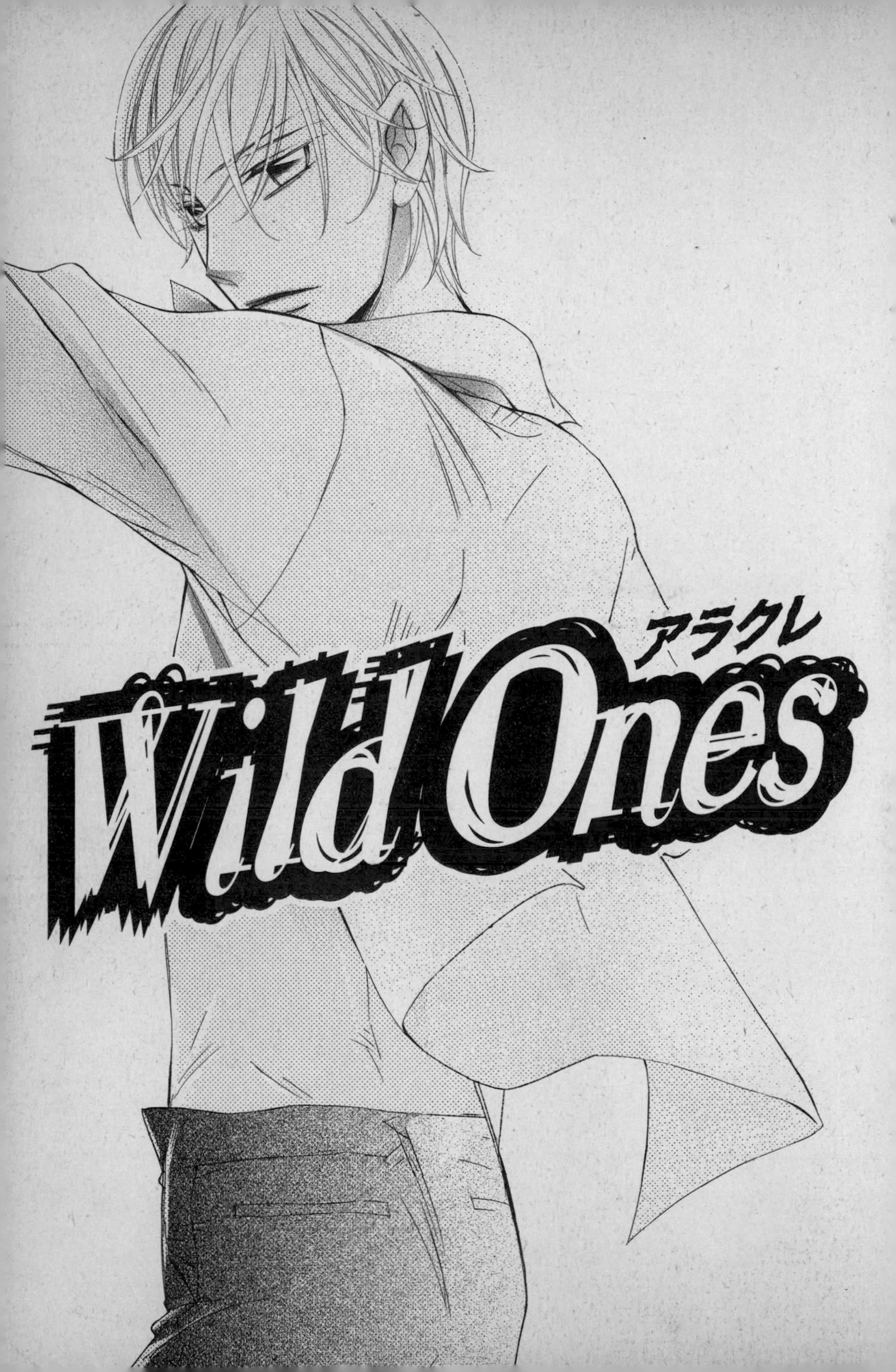
アラクレ
Wild Ones

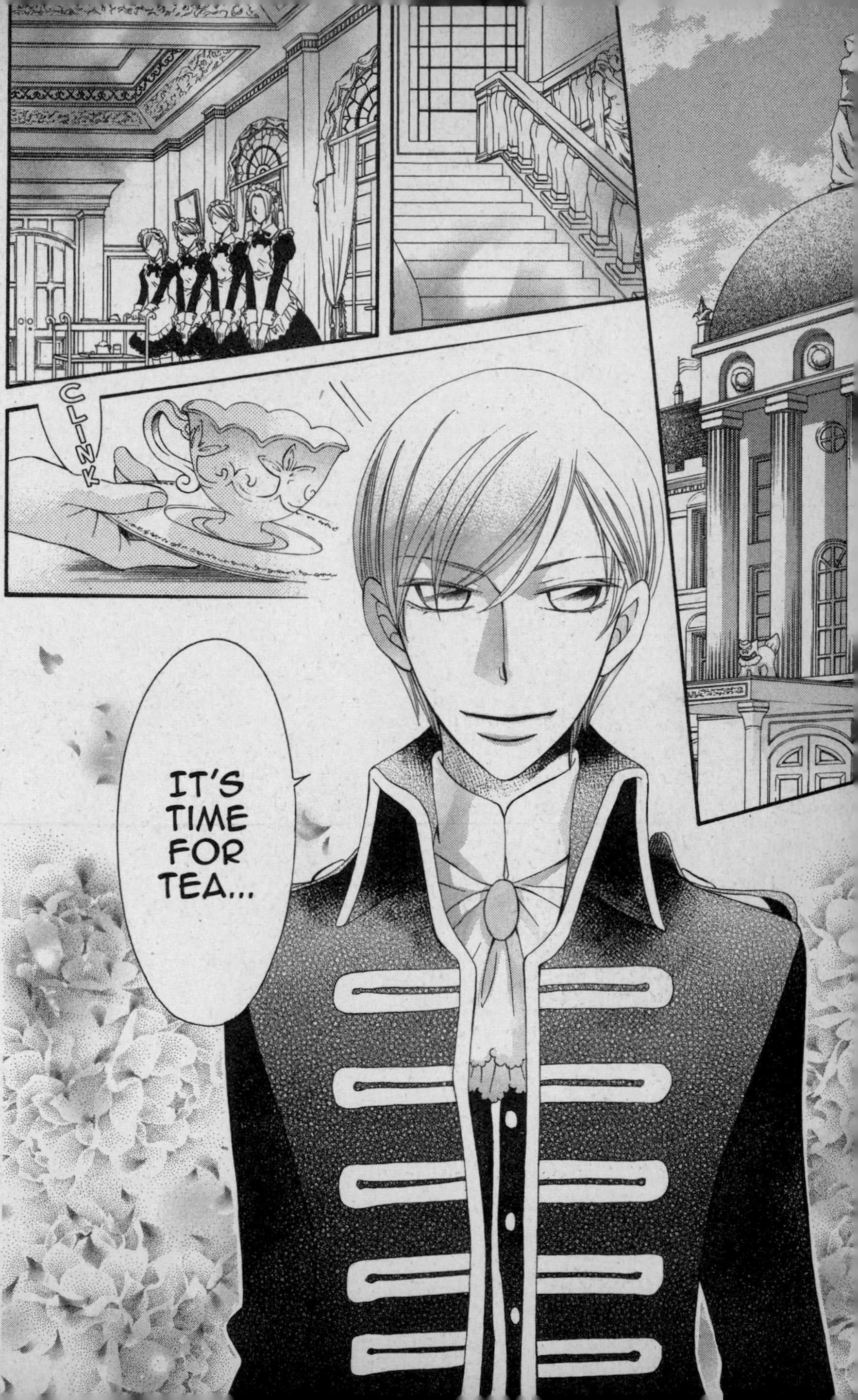
CLINK
IT'S TIME FOR TEA...

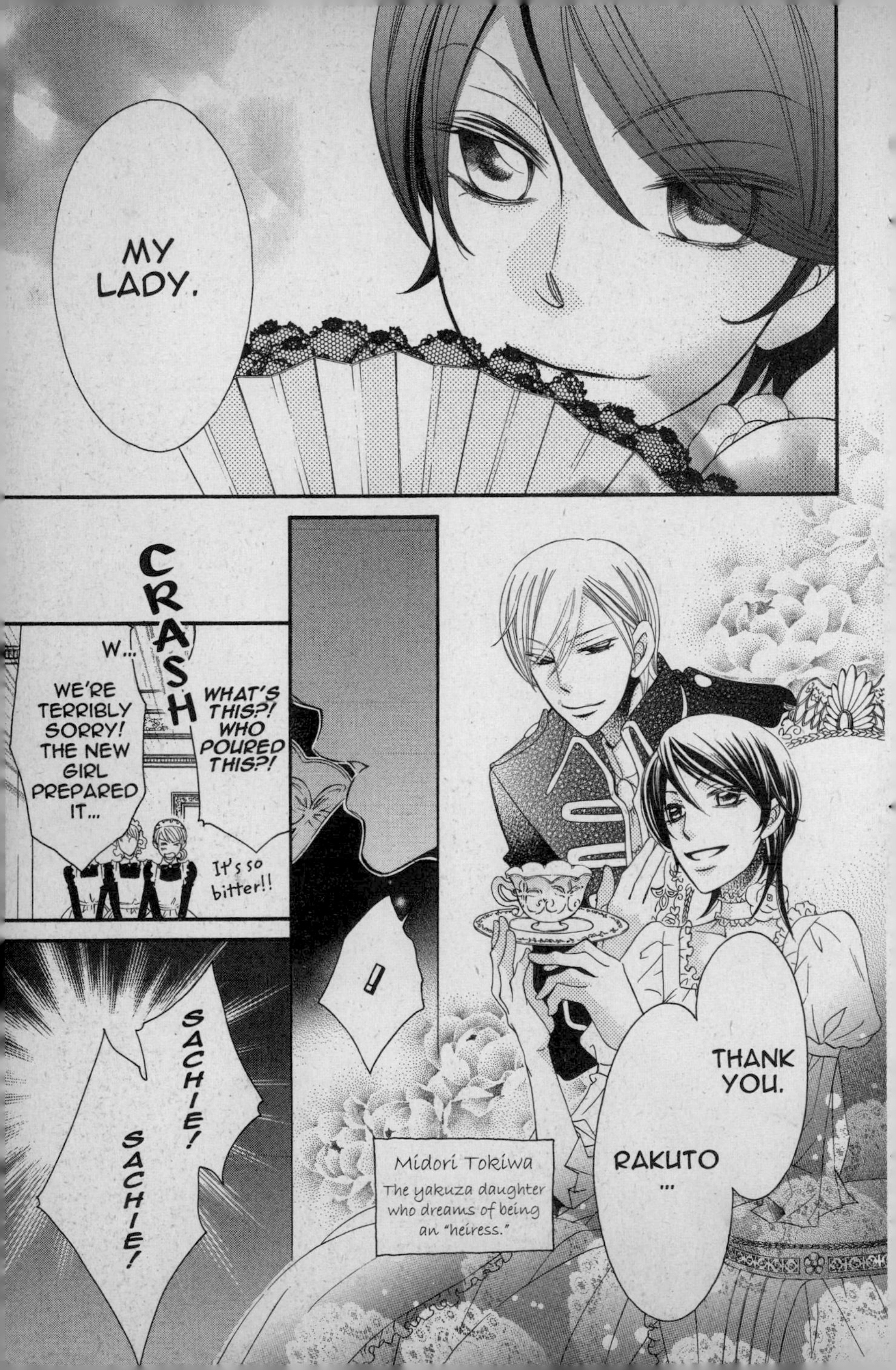
MY LADY.
THANK YOU.
RAKUTO ...
Midori Tokiwa
The yakuza daughter who dreams of being an "heiress."
!
CRASH
WHAT'S THIS?! WHO POURED THIS?!
W...
WE'RE TERRIBLY SORRY! THE NEW GIRL PREPARED IT...
It's so bitter!!
SACHIE!
SACHIE!

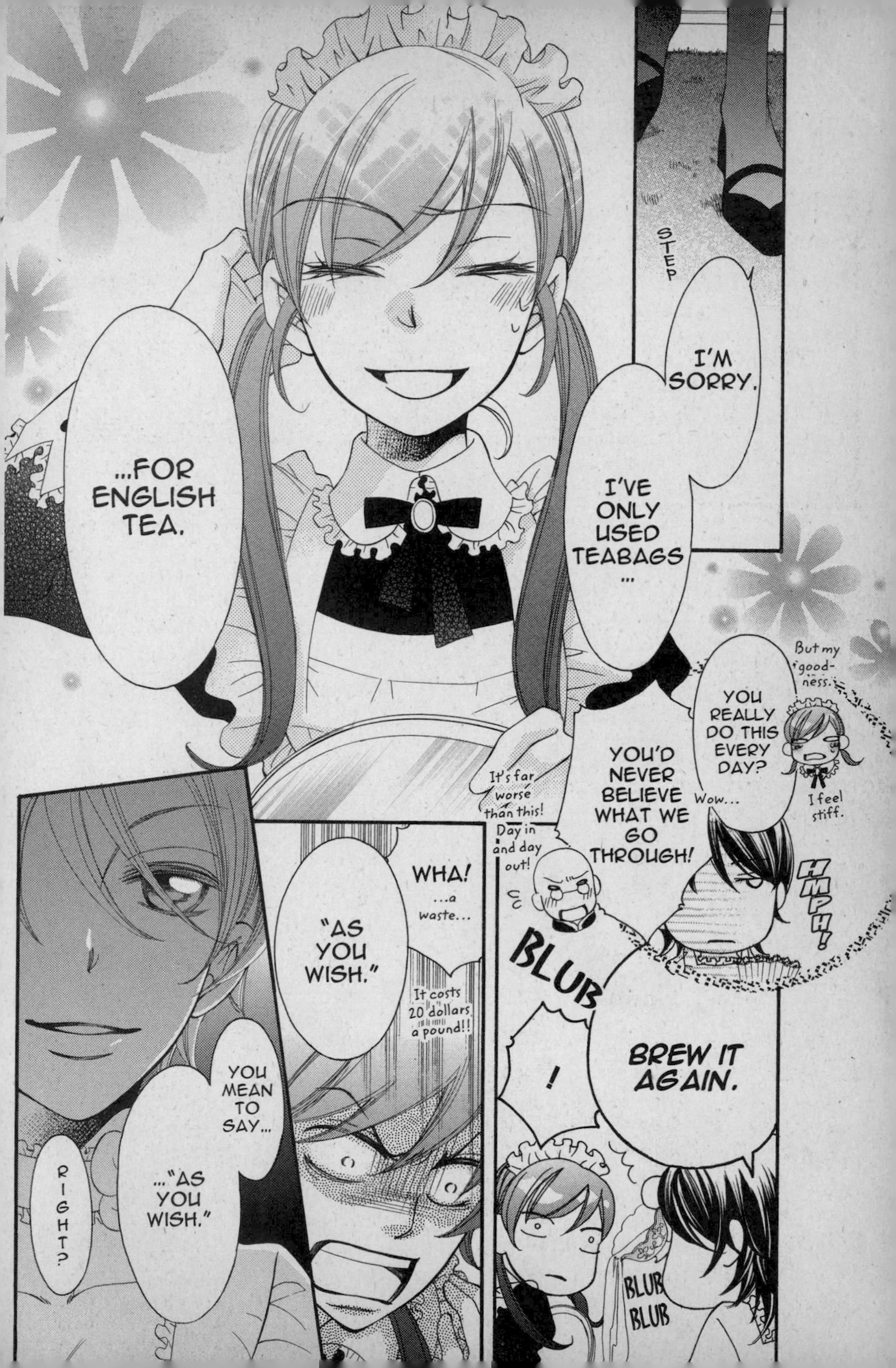
STEP
I'M SORRY.
I'VE ONLY USED TEABAGS ...
...FOR ENGLISH TEA.
But my goodness.
YOU REALLY DO THIS EVERY DAY?
I feel stiff.
Wow...
YOU'D NEVER BELIEVE WHAT WE GO THROUGH!
It's far worse than this! Day in and day out!
HMPH!
BLUB
BREW IT AGAIN.
!
BLUB BLUB
WHA!
...a waste...
"AS YOU WISH."
It costs 20 dollars a pound!!
YOU MEAN TO SAY...
..."AS YOU WISH."
RIGHT?

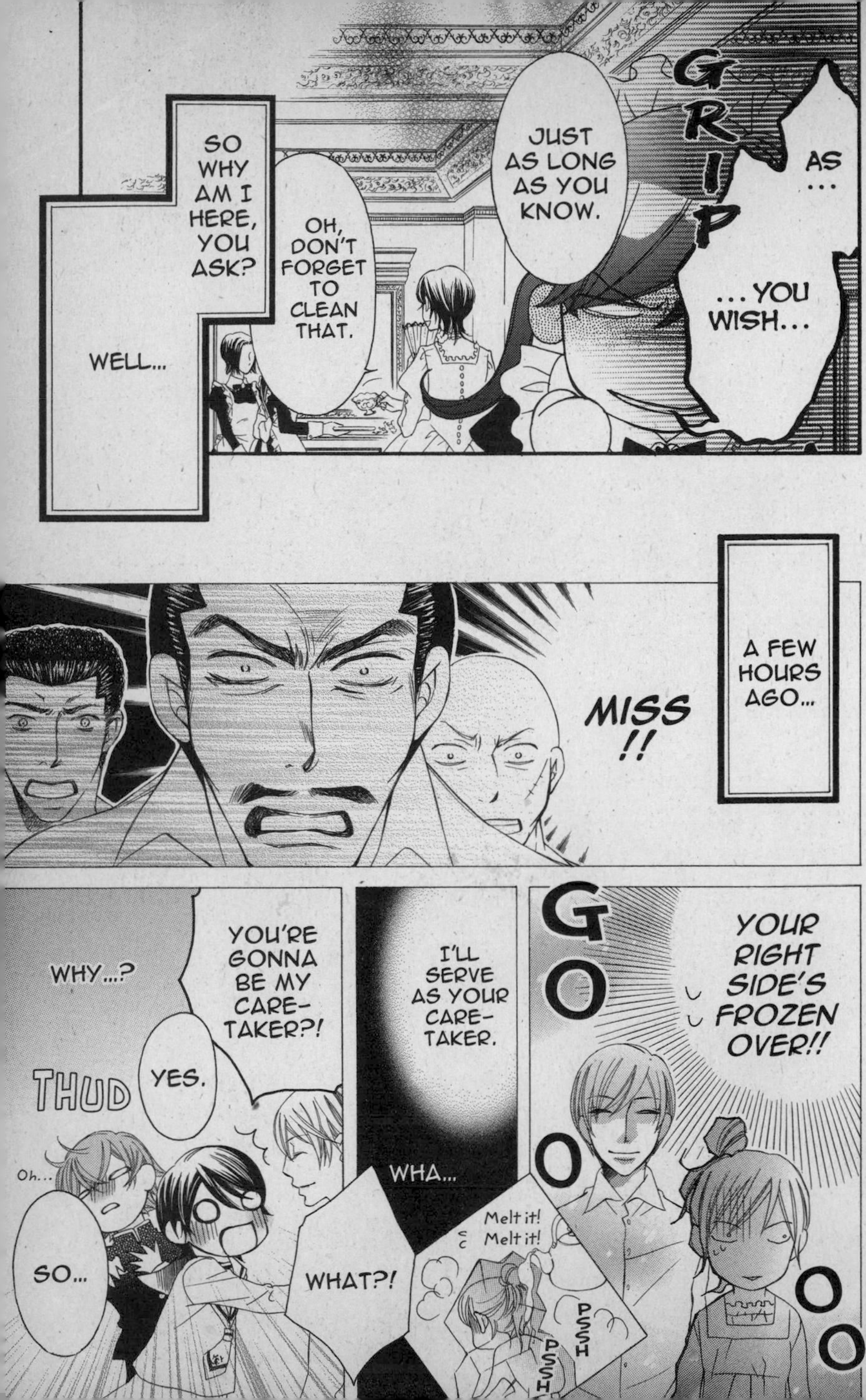
AS...
GRIP
...YOU WISH...
JUST AS LONG AS YOU KNOW.
OH, DON'T FORGET TO CLEAN THAT.
SO WHY AM I HERE, YOU ASK?
WELL...
A FEW HOURS AGO...
MISS!!
GOOOOO
YOUR RIGHT SIDE'S FROZEN OVER!!
Melt it! Melt it!
PSSH
PSSH
I'LL SERVE AS YOUR CARE-TAKER.
WHA...
YOU'RE GONNA BE MY CARE-TAKER?!
WHY...?
YES.
THUD
WHAT?!
Oh...
SO...

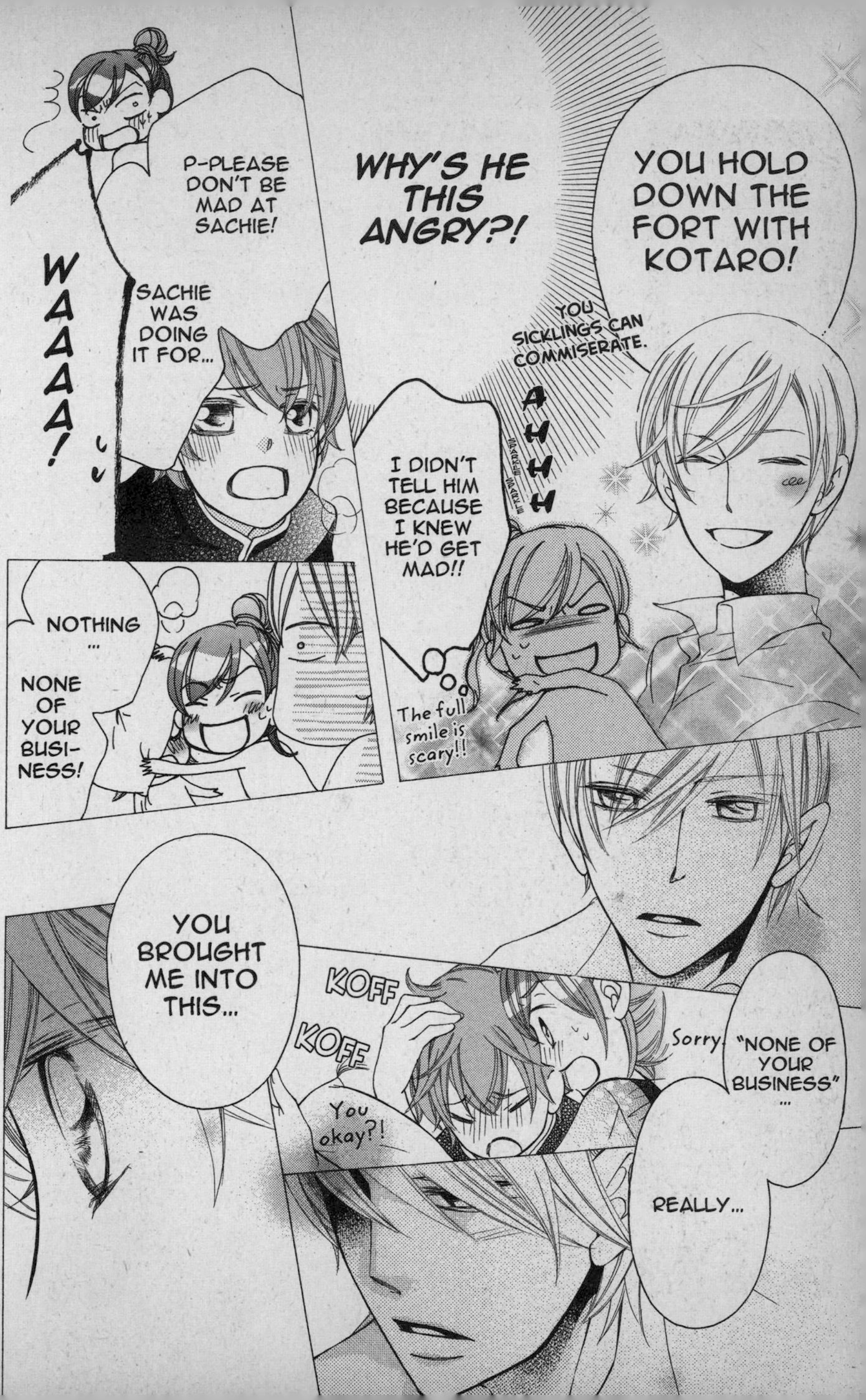
YOU HOLD DOWN THE FORT WITH KOTARO!
YOU SICKLINGS CAN COMMISERATE.
AHHHH
SPARKLE SPARKLE
WHY'S HE THIS ANGRY?!
I DIDN'T TELL HIM BECAUSE I KNEW HE'D GET MAD!!
The full smile is scary!!
P-PLEASE DON'T BE MAD AT SACHIE!
SACHIE WAS DOING IT FOR...
WAAAAA!
NOTHING...
NONE OF YOUR BUSINESS!
"NONE OF YOUR BUSINESS"...
Sorry.
KOFF
KOFF
You okay?!
YOU BROUGHT ME INTO THIS...
REALLY...

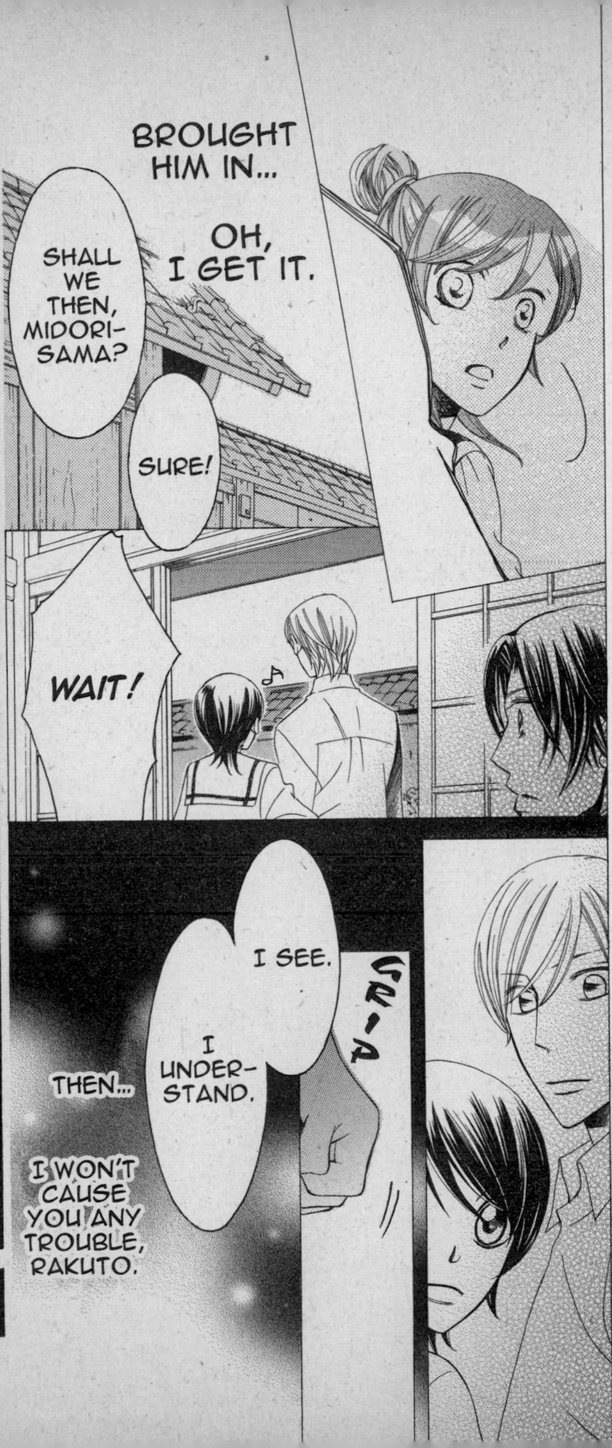
BROUGHT HIM IN...
OH, I GET IT.
SHALL WE THEN, MIDORI-SAMA?
SURE!
WAIT!
SRIP
I SEE.
I UNDER-STAND.
THEN...
I WON'T CAUSE YOU ANY TROUBLE, RAKUTO.

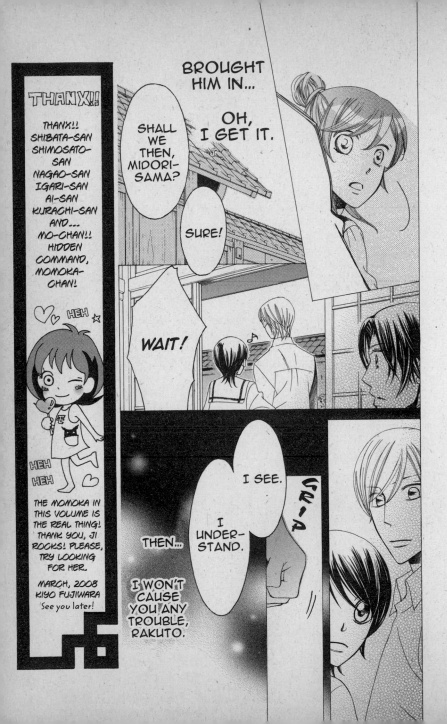

THANX!!

THANX!!
SHIBATA-SAN
SHIMOSATO-SAN
NAGAO-SAN
IGARI-SAN
AI-SAN
KURACHI-SAN
AND...
MO-CHAN!! HIDDEN COMMAND, MOMOKA-CHAN!

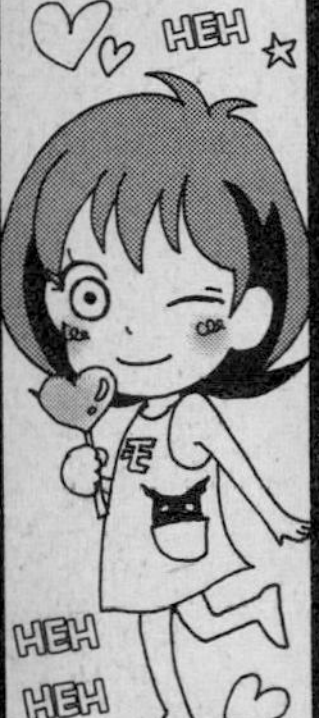
HEH
HEH
HEH

THE MOMOKA IN THIS VOLUME IS THE REAL THING! THANK YOU, JI ROCKS! PLEASE, TRY LOOKING FOR HER.

MARCH, 2008
KIYO FUJIWARA
See you later!

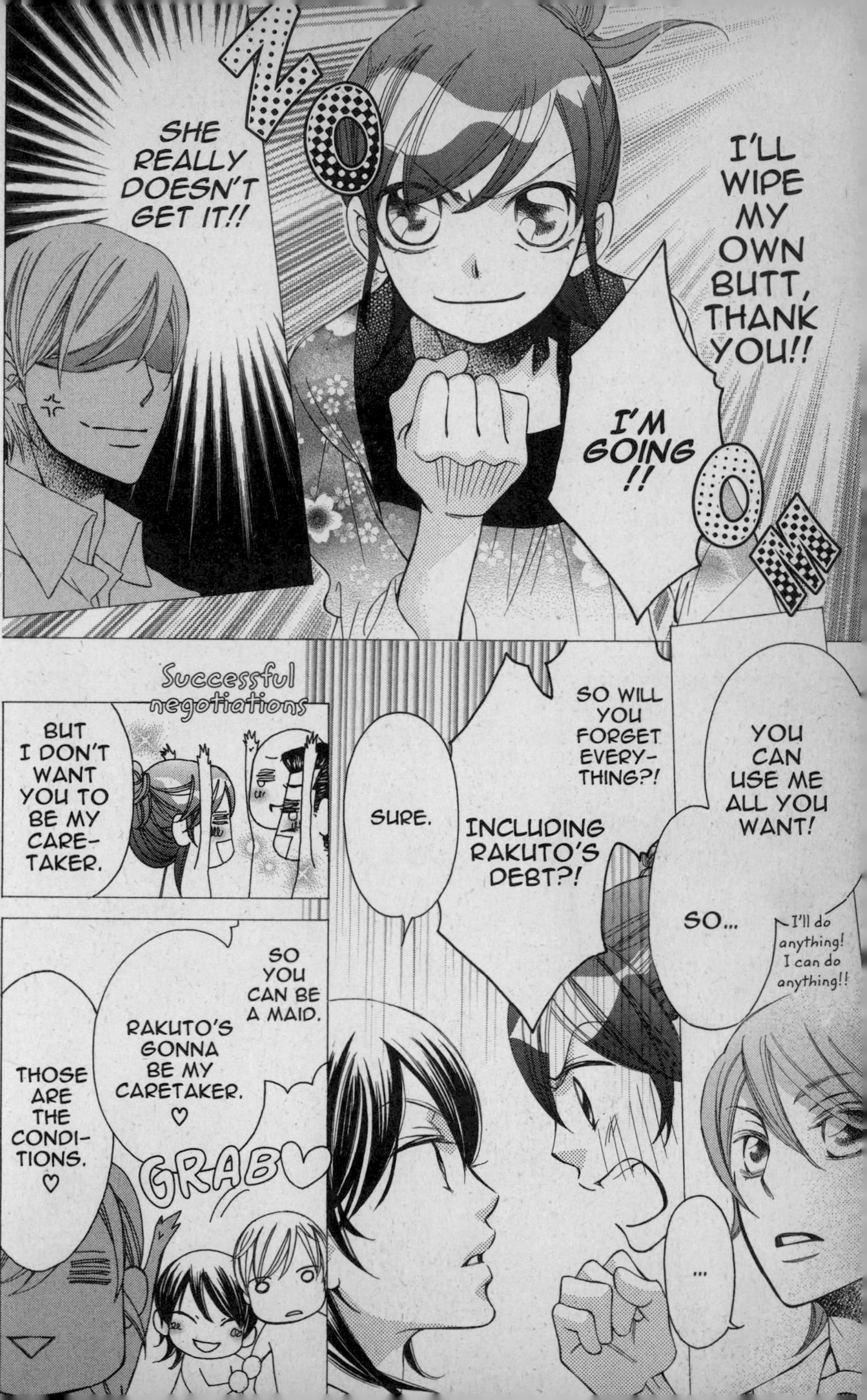
I'LL WIPE MY OWN BUTT, THANK YOU!!
I'M GOING !!
SHE REALLY DOESN'T GET IT!!
YOU CAN USE ME ALL YOU WANT!
SO...
I'll do anything! I can do anything!!
SO WILL YOU FORGET EVERYTHING?!
INCLUDING RAKUTO'S DEBT?!
SURE.
...
Successful negotiations
BUT I DON'T WANT YOU TO BE MY CARETAKER.
SO YOU CAN BE A MAID.
RAKUTO'S GONNA BE MY CARETAKER. ♡
GRAB♡
THOSE ARE THE CONDITIONS. ♡

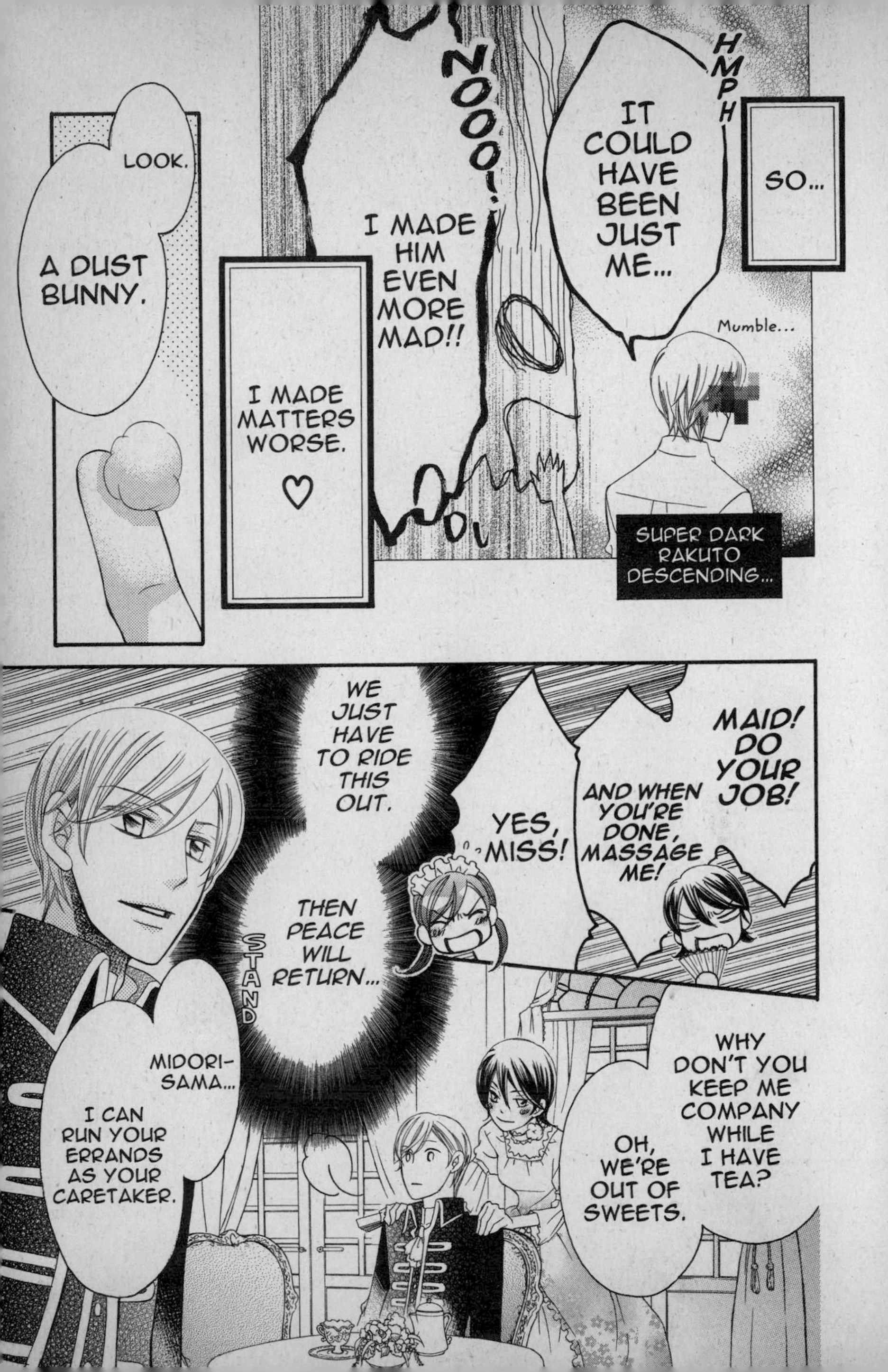
SO...
HMPH
IT COULD HAVE BEEN JUST ME...
Mumble...
SUPER DARK RAKUTO DESCENDING...
NOOOO!!
I MADE HIM EVEN MORE MAD!!
I MADE MATTERS WORSE. ♡
LOOK.
A DUST BUNNY.
MAID! DO YOUR JOB!
AND WHEN YOU'RE DONE, MASSAGE ME!
YES, MISS!
WE JUST HAVE TO RIDE THIS OUT.
THEN PEACE WILL RETURN...
STAND
WHY DON'T YOU KEEP ME COMPANY WHILE I HAVE TEA?
OH, WE'RE OUT OF SWEETS.
MIDORI-SAMA...
I CAN RUN YOUR ERRANDS AS YOUR CARETAKER.

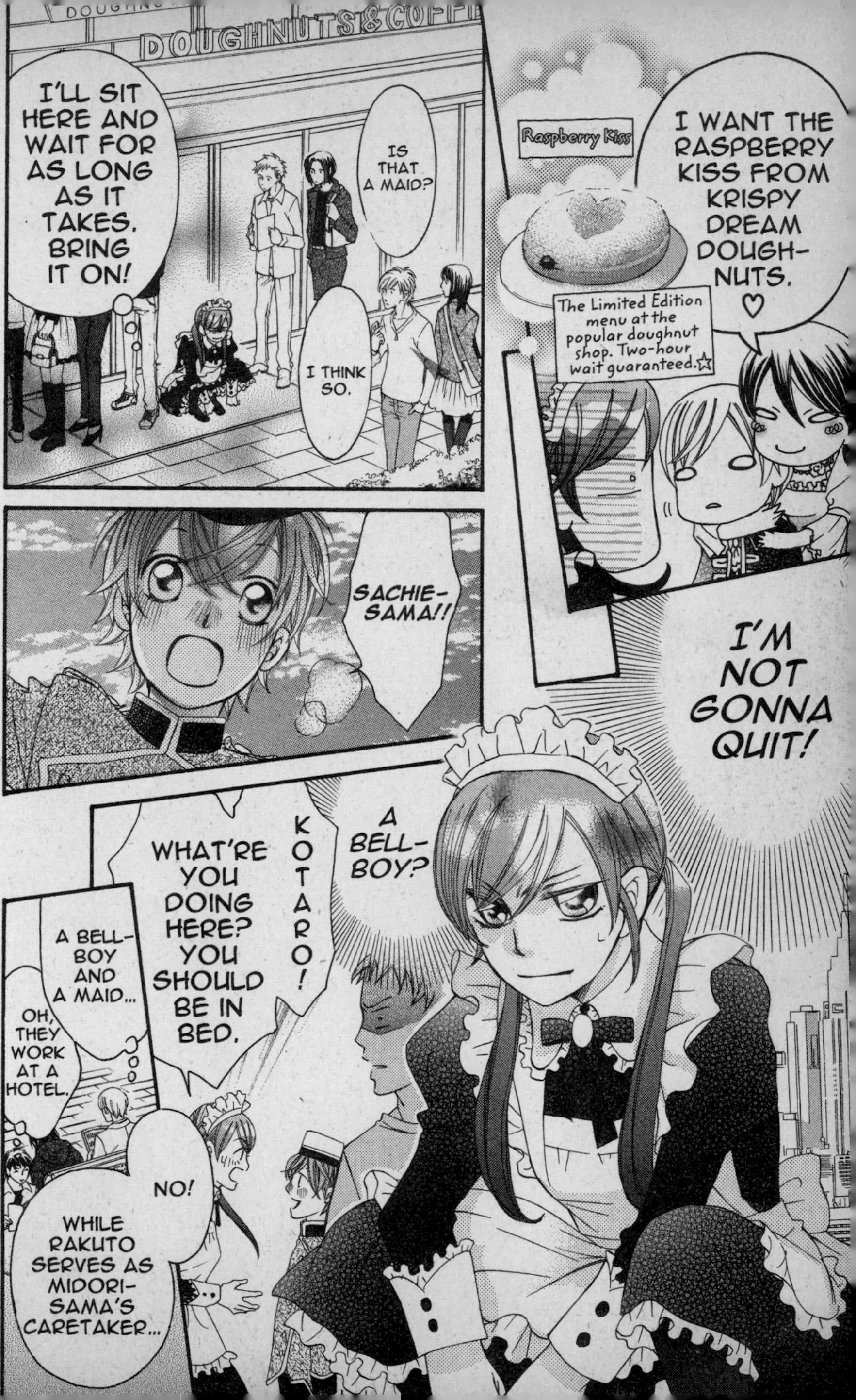
Raspberry Kiss
I WANT THE RASPBERRY KISS FROM KRISPY DREAM DOUGHNUTS. ♡
The Limited Edition menu at the popular doughnut shop. Two-hour wait guaranteed.☆
DOUGHNUTS & COFF
I'LL SIT HERE AND WAIT FOR AS LONG AS IT TAKES. BRING IT ON!
IS THAT A MAID?
I THINK SO.
I'M NOT GONNA QUIT!
SACHIE-SAMA!!
A BELL-BOY?
KOTARO!
WHAT'RE YOU DOING HERE? YOU SHOULD BE IN BED.
A BELL-BOY AND A MAID...
OH, THEY WORK AT A HOTEL.
NO!
WHILE RAKUTO SERVES AS MIDORI-SAMA'S CARETAKER...

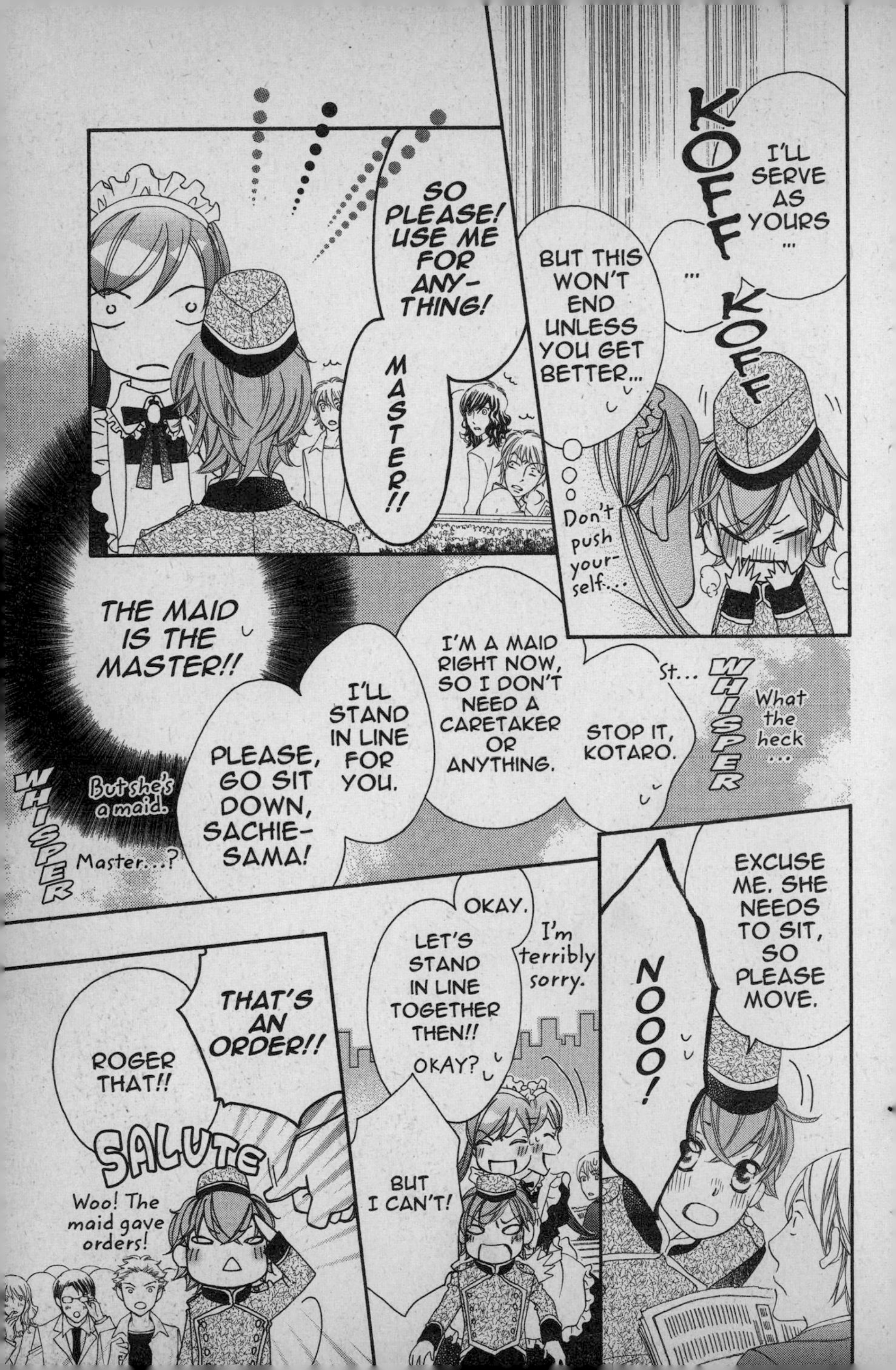
KOFF
I'LL SERVE AS YOURS ...
KOFF
... BUT THIS WON'T END UNLESS YOU GET BETTER...
Don't push yourself...
SO PLEASE! USE ME FOR ANYTHING!
MASTER!!
WHISPER
What the heck...
St...
STOP IT, KOTARO.
I'M A MAID RIGHT NOW, SO I DON'T NEED A CARETAKER OR ANYTHING.
I'LL STAND IN LINE FOR YOU.
PLEASE, GO SIT DOWN, SACHIE-SAMA!
THE MAID IS THE MASTER!!
But she's a maid.
WHISPER
Master...?
EXCUSE ME. SHE NEEDS TO SIT, SO PLEASE MOVE.
NOOO!
OKAY.
I'm terribly sorry.
LET'S STAND IN LINE TOGETHER THEN!!
OKAY?
BUT I CAN'T!
THAT'S AN ORDER!!
ROGER THAT!!
SALUTE
Woo! The maid gave orders!

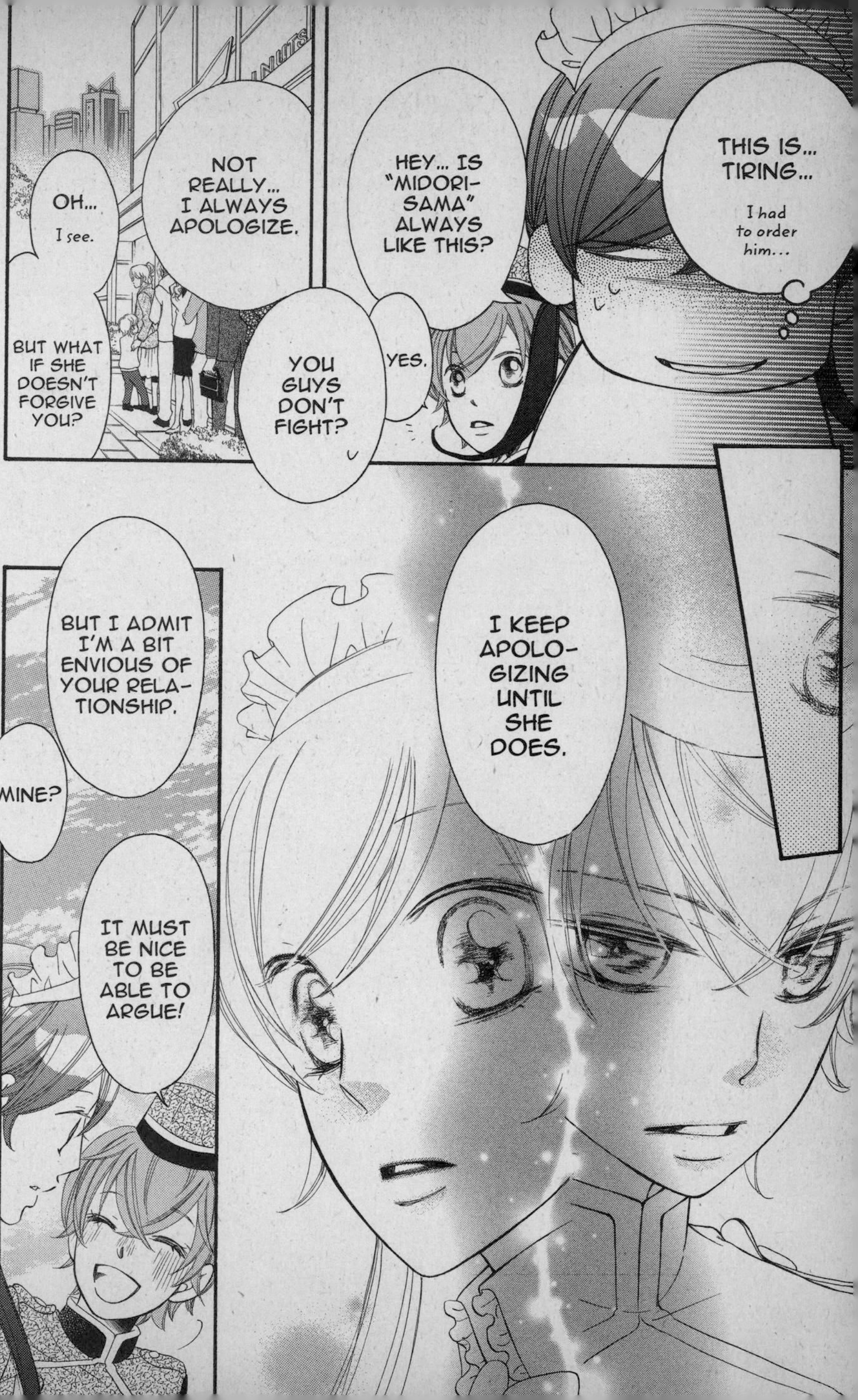
THIS IS... TIRING...
I had to order him...
HEY... IS "MIDORI-SAMA" ALWAYS LIKE THIS?
YES.
YOU GUYS DON'T FIGHT?
NOT REALLY... I ALWAYS APOLOGIZE.
OH... I see.
BUT WHAT IF SHE DOESN'T FORGIVE YOU?
I KEEP APOLOGIZING UNTIL SHE DOES.
BUT I ADMIT I'M A BIT ENVIOUS OF YOUR RELATIONSHIP.
MINE?
IT MUST BE NICE TO BE ABLE TO ARGUE!

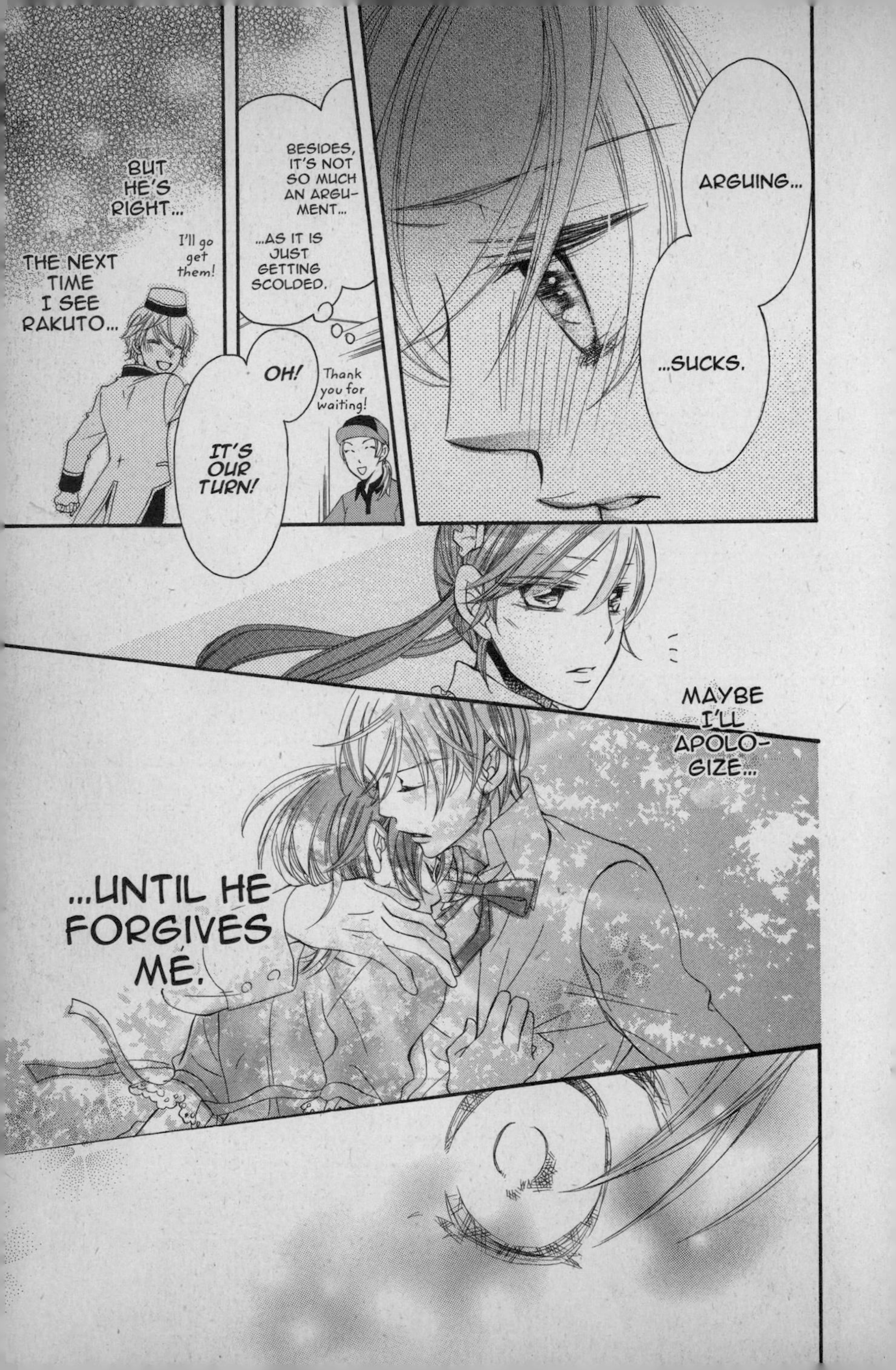
ARGUING...
...SUCKS.
BESIDES, IT'S NOT SO MUCH AN ARGUMENT...
...AS IT IS JUST GETTING SCOLDED.
Thank you for waiting!
OH!
IT'S OUR TURN!
BUT HE'S RIGHT...
I'll go get them!
THE NEXT TIME I SEE RAKUTO...
MAYBE I'LL APOLOGIZE...
...UNTIL HE FORGIVES ME.

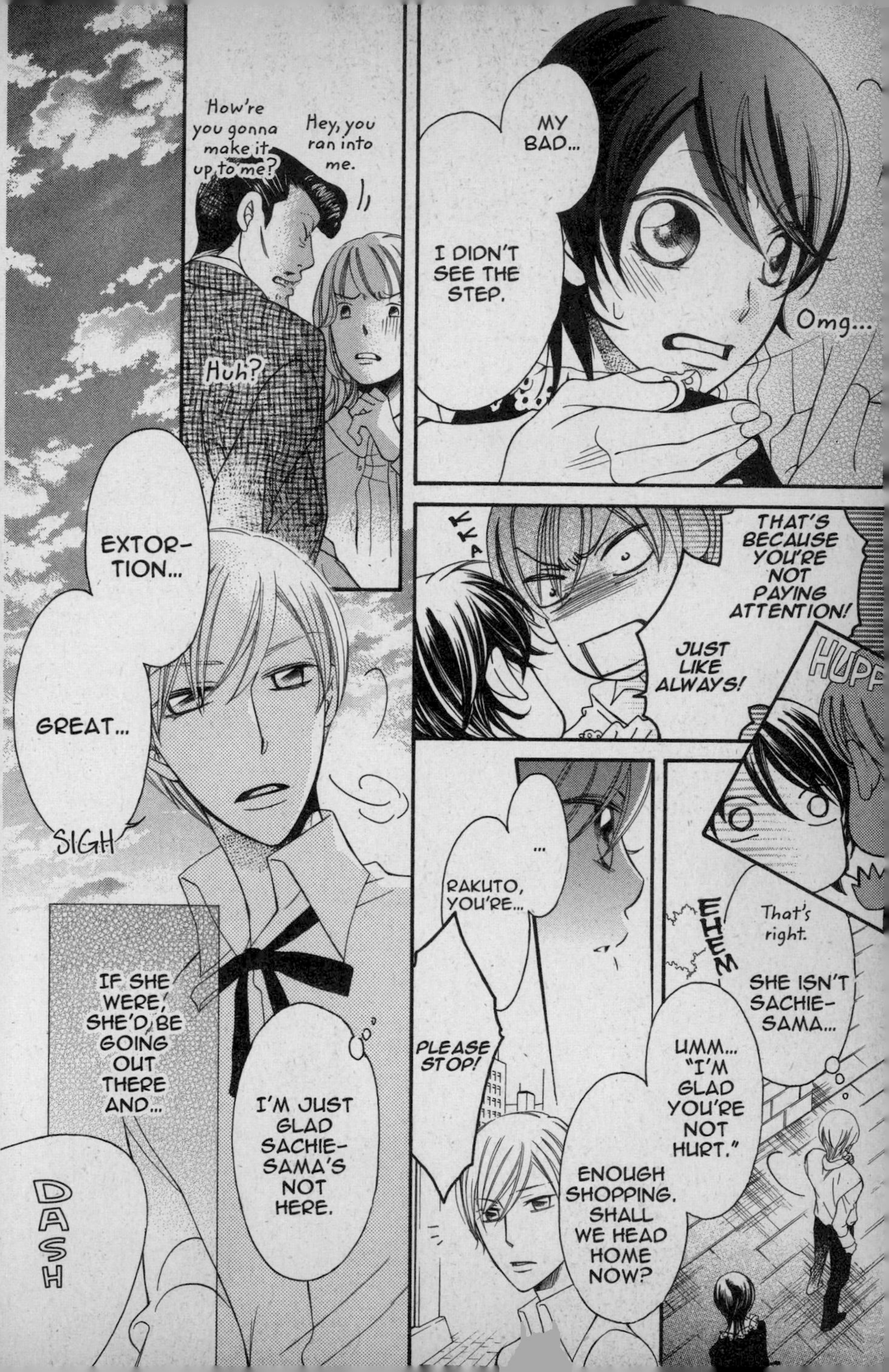
MY BAD...
I DIDN'T SEE THE STEP.
Omg...
KKA
THAT'S BECAUSE YOU'RE NOT PAYING ATTENTION!
JUST LIKE ALWAYS!
HUPP
That's right.
SHE ISN'T SACHIE-SAMA...
EHEM
UMM... "I'M GLAD YOU'RE NOT HURT."
ENOUGH SHOPPING. SHALL WE HEAD HOME NOW?
...
RAKUTO, YOU'RE...
PLEASE STOP!
Hey, you ran into me.
How're you gonna make it up to me?
Huh?
EXTORTION...
GREAT...
SIGH
I'M JUST GLAD SACHIE-SAMA'S NOT HERE.
IF SHE WERE, SHE'D BE GOING OUT THERE AND...
DASH

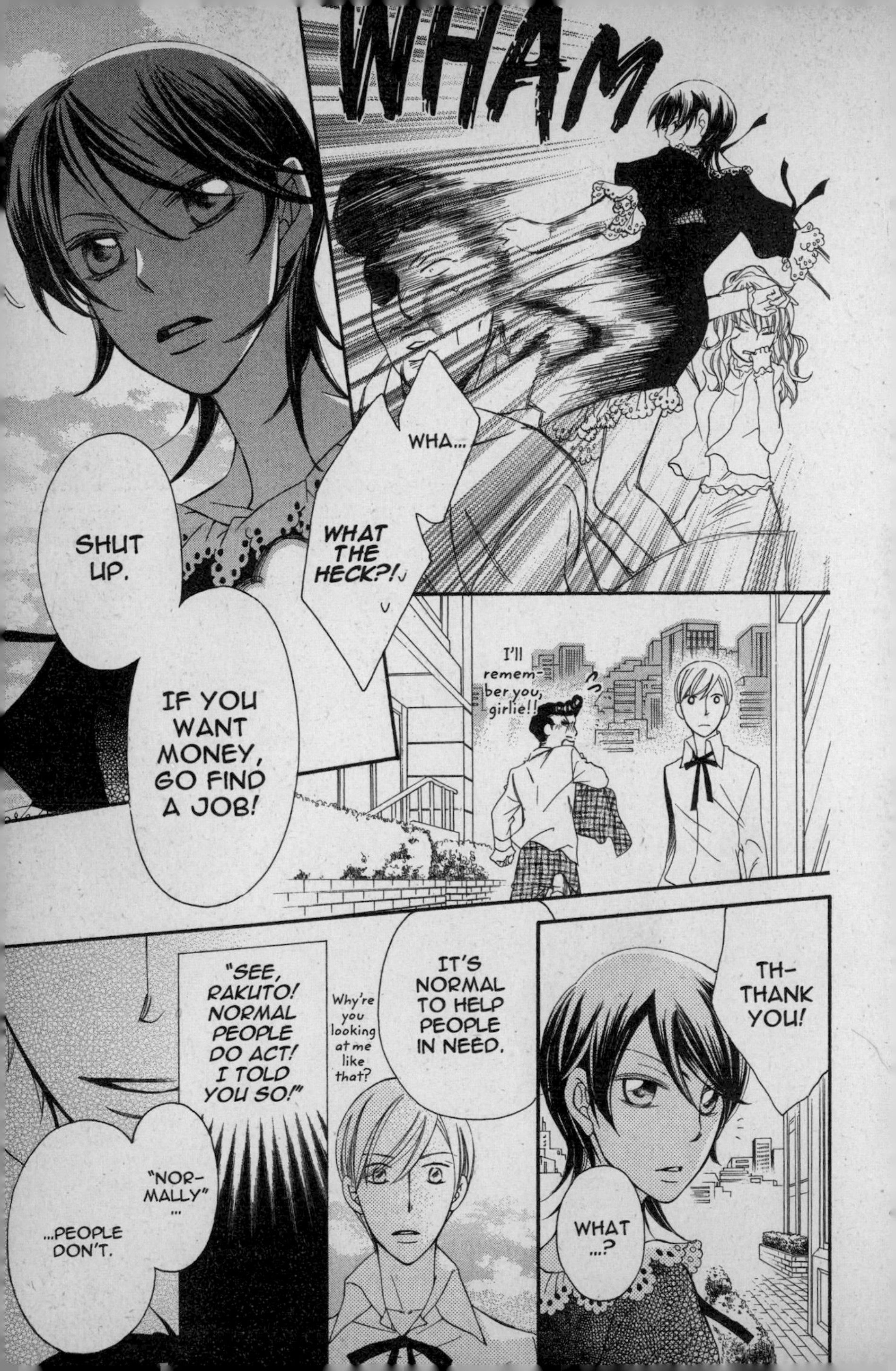
WHAM
WHA...
WHAT THE HECK?!
I'll remember you, girlie!!
SHUT UP.
IF YOU WANT MONEY, GO FIND A JOB!
TH- THANK YOU!
WHAT ...?
IT'S NORMAL TO HELP PEOPLE IN NEED.
Why're you looking at me like that?
"SEE, RAKUTO! NORMAL PEOPLE DO ACT! I TOLD YOU SO!"
"NOR-MALLY" ...
...PEOPLE DON'T.

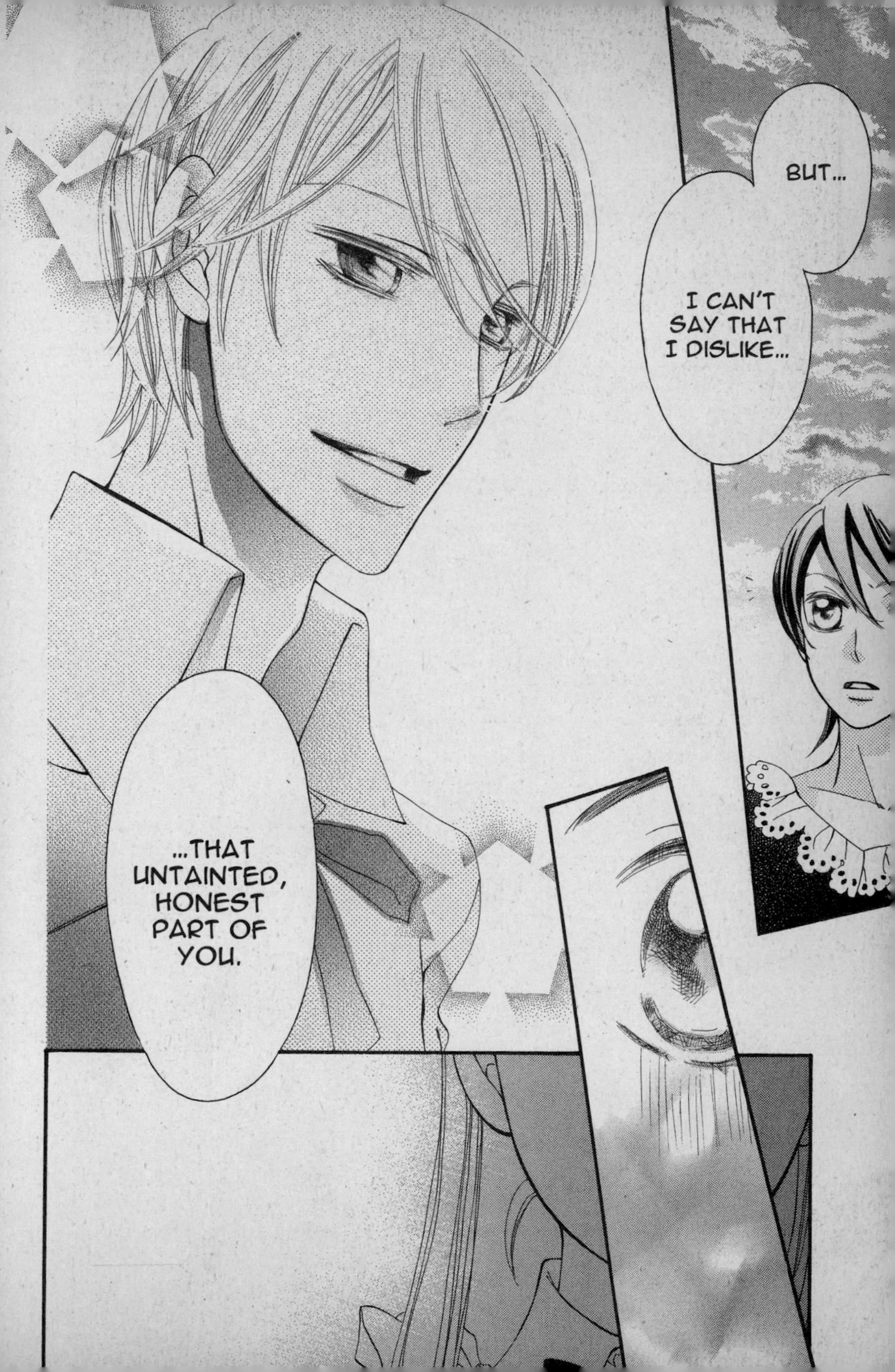
BUT...
I CAN'T SAY THAT I DISLIKE...
...THAT UNTAINTED, HONEST PART OF YOU.

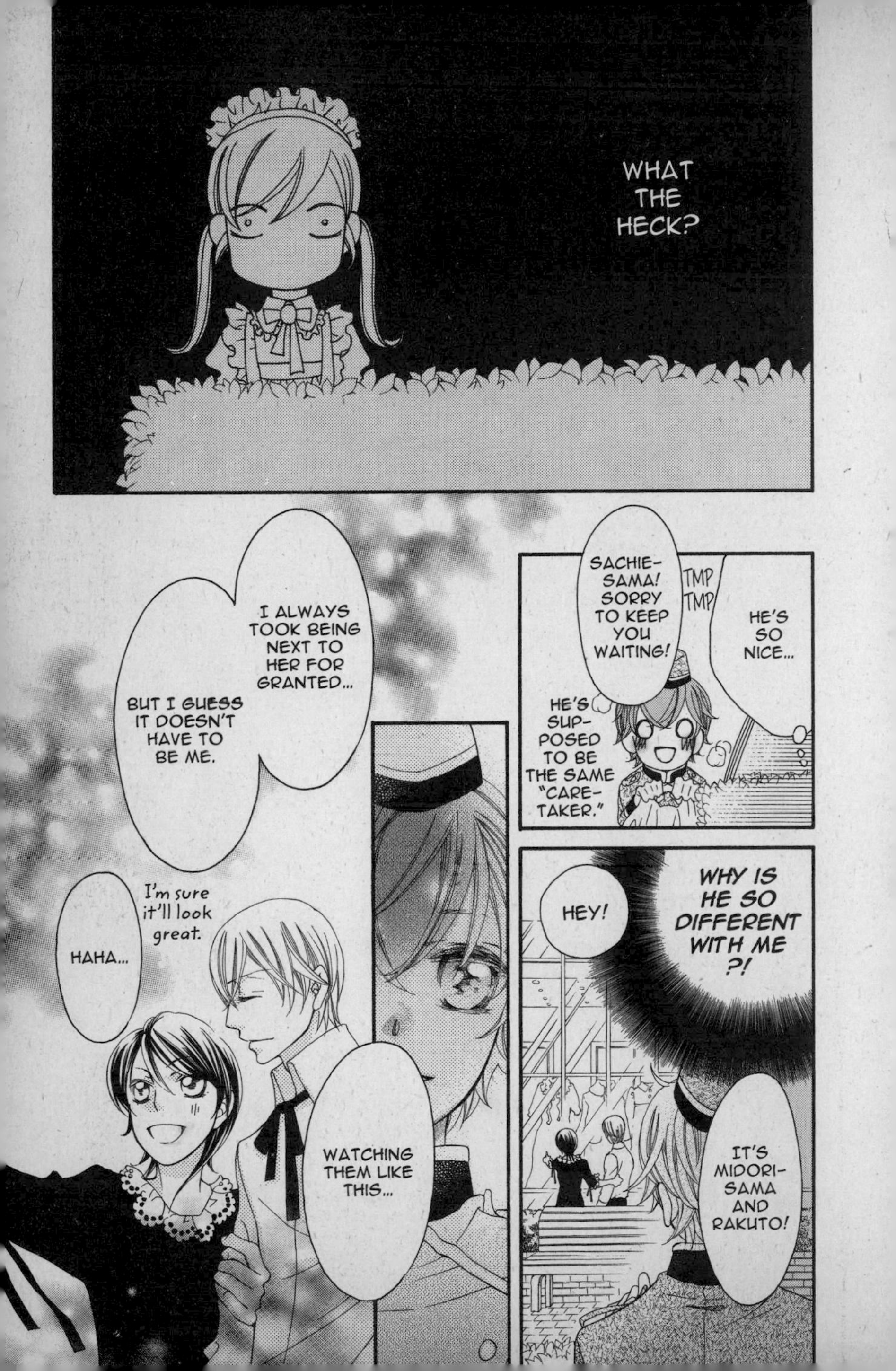
WHAT THE HECK?
HE'S SO NICE...
TMP TMP
SACHIE-SAMA! SORRY TO KEEP YOU WAITING!
HE'S SUP-POSED TO BE THE SAME "CARE-TAKER."
WHY IS HE SO DIFFERENT WITH ME ?!
HEY!
IT'S MIDORI-SAMA AND RAKUTO!
WATCHING THEM LIKE THIS...
I ALWAYS TOOK BEING NEXT TO HER FOR GRANTED...
BUT I GUESS IT DOESN'T HAVE TO BE ME.
I'm sure it'll look great.
HAHA...

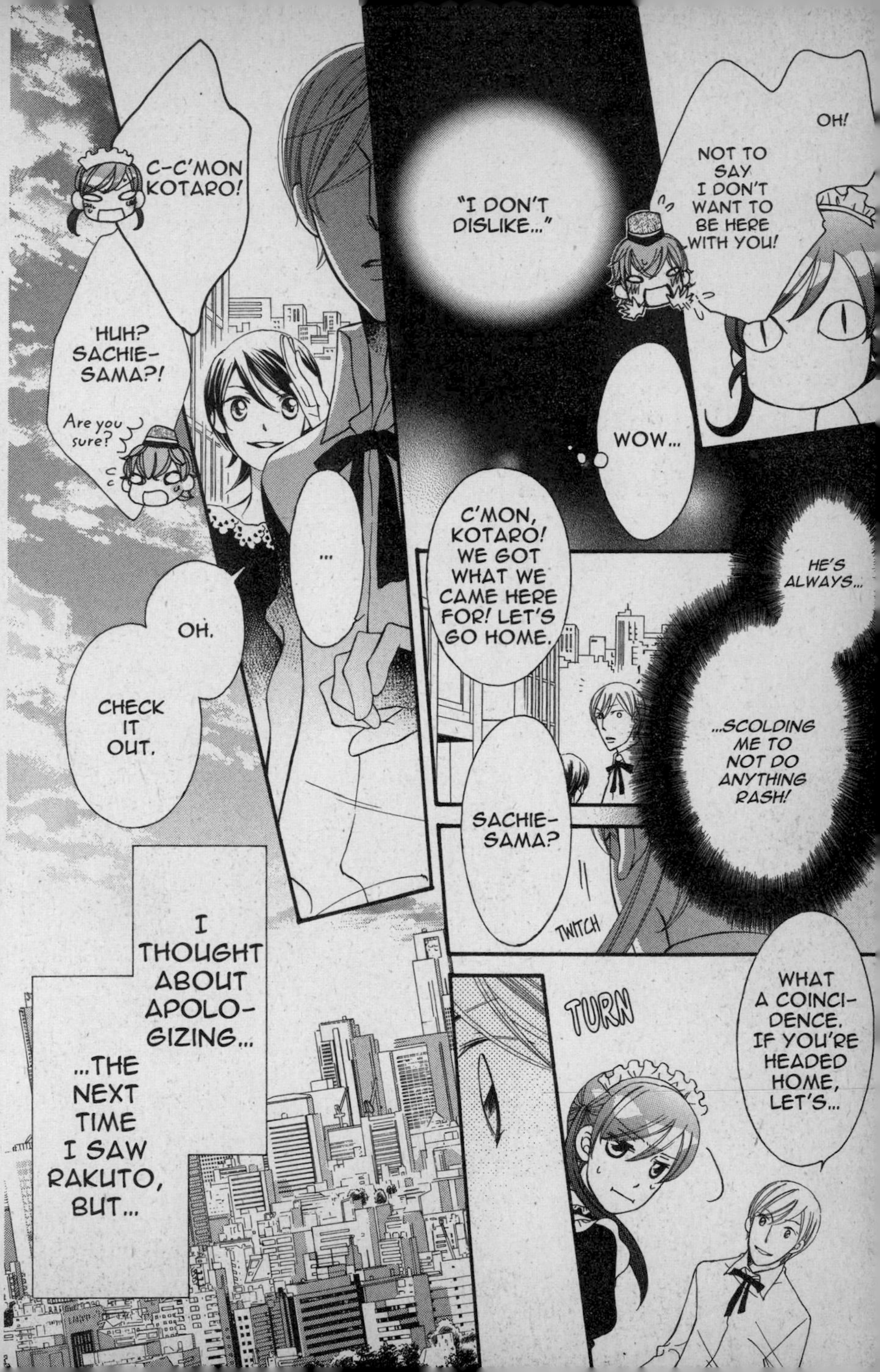
OH!
NOT TO SAY I DON'T WANT TO BE HERE WITH YOU!
"I DON'T DISLIKE..."
WOW...
C-C'MON KOTARO!
HUH? SACHIE-SAMA?!
Are you sure?
...
OH.
CHECK IT OUT.
HE'S ALWAYS...
...SCOLDING ME TO NOT DO ANYTHING RASH!
C'MON, KOTARO! WE GOT WHAT WE CAME HERE FOR! LET'S GO HOME.
SACHIE-SAMA?
TWITCH
WHAT A COINCIDENCE. IF YOU'RE HEADED HOME, LET'S...
TURN
I THOUGHT ABOUT APOLOGIZING...
...THE NEXT TIME I SAW RAKUTO, BUT...

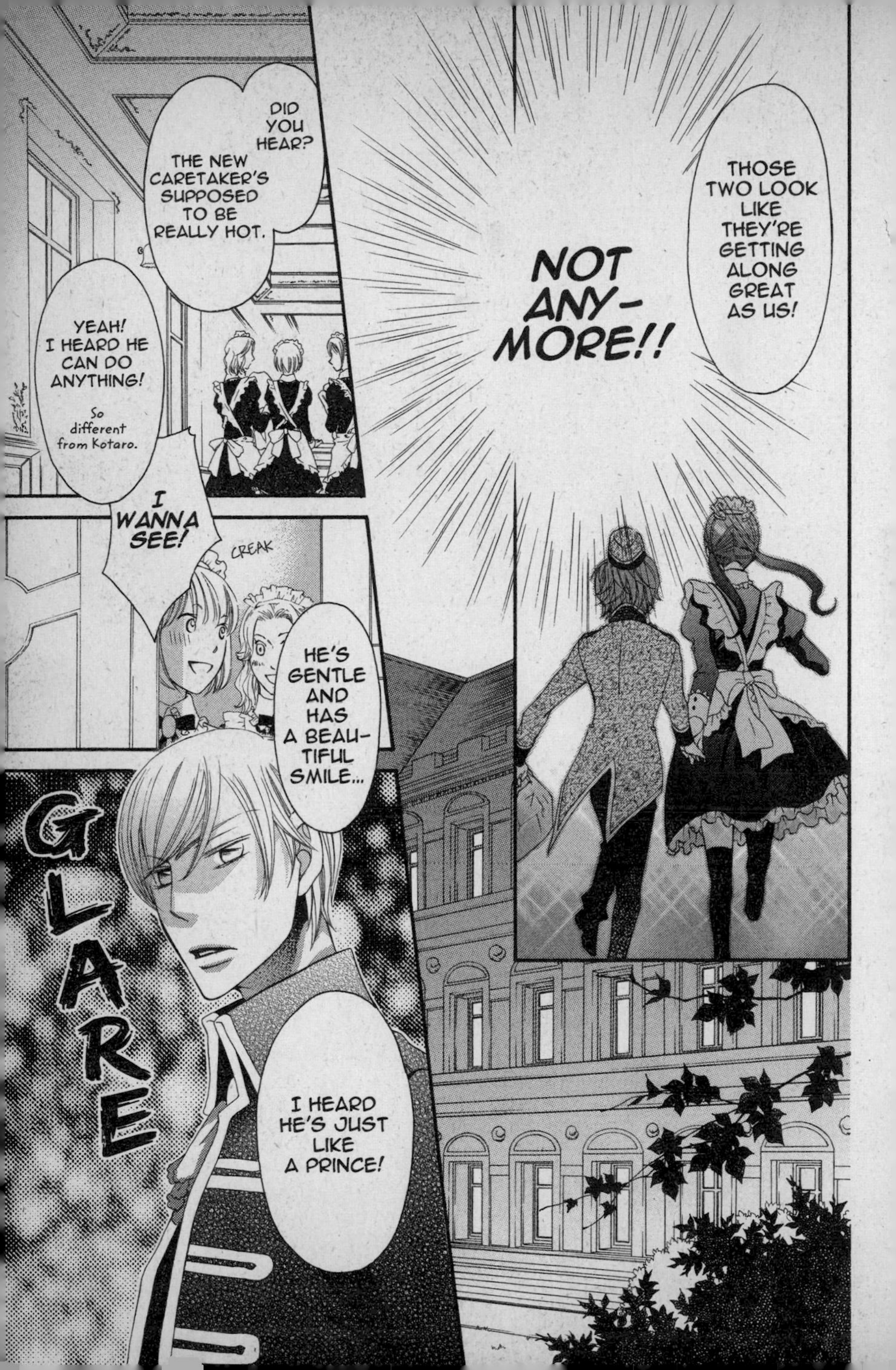
THOSE TWO LOOK LIKE THEY'RE GETTING ALONG GREAT AS US!
NOT ANY-MORE!!
DID YOU HEAR?
THE NEW CARETAKER'S SUPPOSED TO BE REALLY HOT.
YEAH! I HEARD HE CAN DO ANYTHING!
So different from Kotaro.
I WANNA SEE!
CREAK
HE'S GENTLE AND HAS A BEAU-TIFUL SMILE...
GLARE
I HEARD HE'S JUST LIKE A PRINCE!

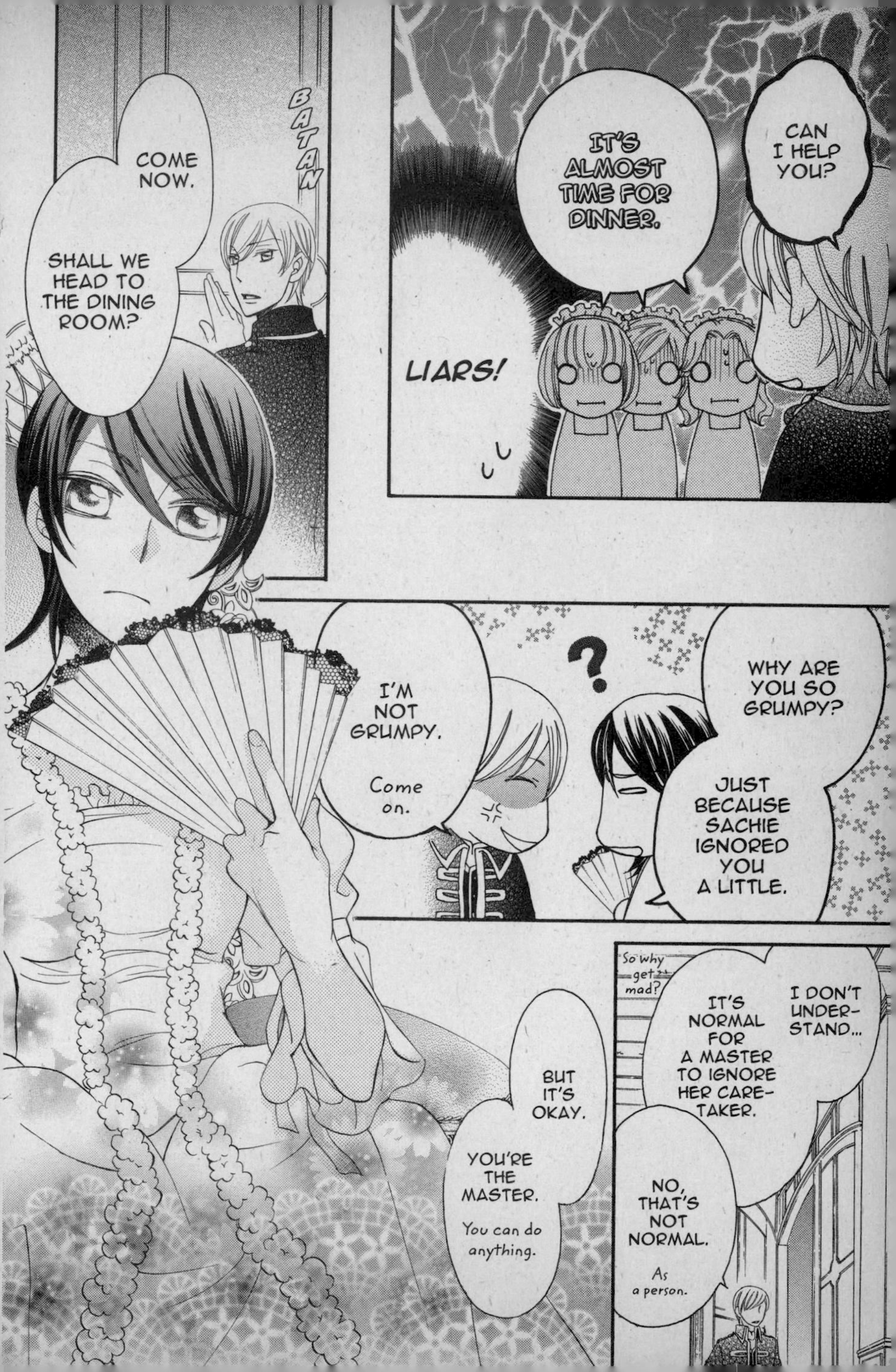
CAN I HELP YOU?
IT'S ALMOST TIME FOR DINNER.
LIARS!
BATAN
COME NOW.
SHALL WE HEAD TO THE DINING ROOM?
WHY ARE YOU SO GRUMPY?
JUST BECAUSE SACHIE IGNORED YOU A LITTLE.
?
I'M NOT GRUMPY.
Come on.
I DON'T UNDER-STAND...
So why get mad?
IT'S NORMAL FOR A MASTER TO IGNORE HER CARE-TAKER.
NO, THAT'S NOT NORMAL.
As a person.
BUT IT'S OKAY.
YOU'RE THE MASTER.
You can do anything.

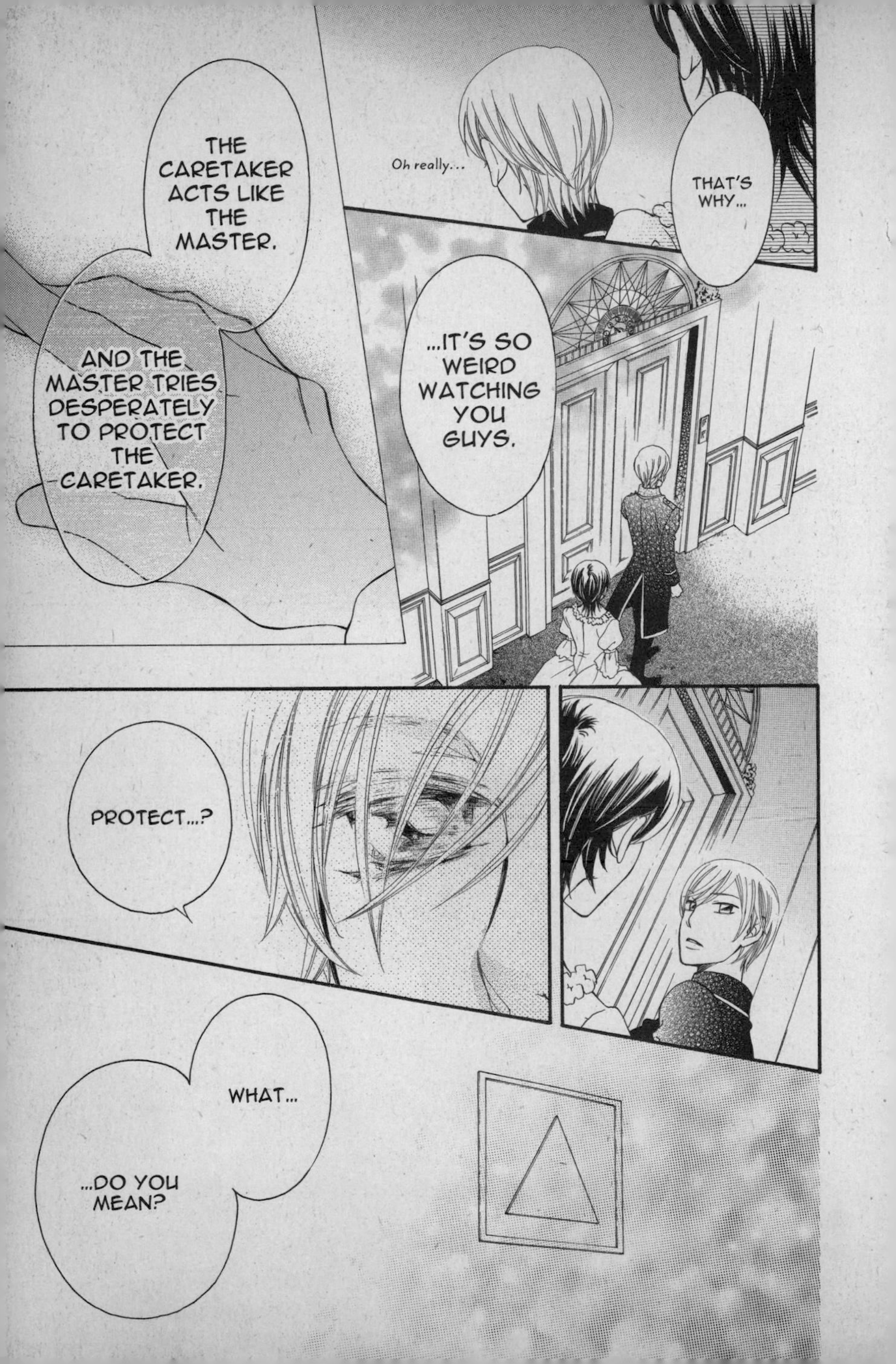
THAT'S WHY...
Oh really...
...IT'S SO WEIRD WATCHING YOU GUYS.
THE CARETAKER ACTS LIKE THE MASTER.
AND THE MASTER TRIES DESPERATELY TO PROTECT THE CARETAKER.
PROTECT...?
WHAT...
...DO YOU MEAN?

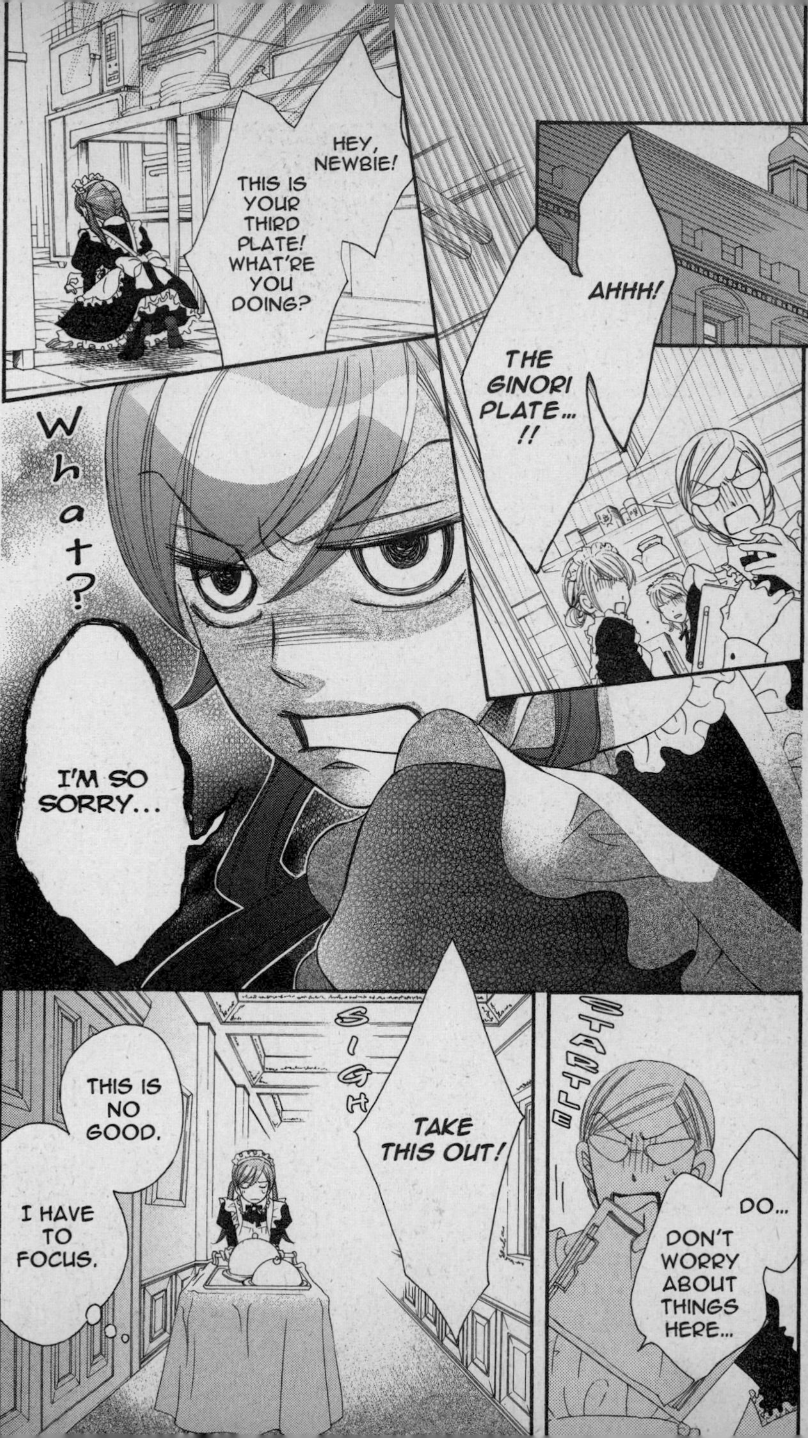
CRASH
AHHH!
THE GINORI PLATE... !!
HEY, NEWBIE!
THIS IS YOUR THIRD PLATE! WHAT'RE YOU DOING?
What?
I'M SO SORRY...
STARTLE
DO...
DON'T WORRY ABOUT THINGS HERE...
SIGH
TAKE THIS OUT!
THIS IS NO GOOD.
I HAVE TO FOCUS.

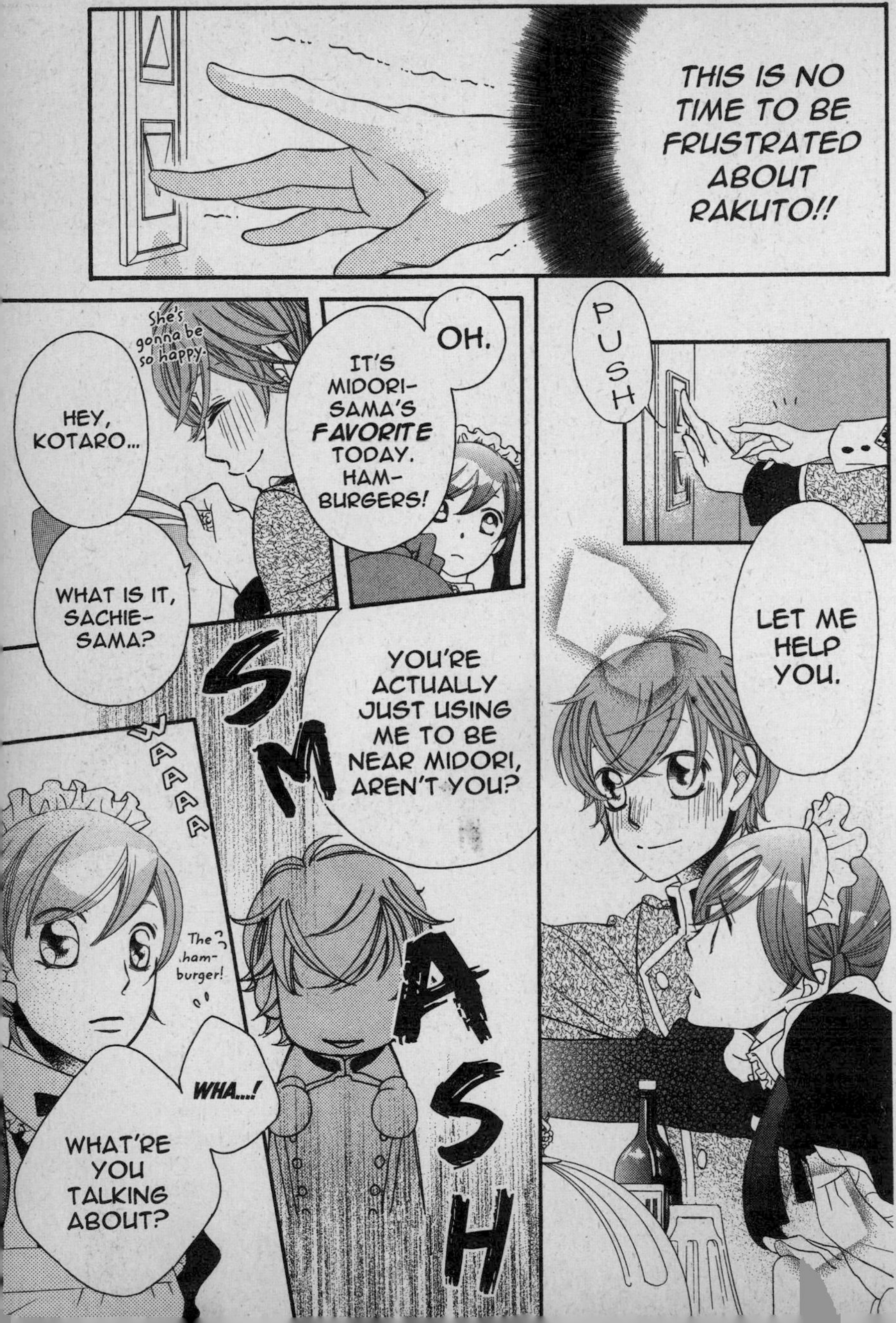
THIS IS NO TIME TO BE FRUSTRATED ABOUT RAKUTO!!
PUSH
LET ME HELP YOU.
OH.
IT'S MIDORI-SAMA'S FAVORITE TODAY. HAMBURGERS!
She's gonna be so happy.
HEY, KOTARO...
WHAT IS IT, SACHIE-SAMA?
YOU'RE ACTUALLY JUST USING ME TO BE NEAR MIDORI, AREN'T YOU?
SMASH
WAAAAA
The hamburger!
WHA...!
WHAT'RE YOU TALKING ABOUT?

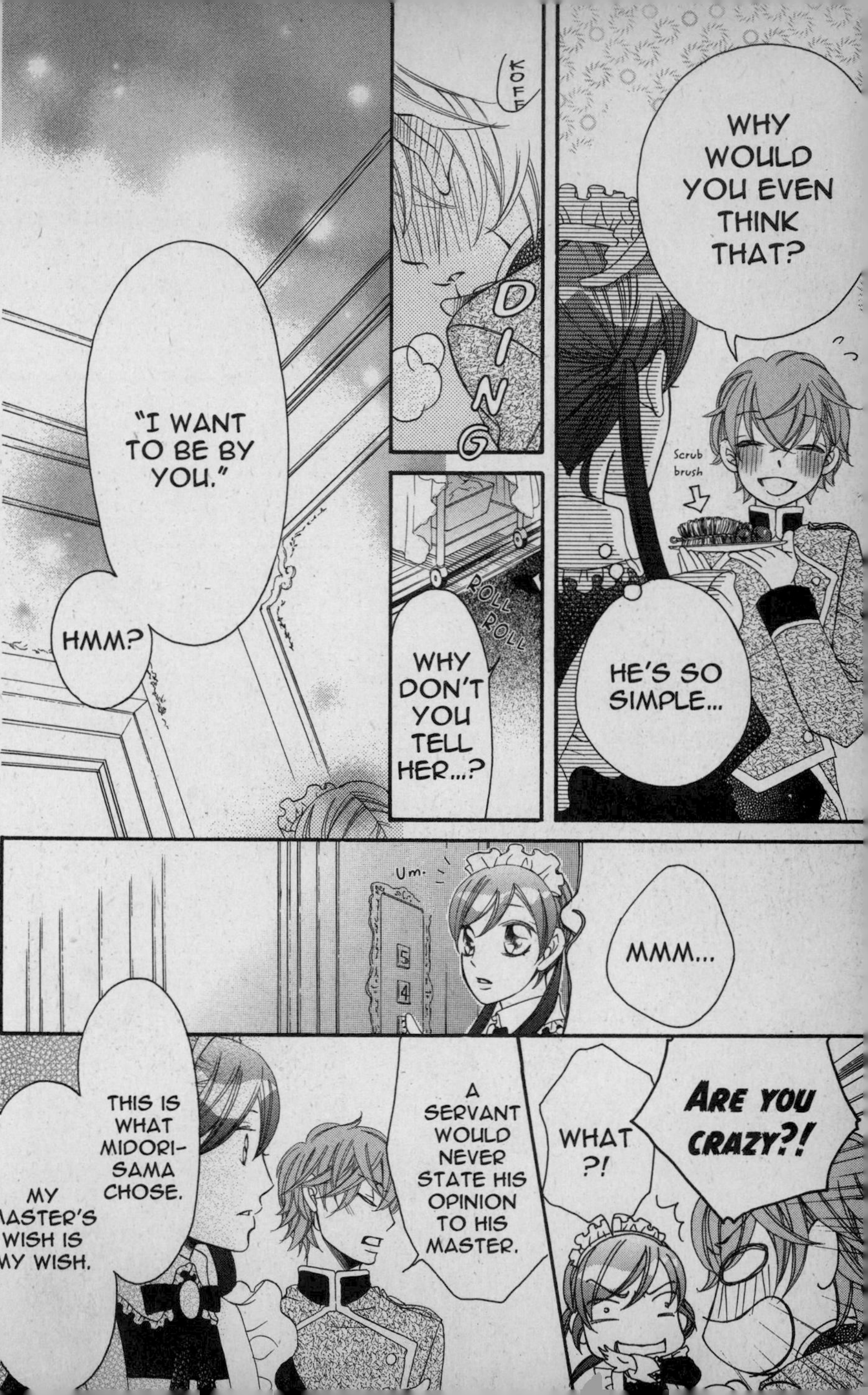
WHY WOULD YOU EVEN THINK THAT?
Scrub brush
HE'S SO SIMPLE...
KOFF
DING
ROLL ROLL
WHY DON'T YOU TELL HER...?
"I WANT TO BE BY YOU."
HMM?
MMM...
Um.
ARE YOU CRAZY?!
WHAT?!
A SERVANT WOULD NEVER STATE HIS OPINION TO HIS MASTER.
THIS IS WHAT MIDORI-SAMA CHOSE.
MY MASTER'S WISH IS MY WISH.

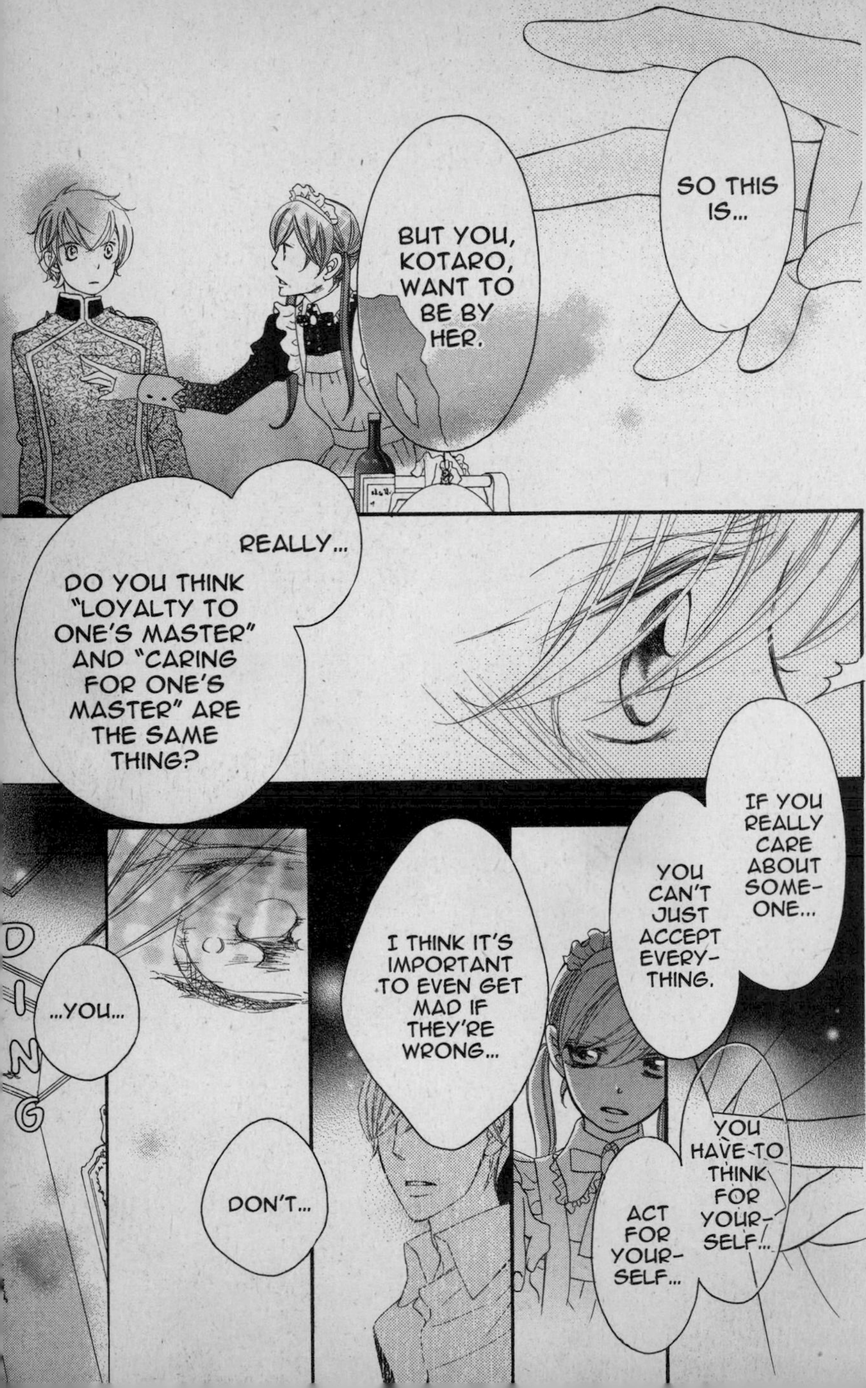
SO THIS IS...
BUT YOU, KOTARO, WANT TO BE BY HER.
REALLY...
DO YOU THINK "LOYALTY TO ONE'S MASTER" AND "CARING FOR ONE'S MASTER" ARE THE SAME THING?
IF YOU REALLY CARE ABOUT SOME-ONE...
YOU CAN'T JUST ACCEPT EVERY-THING.
YOU HAVE TO THINK FOR YOUR-SELF...
ACT FOR YOUR-SELF...
I THINK IT'S IMPORTANT TO EVEN GET MAD IF THEY'RE WRONG...
DON'T...
...YOU...
DING

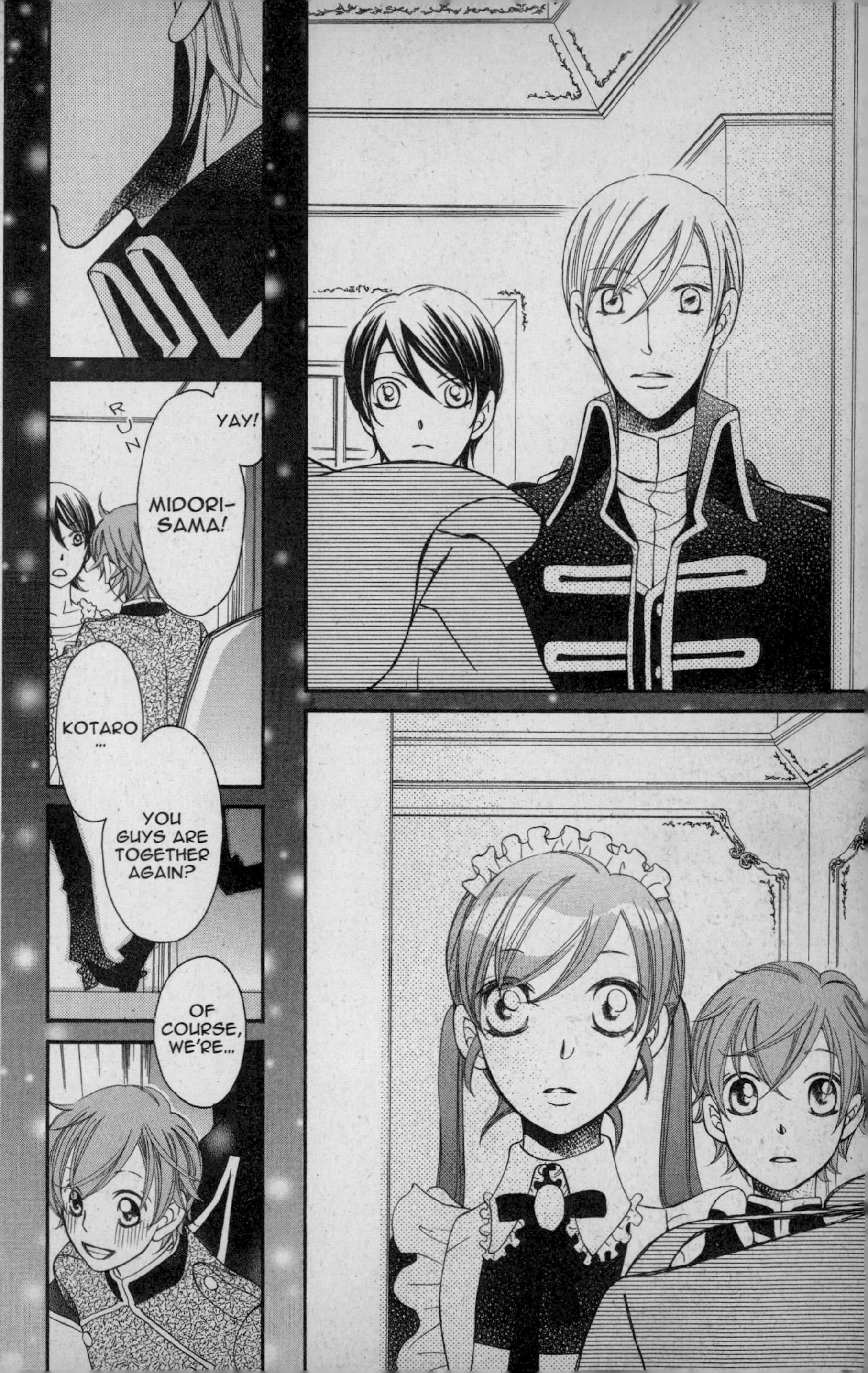
YAY!
RUN
MIDORI-SAMA!
KOTARO...
YOU GUYS ARE TOGETHER AGAIN?
OF COURSE, WE'RE...

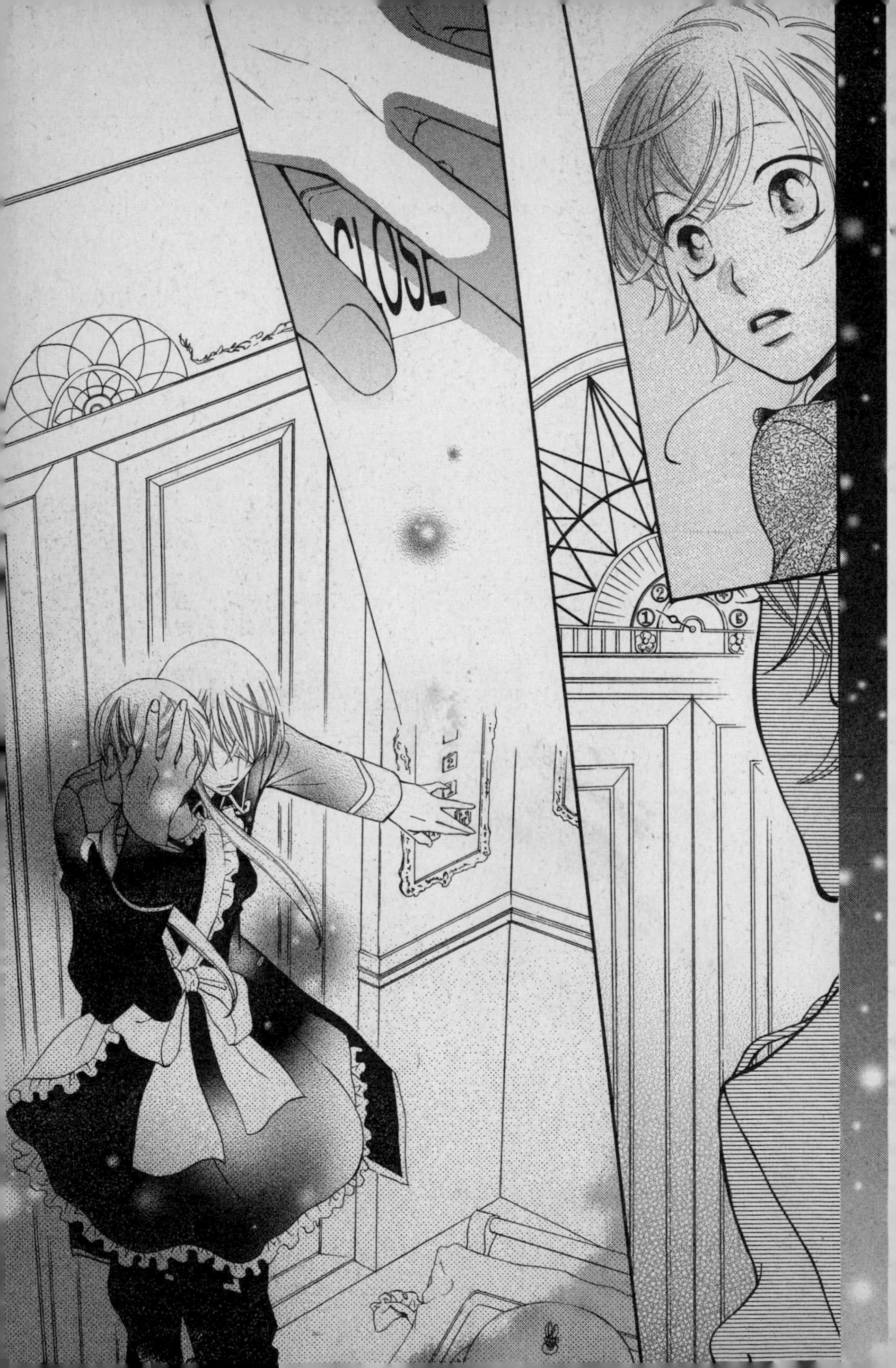
CLOSE

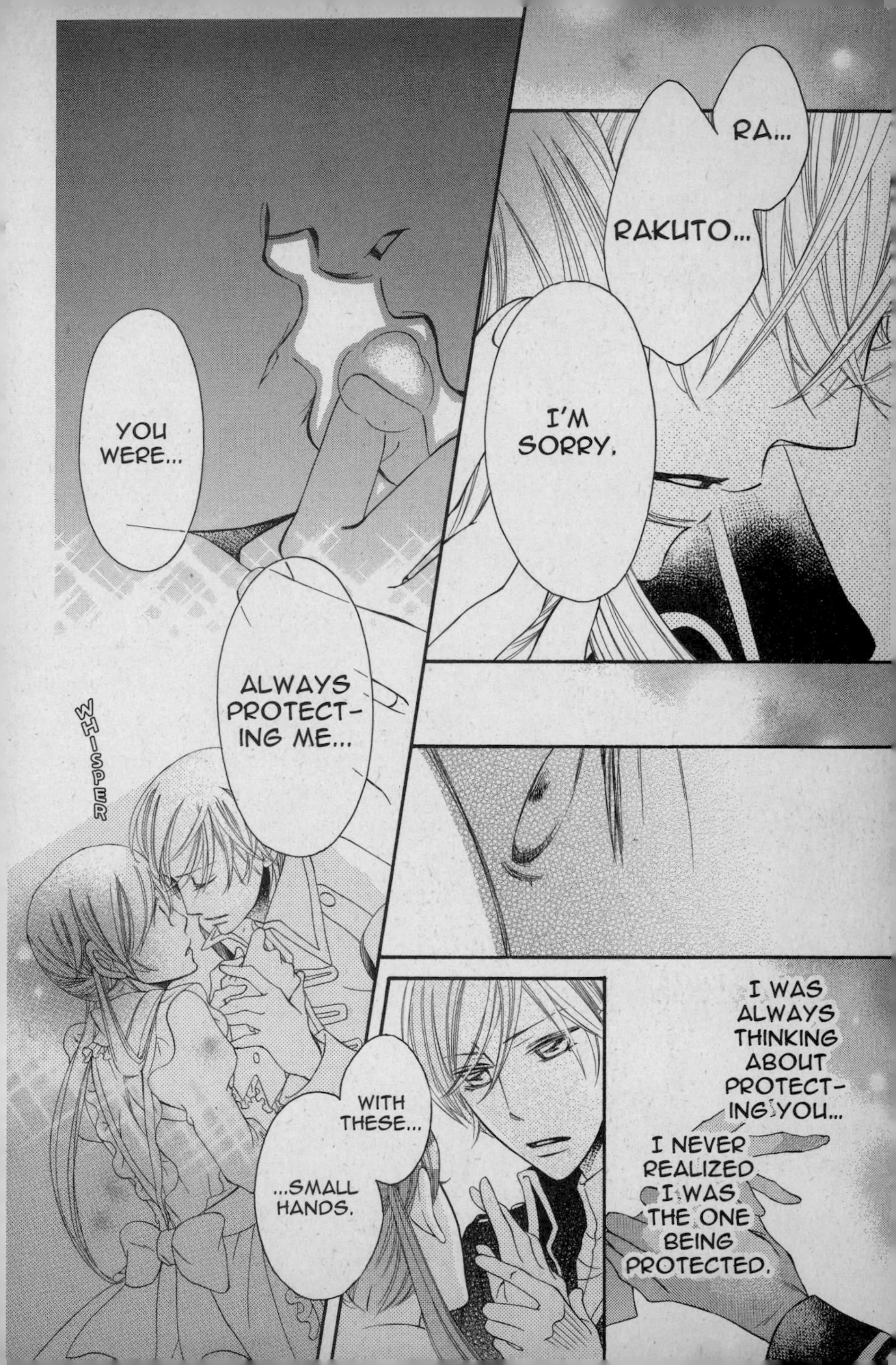
RA...
RAKUTO...
I'M SORRY.
I WAS ALWAYS THINKING ABOUT PROTECTING YOU...
I NEVER REALIZED I WAS THE ONE BEING PROTECTED.
YOU WERE...
ALWAYS PROTECTING ME...
WHISPER
WITH THESE...
...SMALL HANDS.

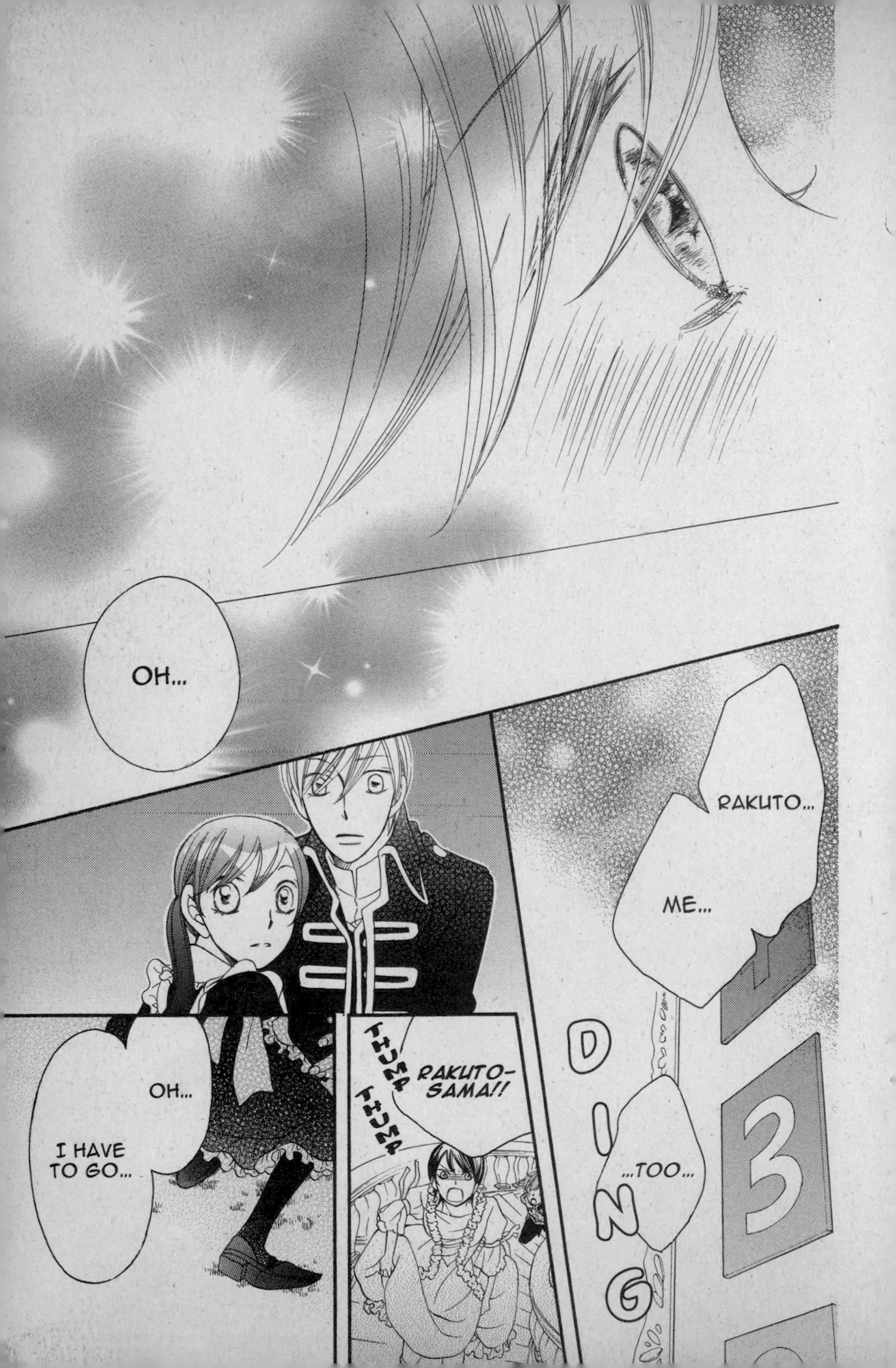
RAKUTO...
ME...
...TOO...
DING
OH...
RAKUTO-SAMA!!
THUMP THUMP
OH...
I HAVE TO GO...

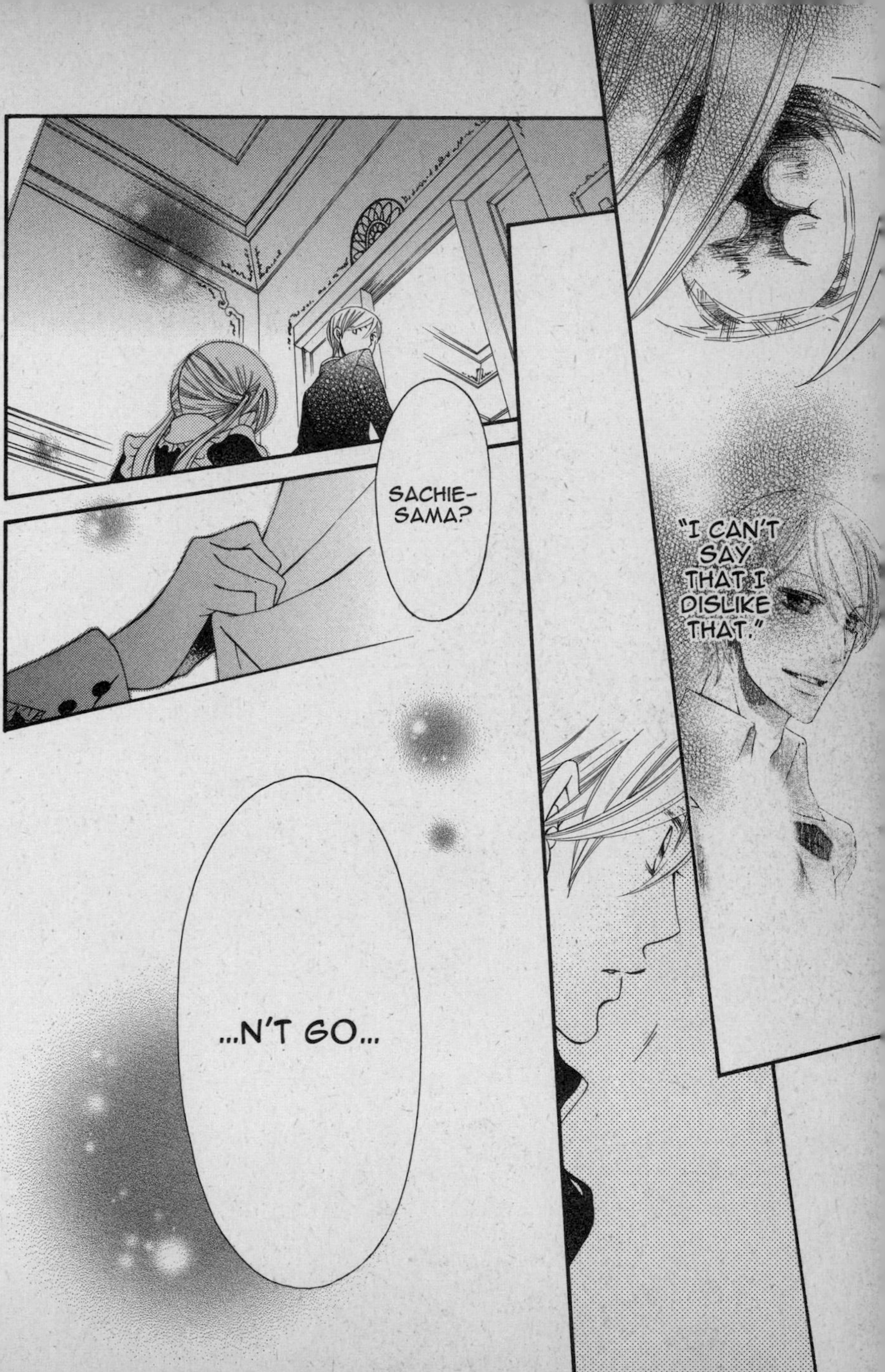
"I CAN'T SAY THAT I DISLIKE THAT."
SACHIE-SAMA?
...N'T GO...

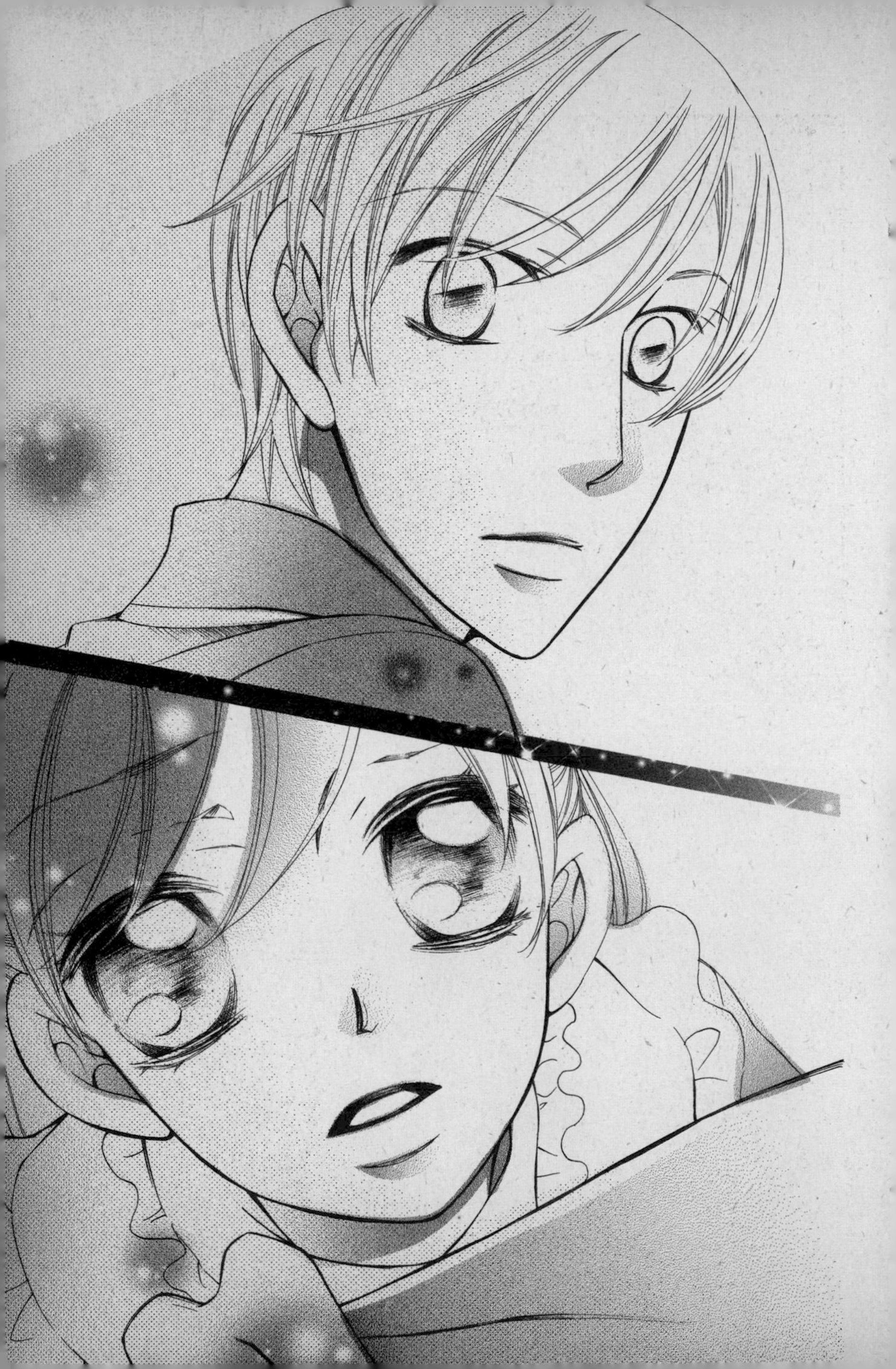

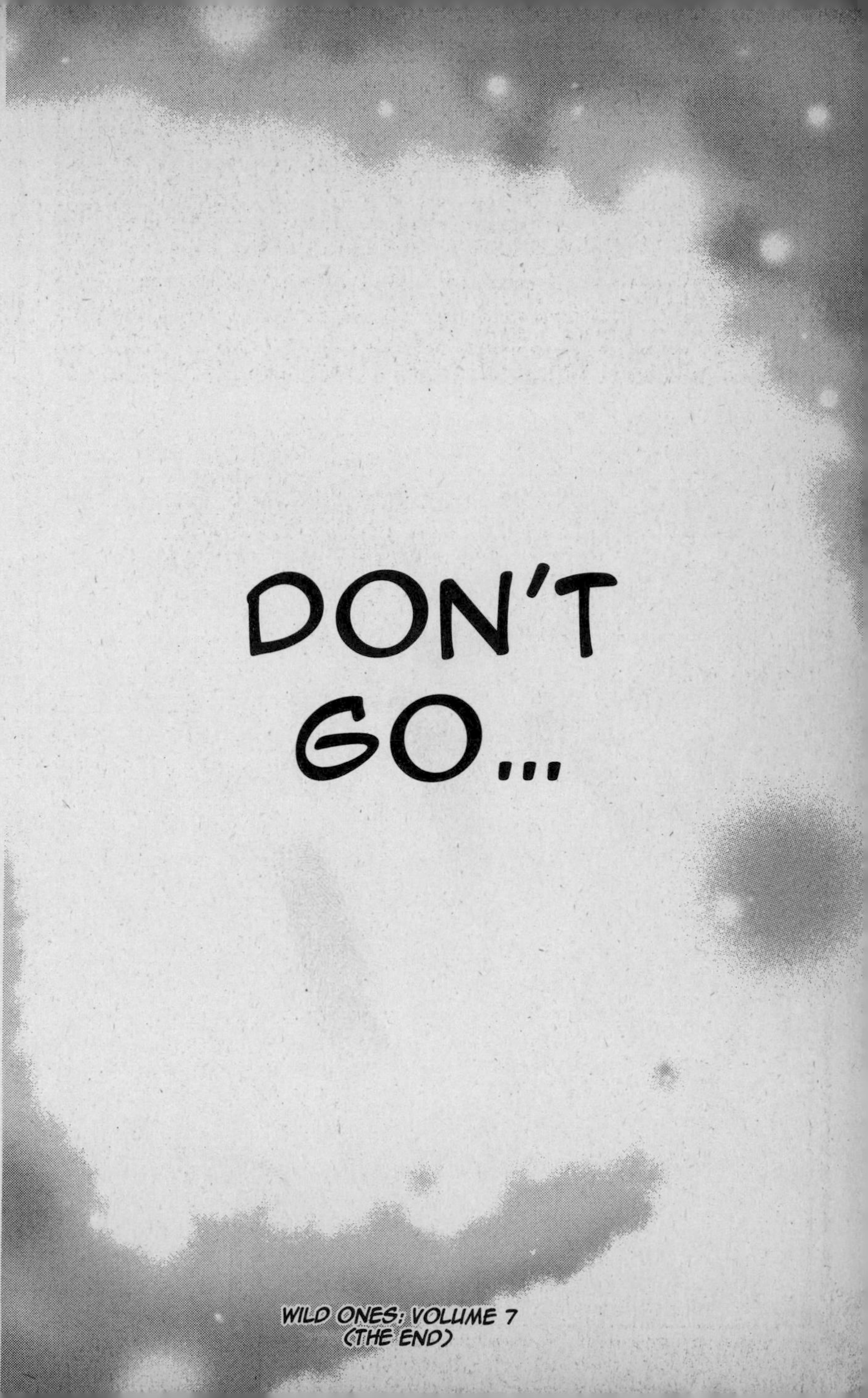
DON'T GO...
WILD ONES: VOLUME 7
(THE END)

WILD ONES SPECIAL INTERVIEW!!

AN EXCLUSIVE INTERVIEW WITH RAKUTO IGARASHI AND AZUMA INUI! A STEP CLOSER TO THEIR TRUE SELVES!

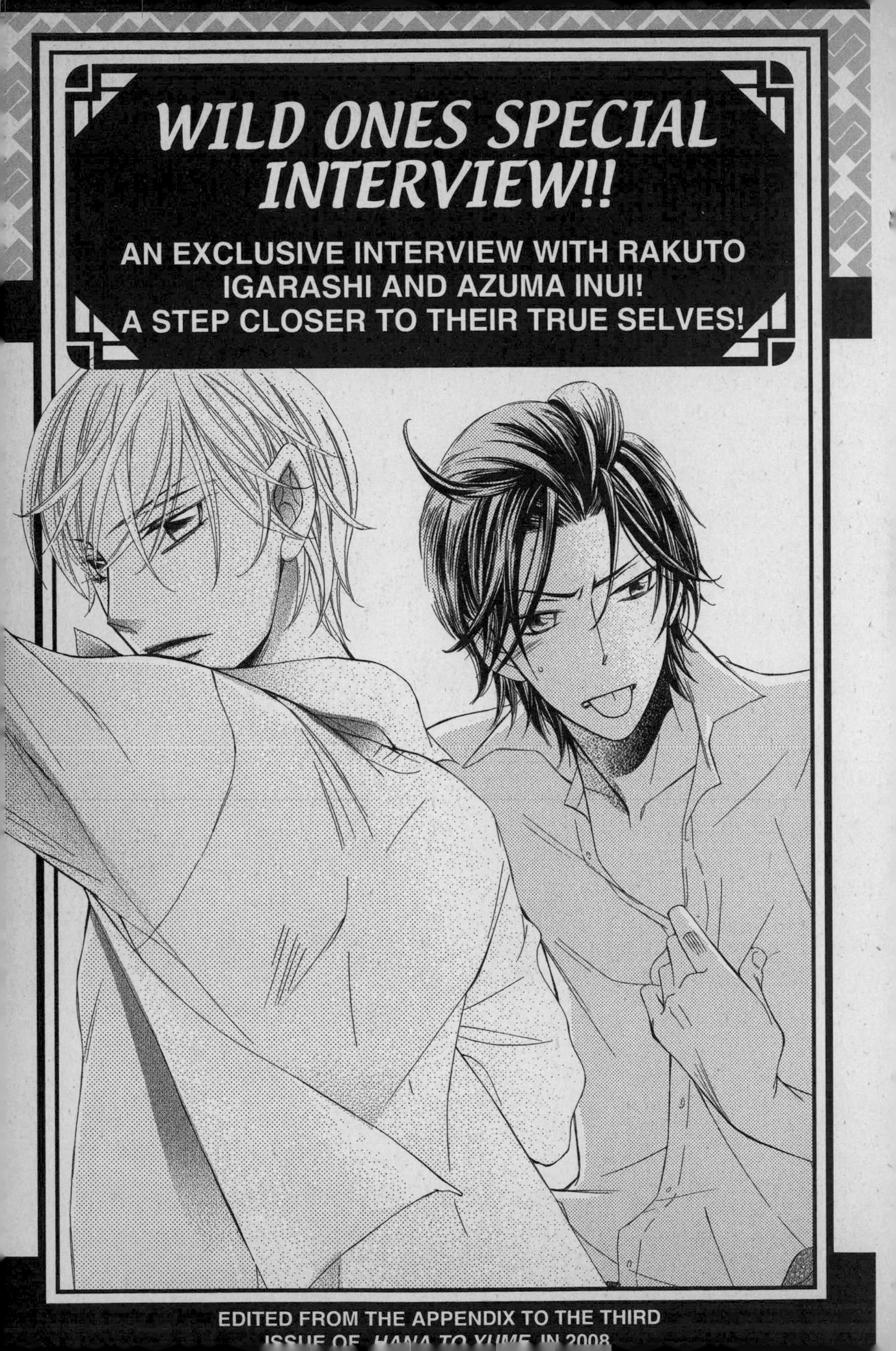

EDITED FROM THE APPENDIX TO THE THIRD ISSUE OF *HANA TO YUME* IN 2008

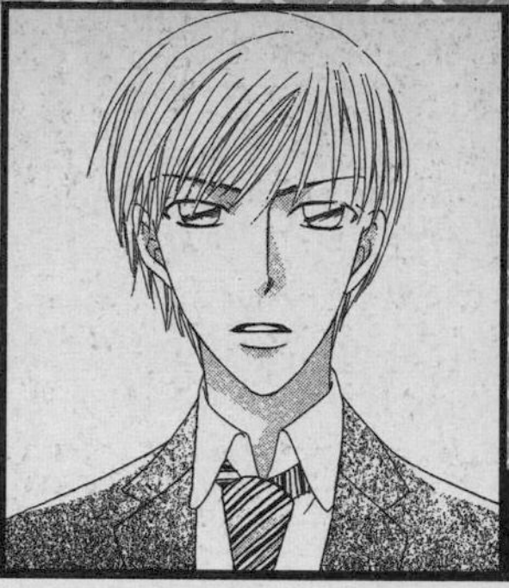

RAKUTO IGARASHI

THE BEAUTIFUL BOY TAKEN IN BY SACHIE'S GRANDFATHER. PROTECTS SACHIE AS HER CARETAKER.

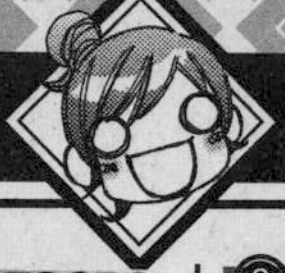

10 QUESTIONS FOR RAKUTO!

① WHAT'S YOUR FAVORITE FOOD?

I EAT ANYTHING. BASICALLY, I DON'T HAVE ANYTHING THAT I DISLIKE.
WHAT ABOUT MANGOS?
OH… THAT… I DON'T REALLY LIKE THAT SENSATION IN YOUR MOUTH… SAME WITH KIWIS. ALTHOUGH, I EAT THEM BOTH.

② FAVORITE ANIMAL?

RABBITS.

③ WHAT DO YOU MAINLY DO ON DAYS OFF?

CLEAN, LAUNDRY, SHOP AND HELP OUT AROUND THE HOUSE.
WHAT ABOUT FUN STUFF?
OH, OF COURSE. CARDS…
I GUESS I STAY INDOORS FOR THE MOST PART. (HEH)

④ SOMETHING YOU'RE WORKING ON?

STAYING FIT. I QUIT TEAM SPORTS AS A THIRD YEAR, BUT I STILL GO TO PRACTICE LIKE I DID BEFORE TO STAY IN SHAPE.

⑤ HOW WOULD YOU DESCRIBE YOURSELF?

A GENTLE, SINCERE GUY...(SORT OF).

⑥ ARE YOU A SADIST OR A MASOCHIST?

I MAY SEEM LIKE A SADIST, BUT I THINK I'M A MASOCHIST TO THE PERSON I LOVE.
I THINK…

⑦ HOW MANY HOURS CAN YOU WAIT FOR A DATE?

I WOULD WAIT TEN MINUTES AND IF SHE DIDN'T COME, I'D GO LOOK FOR HER. SHE'D LIKELY HAVE TAKEN UP A FIGHT SOMEWHERE…

⑧ WHAT KIND OF SUPERPOWER WOULD YOU WANT?

SUPERPOWER… HMM…
TELEPORTATION?

⑨ IF YOU WON A MILLION DOLLARS, HOW WOULD YOU SPEND IT?

I'D TURN IT INTO TWICE AS MUCH MONEY. HOW?
I CAN'T SAY.

⑩ IF YOU COULD ONLY BRING THREE THINGS TO A DESERT ISLAND, WHAT WOULD THEY BE?

WATER AND FOOD. AND THE PERSON DEAREST TO ME.

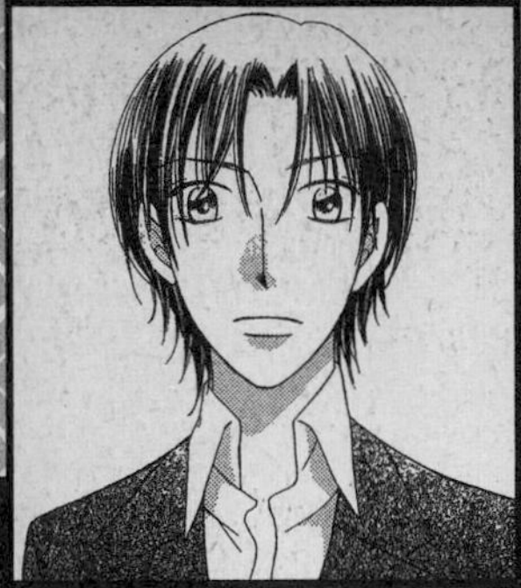

AZUMA INUI

GRANDSON TO A FRIEND OF RAIZO, SACHIE'S GRANDFATHER. IS IN LOVE WITH SACHIE AND IS ARCHENEMY OF RAKUTO, THE CARETAKER.

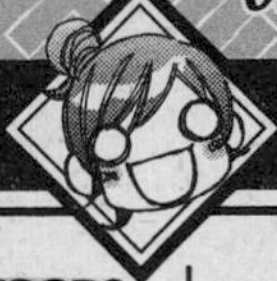

10 QUESTIONS FOR AZUMA!

① WHAT'S YOUR FAVORITE FOOD?

A BEEF BOWL.

② FAVORITE ANIMAL?

ELEPHANTS.

③ WHAT DO YOU MAINLY DO ON DAYS OFF?

I GO VISIT MY GRANDPA.

④ HOW WOULD YOU DESCRIBE YOURSELF?

LATE BLOOMER. (WATCH OUT...!)

⑤ WORDS TO LIVE BY?

A TOUGH SPOT IS AN OPPORTUNITY!!

⑥ HOW MANY HOURS CAN YOU WAIT FOR A DATE?

I'D TRY CALLING HER, AND IF I COULDN'T GET THROUGH, I'D WAIT FOR AS LONG AS IT TAKES. BUT I'D WANT HER TO COME SOON SO I WOULDN'T HAVE TO WORRY.

⑦ WHERE WOULD YOU TAKE A FIRST DATE?

AN AMUSEMENT PARK AND THEN DINNER! OH, BUT THE BEACH IS GOOD TOO. ♥

⑧ DESCRIBE YOUR KIND OF GIRL.

SOMEONE WHO'S FUN TO BE AROUND. SOMEONE WHO HAS A SENSE OF SELF.

⑨ WHAT KIND OF SUPERPOWER WOULD YOU WANT?

HUH...? UMM. X-RAY VISION, MAYBE...

⑩ IF YOU WON A MILLION DOLLARS, HOW WOULD YOU SPEND IT?

I'D TAKE EVERYBODY TO IZU FOR A HOT SPRINGS VACATION!

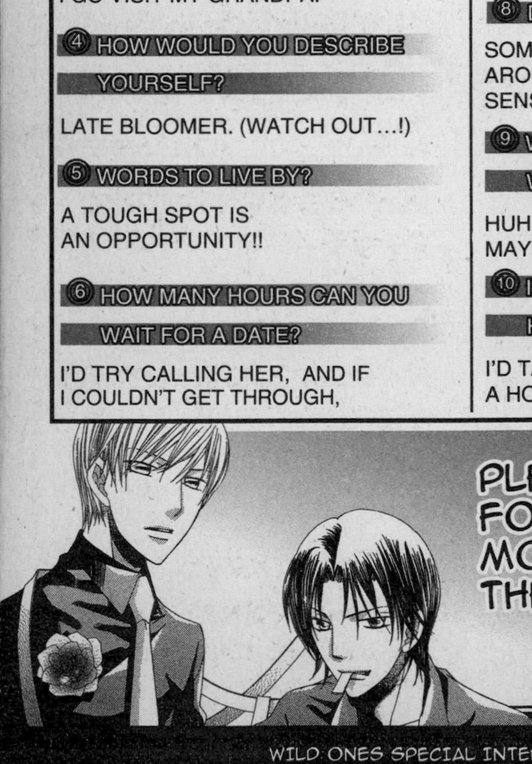

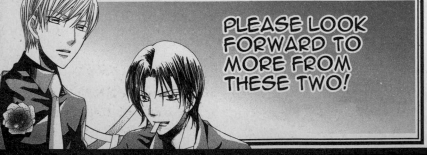

PLEASE LOOK FORWARD TO MORE FROM THESE TWO!

WILD ONES SPECIAL INTERVIEW!! (THE END)

Wanna be part of the *Wild Ones* gang? Then you gotta learn the lingo! Here are some cultural notes to help you out!

San – the most common honorific title; it is used to address people outside one's immediate family and close friends. (On page 101, the author refers to her editor as "Kurachi-san" to show respect and gratitude.)

Sama – the formal version of *san*; this honorific title is used primarily in addressing persons much higher in rank than oneself. *Sama* is also used when the speaker wants to show great respect or deference. (For most of the series, Rakuto calls Sachie "Sachie-sama" in addition to "princess.")

Chan – an informal version of *san* used to address children and females. *Chan* can be used as a term of endearment between women who are good friends. It is also a diminutive, to show close familiarity or a lack of formality.

Sensei – honorific title of respect, used to address teachers as well as professionals such as doctors, lawyers and artists. (Kinoshita-sensei is Rakuto's homeroom teacher.)

NOTES

Page 6, panel 4 – Career Planning Sheet
Japanese high school students have to submit a career planning sheet, listing the colleges or companies that they intend to apply to.

Page 11, panel 4 – Student Council
The student government in Japanese schools is very important, as they organize major school events and the cleaning of the school (often done by students, not a janitorial crew). The student council president is a busy job. It is a sign of how important and diligent Rakuto is that he held the position.

Page 16, panel 3 – Career Path Center
Many Japanese high schools have well-stocked career path centers with detailed information on colleges and technical schools.

Page 34, panel 2 – Tokyo University
Tokyo University is the top-ranked university in Japan. It is a point of great pride for a high school if its students get accepted into Tokyo U.

Page 44, panel 4 – KACHIKOMI - A Challenge
In traditional yakuza culture, one gang will occasionally show up at the headquarters of another gang to challenge them, basically trying to run them out of town and take over their turf. This is why the Asagi Gang always goes ballistic when someone shows up at their house.

Page 68, panel 6 – Compatibility Scale Machine
A popular game machine that matches the compatibility of couples based on some sort of data input. The machine depicted here uses the kanji of people's names, based on an ancient Chinese system of fortune-telling using name characters.

Page 104, panel 4 – HATASHIJO - Letter of Challenge
In traditional samurai and yakuza culture, duels of honor were initiated by *hatashijo*, formal letters of challenge.

Kiyo Fujiwara made her manga debut in 2000 in *Hana to Yume* magazine with *Bokuwane*. Her other works include *Hard Romantic-ker, Help!!* and *Gold Rush 21*. She comes from Akashi-shi in Hyogo Prefecture but currently lives in Tokyo. Her hobbies include playing drums and bass guitar and wearing kimono.

WILD ONES
VOL. 7
The Shojo Beat Manga Edition

STORY AND ART BY
KIYO FUJIWARA

Translation & Adaptation/Mai Ihara
Touch-up Art & Lettering/HudsonYards
Cover Design/Hidemi Dunn
Interior Design/Yuki Ameda
Editor/Jonathan Tarbox

Editor in Chief, Books/Alvin Lu
Editor in Chief, Magazines/Marc Weidenbaum
VP, Publishing Licensing/Rika Inouye
VP, Sales & Product Marketing/Gonzalo Ferreyra
VP, Creative/Linda Espinosa
Publisher/Hyoe Narita

Arakure by Kiyo Fujiwara
© Kiyo Fujiwara 2008
All rights reserved.
First published in Japan in 2008 by HAKUSENSHA, Inc., Tokyo.
English language translation rights arranged with HAKUSENSHA, Inc., Tokyo. The
stories, characters and incidents mentioned in this publication are entirely fictional.

Printed in the U.S.A.

Published by VIZ Media, LLC
P.O. Box 77010
San Francisco, CA 94107

Shojo Beat Manga Edition
10 9 8 7 6 5 4 3 2 1
First printing, June 2009

www.viz.com

store.viz.com

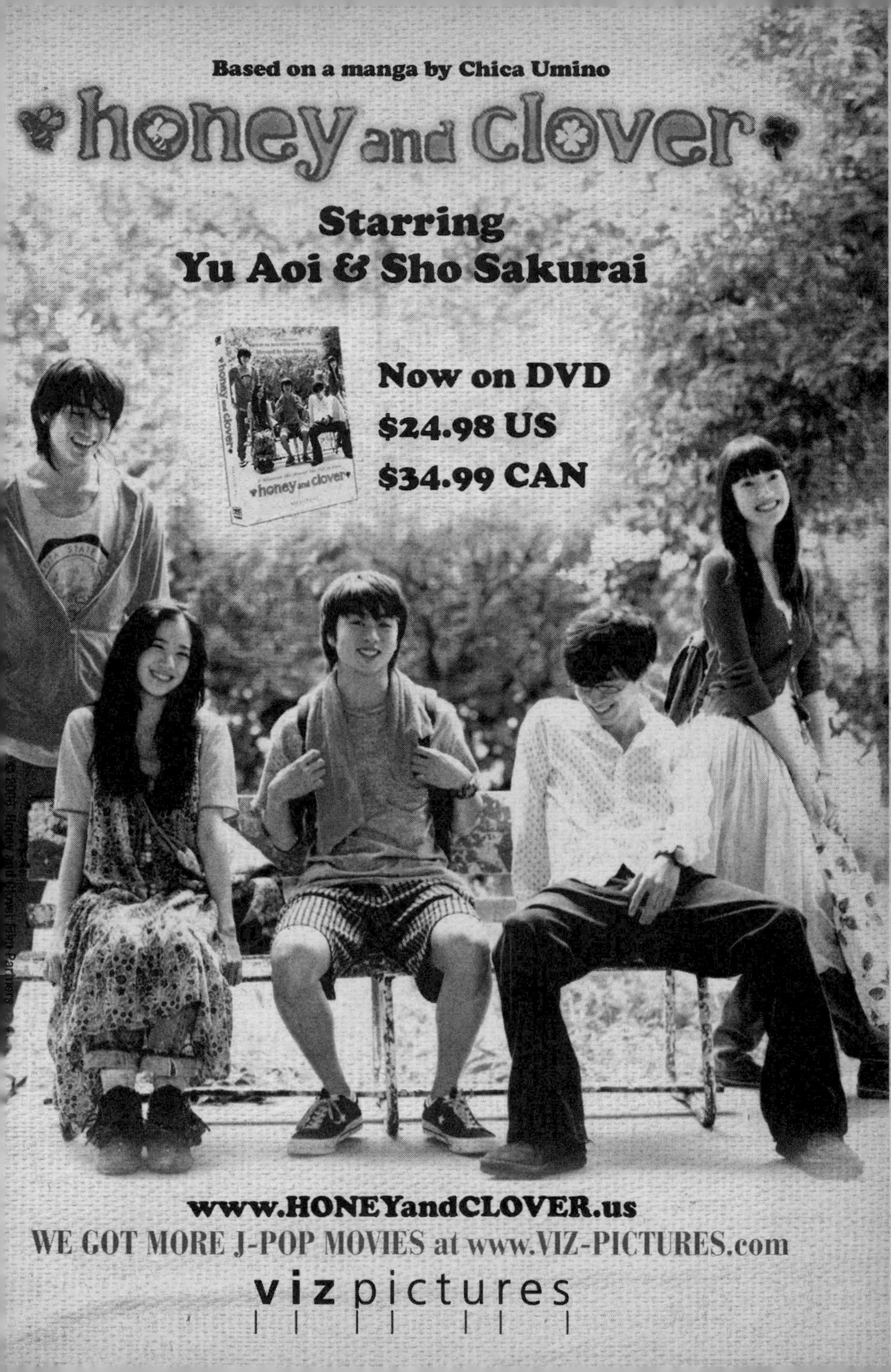
Based on a manga by Chica Umino
honey and clover
Starring
Yu Aoi & Sho Sakurai
Now on DVD
$24.98 US
$34.99 CAN
honey and clover
Honey and Clover Film Partners
www.HONEYandCLOVER.us
WE GOT MORE J-POP MOVIES at www.VIZ-PICTURES.com
viz pictures

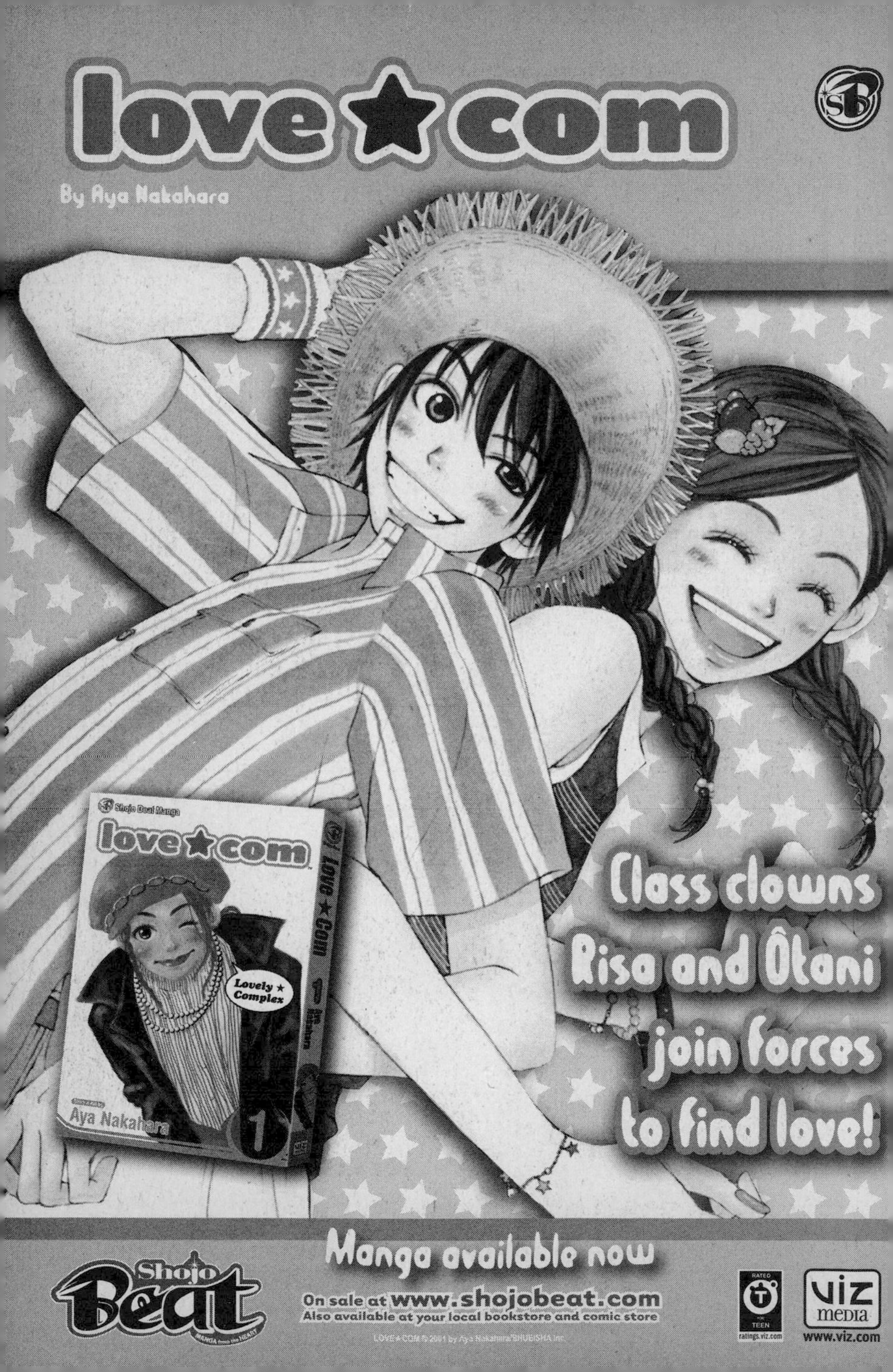
love★com
By Aya Nakahara
Shojo Beat Manga
love★com
Love★Com
Lovely ★ Complex
Aya Nakahara
1
Class clowns Risa and Ôtani join forces to find love!
Manga available now
Shojo Beat
On sale at www.shojobeat.com
Also available at your local bookstore and comic store
RATED T FOR TEEN
ratings.viz.com
VIZ media
www.viz.com
LOVE★COM © 2001 by Aya Nakahara/SHUEISHA Inc.

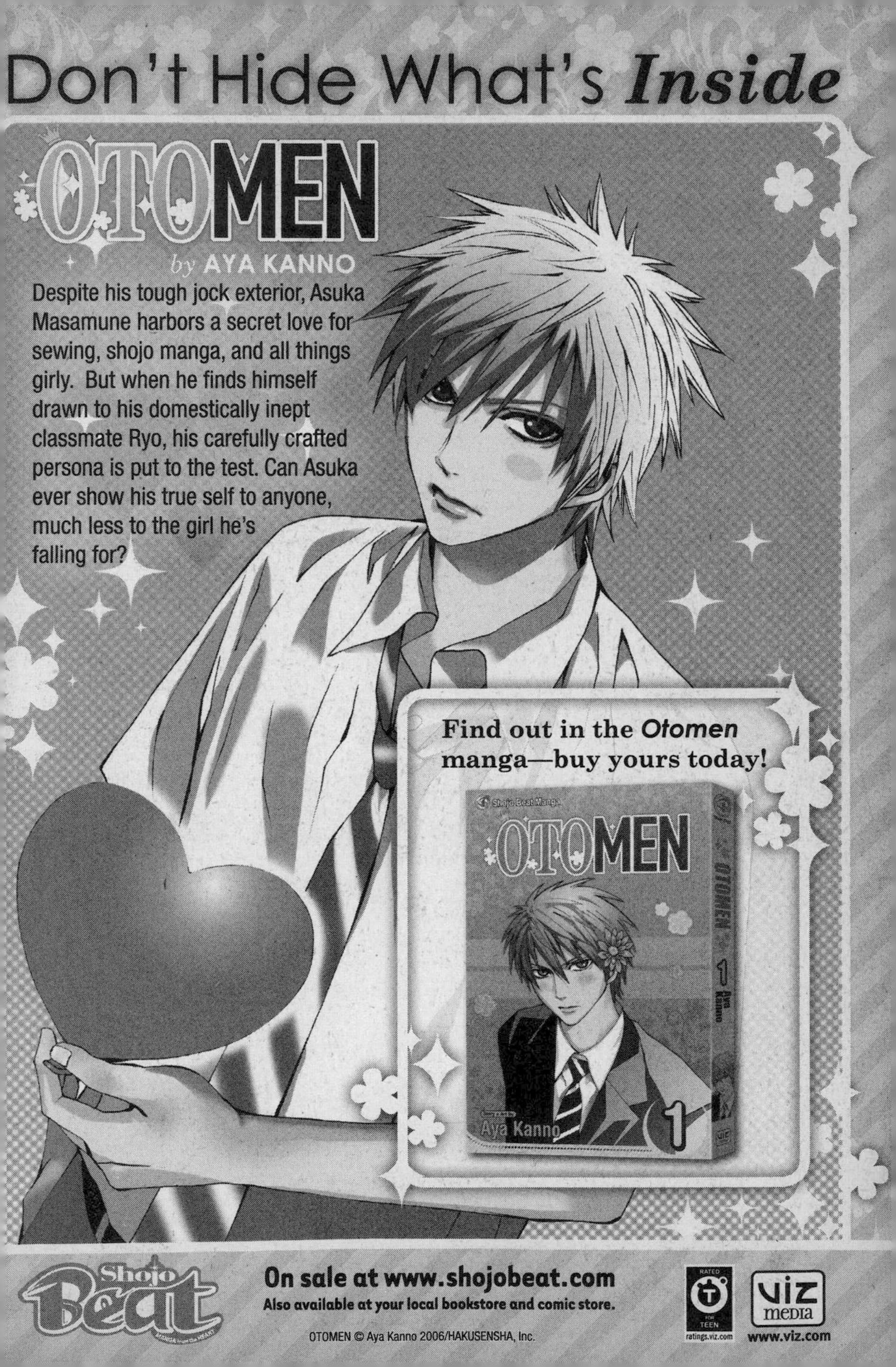

Don't Hide What's Inside
OTOMEN
by AYA KANNO
Despite his tough jock exterior, Asuka Masamune harbors a secret love for sewing, shojo manga, and all things girly. But when he finds himself drawn to his domestically inept classmate Ryo, his carefully crafted persona is put to the test. Can Asuka ever show his true self to anyone, much less to the girl he's falling for?
Find out in the Otomen manga—buy yours today!
Shojo Beat Manga
OTOMEN
1
Aya Kanno
Shojo Beat
On sale at www.shojobeat.com
Also available at your local bookstore and comic store.
OTOMEN © Aya Kanno 2006/HAKUSENSHA, Inc.
RATED T FOR TEEN
ratings.viz.com
VIZ MEDIA
www.viz.com

Tell us what you think about Shojo Beat Manga!

Our survey is now available online. Go to:

shojobeat.com/mangasurvey

Help us make our product offerings better!

THE REAL DRAMA BEGINS IN...